The LIBOR Market Model in Practice

For other titles in the Wiley Finance Series
please see www.wiley.com/finance

The LIBOR
market model
in practice

"This book is a valuable aid to interest-rate quants aiming at an efficient implementation of a LIBOR market model. The numerous recipes provided help develop robust calibration routines and time-saving pricing algorithms."

   —Fabio Mercurio, PhD, Head of Financial
      Modelling, Banca IMI

"Is it coincidence or destiny that yet another group of BGM authors (Bachert, Gatarek and Maksymiuk) formed, this time to write an unprecedented and already classic text book on market model theory? Providing numerous numerical illustrations, it forms the ideal starting point for anyone wanting to master market model skills."

   —Raoul Pietersz

"A book 'by quants for quants' with a number of recent developments concerning the LIBOR market model that have never been collected into a single source before. Unnecessary mathematical sophistication is avoided in order to allow as large a public as possible to benefit from the book, and a careful attention to market-driven problems avoids the introduction and development of theoretical tools that are never used in practice. This is an important addition to the available literature from one of the researchers who historically contributed to establish and formalise this increasingly central model for interest rate derivatives."

   —Damiano Brigo, author of
      *Interest Rate Models – Theory and Practice
      with Smile, Inflation and Credit*

About the authors

DARIUSZ GATAREK is credit risk analyst at Glencore UK Ltd. He is also professor at the WSB-National Louis University and the Polish Academy of Sciences. Dariusz has published a number of papers on financial models including his well-known work with Alan Brace and Marek Musiela on Brace-Gatarek-Musiela (BGM) models of interest rates dynamics and is a frequent speaker at conferences worldwide.

PRZEMYSLAW BACHERT is a senior financial engineer in the Global Financial Services Risk Management Group at Ernst and Young. He gained his Ph.D. in Economics from the University of Lodz. He is responsible for structure derivatives valuation and the implementation of risk management systems. Przemyslaw also teaches in the Ernst and Young Academy of Business for the Financial Engineering course, which covers the LIBOR Market Model.

ROBERT MAKSYMIUK is a senior financial engineer in the Global Financial Services Risk Management Group at Ernst and Young where he is responsible for structured derivatives pricing and the implementation of risk management systems. Robert also teaches in the Ernst and Young Academy of Business for the Financial Engineering course, which covers the LIBOR Market Model.

The LIBOR Market Model in Practice

**Dariusz Gatarek,
Przemyslaw Bachert and Robert Maksymiuk**

John Wiley & Sons, Ltd

Other Wiley Editorial Offices

John Wiley & Sons Inc., 111 River Street, Hoboken, NJ 07030, USA

Jossey-Bass, 989 Market Street, San Francisco, CA 94103-1741, USA

Wiley-VCH Verlag GmbH, Boschstr. 12, D-69469 Weinheim, Germany

John Wiley & Sons Australia Ltd, 42 McDougall Street, Milton, Queensland 4064, Australia

John Wiley & Sons (Asia) Pte Ltd, 2 Clementi Loop #02-01, Jin Xing Distripark, Singapore 129809

John Wiley & Sons Canada Ltd, 6045 Freemont Blvd, Mississauga, ONT, L5R 4J3, Canada

Wiley also publishes its books in a variety of electronic formats. Some content that appears in print may not be
available in electronic books.

Library of Congress Cataloging in Publication Data

Gatarek, Dariusz.
  The LIBOR market model in practice / Dariusz Gatarek, Przemyslaw Bachert, and Robert Maksymiuk.
    p. cm.
  ISBN-13: 978-0-470-01443-1
  ISBN-10: 0-470-01443-1
  1. Interest rates—Mathematical models. 2. Interest rate futures—Mathematical models. I. Bachert,
  Przemyslaw. II. Maksymiuk, Robert. III. Title. IV. Title: London Interbank Offer Rate market model
  in practice.
  HG1621.G38 2007
  332.1′13—dc22

                                                                                              2006028049

British Library Cataloguing in Publication Data

A catalogue record for this book is available from the British Library

ISBN-13: 978-0-470-01443-1 (HB)
ISBN-10: 0-470-01443-1 (HB)

Typeset in 10/12pt Times by Integra Software Services Pvt. Ltd, Pondicherry, India

This book is printed on acid-free paper responsibly manufactured from sustainable forestry
in which at least two trees are planted for each one used for paper production.

Contents

Acknowledgments

The book would be never written without support of many people. We would like to thank our teachers Jerzy Zabczyk, Marek Musiela, Marek Rutkowski, Wladyslaw Milo, Alan Brace and Farshid Jamshidian. We also acknowledge strong support from our executives and friends, namely Evan Kalimtgis, Kostas Kalimtgis, Steven Isaacs, Milos Brajovic, Matt Johnson, Panos Gevros, Athanasious Stavrou, Phil Burford and Michael Dorgan form Glencore as well as Duleep Aluwihare and Piotr Gajek from Ernst and Young. We are indebted to Damiano Brigo, Fabio Mercurio and Raoul Pietersz for numerous very helpful discussions. We would like to thank Caitlin Cornish and Emily Pears for their continuous support from Wiley. The remarks and edits by Simon Pascoe, who did a great job reading the final manuscript, are of special value. Without the strong support and patience from our families, we would never complete the book. The responsibility for all remaining errors is obviously ours and only ours.

About the Authors

Dariusz Gatarek is credit risk analyst at Glencore UK Ltd. He is also professor at the WSB-National Louis University and the Polish Academy of Sciences. He joined Glencore UK Ltd from NumeriX LLC, where he was Director of Research specializing in interest rate derivatives pricing. Before that he was involved in valuing derivatives and designing risk management systems for capital adequacy within the consultancy Deloitte and Touche and several banks. Dariusz has published a number of papers on financial models including his well-known work with Alan Brace and Marek Musiela on Brace-Gatarek-Musiela (BGM) models of interest rates dynamics and he is a frequent speaker at conferences worldwide.

Przemyslaw Bachert is a senior financial engineer in the Global Financial Services Risk Management Group at Ernst and Young. He gained his Ph.D. in Economics from the University of Lodz. Przemyslaw is responsible for structure derivatives valuation and implementation of risk management systems. He has spent the last six years working with financial institutions in Europe, the Middle East and China to enhance their risk management capabilities including Algorithmics parameterization. Prior to joining Ernst and Young, Przemyslaw was a Financial Analyst at Bank Handlowy in Warsaw (Citigroup) where he was responsible for quantitative maintenance of the front office system Kondor+. He also teaches at the Ernst and Young Academy of Business for the Financial Engineering course which covers the LIBOR Market Model.

Robert Maksymiuk is a senior financial engineer in the Global Financial Services Risk Management Group at Ernst and Young where he is responsible for structured derivatives pricing and implementation of risk management systems. He has worked for several financial institutions in Europe and the Middle East and his activity covered implementation of the Algo Suite risk management system. Prior to joining Ernst and Young Robert worked in the BRE Bank where he worked together with Dariusz Gatarek and he was engaged in quantitative research. Robert also teaches at the Ernst and Young Academy of Business on the Financial Engineering course which covers the LIBOR Market Model.

Introduction

The LIBOR Market Model (LMM) is the first model of interest rates dynamics consistent with the market practice of pricing interest rate derivatives. The model was created in 1994 by Kristian Miltersen, Klaus Sandmann and Dieter Sondermann (1997), then developed in 1995 to a form applicable in practice by Alan Brace, Dariusz Gatarek and Marek Musiela (1997). Its current form (including the name) belongs to Farshid Jamshidian (1997) and is based an abstract formulation of LMM by Marek Musiela and Marek Rutkowski (1997a). The LMM is also called Brace-Gatarek-Musiela (BGM) model. Some authors claim that the model was discovered independently, that is not true – there was close collaboration between the Bonn group (Miltersen, Sandmann and Sondermann), the Sydney group (Brace, Gatarek and Musiela), Marek Rutkowski in Warsaw and Farshid Jamshidian in London. Its popularity is a result of consistency with practice, allowing the pricing of vanilla products in LMM to be reduced to using standard market formulae. However ease of use does not suffice to win the market, and there are numerous theoretical advantages to the LMM as well. The LMM was preceded by so called short rate models – where the dynamics of all interest rates was determined by the dynamics of the overnight rate. This is a counterintuitive property but practitioners learned how to apply it to a relatively high degree of effectiveness. The next stage was the seminal Heath-Jarrow-Morton (HJM) model (1992), where attention was shifted correctly from the artificial notion of the short rate to the whole term structure of interest rates – a mathematically interesting problem of random dynamics in infinite dimension. We may say that all questions were already answered, the main contribution of the LMM is one more shift of attention to instantaneous forward rates and, interesting for theorists, to forward rates with market compounding – quarterly, semi-annual, annual, etc. The history of science has told us that the simple and obvious properties are the most difficult to spot.

Why one more book on LMM? In almost all books dealing with derivatives pricing, there is a chapter on the LMM, for example ten books[1] deal entirely or for large parts with the LMM. One thing is sure – a new book on the LMM must be really new. What is (in our opinion) new in this book is the full practitioner's approach – a quantitative analyst, being the target reader of our book, is neither a less gifted version of an academic researcher nor an operator of pricing software nor just a trader's associate. We tried to adopt the specific

---

[1] Brigo and Mercurio, 2001; Hunt and Kennedy, 1999; Jaeckel, 2002; Joshi, 2003; Musiela and Rutkowski, 1997b; Pelsser, 2000; Rebonato, 2002, 2004; Schoenmakers, 2005; Zühlsdorff, 2002.

language of a quantitative analyst to the largest possible level – borrowing from the language of a trader or of an academia theorist as little as necessary. It is one of first books entirely by quants for quants. In the theoretical part, we try to be as rough as possible – we do not deal with issues like capital asset pricing, security replication, complete markets, mean-variance hedging, existence and uniqueness of martingale measures and other issues, instead we refer the reader to other sources such as Musiela and Rutkowski, 1997b; Bjork, 2004; Shreve, 2004, 2005. In our very personal but justified view, they have very little impact on every day pricing of financial derivatives. We try to replicate the way of thinking of a quantitative analyst – mathematical notions must be kept in mind but they are treated in a way closer to physics rather than mathematics: computational efficiency is more important than mathematical rigour. On the other hand, except for basic mathematical ideas, we derive all used properties, and at the same time try to make the book as self-contained as possible. In the practical parts our attention is focused on concrete financial applications rather than the full presentation of the numerical method, which may make it a tough read and indeed to some extent slightly messy. This is because no-one before, to our knowledge, has used this kind of presentation.

The book is self-contained but advanced, we do not recommend it as a first textbook in derivatives pricing. Most parts of this book were not published in full extent before and we cover new and important issues such as various drift approximations, various parametric and nonparametric calibrations, the uncertain volatility approach to smile modelling, a version of the HJM model based on market observables and the duality between BGM and HJM models. We decided to divide the book into three parts – theory, calibration and numerical pricing methods.

In the first part we deal with the mathematical background of the BGM and HJM models and the models themselves. We start with the shortest ever summary on probability theory and stochastic processes. We present new compact proofs on change of numeraire and forward measure formulas.

Then we present both models in parallel, both in the spot and forward measures. Special attention is paid to analogies between the models. In addition we give a brief summary on most important short rate models: Vasiček (1997), Cox-Ingersoll-Ross (1985) and Black-Karasiński (1991) and their relation to HJM model. We close the section with cap and floor formulae in BGM and HJM models.

In the next section we give basic information on tree and Monte Carlo simulation of the BGM and HJM models in larger dimensions, particularly focussing on Principal Component Analysis and Cholesky decomposition. We give new formulae for a multidimensional trinomial tree approximation for correlated diffusions.

The next section is entirely devoted to pricing of swaptions. There exists a swap-related counterparty of the LIBOR market model called the swap market model (Jamshidian, 1997) but to our knowledge is rarely used in practice. Therefore we have decided to restrict ourselves to swaption pricing in the LIBOR market model, which in practice coincides with swap market model. In this section we give market conventions for pricing swaptions by the Black formula. We give three accurate approximations to swaption prices with the BGM and HJM models: linear, semilinear and nonlinear. We study the problem of volatility parameterisation and propose six methods: parametric by Rebonato (2002), parameterised, separated, time homogeneous, universal and locally single factor. We close the section with a numerical example dealing with the separated calibration approach and its relation to the string model of Longstaff-Schwartz-Santa Clara for the BGM model (2001).

In the next section we investigate the problem of volatility smile modelling in the interest rate derivatives world. We start with presenting exact nature of the volatility smile, how the smile is quoted for interest rate derivatives and what the difference is in the methodology between smile modelling for equity and currency and smile modelling for interest rates. In particular we study the problem of smile modelling for long term options, its relation to the ergodicity of stochastic processes and its implications for interest rate volatility smiles. We propose two methods for smile modelling: the shifted BGM model and the uncertain volatility displaced BGM model. We prove that the shifted BGM model forms an interpolation between BGM and HJM models. We finish the section with a simple approach to smile modeling by 'mixing' the BGM and HJM models.

The last section of the theoretical part is devoted to the single dimensional BGM and HJM models – giving an extremely easy method of pricing certain interest derivatives, constant maturity swaps (CMS) in particular. We present the dynamics of CMS rates in both BGM and HJM models and discuss calibration to co-terminal swaptions and smile modelling issues.

The second part of the book deals with practical issues related to calibration and is designed as a manual allowing the reared to implement the presented algorithms in an easy way. We present the most popular calibration algorithms of the LIBOR Market Model used in practice. Although descriptions are restricted only to at-the-money (ATM) volatilities the presented step-by-step procedure of calibration is very detailed and can really help the beginning quant to understand the matter.

The chapters containing calibration algorithms are organized in the following way. Chapter 7 presents the first necessary steps in calibration. We present the market data set used in all calibration procedures. All the market data are taken from a particular working day and contains discount factors bootstrapped from par interest rates (LIBOR's, FRA, IRS), at-the-money cap volatilities and swaption volatilities. We deal with EUR currency in all the calibration chapters.

The next part in the chapter describes the nature of caps and ways of determining resets and payments. That may seems to be easy but provides a short introduction for some of the readers may not be familiar with nature of the cap mechanism. For that case is seems to be useful to show the interpretation of cap quotes.

After that we present a big section describing calibration algorithms to caps. Presented in the book the calibration algorithms to caps are the simplest algorithms used in practice and do not require the use of any optimization techniques. All the algorithms are presented in a high level of detail. Because calibration of the LIBOR Market Model requires knowing how to price caps, the standard Black formula for caplets is also presented both theoretically and practically. Next we present the market standard of determining strikes for caps through deriving forward swap rates.

The next part of the chapter is dedicated to stripping caplet volatilities from cap quotes which is the last step before presenting the final calibration to caps. In the calibration some definitions are introduced and recalled. This includes instantaneous and piecewise constant instantaneous volatilities and also time homogeneity. Two ways of calculating volatility structures are provided: piecewise constant instantaneous volatilities depending on time to maturity and piecewise constant instantaneous volatilities depending on the maturity of the underlying forward rate. Both approaches have examples of usage of them in practice. One of the example shows that time homogeneity assumption may lead to negative instantaneous volatilities.

Chapter 8 introduces calibration algorithms to swaptions. First we present one of the popular approaches of BGM calibration what is called the separated approach. The separated approach provides a direct way of calibrating the model to the full set of swaptions. As a result of some computations we show the variance-covariance matrices and also perform some analysis to compute eigenvectors and eigenvalues. We compare results between the many variants of the separated approach by computing theoretical swaption volatilities and root mean squared errors between them and market swaption volatilities.

In the next paragraph we develop the previously demonstrated separated approach by adding an optimization algorithm. As the target function we set a root mean squared error for differences between the theoretical and market swaption volatilities. We minimize that function but with several restrictions for the VCV. We postulate that the VCV matrix must be positive definite. For that case we implement a subalgorithm for reducing the VCV matrix by removing all eigenvectors associated with negative eigenvalues. We present all necessary steps for that calibration algorithm so that it can be utilised in practice. We present the whole calibration algorithm in Matlab code.

Next we move to another widely used approach of calibration to swaptions which is called the locally single factor approach. We present algorithms in a detailed way and present results of instantaneous volatility calculations.

After that we present a nonparametric calibration to swaptions using historical correlations. First we show that we have to compute the matrix of historical correlations of forward rates. We give an example for EUR market and show some unexpected results that a lot of historical correlations have negative signs. That may suggest that market of forward rates is not as effective as everybody assumes.

We move afterwards to another widely used technique of BGM calibration which is calibration to co-terminal swaptions. Analysing the results we can observe a typical hump of volatility between one and three years. Our results are also similar to those obtained via calibration to caps.

Chapter 9 turns to look at nonparametric calibration to caps and swaptions based on the Rebonato approach. This is a very popular algorithm allowing one to obtain the implied instantaneous correlations of forward rates. First we derive the annual caplet volatilities driven by a dynamic of annual forward rates from the dynamics of quarterly forward rates. Having done that we then compute the forward swap rates. Our goal is to find such instantaneous correlations of LIBOR rates, which together with the instantaneous volatilities obtained from caplet prices will give a negligible difference between the Black and LFM swaption prices. For that reason we also recall the Black closed formula for swaptions and also approximations to LFM Black squared swaption volatilities as well as swap rates expressed as linear combination of forward rates. In the calibration we consider a piecewise – constant instantaneous volatility structure. Finally we present theoretical and market volatilities of swaptions together with differences between them after calibration.

The last part of the chapter is a simultaneously parametric calibration to caps and swaptions. After the derivation of caplet prices from cap prices we present all the necessary steps of the algorithm including: the structure of parametric functions, optimization algorithms and minimization functions. Finally we present the results.

It is worth bearing in mind that all calibration algorithms presented in the chapter contain detailed steps allowing for them to be implemented in practice. Many theoretical aspects are presented on diagrams and schemas in a simple manner. Additionally a lot of examples are provided which we feel help the reader to really understand the matter. Finally results of each algorithm are presented and commented upon. The results obtained via different algorithms can be used to value some interest rate derivatives and analyse the impact of various techniques of calibrations on the fair value of exotic products.

The last and third part of the book deals with using numerical methods in the pricing of derivatives. The pricing algorithms are again described at very high level of detail and they are supported by numerical examples of 'step-by-step' calculations. The presented methods are focused on pricing Bermudian and American claims, i.e. problem of optimal stopping. Generally these methods can be split into two main groups:

(1) Trees
(2) Monte Carlo simulations

Chapter 10 presents different methods of drift approximation in the BGM model and the application these methods to derivatives pricing. The first part of this chapter describes different methods of drift approximation ranging from the simplest 'frozen drift' to a method based on the Brownian Bridge. The second part of the chapter presents unpublished constructions of recombining binomial and trinomial trees basing upon a Brownian Bridge drift approximation. We present four basis construction algorithms in the following sections:

7. Binomial tree construction for $L_n^A(t)$
8. Binomial tree construction for $L_n^D(t)$
10. Trinomial tree construction for $L_n^A(t)$
11. Trinomial tree construction for $L_n^D(t)$

Section 13 describes an approximation of annuities presenting the improvement that applied to each of the aforementioned four basis constructions to improve its accuracy, especially for very high volatilities of forward LIBORs (40%–70%). Although descriptions of the tree construction is limited to the one dimensional case it can be easily generalized to multidimensional cases. The third part of the chapter compares the accuracy of different methods of drift approximation and shows that the tree constructions based on Brownian Bridge approximations seem to outperform other approximations. The last part of the chapter presents a complete application of the constructed binomial tree for pricing a Bermudian swaption – starting from the calibration model to co-terminal European swaptions by a tree construction to calculating the value of the priced swaption.

Chapter 11 presents an alternative approach for the HJM and BGM – the LIBOR Functional Markov Model. The first part of the chapter describes a theoretical construction of the one dimensional version of the model. Our description is based on that of Bennett and Kennedy (2005). Unlike in case of the HJM and BGM, the dynamic of the interest rate term structure in the LIBOR Functional Markov Model is not given by an analytical SDE. It is derived from market prices of caps by a numerical construction. The second part of the chapter describes constructions of binomial trees. This description is supported by numerical 'step-by-step' example of such a construction.

Chapter 12 gives an overview of different methods of pricing Bermudian claims: recombining trees/lattices, stochastic mesh, direct methods, additive noise, Longstaff-Schwartz. Two of presented approaches:

1. Recombining trees/lattices
2. Longstaff-Schwartz

are widely used in practice. The exact implementation of these approaches are described in Chapters 13 and 10.

Chapter 13 presents several algorithms that use Least Squares Monte Carlo to estimate a stopping boundary. All the presented algorithms use one or two sets of Monte Carlo scenarios for the evolution of interest rates (Forward LIBORs). The first part of the chapter presents five different algorithms based on the LSM approach. The second part describes numerical 'step-by- step' examples of some of the algorithms described in the first part. The third part of the chapter presents results of a valuation of a Bermudian Swaption using each of the derived algorithms. The fourth part presents an estimation of the differences between the real derivative value and the expected value of its estimator and therefore shows reasons for under- and overpricing that appear during valuation with LSM approaches. The last part is a trial valuation algorithm taking into account the results of their application to Bermudian swaption pricing (i.e. in third part of the chapter) as well as the theoretical divagation from fourth part of the chapter.

INDEX OF NOTATIONS FOR THE ENTIRE BOOK

$A_{nN}(t) = \sum\limits_{i=n+1}^{N} B(t, T_i)$ — annuity associated to a swap

$B(t, T)$ — discount factors on the period $[t, T]$

$C_{kl}(s, T) = \int\limits_{s}^{T} \gamma_l(t) \cdot \gamma_k(t) dt$ — BGM covariance

$D_n(t) = \dfrac{B(t, T_{n-1})}{B(t, T_n)}$ — forward compound factors

$d_1 = \dfrac{\ln(X(0)/K) + \sigma^2 T/2}{\sigma\sqrt{T}}$ — in Black formula

$d_2 = d_1 - \sigma\sqrt{T}$ — in Black formula

δ — accrual period

E — expected (mean) value

E_n — expected value under forward measure P_n

E_{nN} — expected value under forward swap measure P_{nN}

$\eta_n(t) = \Sigma(t, T_n) - \Sigma(t, T_{n-1})$ — volatility of forward compound factors

$\eta_{nN}(t)$ — HJM volatility of forward swap rates

$F_{kl}(s, T) = \int\limits_{s}^{T} \eta_l(t) \cdot \eta_k(t) dt$ — HJM covariance

$\Phi^i = \begin{bmatrix} \varphi^i_{11} & \varphi^i_{12} & \cdots & \varphi^i_{1N} \\ \varphi^i_{21} & \varphi^i_{22} & \cdots & \varphi^i_{2N} \\ \cdots & \cdots & \cdots & \cdots \\ \varphi^i_{N1} & \varphi^i_{N2} & \cdots & \varphi^i_{NN} \end{bmatrix}$ — BGM covariance matrix

$\varphi^i_{kl} = C_{kl}(0, T_i)$ — BGM covariance

$\gamma_n(t)$ — volatility of forward LIBOR rates

$\gamma_{nN}(t)$ — BGM volatility of forward swap rates

K — strike price

$K_n(t) = \dfrac{\delta L_n(t)}{1 + \delta L_n(t)}$ — volatility component

k_n — LIBOR shift

$k_{nN} = \sum\limits_{i=n+1}^{N} u_i(0)k_i$ — swap shift

$L_n(t) = \delta^{-1}\left(\dfrac{B(t, T_{n-1})}{B(t, T_n)} - 1\right)$ — forward LIBOR rates

$M^n_k(t) = \int\limits_{0}^{t} \gamma_n(s) \cdot dW_k(s)$ — BGM martingale

$\mu^i_{kl} = F_{kl}(0, T_i)$ — HJM covariance

N — Principal notional

$N^n_k(t) = \int\limits_{0}^{t} \eta_n(s) \cdot dW_k(s)$ — HJM martingale

P — probability

P_n –   forward measure

P_{nN} –   forward swap measure

$$\Pi^i = \begin{bmatrix} \mu_{11}^i & \mu_{12}^i & \cdots & \mu_{1N}^i \\ \mu_{21}^i & \mu_{22}^i & \cdots & \mu_{2N}^i \\ \cdots & \cdots & \cdots & \cdots \\ \mu_{N1}^i & \mu_{N2}^i & \cdots & \mu_{NN}^i \end{bmatrix}$$ –   HJM covariance matrix

$r(t)$ –   short rate

$\widetilde{R}_{nN}^i(t)$ –   HJM swaption volatility weight

$R_{nN}^i(t)$ –   BGM swaption volatility weight

$$S_{nN}(t) = \frac{\sum\limits_{i=n+1}^{N} B(t, T_i) L_i(t)}{A_{nN}(t)}$$ –   forward swap rates

$Swaption_{nN}(0, K)$ –   swaption price

$\Sigma(t, T)$ –   volatility of discount factors

σ_{nN} –   market swaption volatility

T –   time

T_n –   time grid

$$u_j(t) = \frac{B(t, T_j)}{A_{nN}(t)}$$ –   weight function

$W(t)$ –   Wiener process or Brownian motion

$$W_n(t) = W(t) + \int_0^t \Sigma(s, T_n) ds$$ –   Wiener process under forward measure

$$W_{nN}(t) = W(t) + \int_0^t \frac{\sum\limits_{i=n+1}^{N} B(s, T_i) \Sigma(s, T_i)}{A_{nN}(t)} ds$$ –   Wiener process under forward swap measure

$X_0(t)$ –   savings account

Part I
Theory

Part I
Theory

1

Mathematics in a Pill

The purpose of this chapter is to give a brief outline of the probability theory underlying the mathematics inside the book, and to introduce necessary notation and conventions which are used throughout.

1.1 PROBABILITY SPACE AND RANDOM VARIABLES

A probability triple (Ω, Σ, P) consists of the following components:

1. A set Ω of elementary outcomes called the *sample space*.
2. A σ-algebra Σ of possible *events* (subsets of Ω).
3. A *probability function* $P : \Sigma \to [0,1]$ that assigns real numbers between 0 and 1 called probabilities to the events in Σ.

The *conditional probability* of A given B is defined as follows:

$$P(A|B) = P(A \cap B)/P(B).$$

Two events are said to be *independent* if the following three (equivalent) conditions hold:

1. $P(A \cap B) = P(A)P(B)$
2. $P(A) = P(A|B)$
3. $P(B) = P(B|A)$

A random variable $X : \Omega \to G$ is a measurable function from a probability space Ω into a Banach space G known as the state space.

We say that random two variables X and Y are independent if for all events A and B

$$P(X \in A, Y \in B) = P(X \in A)P(Y \in B).$$

We define expected (mean) value EX of the random variable X as the integral

$$EX = \int_\Omega X(\omega)P(d\omega),$$

and define the variance DX as

$$DX = \int_\Omega (X(\omega) - EX) \otimes (X(\omega) - EX)P(d\omega).$$

where $\otimes$ stands for tensor product. We may define the conditional expectation of a random variable X with respect to a σ-algebra $\Xi \subset \Sigma$. It is the only random variable $E(X|\Xi)$ such that for all $A \in \Xi$

$$\int_A X(\omega)P(d\omega) = \int_A E(X|\Xi)(\omega)P(d\omega).$$

If the state space is the real line R, we define the distribution function $F(x)$ (also called the cumulative density function or probability distribution function) as the probability that a real random variable X takes on a value less than or equal to a number x.

$$F(x) = P(X < x).$$

If the function F is differentiable, its derivative $f(x)$ is called the density function:

$$f(x) = F'(x).$$

1.2   NORMAL DISTRIBUTIONS

A normal (Gaussian) distribution on R with mean $EX = \mu$ and variance $DX = \sigma^2$ is a probability distribution with probability function

$$f(t) = \frac{1}{\sigma\sqrt{2\pi}} \exp\left\{-\left(\frac{(t-\mu)^2}{2\sigma^2}\right)\right\}. \tag{1.1}$$

Figure 1.1   Gaussian distribution.

We also have the result that the sum of two normal variables is also a normal variable. A normal variable with mean $\mu = 0$ and variance $\sigma = 1$ is called a standard normal. We denote the cumulative distribution by N. A vector of M normal variables is called a multidimensional normal variable.

1.3   STOCHASTIC PROCESSES

Let $F_t \subset \Sigma$ be a family of increasing σ-algebras. We define the probability quadruple (Ω, F_t, Σ, P) as a standard probability setting for all dynamic models used in this book. A stochastic process is an indexed collection of F_t-measurable random variables $X(t)$, each of which is defined on the same probability triple (Ω, Σ, P) and takes values on the same codomain – in our case the interval $[0, T]$. In a continuous stochastic process the index set is continuous, resulting in an infinite number of random variables. A particular stochastic process is determined by specifying the joint probability distributions of the various random variables $X(t)$.

1.4   WIENER PROCESSES

A continuous-time stochastic process $W(t)$ with the following properties

- $W(0) = 0$,
- W has continuous paths,
- $W(s)$ and $(W(t) - W(s))$ are independent random variables for any $0 < s < t$,
- $W(t)$ has Gaussian distribution with mean 0 and variance t

is called Wiener process or Brownian motion. It was introduced by Louis Bachelier in 1900 as a model of stock prices. A vector of N independent Wiener processes is called a multidimensional Wiener process. The general shape of such a process is seen in the example below.

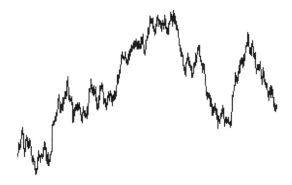

Figure 1.2   Wiener process.

1.5   GEOMETRIC WIENER PROCESSES

The following stochastic process

$$X(t) = X(0) \exp\left\{ \mu t + \sigma W(t) - \frac{\sigma^2}{2} t \right\} \tag{1.2}$$

is called geometric Wiener process. The coefficient μ is called the drift and the coefficient σ is called the volatility.

1.6 MARKOV PROCESSES

A stochastic process X whose future probabilities are determined by its most recent values is called or is said to be Markov. This can be described mathematically in the following manner

$$P(X(T) \in A | X(s), s \leq t) = P(X(T) \in A | X(t)).$$

1.7 STOCHASTIC INTEGRALS AND STOCHASTIC DIFFERENTIAL EQUATIONS

If Y is a predictable stochastic process such that

$$P\left(\int_0^t |Y(s)|^2 \, ds < \infty \right) = 1,$$

we may define the stochastic integral with respect to the Wiener process $W(t)$ to be

$$C(t) = \int_0^t Y(s) \cdot dW(s). \tag{1.3}$$

If the process Y is deterministic then C is Gaussian with independent increments. The stochastic integral has the following properties:

$$EC(t) = 0 \text{ and } EC^2(t) = E \int_0^t |Y(s)|^2 \, ds.$$

We say that Y satisfies the Ito stochastic differential equation

$$dY(t) = f(t, Y(t))dt + g(t, Y(t)) \cdot dW(t),$$
$$Y(0) = y. \tag{1.4}$$

If

$$Y(t) = Y(0) + \int_0^t f(s, Y(s))ds + \int_0^t g(s, Y(s)) \cdot dW(s).$$

If f and g are deterministic functions with properties that ensure uniqueness of solution, then the process Y is a Markov process. A Geometric Wiener process satisfies the following stochastic equation:

$$dX(t) = \mu X(t)dt + \sigma X(t)dW(t). \tag{1.5}$$

1.8   ITO'S FORMULA

Let the process Y satisfy the Ito equation:

$$dY(t) = f(t)dt + g(t) \cdot dW(t)$$

and let F be a smooth function. By applying the Ito formula we produce the stochastic equation satisfied by the process $F(t, Y(t))$:

$$dF(t, Y(t)) = \left(\frac{\partial F}{\partial t} + \frac{1}{2} \frac{\partial^2 F}{\partial Y^2} |g(t)|^2 \right) dt + \frac{\partial F}{\partial Y} dY(t). \qquad (1.6)$$

1.9   MARTINGALES

The N-dimensional stochastic process $M(t)$ is a martingale with respect to F_t if $E|C(t)| < \infty$ and the following property also holds:

$$M(t) = E\left(M(T)|F_t\right).$$

Every stochastic integral (and hence any Wiener process) is a martingale. However, a Geometric Wiener process is a martingale only if $\mu = 0$. Any continuous martingale M can be represented as an Ito integral, i.e.

$$M(t) = \int\limits_0^t Y(s) \cdot dW(s)$$

for some predictable process Y. A martingale can be considered as a model of a fair game and therefore can be considered a proper model of financial markets.

1.10   GIRSANOV'S THEOREM

Let M be a positive continuous martingale, such that $M(0) = 1$. Then there exists a predictable stochastic process $\sigma(t)$ such that

$$dM(t) = -\sigma(t)M(t)dW(t)$$

or, equivalently

$$M(t) = \exp\left\{ -\frac{1}{2} \int\limits_0^t \sigma^2(s)ds - \int\limits_0^t \sigma(s)dW(s) \right\}.$$

If we now define new probability measure E_T by

$$P_T(A) = \int\limits_\Omega I_A(\omega)M(T, \omega)P(d\omega).$$

then P_T is a probability measure under which the stochastic process

$$W_T(t) = W(t) + \int_0^t \sigma(s)\,ds$$

is a Wiener process.

1.11 BLACK'S FORMULA (1976)

Let the stochastic process X satisfy the equation:

$$dX(t) = \sigma X(t)\,dW(t).$$

Let C represent the (undiscounted) payoff from a European call option, so that $C = E\,(X(T) - K)^+$. Then C is given by the Black'76 formula:

$$C = X(0)N(d_1) - KN(d_2),   \tag{1.7}$$

where

$$d_1 = \frac{\ln(X(0)/K) + \sigma^2 T/2}{\sigma\sqrt{T}},$$

$$d_2 = d_1 - \sigma\sqrt{T}.$$

1.12 PRICING DERIVATIVES AND CHANGING OF NUMERAIRE

We can introduce a general abstract approach to derivatives pricing as follows: We are given a set of positive continuous stochastic processes $X_0(t), X_1(t), \ldots, X_N(t)$ representing market quantities; these could be stock prices, interest rates, exchange rates, etc. We assume that the market is arbitrage-free, so that the quantities $M_1(t) = \frac{X_1(t)}{X_0(t)}, \ldots, M_N(t) = \frac{X_N(t)}{X_0(t)}$ are martingales, where $X_0(t)$ is called a basic asset – a numeraire. Pricing European derivatives maturing at time T consists of calculating functionals of the form:

$$Price = E\left\{\frac{\varsigma}{X_0(T)}\right\},$$

where ς is a random variable representing the payoff at time T. The process $X_0(t)$ is understood as the time value of money, i.e. comparable to a savings account, so we have to assume that $X_0(0) = 1$. If we define N new probability measures by

$$P_i(A) = X_i^{-1}(0) \int_\Omega I_A(\omega) M_i(T, \omega) P(d\omega).$$

then this leads to the following theorem:

Theorem. The processes $\frac{X_0(t)}{X_i(t)}, \frac{X_1(t)}{X_i(t)}, \ldots, \frac{X_N(t)}{X_i(t)}$ are martingales under the measure P_i.

Proof. Let ς be an F_t-measurable random variable.

$$X_i(0)E_i\left\{\frac{X_j(t)}{X_i(t)}\varsigma\right\} = E\left\{\frac{X_j(t)}{X_i(t)}\frac{X_i(t)}{X_0(t)}\varsigma\right\} = EM_j(t)\varsigma = E\varsigma E\left(M_j(T)|F_t\right)$$

$$= EE\left(M_j(T)\varsigma|F_t\right) = EM_j(T)\varsigma = E\left\{\frac{X_j(T)}{X_i(T)}\frac{X_i(T)}{X_0(T)}\varsigma\right\} = X_i(0)E_i\left\{\frac{X_j(T)}{X_i(T)}\varsigma\right\}.$$

This simple theorem is extremely important. In pricing derivatives the savings account $X_0(t)$ can be replaced by any other tradable asset – we can change the numeraire, which may allow us to simplify certain calculations, for example we have

$$Price = E\left\{\frac{\varsigma}{X_0(T)}\right\} = E\left\{\frac{\varsigma}{X_1(T)}\frac{X_1(T)}{X_0(T)}\right\} = X_1(0)E_1\left\{\frac{\varsigma}{X_1(T)}\right\}.$$

1.13 PRICING OF INTEREST RATE DERIVATIVES AND THE FORWARD MEASURE

The theory of interest rate derivatives is in some sense simple because it relies only on one basic notion – the time value of money. Let us start with some basic notions: denote by $B(t, T)$ be discount factors on the period $[t, T]$ – understood as value at time t of an obligation to pay \$1 at time T. Payment of this dollar is certain; there is no credit risk involved. This obligation is also called a zero-coupon bond. We assume that zero-coupon bonds with all maturities are traded and this market is absolutely liquid – there are no transaction spreads. These assumptions are quite sensible since the money, bond and swap markets are very liquid with spreads not exceeding several basis points. Notice several obvious properties of discount factors:

$$0 < B(t, T) \le B(t, S) \le 1 \text{ if } S \le T \text{ and } B(T, T) = 1.$$

Let $X_0(t)$ be the savings account then all tradable assets $\xi(t)$ satisfy the arbitrage property that

$$\frac{\xi(t)}{X_0(t)} \text{ is a martingale.}$$

In particular we have that

$$M(t, T) = \frac{B(t, T)}{X_0(t)B(0, T)}$$

is a positive continuous martingale. We assume that the savings account is a process with finite variation – existence and uniqueness of a savings account may be a subject to a fascinating mathematical investigation. Since this problem is completely irrelevant to pricing issues – we refer to Musiela and Rutkowski (1997b) stating only that it is satisfied for all practical models. The savings account is of little interest because it is not a tradable asset, hence its importance is rather of mathematical character and practitioners try get rid of all notions not related to trading as soon as possible. We adopt this principle and will shortly remove the notion of savings account from our calculations.

There exists a d-dimensional stochastic process $\Sigma(t, T)$ a d-dimensional Brownian motion and such that

$$dB(t, T) = -B(t, T)(-d \ln X_0(t) + \Sigma(t, T) \cdot dW(t))$$

and

$$dM(t, T) = -M(t, T)\Sigma(t, T) \cdot dW(t).$$

Remark. The d-dimensional representation is not unique, however uniqueness does hold for the single dimensional representation. Since most financial models are multidimensional we have chosen the less elegant d-dimensional representation. The dot stands for scalar product.

Therefore

$$M(t, T) = \exp\left\{ -\frac{1}{2}\int_0^t |\Sigma(s, T)|^2 ds - \int_0^t \Sigma(s, T) \cdot dW(s) \right\}$$

and

$$B(t, T) = B(0, T)X_0^{-1}(t)\exp\left\{ -\frac{1}{2}\int_0^t |\Sigma(s, T)|^2 ds - \int_0^t \Sigma(s, T) \cdot dW(s) \right\}. \qquad (1.8)$$

Since $B(T, T) = 1$, $M(T, T)B(0, T) = X_0^{-1}(T)$.

The pricing of European interest rate derivatives consists of finding expectation of discounted values of cash flows

$$E\left(X_0^{-1}(t)\xi \right),$$

where ξ is an F_T-measurable random variable – the intrinsic value of the claim. Define the probability measure E_T by

$$E_T\varsigma = E\varsigma M(T, T)$$

for any random variable ς. By the Girsanov theorem E_T is a probability measure under which the process

$$W_T(t) = W(t) + \int_0^t \Sigma(s, T)ds$$

is a Wiener process. Now

$$EX_0^{-1}(T)\xi = B(0, T)EM(T, T)\xi = B(0, T)E_T\xi.$$

We may take discounting with respect to multiple cash flows as in the case of swaptions. Let δ be accrual period for both interest rates and swaps. For simplicity, we assume it is constant. Define consecutive grid points as $T_{i+1} = T_i + \delta$ for a certain initial $T = T_0 < \delta$. To ease the notation, we set $E_n = E_{T_n}$ and $W_n = W_{T_n}$. The forward compound factors and forward LIBOR rates are defined as

$$\delta L_n(t) + 1 = D_n(t) = \frac{B(t, T_{n-1})}{B(t, T_n)} \tag{1.9}$$

and forward swap rates as

$$S_{nN}(t) = \frac{\sum\limits_{i=n+1}^{N} B(t, T_i) L_i(t)}{A_{nN}(t)} = \frac{B(t, T_n) - B(t, T_N)}{\delta A_{nN}(t)}$$

where

$$A_{nN}(t) = \sum_{i=n+1}^{N} B(t, T_i).$$

Now let

$$C(S_{nN}) = \sum_{i=n+1}^{N} X_0^{-1}(T_i) = \sum_{i=n+1}^{N} B(0, T_i) M(T_i, T_i).$$

Thus the pricing of European swap derivatives consists of finding

$$E(C(S_{nN})\xi),$$

where ξ is an $F_{T_{n+1}}$-measurable random variable – the intrinsic value of the claim. Since $M(t, T)$ is a positive continuous martingale we also have that the following is a positive continuous martingale:

$$M(t, S_{nN}) = \frac{\sum\limits_{i=n+1}^{N} B(0, T_i) M(t, T_i)}{A_{nN}(0)} = \frac{\sum\limits_{i=n+1}^{N} B(t, T_i)}{X_0(t) A_{nN}(0)}.$$

Moreover

$$dM(t, S_{nN}) = -\frac{\sum\limits_{i=n+1}^{N} B(0, T_i) M(t, T_i)}{A_{nN}(0)} \cdot \frac{\sum\limits_{i=n+1}^{N} B(0, T_i) M(t, T_i) \Sigma(t, T_i)}{\sum\limits_{i=n+1}^{N} B(0, T_i) M(t, T_i)} dW(t)$$

$$= -M(t, S_{nN}) \frac{\sum\limits_{i=n+1}^{N} B(t, T_i) \Sigma(t, T_i)}{A_{nN}(t)} dW(t).$$

Therefore E_{nN} defined by

$$E_{nN}\varsigma = E_{\varsigma}M(T_{n+1}, S_{nN})$$

is a probability measure under which the process

$$W_{nN}(t) = W(t) + \int_0^t \frac{\sum_{i=n+1}^N B(s, T_i)\Sigma(s, T_i)}{A_{nN}(t)} ds \qquad (1.10)$$

is a Wiener process. Hence

$$EC(S_{nN})\xi = \sum_{i=n+1}^N B(0, T_i)EM(T_i, T_i)\xi$$

$$= \sum_{i=n+1}^N B(0, T_i)EM(T_{n+1}, T_i)\xi = A_{nN}(0)E_{nN}\xi.$$

Moreover

$$M(t, S_{nN})S_{nN}(t) = \frac{\sum_{i=n+1}^N B(t, T_i)}{X_0(t)A_{nN}(0)} \frac{B(t, T_n) - B(t, T_N)}{A_{nN}(t)} = \frac{B(t, T_n) - B(t, T_N)}{X_0(t)A_{nN}(0)}.$$

Therefore $S_{nN}(t)M(t, S_{nN})$ is a martingale under the measure E, and then the forward swap rate $S_{nN}(t)$ is a martingale under E_{nN}.

2

Heath-Jarrow-Morton and Brace-Gatarek-Musiela Models

2.1 HJM AND BGM MODELS UNDER THE SPOT MEASURE

The purpose of this section is to derive stochastic equations for interest rates dynamics in both the HJM and BGM models. Since the models can be considered as twins, they will be studied in parallel. We will extensively use the Ito formula. By (1.8),

$$D_n(t) = \frac{B(0, T_{n-1})}{B(0, T_n)} \exp\left\{ -\frac{1}{2} \int_0^t \left(|\Sigma(s, T_{n-1})|^2 - |\Sigma(s, T_n)|^2 \right) ds \right. $$
$$\left. - \int_0^t (\Sigma(s, T_{n-1}) - \Sigma(s, T_n)) \cdot dW(s) \right\}.$$

By the Ito formula $D_n(t)$ satisfies

$$dD_n(t) = \Sigma(t, T_n) \cdot (\Sigma(t, T_n) - \Sigma(t, T_{n-1})) \, D_n(t) dt + D_n(t) \, (\Sigma(t, T_n) - \Sigma(t, T_{n-1})) \cdot dW(t).$$

The HJM model is constructed as follows: Setting $\Sigma(t, T)$ to be deterministic and denoting $\eta_n(t) = \Sigma(r, T_n) - \Sigma(t, T_{n-1})$ we get an equation similar to Black-Scholes:

$$dD_n(t) = \Sigma(t, T_n) \cdot \eta_n(t) D_n(t) dt + D_n(t) \eta_n(t) \cdot dW(t). \tag{2.1}$$

Hence if we set $\Sigma(t, s) = 0$ for $s \leq t + \delta$ we have

$$\Sigma(t, T_n) = \sum_{T_j > t+\delta}^{n} \eta_j(t).$$

In a similar manner, the BGM model is constructed as follows: Since $\delta dL_n(t) = dD_n(t)$

$$dL_n(t) = \Sigma(t, T_n) \cdot (\Sigma(t, T_n) - \Sigma(t, T_{n-1})) \left(L_n(t) + \delta^{-1} \right) dt$$
$$+ \left(L_n(t) + \delta^{-1} \right) (\Sigma(t, T_n) - \Sigma(t, T_{n-1})) \cdot dW(t).$$

Then, set the linear diffusion parameter

$$L_n(t) \gamma_n(t) = (\Sigma(t, T_n) - \Sigma(t, T_{n-1})) \left(L_n(t) + \delta^{-1} \right),$$

where $\gamma(t)$ is the LIBOR volatility. Therefore

$$\Sigma(t, T_n) = \Sigma(t, T_{n-1}) + K_n(t) \gamma_n(t) \text{ with } K_n(t) = \frac{\delta L_n(t)}{1 + \delta L_n(t)}.$$

Hence

$$\Sigma(t, T_n) = \sum_{T_j > t + \delta}^{n} K_j(t)\gamma_j(t)$$

finally if we set $\Sigma(t, s) = 0$ for $s \leq t + \delta$ then

$$dL_n(t) = \Sigma(t, T_n) \cdot \gamma_n(t)L_n(t)dt + L_n(t)\gamma_n(t) \cdot dW(t). \qquad (2.2)$$

By the standard fixed point method and Picard theorem, there exist unique solutions for the equations (2.1) and (2.2) by Lipschitz continuity of parameters, for details we refer to Doberlein and Schweizer (2001) and Shreve (1988). Indeed, the equation (2.1) is linear, hence it defines a geometric Brownian motion. The equation (2.2) is nonlinear and may be solved by induction with respect to n. Notice that the BGM (2.2) and HJM (2.1) models may be studied in parallel and we will use this approach in this chapter. As it will be shown later, forward rate models are used only under forward measures, hence assumptions that $\Sigma(t, s) = 0$ for $s \leq t + \delta$ are not restrictive. Determining of bond volatilities $\Sigma(t, T)$ is indeed equivalent to construction of a term structure model.

Warning for rigorous mathematicians. The derivation of the HJM and BGM equations was done in the way known from physics – assuming that all qualitative assumptions are satisfied, we then derive the proper form of the equation. The mathematical approach is different – we prove non-arbitrage property while constructing a model. Those who wish to look at a more rigorous method are referred to Musiela and Rutkowski (1997b); Karatzas and Shreve (1988), at least for this part of the theory.

For historical reasons the HJM model is not formulated in the form (2.1) but as a differential one. Assuming that $B(t, T)$ is differentiable with respect to T and

$$B(t, T) = \exp\left\{ -\int_t^T r(t, s)ds \right\}.$$

Then obviously the savings account $X_0(t)$ is defined as

$$X_0(t) = \exp\left\{ \int_0^t r(s)ds \right\} \text{ with } r(s) = r(s, s).$$

Hence

$$\frac{B(t, T)}{X_0(t)} = E\exp\left\{ -\int_0^t r(s)ds - \int_t^T r(t, s)ds \right\}.$$

Assume that Y has bounded variation and $r(\cdot, T)$ is an Ito process, i.e.

$$dr(t, T) = a(t, T)dt + \sigma(t, T) \cdot dW(t), \qquad (2.3)$$

where W is a Wiener process, a and σ are stochastic processes. We can now present

Theorem. For any $0 \leq t \leq T < \infty$

$$a(t, T) = \sigma(t, T) \cdot \int_t^T \sigma(t, s) ds.$$

Proof. By the Ito formula

$$d\frac{B(t, T)}{X_0(t)} = \frac{B(t, T)}{X_0(t)} \{r(t) - r(t)\} dt$$

$$+ \frac{B(t, T)}{X_0(t)} \left\{ \frac{1}{2} \left| \int_t^T \sigma(t, s) ds \right|^2 dt - \int_t^T a(t, s) ds dt - \int_t^T \sigma(t, s) ds \cdot dW(t) \right\}.$$

To ensure the martingale property for $\frac{B(t,T)}{X_0(t)}$ for any $0 \leq t \leq T$, we must have

$$\frac{1}{2} \left| \int_t^T \sigma(t, s) ds \right|^2 = \int_t^T a(t, s) ds$$

and therefore

$$a(t, T) = \sigma(t, T) \cdot \int_t^T \sigma(t, s) ds.$$

Hence the equation (2.3) becomes

$$dr(t, T) = \sigma(t, T) \cdot \int_t^T \sigma(t, s) ds dt + \sigma(t, T) \cdot dW(t). \tag{2.4}$$

The equation (2.4) is called Heath-Jarrow-Morton equation and normally in literature the model is formulated as above rather than (2.1). Justification for this formulation is hard to find, and in fact appears only to be done for historical reasons. The instantaneous rates $r(t, T)$ are not quoted by the market, while LIBOR rates L_n and hence compound factors D_n are. People normally discretise the equation (2.4) – taking $r(t, T)$ for a short term (say, one week) interest rate, and such an approximated model is used in valuation of derivatives. We, however, do not recommend this procedure as a short cut, which is longer than the regular way.

There is one reason for which the form (2.4) should be present in this book. The rate $r(t)$ is called short rate and has very intuitive interpretation as the interest rate on a very short period – overnight for instance. There exists a large class of interest rate models, called short rate models based on some mathematically correct but counterintuitive property. Since they are still used in practice, they deserve several comments. Let us start with this property: Since $B(T, T) = 1$ and

$$B(t, T) \exp\left\{ -\int_0^t r(s) ds \right\}$$

is a martingale,

$$B(t, T) = E \left\{ \exp \left(-\int_t^T r(s)ds \right) \middle| F_t \right\}. \tag{2.5}$$

We may assume that $r(s)$ is a Markov process, which in practice means that $r(s)$ satisfies the following stochastic differential equation

$$dr(t) = a(t, r(t))dt + \sigma(t, r(t))dW(t)$$

for sufficiently regular functions a and σ. By the Markov property

$$B(t, T) = E \left\{ \exp \left(-\int_t^T r(s)ds \right) \middle| F_t \right\} = E \left\{ \exp \left(-\int_t^T r(s)ds \right) \middle| r(t) \right\} = h(t, T, r(t))$$

for some deterministic function h. The functions a and σ obviously determine the function h, at least with help of a numerical procedure. Traders however will never agree that the dynamics of all interest rates are determined by dynamics of the overnight rate. However in practice the short rate is never used and the single factor, identified by mathematicians as the short rate, is rather understood as a parameterization of a medium or long term rate. By the Ito formula, every short rate model is a HJM model, i.e. there exist deterministic functions F and G such that:

$$r(t, T) = F(t, T, r(t)) \tag{2.6}$$

and

$$\sigma(t, T) = G(t, T, r(t)). \tag{2.7}$$

Formulae (2.6) and (2.7) have no important practical implication but show relation between various interest rate models. We present an overview of three short rate models which are of special interest from practical point of view: Vasiček, Cox-Ingersoll-Ross and Black-Karasiński.

2.2   VASIČEK MODEL

In the Vasiček model (Vasiček, 1977) the short rate follows the Ito equation:

$$dr(t) = a(b - r(t))dt + \sigma dW(t), \tag{2.8}$$

where a, b and σ are given constants. We may calculate that the discount factors are given by the formula

$$B(t, T) = A(T - t) \cdot e^{C(T-t)r(t)}, \tag{2.9}$$

where for $a \neq 0$

$$C(t) = \frac{e^{-at} - 1}{a},$$

$$A(t) = \exp \left\{ \frac{(C(t) - t)(a^2 b - \sigma^2/2)}{a^2} - \frac{\sigma^2 C(t)^2}{4a} \right\}.$$

If $a = 0$, then $C(t) = t$ and

$$A(t) = \exp \left\{ \sigma^2 t^3/6 \right\}.$$

The Vasiček model with added time dependennce in the parameter $b(t)$ calculated to fit the initial yield curve is called the Hull-White model.

2.3 COX-INGERSOLL-ROSS MODEL

In the Cox-Ingersoll Ross (1985) model the short rate follows the Ito equation:

$$dr(t) = a(b - r(t))dt + \sigma \sqrt{r(t)} dW(t), \tag{2.10}$$

where a, b and σ are constants. We may calculate that the discount factors are given by the formula (2.9), where

$$C(t) = \frac{2 \left(e^{\delta t} - 1 \right)}{(\delta + a) \left(e^{\delta t} - 1 \right) + 2\delta},$$

$$A(t) = \left\{ \frac{2\delta e^{(a+\delta)t/2}}{(\delta + a) \left(e^{\delta t} - 1 \right) + 2\delta} \right\}^{\frac{2ab}{\sigma^2}},$$

$$\delta = \sqrt{a^2 + 2\sigma^2}.$$

The formula (2.9) is crucial – it states that the bond prices is an exponent of an affine function of the short rate. Duffie and Singleton (1997) proved that only the Vasiček (1977) and Cox-Ingersoll-Ross (1985) models follow the exponential affine property.

2.4 BLACK-KARASIŃSKI MODEL

In the Black-Karasiński (1991) model the short rate is given by the formula $r(t) = e^{f(t)}$, where f follows the Ito equation:

$$df(t) = a(b - f(t))dt + \sigma dW(t).$$

There is known no closed form representation for $B(t, T)$ and it has to be calculated by numerical methods. The popular Black-Derman-Toy (1990) model is a special case of Black-Karasiński model. All three models, when used in practice, will have time-dependent parameter $b(t)$ to fit initial yield curve.

2.5 HJM AND BGM MODELS UNDER THE FORWARD MEASURES

In order to avoid repeating formula we introduce the following convention:

$$\sum_{j=k+1}^{n} a_j = -\sum_{j=n+1}^{k} a_j \tag{2.11}$$

for $n \leq k$. Recall that the process

$$W_k(t) = W(t) + \int_0^t \Sigma(s, T_k) ds$$

is a Wiener process under the measure E_k. The compound factors $D_n(t)$ in the HJM model and forward LIBORs $L_n(t)$ in the BGM model, follow the equations:

$$dD_n(t) = -D_n(t) \sum_{j=n+1}^{k} \eta_j(t) \cdot \eta_n(t) dt + D_n(t) \eta_n(t) \cdot dW_k(t) \tag{2.12}$$

and

$$dL_n(t) = -L_n(t) \sum_{j=n+1}^{k} K_j(t) \gamma_j(t) \cdot \gamma_n(t) dt + L_n(t) \gamma_n(t) \cdot dW_k(t). \tag{2.13}$$

Under the swap measure E_{nN} for $n < k$, we have that the compound factors $D_k(t)$ in the HJM model and forward LIBORs $L_k(t)$ in the BGM model, follow the equations:

$$dD_k(t) = D_k(t) \eta_k(t) \cdot \left(dW_{nN}(t) + \sum_{j=n+2}^{k} \eta_j(t) dt - \sum_{j=n+1}^{N-1} \frac{A_{jN}(t)}{A_{nN}(t)} \eta_{j+1}(t) dt \right) \tag{2.14}$$

and

$$dL_k(t) = L_k(t) \gamma_k(t) \cdot \left(dW_{nN}(t) + \sum_{j=n+2}^{k} K_j(t) \gamma_j(t) dt - \sum_{j=n+1}^{N-1} \frac{K_{j+1}(t) A_{jN}(t)}{A_{nN}(t)} \gamma_{j+1}(t) dt \right). \tag{2.15}$$

And finally

$$dL_n(t) = L_n(t) \gamma_n(t) \cdot dW_n(t),$$

hence

$$E \frac{(L_n(T_{n-1}) - K)^+}{X_0(T_n)} = B(0, T_n) E_n (L_n(T_{n-1}) - K)^+ = B(0, T_n) (L_n(0) N(d_1) - K N(d_2)),$$

where

$$d_1 = \frac{\ln(L_n(0)/K) + \sigma^2/2}{\sigma},$$

$$d_2 = d_1 - \sigma,$$

and we have

$$\sigma^2 = \int\limits_{s}^{T_{n-1}} |\gamma_n(t)|^2 dt.$$

This is one of main reasons for the popularity of BGM model – caplet pricing coincides with the market convention of using the Black'76 formula. Similarly a analogy holds for the HJM model as well, although differs from the market convention:

$$dD_n(t) = D_n(t)\eta_n(t) \cdot dW_n(t),$$

hence

$$E\frac{(L_n(T_{n-1}) - K)^+}{X_0(T_n)} = E\frac{(D_n(T_{n-1}) - (\delta K + 1))^+}{\delta X_0(T_n)}$$

$$= \delta^{-1} B(0, T_n) E_n (D_n(T_{n-1}) - (\delta K + 1))^+$$

$$= B(0, T_n) \left((L_n(0) + \delta^{-1})N(d_1) - (K + \delta^{-1})N(d_2) \right),$$

where

$$d_1 = \frac{\ln(\delta L_{n-1}(0) + 1) - \ln(\delta K + 1) + \widetilde{\sigma}^2/2}{\widetilde{\sigma}},$$

$$d_2 = d_1 - \widetilde{\sigma},$$

and

$$\widetilde{\sigma}^2 = \int\limits_{0}^{T_{n-1}} |\eta_n(t)|^2 \, dt.$$

We have never seen a situation where pricing of interest rated derivatives is most suitable under the spot measure. In our experience – interest rate derivatives should be priced under suitable forward measure. To be honest – the proper choice of the most convenient forward measure is not straightforward and may be tricky.

3
Simulation

3.1 SIMULATION OF HJM AND BGM MODELS UNDER THE FORWARD MEASURE

Again by the Ito formula $D_k(t)$ in the HJM model and forward LIBORs $L_n(t)$ in the BGM model, are given by the formulae:

$$D_n(t) = D_n(0) \exp\left(-F_{jn}(0, t) - \frac{1}{2}F_{nn}(0, t) + N_k^n(t)\right) \tag{3.1}$$

and

$$L_n(t) = L_n(0) \exp\left(-\int_0^t \sum_{j=n+1}^k K_j(s)\gamma_j(s) \cdot \gamma_n(s)ds - \frac{1}{2}C_{nn}(0, t) + M_k^n(t)\right), \tag{3.2}$$

where

$$N_k^n(t) = \int_0^t \eta_n(s) \cdot dW_k(s), \tag{3.3}$$

$$M_k^n(t) = \int_0^t \gamma_n(s) \cdot dW_k(s), \tag{3.4}$$

$$F_{kl}(s, T) = \int_s^T \eta_l(t) \cdot \eta_k(t)dt, \tag{3.5}$$

and

$$C_{kl}(s, T) = \int_s^T \gamma_l(t) \cdot \gamma_k(t)dt. \tag{3.6}$$

We have arrived at an important difference between the two twins: in the case of HJM model (3.1) forms a closed formula, where for the BGM model (3.2) is a just alternative representation. Clearly

$$E_k N_k^n(t) = E_k M_k^n(t) = 0,$$

$$E_k N_k^n(t)N_k^m(t) = F_{mn}(0, t)$$

and

$$E_k M_k^n(t) M_k^m(t) = C_{mn}(0, t).$$

Since our compound factors $D_n(t)$ are deterministic functions of the zero-mean Gaussian process with independent increments $\{N_k^1(t), \ldots, N_k^d(t)\}$ with given correlations $F_{mn}(0, t)$, it suffices to simulate $\{N_k^1(t), \ldots, N_k^d(t)\}$. The simulation scheme for BGM is not that easy but also not very sophisticated:

$$L_n(t + \Delta t) = L_n(t) \exp\left(-\sum_{j=n+1}^{k} K_j(t) C_{jn}(t, t + \Delta t) - \frac{1}{2} C_{nn}(t, t + \Delta t) + \Delta M_k^n(t)\right), \quad (3.7)$$

where

$$\Delta M_k^n(t) = \int_{t}^{t+\Delta t} \gamma_n(s) \cdot dW_k(s) = M_k^n(t + \Delta t) - M_k^n(t).$$

In both cases the deterministic functions $C_{mn}(s, t)$ and $F_{mn}(s, t)$ determine dynamics of the compound factors and LIBOR rates and volatility terms $\gamma_n(t)$ and $\eta_n(t)$ are redundant. Simulation of HJM model was here reduced to generation of multidimensional Gaussian variables. We present it briefly for the sake of completeness.

3.2   MONTE CARLO SIMULATION OF MULTIDIMENSIONAL GAUSSIAN VARIABLES

Let

$$\Sigma = \begin{bmatrix} \sigma_{11} & \sigma_{21} & \cdots & \sigma_{N1} \\ \sigma_{12} & \sigma_{22} & \cdots & \sigma_{N2} \\ \cdots & \cdots & \cdots & \cdots \\ \sigma_{1N} & \sigma_{2N} & \cdots & \sigma_{NN} \end{bmatrix}$$

be the covariance matrix of $F_{mn}(s, t)$ or $C_{mn}(s, t)$ in our case. Our task is to generate a pseudo-random zero-mean vector with covariance matrix Σ. We use the scheme in Figure 3.1 in order to accomplish this task.

Random numbers generation

The most popular generator of uniformly distributed on [0,1] (pseudo) random numbers is the affine generator (Wieczorkowski and Zieliński, 1997):

$$x_n = (a x_{n-1} + b) \bmod(c), \quad X_n = x_n/c.$$

Generators based on genetic algorithms are popular as well. Random numbers $Y = \left(N^{-1}(X_n), N^{-1}(X_{n+1}), \ldots, N^{-1}(X_{n+m})\right)$ are random normally distributed random vectors with covariance matrix I, where N is the cumulative distribution of standard normal random variables. There exist more sophisticated and efficient generators of normally distributed random vectors, we refer to Wieczorkowski and Zieliński (1997).

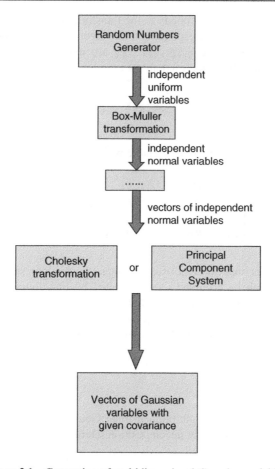

Figure 3.1 Generation of multidimensional Gaussian variables.

Principal Components Analysis (PCA)

Due to the fact that the covariance matrix is symmetric positive we are able to transform it in the following way:

$$\hat{\Sigma} = P\Sigma P',$$

where matrix P is orthonormal, i.e.: $PP' = I$, and matrix $\hat{\Sigma}$ is diagonal of the form:

$$\hat{\Sigma} = \begin{bmatrix} \lambda_1 & 0 & \ldots & 0 \\ 0 & \lambda_2 & \ldots & 0 \\ \ldots & \ldots & \ldots & \ldots \\ 0 & 0 & \ldots & \lambda_N \end{bmatrix},$$

where

$$\lambda_1 \geq \lambda_2 \geq \ldots \ldots \geq \lambda_N \geq 0.$$

The foregoing transformation corresponds to the transformation by rotation of coordinates; the i-th column of the matrix P corresponding to the eigenvalue λ_i is called i-th eigenvector. Let $\Xi = (\xi_1, \xi_2, \ldots, \xi_N)$, where $\xi_1, \xi_2, \ldots, \xi_N$ are independent identically distributed standard random variables. Then the random vector

$$B = \sqrt{\hat{\Sigma}} P \Xi = \sum_{i=1}^{N} \xi_i \sqrt{\lambda_i} P_i$$

is a multidimensional Gaussian random variable with covariance matrix Σ, where

$$P = \begin{bmatrix} p_{11} & p_{21} & \cdots & p_{N1} \\ p_{12} & p_{22} & \cdots & p_{N2} \\ \cdots & \cdots & \cdots & \cdots \\ p_{1N} & p_{2N} & \cdots & p_{NN} \end{bmatrix} \text{ and } P_i = \begin{bmatrix} p_{i1} \\ p_{i2} \\ \cdots \\ p_{iN} \end{bmatrix}.$$

When λ_1 is much larger than the rest of eigenvalues the random vector $Y = \sqrt{\hat{\Sigma}} P \Xi$ with covariance matrix Σ can be accurately approximated by one-dimensional random vector $\tilde{Y} = \xi_1 \sqrt{\lambda_1} P_1$ with covariance matrix $\tilde{\Sigma} = \lambda_1 P_1' P_1$.

This means that the eigenvector P_1 describes a large part of the matrix Σ and therefore is called principal component. This approach can be easily generalized to more components.

Cholesky decomposition

An alternative way of generating multidimensional Gaussian random variable with given covariance matrix Σ is via Cholesky decomposition. Define a triangular matrix A by

$$A = \begin{bmatrix} a_{11} & 0 & \cdots & 0 \\ a_{12} & a_{22} & \cdots & 0 \\ \cdots & \cdots & \cdots & 0 \\ a_{1N} & a_{2N} & \cdots & a_{NN} \end{bmatrix},$$

where

$$a_{ii} = \sqrt{\sigma_{ii} - \sum_{k=1}^{i-1} a_{ki}^2}$$

and

$$a_{ij} = \frac{\sqrt{\sigma_{ij} - \sum_{k=1}^{i-1} a_{ki} a_{kj}}}{a_{ii}}.$$

Then $\Sigma = AA'$ and the random vector $A'\Xi$ is a multidimensional Gaussian random variable with covariance matrix Σ.

3.3   TRINOMIAL TREE SIMULATION OF MULTIDIMENSIONAL GAUSSIAN VARIABLES

The construction of trinomial trees has the following graphical representation:

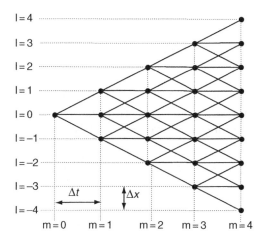

Figure 3.2   Example of a trinomial tree.

Let our simulated Gaussian process $G_i^n = N_k^n(T_i)$ (or $G_i^n = M_k^n(T_i)$, or other) admit the representation

$$G_i^n = \sum_{k=1}^{i} Y_k^n. \tag{3.8}$$

Let $Y_k = (Y_k^1, Y_k^2, \ldots, Y_k^p)$ be a sequence of independent random vectors with covariance matrices

$$\Psi_k = \begin{bmatrix} \psi_{11}^k & \psi_{12}^k & \cdots & \psi_{1p}^k \\ \psi_{21}^k & \psi_{22}^k & \cdots & \psi_{2p}^k \\ \cdots & \cdots & \cdots & \cdots \\ \psi_{p1}^k & \psi_{p2}^k & \cdots & \psi_{pp}^k \end{bmatrix}.$$

The random variables $(Y_k^1, Y_k^2, \ldots, Y_k^p)$ can be approximated by trinomial random variables $(Z_k^1, Z_k^2, \ldots, Z_k^p)$. Let

$$a^2 = \max_{1 \le l \le p} \max_{0 \le k \le N} \psi_{ll}^k.$$

Let $(Z_k^1, \ldots, Z_k^p)_{k=0,\ldots,N}$ be independent random variables on $\{-a, 0, a\}^p$. Define probabilities as

$$b_{i_1, i_2, \ldots, i_p}^k = P\left(Z_k^{i_1} = i_1 a, Z_k^{i_2} = i_2 a, \ldots, Z_k^{i_p} = i_p a\right) \text{ for } i_1, i_2, \ldots, i_p = -1, 0, 1,$$

$$b_i^{kj} = \frac{\psi_{jj}^k}{2a^2} \text{ if } i \neq 0,$$

$$b_i^{kj} = \left(1 - \frac{\psi_{jj}^k}{a^2}\right) \text{ if } i = 0,$$

$$b_{i_1,i_2,\ldots,i_k}^k = \prod_{j=1}^{p} b_{i_j}^{kj} + \frac{\sum\limits_{l \neq j} i_l i_j \psi_{lj}^k \prod\limits_{l \neq m \neq j} b_{i_m}^{km}}{4a^2}.$$

We preserve the expectations and variances of the variables Y_k^l i.e. $EY_k^l = EZ_k^l = 0$, $E\left(Y_k^l Y_k^i\right) = E\left(Z_k^l Z_k^i\right) = \psi_{li}^k$ and $E\left(Y_k^l\right)^2 = E\left(Z_k^l\right)^2 = \psi_{ll}^k$. To make things more clear let us give the formulae above for the most important two-dimensional case which is when $p = 2$.

$$b_{1,0}^k = b_{-1,0}^k = \frac{\psi_{11}^k}{2a^2}\left(1 - \frac{\psi_{22}^k}{a^2}\right),$$

$$b_{0,1}^k = b_{0,-1}^k = \frac{\psi_{22}^k}{2a^2}\left(1 - \frac{\psi_{11}^k}{a^2}\right)$$

$$b_{0,0}^k = \left(1 - \frac{\psi_{11}^k}{a^2}\right)\left(1 - \frac{\psi_{22}^k}{a^2}\right),$$

$$b_{-1,-1}^k = b_{1,1}^k = \frac{\psi_{11}^k \psi_{22}^k + a^2 \psi_{12}^k}{4a^4},$$

$$b_{1,-1}^k = b_{-1,1}^k = \frac{\psi_{11}^k \psi_{22}^k - a^2 \psi_{12}^k}{4a^4}.$$

The process $\sum\limits_{i=0}^{k}\left(Z_i^1,\ldots,Z_i^p\right)$ is a Markov process on the net $\{\ldots, -2a, -a, 0, a, 2a, \ldots\}^p$.

Swaption Pricing and Calibration

Take grid points T_1, T_2, ... being consecutive maturities for both options and their underlying swaps. A European payer swaption with strike K, maturing at some date T_n gives the holder the right to pay fixed cashflows δK at T_k, for $k = n+1, \ldots, N$ in exchange for LIBOR on a \$1 notional. Its price is given by

$$Swaption_{nN}(0) = \delta E \left\{ \sum_{i=n+1}^{N} X_0^{-1}(T_i)\, (S_{nN}(T_n) - K)^+ \right\}$$

$$= \delta E \left\{ X_0^{-1}(T_n)\, (S_{nN}(T_n) - K)^+ E \left(\sum_{i=n+1}^{N} \frac{X_0(T_n)}{X_0(T_i)} \middle| F_{T_n} \right) \right\}$$

$$= E \left\{ X_0^{-1}(T_n) I_{\{S_{nN}(T_n) > K\}} \left(1 - B(T_n, T_N) - \delta K \sum_{i=n+1}^{N} B(T_n, T_i) \right) \right\}.$$

By the forward measure paradigm

$$Swaption_{nN}(0) = \delta A_{nN}(0) E_{nN}\, (S_{nN}(T_n) - K)^+ .$$

Let us start with practical issues on swaption pricing. In practice swap options are priced by the Black formula (call option, strike $= K$, option maturity $= T$)

$$Swaption_{nN}(0) = \delta A_{nN}(0)\, (S_{nN}(0)N(d_1) - KN(d_2)), \tag{4.1}$$

where

$$d_1 = \frac{\ln(S_{nN}(0)/K) + T_n \sigma_{nN}^2/2}{\sigma_{nN}\sqrt{T_n}}, \tag{4.2}$$

$$d_2 = d_1 - \sigma_{nN}\sqrt{T_n}. \tag{4.3}$$

A typical swaption quotation from Tullet is displayed in Figure 4.1

By calibration we usually understand determining the set of instantaneous volatilities $\Gamma(t) = [\gamma_1(t), \gamma_2(t), \ldots, \gamma_N(t)]$. If we are able to do it we are thus able to price everything, at least in theoretical sense. In practice we do not have enough data to determine instantaneous volatilities, so some silent assumptions must be imposed. In most, if not all cases, we assume some interpolation between grid points – imposed by some

	1Y	2Y	3Y	4Y	5Y	6Y	7Y	8Y	9Y	10Y	
			(c) 2004 Tullett Financial Information 15–Apr–2004 07 : 45								
			NOK Swaption Yield Volatility								
1M	32.8	26.6	23.5	21.9	20.9	19.5	18.4	17.4	16.6	15.9	1M
3M	32.3	26.3	23.4	21.8	20.8	19.5	18.4	17.5	16.7	16.1	3M
6M	30.3	25.2	22.7	21.2	20.1	19.0	17.9	17.1	16.3	15.8	6M
1Y	26.1	22.8	20.8	19.3	18.2	17.3	16.4	15.7	15.1	14.6	1Y
2Y	20.7	18.9	17.5	16.5	15.5	14.9	14.4	13.9	13.6	13.2	2Y
3Y	17.9	16.5	15.5	14.5	13.6	13.2	12.9	12.6	12.3	12.1	3Y
4Y	15.6	14.8	13.8	12.9	12.0	11.8	11.7	11.5	11.4	11.2	4Y
5Y	14.5	13.4	12.5	11.7	11.0	10.9	10.7	10.6	10.5	10.4	5Y
7Y	12.8	12.0	11.4	10.9	10.2	10.2	10.1	9.98	9.95	9.90	7Y
10Y	12.3	11.5	11.0	10.5	9.84	9.84	9.81	9.74	9.66	9.57	10Y
	1Y	2Y	3Y	4Y	5Y	6Y	7Y	8Y	9Y	10Y	

Figure 4.1 Swaption quotation.

model assumptions. Before we pass to calibration let us collect some simple properties of volatilities. Define the covariance matrix

$$
\Phi^i = \begin{bmatrix} \varphi^i_{11} & \varphi^i_{12} & \cdots & \varphi^i_{1N} \\ \varphi^i_{21} & \varphi^i_{22} & \cdots & \varphi^i_{2N} \\ \cdots & \cdots & \cdots & \cdots \\ \varphi^i_{N1} & \varphi^i_{N2} & \cdots & \varphi^i_{NN} \end{bmatrix},
\tag{4.4}
$$

where, for $i < k$ and $i < l$, we define the entries of the matrix by

$$
\varphi^i_{kl} = C_{kl}(0, T_i) = \int_0^{T_i} \gamma_l(t) \cdot \gamma_k(t)\, dt
$$

and let us also define the matrix

$$
\Pi^i = \begin{bmatrix} \mu^i_{11} & \mu^i_{12} & \cdots & \mu^i_{1N} \\ \mu^i_{21} & \mu^i_{22} & \cdots & \mu^i_{2N} \\ \cdots & \cdots & \cdots & \cdots \\ \mu^i_{N1} & \mu^i_{N2} & \cdots & \mu^i_{NN} \end{bmatrix},
\tag{4.5}
$$

where again for $i < k$ and $i < l$, the entries are given by

$$
\mu^i_{kl} = F_{kl}(0, T_i) = \int_0^{T_i} \eta_l(t) \cdot \eta_k(t)\, dt.
$$

All further theory deals with both Φ^i and Π^i exactly in the same sense, therefore we restrict our attention to the matrix Φ^i only. The notion of correlation may be defined twofold: as an instantaneous correlation:

$$
corr_{kl}(t) = \frac{\gamma_l(t) \cdot \gamma_k(t)}{\sqrt{\gamma_k(t) \cdot \gamma_k(t)}\sqrt{\gamma_l(t) \cdot \gamma_l(t)}}
$$

or as a terminal correlation

$$corr_{kl}(t, T) = \frac{C_{kl}(t, T)}{\sqrt{C_{kk}(t, T)C_{ll}(t, T)}}.$$

If we know our volatility interpolation scheme, the calibration of the models reduces to calculation of the matrices Φ^i. We can make some simple conclusions after a little mathematics – there are $\frac{N(N+1)}{2}$ swaptions and caplets in the period $[0, N]$ (N = option expiry + swap tenor). On the other hand all Φ^k's have

$$\sum_{k=1}^{N} \frac{k(k+1)}{2} = \frac{N(N+1)(N+2)}{6}$$

free parameters. Hence there are many possible calibrations (and indeed perhaps too many) of the BGM and HJM models and our choice should thus depend on our aim. Unlike the short rate models, we have enough freedom to model the volatility structure of forward rate models. There may be several specifications of the model volatility and we will describe them in later sections in this book.

4.1   LINEAR PRICING IN THE BGM MODEL

Since $S_{nN}(t)$ is a positive martingale with respect to the measure E_{nN} it follows the dynamics

$$dS_{nN}(t) = S_{nN}(t)\gamma_{nN}(t) \cdot dW_{nN}(t), \tag{4.6}$$

where $\gamma_{nN}(t)$ is the stochastic instantaneous volatility of $S_{nN}(t)$. On the other hand

$$dS_{nN}(t) = \sum_{i=n+1}^{N} \frac{\partial S_{nN}(t)}{\partial L_i(t)} L_i(t)\gamma_i(t) \cdot dW_{nN}(t) = S_{nN}(t) \sum_{i=n+1}^{N} R_{nN}^i(t)\gamma_i(t) \cdot dW_{nN}(t), \tag{4.7}$$

where

$$R_{nN}^{i+1}(t) := \frac{\partial \ln S_{nN}(t)}{\partial \ln L_{i+1}(t)} = K_{i+1}(t)\frac{B(t, T_n)A_{iN} + B(t, T_N)A_{ni}(t)}{(B(t, T_n) - B(t, T_N))A_{nN}(t)}.$$

Obviously we have

$$\gamma_{nN}(t) = \sum_{k=n+1}^{N} R_{nN}^k(t)\gamma_k(t). \tag{4.8}$$

If we make rough assumption that $\frac{B(t,T_i)}{A_{nN}(t)}$ does not depend on $L_k(t)$ we get an attractive 'brute force' approximation

$$R_{nN}^i(t) \cong \frac{B(t, T_i)L_i(t)}{\sum_{k=n+1}^{N} B(t, T_k)L_k(t)} = \frac{\delta B(t, T_i)L_i(t)}{B(t, T_n) - B(t, T_N)} = \frac{B(t, T_{i-1}) - B(t, T_i)}{B(t, T_n) - B(t, T_N)}$$

for which swap volatility becomes just a weighed average of the LIBOR volatilities:

$$\gamma_{nN}(t) = \frac{\sum\limits_{k=n+1}^{N} B(t, T_k) L_k(t) \gamma_i(t)}{\sum\limits_{k=n+1}^{N} B(t, T_k) L_k(t)}.$$

We may approximate $R^k_{nN}(t)$ by $R^k_{nN}(0)$. This makes sense if most of the interest rate movements are parallel shifts. Hence

$$T_k \sigma^2_{kN} = \int\limits_0^{T_k} \gamma^2_{kN}(t) dt \cong \sum\limits_{l=k+1}^{N} \sum\limits_{i=k+1}^{N} R^i_{kN}(0) \varphi^k_{il} R^l_{kN}(0). \tag{4.9}$$

We call this pricing linear since both drift term in swap rate dynamics and swaption variance term are linear with respect to swap rate and correlation terms respectively.

4.2   LINEAR PRICING OF SWAPTIONS IN THE HJM MODEL

The European swaption price is given by (4.1). Since $1 + \delta S_{nN}(t)$ is a positive martingale with respect to the measure E_{nN}

$$d\left(\delta S_{nN}(t) + 1\right) = \left(\delta S_{nN}(t) + 1\right) \eta_{nN}(t) \cdot dW_{nN}(t), \tag{4.10}$$

where $\eta_{nN}(t)$ is the stochastic instantaneous volatility of $\delta S_{nN}(t) + 1$. On the other hand

$$d\left(\delta S_{nN}(t) + 1\right) = \sum\limits_{i=n+1}^{N} \frac{\partial\left(\delta S_{nN}(t) + 1\right)}{\partial D_i(t)} D_i(t) \eta_i(t) \cdot dW_{nN}(t). \tag{4.11}$$

Denote

$$\widetilde{R}^i_{nN}(t) = \frac{A_{i-1,N}(t)}{A_{nN}(t)} - \frac{A_{i-1,N-1}(t)}{A_{n-1,N-1}(t)}. \tag{4.12}$$

Then

$$\eta_{nN}(t) = \sum\limits_{k=n+1}^{N} \widetilde{R}^k_{nN}(t) \eta_k(t). \tag{4.13}$$

If we again make a rough assumption that $\frac{B(t,T_i)}{A_{nN}(t)}$ does not depend on $D_k(t)$ (i.e. in a similar way to when we were working with the HLM model) we again get an attractive 'brute force' approximation

$$\widetilde{R}^i_{nN}(t) \cong \frac{B(t, T_i) D_i(t)}{\sum\limits_{k=n+1}^{N} B(t, T_k) D_k(t)} = \frac{B(t, T_{i-1})}{A_{n-1,N-1}(t)}$$

and hence the swap volatility becomes just a weighed average of the compound factor volatilities:

$$\eta_{nN}(t) = \frac{\sum_{k=n}^{N-1} B(t, T_k)\eta_{i+1}(t)}{A_{n-1,N-1}(t)}.$$

We may approximate $\tilde{R}_{nN}^k(t)$ by $\tilde{R}_{nN}^k(0)$ again in a similar way to before which makes sense if most of the interest rate movements are parallel shifts.

Since market volatilities are quoted in lognormal terms and HJM model is a Gaussian one, they should be transformed to their (equivalent) Gaussian form. The at-the-money swaption price is given by:

$$Swaption_{nN}(0) = \delta A_{nN}(0) \left(S_{nN}(0) N \left(\frac{\sigma_{nN}\sqrt{T_n}}{2} \right) - S_{nN}(0) N \left(-\frac{\sigma_{nN}\sqrt{T_n}}{2} \right) \right)$$

$$= \delta A_{nN}(0) S_{nN}(0) \left(2N \left(\frac{\sigma_{nN}\sqrt{T_n}}{2} \right) - 1 \right) \tag{4.14}$$

where the transformation to Gaussian form consists of finding sequence of market Gaussian standard deviations θ_{nN} satisfying

$$Swaption_{nN}(0) = A_{nN}(0) \left((\delta S_{nN}(0) + 1) N \left(\frac{\theta_{nN}}{2} \right) - (\delta S_{nN}(0) + 1) N \left(-\frac{\theta_{nN}}{2} \right) \right). \tag{4.15}$$

Hence (4.14) reduces to

$$\delta S_{nN}(0) N \left(\frac{\sigma_{nN}\sqrt{T_n}}{2} \right) + \frac{1}{2} = (1 + \delta S_{nN}(0)) N \left(\frac{\theta_{nN}}{2} \right).$$

The equation (4.14) can be easily solved by Newton method or bisection. Since the θ_n are very small, the one-step Newton method gives satisfactory results. Taking two or three steps makes the approximation almost perfect.
Hence

$$\theta_{kN}^2 = \int_0^{T_k} \eta_{kN}^2(t)dt \cong \sum_{l=k+1}^{N} \sum_{i=k+1}^{N} \tilde{R}_{kN}^i(0)\mu_{il}^k R_{kN}^l(0). \tag{4.16}$$

4.3   UNIVERSAL VOLATILITY FUNCTION

The volatility structure of the LIBOR market model is so rich that the model can be calibrated to a given instantaneous correlation and all swaption process in the same time. Let Ψ be a correlation matrix (historic for instance) of forward LIBORs and let the matrices $\Phi^k - \Phi^{k-1}$ be of the form: $\varphi_{ij}^k - \varphi_{ij}^{k-1} = \varphi_i^k \varphi_j^k \psi_{ij}$, setting $\varphi_{ij}^{-1} = 0$. Then

$$T_k \sigma_{k,k+1}^2 = \sum_{j=0}^{k} \left(\varphi_{k+1}^j \right)^2,$$

$$T_m \sigma_{mN}^2 = \sum_{j=0}^{k} \sum_{l=m+1}^{N} \sum_{i=m+1}^{N} R_{mN}^i(0) \varphi_l^j \psi_{il} \varphi_i^j R_{mN}^l(0).$$

We call that approach universal because of ability to simultaneous fit to both: swaption prices and given correlation. The everlasting discussion of 'implied versus historic' threatens the problem of determining the swaption correlation matrix. Not all authors are aware that it possible to calibrate to historic correlation and swaption prices in the same time. We have the following formulae for φ_{m+1}^m:

$$\varphi_1^0 = \sigma_{01}, \quad \varphi_{k+1}^k = \sqrt{ T_k \sigma_{k,k+1}^2 - \sum_{j=0}^{k-1} \left(\varphi_{k+1}^j \right)^2 }$$

and the following quadratic equation for φ_N^m:

$$\left(\varphi_N^m R_{mN}^N(0) \right)^2 + 2 \varphi_N^m R_{mN}^N(0) \sum_{i=m+1}^{N-1} R_{mN}^i(0) \psi_{iN} \varphi_i^m - T_m \sigma_{mN}^2$$

$$= - \sum_{j=0}^{m-1} \sum_{l=m+1}^{N} \sum_{i=m+1}^{N} R_{mN}^i(0) \varphi_l^j \psi_{il} \varphi_i^j R_{mN}^l(0) - \sum_{l=m+1}^{N-1} \sum_{i=m+1}^{N-1} R_{mN}^i(0) \varphi_l^m \psi_{il} \varphi_i^m R_{mN}^l(0). \tag{4.17}$$

The assumption that the covariance matrices Φ^i are of single factor means that $\varphi_{ij}^k - \varphi_{ij}^{k-1} = \varphi_i^k \varphi_j^k$. Under this assumption we have the following simple approximate formulae:

$$T_k \sigma_{k,k+1}^2 = \sum_{j=0}^{k} \left(\varphi_{k+1}^j \right)^2,$$

$$T_k \sigma_{kN}^2 = \sum_{j=0}^{k} \left(\sum_{i=k+1}^{N} R_{kN}^i(0) \varphi_i^j \right)^2. \tag{4.18}$$

A locally single factor approximation provides a direct way of calibrating the model to the full set of $\frac{N(N+1)}{2}$ swaptions in the following manner:

$$\varphi_1^0 = \sigma_{01},$$

. . . .

$$\varphi_{k+1}^k = \sqrt{T_k \sigma_{k,k+1}^2 - \sum_{j=0}^{k-1} \left(\varphi_{k+1}^j \right)^2}, \tag{4.19}$$

. . . .

$$\varphi_n^k = \frac{\sqrt{T_k \sigma_{kn}^2 - \sum_{j=0}^{k-1} \left(\sum_{i=k+1}^{n} R_{kn}^i(0)\varphi_i^j \right)^2 - \sum_{i=k+1}^{n-1} R_{kn}^i(0)\varphi_i^k}}{R_{kn}^n(0)}. \tag{4.20}$$

It is possible to calibrate the single-factor model to the full set of caps and swaptions prices provided the condition below holds:

$$T_k \sigma_{kN}^2 \geq \sum_{j=0}^{k-1} \left(\sum_{i=k+1}^{N} R_{kN}^i(0)\varphi_i^j \right)^2.$$

Notice that although the model is locally single factor, the actual dynamics of $S_{kN}(t)$ is driven by more factors.

4.4   TIME HOMOGENEOUS VOLATILITY

For a time homogeneous model, where $\gamma_k(t) = \gamma(T_k - t)$

$$\varphi_{kl}^i = \int_0^{T_i} \gamma(T_l - t) \cdot \gamma(T_k - t) dt.$$

Hence if $\delta = T_0$ then we have that

$$\varphi_{kl}^i = \int_0^{T_i} \gamma(T_l - t) \cdot \gamma(T_k - t) dt = \sum_{j=0}^{i} \varphi_{k-j,l-j}^0.$$

Hence for the time homogeneous model

$$T_k \sigma_{kN}^2 = \int_0^{T_k} \gamma_{kN}^2(t) dt \cong \sum_{j=0}^{k} \sum_{l=k+1}^{N} \sum_{i=k+1}^{N} R_{kN}^i(0)\varphi_{i-j,l-j}^0 R_{kN}^l(0).$$

There are $\frac{N(N+1)}{2}$ free parameters in the matrix Φ^0. Analogously for the time homogeneous model

$$\varphi_{11}^0 = T_0 \sigma_{01}^2,$$

$$\varphi_{kk}^0 = T_0 \sigma_{k-1,k}^2 - \sum_{j=0}^{k-1} \varphi_{jj}^0,$$

$$\varphi^0_{k+1,N} =$$

$$\frac{T_k \sigma^2_{kN} - \sum\limits_{j=1}^{k} \sum\limits_{l=k+1}^{N} \sum\limits_{i=k+1}^{N} R^i_{kN}(0)\varphi^0_{i-j,l-j} R^l_{kN}(0) - \sum\limits_{l=k+1}^{N} \sum\limits_{i=k+1}^{N} R^i_{kN}(0)\varphi^0_{il} R^l_{kN}(0) + 2R^{k+1}_{kN}(0)\varphi^0_{k+1,N} R^N_{kN}(0)}{2R^{k+1}_{kN}(0)R^N_{kN}(0)}.$$

4.5   SEPARATED VOLATILITY

If we assume that

$$\varphi^i_{kl} = \Lambda_i \varphi_{kl},$$

where Λ_i are positive numbers and

$$\Phi = \begin{bmatrix} \varphi_{11} & \varphi_{12} & \cdots & \varphi_{1N} \\ \varphi_{21} & \varphi_{22} & \cdots & \varphi^i_{2N} \\ \cdots & \cdots & \cdots & \cdots \\ \varphi_{N1} & \varphi_{N2} & \cdots & \varphi_{NN} \end{bmatrix}$$

is a covariance matrix we may calibrate the model perfectly. With these assumptions this approach will be called separated. If we assume that $\varphi_{kk} = 1$ for all k, Φ is obviously a correlation matrix, although we do not want to restrict ourselves to that class. The volatility functions $\gamma_n(t)$ can be represented as $\gamma_n(t) = \lambda(t)\varsigma_n$, where $\lambda(t)$ is a scalar function satisfying

$$\Lambda_k = \int_0^{T_k} \lambda^2(t)dt$$

and ς_i are volatility vectors. In the case when $\Lambda_k = T_k$ represents the situation when $\lambda(t) \equiv 1$ and is called by Longstaff, Santa-Clara and Schwartz (2001) a string model.

Let $\lambda_1 > \lambda_2 > \ldots > \lambda_N$ denote the eigenvalues of the matrix Φ with respective eigenvector basis $[e_{11}, e_{12}, \ldots, e_{1N}], [e_{21}, e_{22}, \ldots, e_{2N}], \ldots, [e_{N1}, e_{N2}, \ldots, e_{NN}]$. Then by Principal Component Analysis $M^n(t)$ admits the representation:

$$M^n(t) = \sum_{i=1}^{N} \sqrt{\lambda_i} e_{in} \int_0^t \lambda(s)dW^i(s).$$

The dimension of the problem can be reduced (usually to dimension 2 or 3) by removing eigenvectors corresponding to very small eigenvalues. Under our assumption we have the following simple formulae:

$$T_{k-1}\sigma^2_{k-1,k} = \Lambda_{k-1}\varphi_{kk},$$

$$T_k \sigma^2_{kN} = \Lambda_k \sum_{l=k+1}^{N} \sum_{i=k+1}^{N} R^i_{kN}(0)\varphi_{il} R^l_{kN}(0). \tag{4.21}$$

The separated approach provides a direct way of calibrating the model to the full set of $\frac{N(N+1)}{2}$ swaptions, even via closed form formulae:

$$\varphi_{kk} = \frac{T_{k-1}\sigma_{k-1,k}^2}{\Lambda_{k-1}},$$

. . . .

$$\varphi_{k+1,N} = \frac{T_k\sigma_{kN}^2 - \Lambda_k\left(\sum_{l=k+1}^{N}\sum_{i=k+1}^{N}R_{kN}^i(0)\varphi_{il}R_{kN}^l(0) - 2R_{kN}^{k+1}(0)\varphi_{k+1,N}R_{kN}^N(0)\right)}{2\Lambda_k R_{kN}^{k+1}(0)R_{kN}^N(0)}. \tag{4.22}$$

Note that the formulae above are recursive in an unusual way. First we calculate parameters on the diagonal and the pass to the lower-left and upper-right corners. We must also remark that when we assume time-homogeneity this already determines the form of the calibration and the number of factors. Separated calibration leaves one free parameter to be determined by the user – D_k. It may be considered as an emergency parameter – by manipulating D_k we may control the number of factors and the positivity of the covariance matrix Φ. The separated approach may be also useful to input the covariance matrix but here we must limit the number of swaptions. Let Ψ be a correlation matrix of forward LIBORs and let the matrix Φ be of the form: $\varphi_{ij} = k_i k_j \psi_{ij}$. In order to avoid non-unique solutions we force $k_N = 1$.

$$T_{i-1}\sigma_{i-1,i}^2 = \Lambda_{i-1}k_i^2,$$

$$T_m\sigma_{mN}^2 = \Lambda_m \sum_{l=m+1}^{N}\sum_{i=m+1}^{N} R_{mN}^i(0)k_l\psi_{il}k_i R_{mN}^l(0). \tag{4.23}$$

We can perform the calibration as follows

$$\Lambda_{N-1} = T_{N-1}\sigma_{N-1,N}^2,$$

$$T_m\sigma_{m,m+1}^2 = \Lambda_m k_{m+1}^2,$$

$$T_m\sigma_{mN}^2 = \Lambda_m \left\{ \left(k_{m+1}R_{mN}^{m+1}(0)\right)^2 + 2k_{m+1}R_{mN}^{m+1}(0)\sum_{i=m+2}^{N}R_{mN}^i(0)\psi_{il}k_i \right.$$

$$\left. + \sum_{l=m+2}^{N}\sum_{i=m+2}^{N}R_{mN}^i(0)k_l\psi_{il}k_i R_{mN}^l(0) \right\},$$

which leads to quadratic equation:

$$\left(\frac{\sigma_{mN}^2}{\sigma_{n,m+1}^2} - R_{mN}^{m+1}(0)^2\right)k_{m+1}^2 = 2k_{m+1}R_{mN}^{m+1}(0)\sum_{i=m+2}^{N}R_{mN}^i(0)\psi_{i,m+1}k_i$$

$$+ \sum_{l=m+2}^{N}\sum_{i=m+2}^{N}R_{mN}^i(0)k_l\psi_{il}k_i R_{mN}^l(0).$$

An important special case is the single factor model, i.e. when $\psi_{ij} = 1$. In such case we have the equalities:

$$T_{i-1}\sigma_{i-1,i}^2 = D_{i-1}k_i^2,$$

$$T_m\sigma_{mN}^2 = \Lambda_m \sum_{l=m+1}^{N} \sum_{i=m+1}^{N} R_{mN}^i(0)k_l k_i R_{mN}^l(0). \tag{4.24}$$

$$\Lambda_{N-1} = T_{N-1}\sigma_{N-1,N.}^2$$

Hence

$$T_m\sigma_{m,m+1}^2 = \Lambda_m k_{m+1}^2,$$

$$T_m\sigma_{mN}^2 = \Lambda_m \left\{ k_{m+1}R_{mN}^{m+1}(0) + \sum_{i=m+2}^{N} R_{mN}^i(0)k_i \right\}^2,$$

which again leads to a quadratic equation:

$$\left(\frac{\sigma_{mN}^2}{\sigma_{n,m+1}^2} - R_{mN}^{m+1}(0)^2 \right) k_{m+1}^2 = 2k_{m+1}R_{mN}^{m+1}(0) \sum_{i=m+2}^{N} R_{mN}^i(0)k_i + \left(\sum_{i=m+2}^{N} R_{mN}^i(0)k_i \right)^2.$$

Example of separated calibration

The example is entirely based on Krynicki (2003). We decided to deal with separated approach because it gives us best control over the number of factors – an issue extremely important when considering the speed of pricing and hedging swaptions and the pricing of exotic products, particularly of Bermudan style. Let us consider the USD data of 28th April 2003 from Table 4.1 below. Volatilities are quoted in percentages.

Table 4.1 Swaption quotations

		Swap maturity							
		2Y	3Y	4Y	5Y	6Y	7Y	8Y	9Y	10Y
Option maturity	1M	55.50	47.10	42.90	40.50	37.40	34.30	32.60	30.80	29.10
	1Y	49.60	43.20	39.30	36.50	34.30	32.00	30.60	29.30	27.90
	2Y	38.00	34.80	32.40	30.50	29.10	27.70	26.70	25.60	24.60
	3Y	31.70	29.70	28.00	26.70	25.60	24.50	23.70	22.90	22.10
	4Y	27.50	26.00	4.90	23.90	23.10	22.30	21.60	20.80	20.10
	5Y	24.40	23.40	22.50	21.70	21.00	20.20	19.60	19.00	18.40
	6Y	22.50	21.60	20.80	20.10	19.50	18.90	18.30	17.80	17.30
	7Y	20.60	19.90	19.20	18.50	18.00	17.50	17.00	16.60	16.10
	8Y	19.30	18.70	18.00	17.40	17.00	16.50	16.10	15.70	15.30
	9Y	17.90	17.40	16.90	16.40	16.00	15.60	15.20	14.80	14.40
	10Y	16.60	16.20	15.70	15.30	15.00	14.60	14.30	13.90	13.60

We calculate the following parameters:

$$\Lambda_0 = 0.07900, \quad \Lambda_6 = 2.44949,$$
$$\Lambda_1 = 0.88650, \quad \Lambda_7 = 2.64575,$$
$$\Lambda_2 = 1.41421, \quad \Lambda_8 = 2.82843,$$
$$\Lambda_3 = 1.73205, \quad \Lambda_9 = 3.00000,$$
$$\Lambda_4 = 2.00000, \quad \Lambda_{10} = 3.16228$$
$$\Lambda_5 = 2.23607,$$

which lead us to the following eigenvalues:

$$\lambda_1 = 105.9\% \quad \lambda_6 = 9.5\%$$
$$\lambda_2 = 49.9\% \quad \lambda_7 = 6.6\%$$
$$\lambda_3 = 27.4\% \quad \lambda_8 = 4.3\%$$
$$\lambda_4 = 19.4\% \quad \lambda_9 = -2.3\%$$
$$\lambda_5 = -13.5\% \quad \lambda_{10} = 1.0\%$$

Removing of eigenvectors associated to negative eigenvalues leads to insignificant mispricing of some options. Reduction of the number of factors to three also has minimal impact on the pricing. For the string model of Longstaff, Santa-Clara and Schwartz, (i.e. when $\Lambda_i = T_i$) the situation however is different. Our eigenvalues are the equal to:

$$\lambda_1 = 127.6\% \quad \lambda_6 = 6.0\%$$
$$\lambda_2 = -29.2\% \quad \lambda_7 = -4.1\%$$
$$\lambda_3 = 29.2\% \quad \lambda_8 = 2.3\%$$
$$\lambda_4 = -16.6\% \quad \lambda_9 = -1.2\%$$
$$\lambda_5 = 14.4\% \quad \lambda_{10} = -0.8\%$$

Because of the large negative eigenvalues the model is misspecified, hence option prices may very dependent of choice of calibration swaptions.

4.6 PARAMETRIZED VOLATILITY

Let X_k^n be defined as

$$X_0^n = \int_0^{T_0} \gamma_n(t)dW(t), \tag{4.25}$$

$$X_k^n = \int_{T_{k-1}}^{T_k} \gamma_n(t)dW(t). \tag{4.26}$$

In addition we let the matrix $\widetilde{\Phi}^k$ be the covariance matrix of the random variables $X_{k,k=0,1,\dots,n-1}^n$ (with entries to be determined below). If,

$$X_k^n = \sum_{l=1}^p q_l^n Y_k^l \tag{4.27}$$

for some numbers q_l^n and any n, where $(Y_k^1, Y_k^2, \ldots, Y_k^p)$ are independent p-dimensional Gaussian random variables, we say that dynamics of $L_{n,n=1,2,\ldots}$ is of p-factors. The dynamics of the LIBOR rates $L_n(t)$ can be represented as

$$dL_n(t) = drift \cdot dt + L_n(t) \sum_{i=1}^{p} \sum_{l=1}^{p} q_l^n s^{li}(t) dW_i(t),$$

where $W_i(t)$ are independent Wiener processes and $s^{li}(t)$ are volatility functions. Denote $\psi_{li}^k = E(Y_k^l Y_k^i)$. Hence the covariance matrix $\widetilde{\Phi}^k$ is of the form

$$\widetilde{\varphi}_{mn}^k = \sum_{i=1}^{p} \sum_{l=1}^{p} q_l^m q_i^n \psi_{il}^k \qquad (4.28)$$

and the relation between swaption market volatility and model parameters can be written as

$$T_n \sigma_{nN}^2 = \sum_{l=1}^{p} \sum_{i=1}^{p} \sum_{j=0}^{n} A_{nN}^l \psi_{li}^j A_{nN}^i, \qquad (4.29)$$

where

$$A_{nN}^l = \sum_{k=n+1}^{N} R_{nN}^k(0) q_l^k.$$

The calibration of the model to swaptions (caplets and floorlets are considered as trivial one-period swaptions) consists of determining the parameter pairs $(q_l^n, \psi_{li}^k)_{l,i=1,\ldots,p,k,n=1,2,\ldots}$ to satisfy the equation (4.9) for a given set of swaption volatilities σ_{nN}. Once more let us make some arithmetical calculations. There are $N(N+1)/2$ swaptions and caplets in the period $[0, N]$. The p-factors model has $N\left(\frac{p(p+1)}{2} + p\right)$ free parameters. Therefore to calibrate the model perfectly both these numbers have to be approximately the same size. Hence $N \approx p(p+3) - 1$. Results are surprising: two factors can calibrate the model up to ten years, three factors work successfully up to twenty years. Since not all the swaptions are liquid, a two factor calibration is satisfactory in most cases.

4.7   PARAMETRIC CALIBRATION TO CAPS AND SWAPTIONS BASED ON REBONATO APPROACH

The first part of calibration is to fit the instantaneous volatilities to the observable market caplet prices. Having a set of caplet implied volatilities $\{\sigma_i^{caplet}(t), i = 1, \ldots, N\}$ we can set functions:

$$I_{j,i}(v) = \int_{T_j}^{T_i} |f(T_i - t)|^2 dt$$

where for $f(T_i - t)$ we can choose $f(t) = v_1 + (v_2 + v_3(T_i - t))e^{-v_4(T_i - t)}$.

The three stage procedure of calibration based on the Rebonato approach can be written as:

1. Obtain estimates of v:

2.
$$\hat{v} = \arg\min_v \left| \sum_{i=1}^{N} \left[\sigma_i^{caplet} (t)^2 (T_i - t) - \sum_{j=1}^{i} I_{j,i}(v) \right]^2 \right|$$

3. Setting $g(t_j) = 1 + \varepsilon_j$ for reset times T_j and estimate $\varepsilon = \{\varepsilon_j\}$ as:

4.
$$\hat{\varepsilon} = \arg\min_\varepsilon \left| \sum_{i=1}^{N} \left[\sigma_i^{caplet} (t)^2 (T_i - t) - \sum_{j=1}^{i} I_{j,i}(\hat{v})(1 + \varepsilon_j) \right]^2 \right|$$

5. Setting $1 + \delta_i$ for reset times T_i as:

$$1 + \hat{\delta} = \sum_{i=1}^{N} \frac{\sigma_i^{caplet} (t)^2 (T_i - t)}{\sum_{j=1}^{i} I_{j,i}(\hat{v})(1 + \hat{\varepsilon}_j)}$$

Thus we can write the functional form for ε as:

$$\varepsilon(T_i - t) = g_1 + g_2 \cos[g_3(T_i - t)]$$

We thus have that most of σ_i^{caplet} values are explained by the function $f(t)$. Most of the rest are explained by function $g(t)$ and the remainder are explained by $1 + \delta$.

The second part of calibration is fitting to the swaptions. We will use the Rebonato approximation formula for swaptions where the LFM Black squared swaption volatility can be approximated by

$$\left(v_{n,N}^{LFM}\right)^2 = \sum_{i,j=n+1}^{N} \frac{w_i(0) w_j(0) L_i(0) L_j(0) \rho_{i,j}}{S_{n,N}(0)^2} \int_0^{T_n} \sigma_i(t) \sigma_j(t) dt$$

and the swap rates are expressed as a linear combination of forward rates

$$S_{n,N}(0) = \sum_{i=n+1}^{N} w_i(t) L_i(t) \overset{assumption}{=} \sum_{i=n+1}^{N} w_i(0) L_i(0).$$

For the purpose of the calibration all $w_i(t)$ and $L_i(t)$ are frozen to the value at time 0.

The instantaneous correlations in that approach can be approximated by:

$$\rho_{i,j} = \cos(\Phi_i - \Phi_j) - \sin(\Phi_i)\sin(\Phi_j)\left[1 - \cos(\Theta_i - \Theta_j)\right]$$

where Φ_i, Θ_i will have the following functional forms:

$$\Theta_i = \theta_1 + [\theta_2 + \theta_3(T_i - t)] e^{-\theta_4(T_i - t)}$$
$$\Phi_i = \phi_1 + [\phi_2 + \phi_3(T_i - t)] e^{-\phi_4(T_i - t)}.$$

Our calibration to swaptions is based on a local algorithm of minimization for finding the best fitting parameters θ and ϕ starting from certain initial guesses and with the restriction that all $\rho_{i,j} > 0$.

4.8 SEMILINEAR PRICING OF SWAPTIONS IN THE BGM MODEL

In the formula (4.1) we assume both lognormality of the swap rate in the BGM model and linear dependence of swap volatility with respect of forward LIBOR in the BGM model volatility. If we allow the dependence of swap volatility with respect of forward LIBOR to be nonlinear, keeping the lognormality of the swap rate, we get a more accurate approximation of swaption prices. All volatility parameterisations are independent of approximation of swaption prices, although the semilinear approximation provides no closed formulae for model volatilites.

Approximation 1. Let $T = T_n$. Then the distribution of swap rate $S_{nN}(T)$ under swap measure E_{nN} can be approximated as lognormal, with the variance of $\ln S_{nN}(T)$ equal to:

$$
V = \sum_{j,k=n+1}^{N} Q_{nN}^{jk}(0) \int_0^T \gamma_j(t) \cdot \gamma_k(t)\, dt
$$

$$
+ \sum_{j,k,l=n+1}^{N} \frac{\partial Q_{nN}^{jk}(0)}{\partial L_l(0)} L_l(0) \int_0^T C_{jk}(t,T)\, \gamma_l(t) \cdot J_l(t)\, dt
$$

$$
+ \sum_{j,k,l,m=n+1}^{N} \frac{1}{2} \frac{\partial^2 Q_{nN}^{jk}(0)}{\partial L_l(0)\partial L_m(0)} L_l(0) L_m(0) \int_0^T C_{jk}(t,T)\, \gamma_l(t) \cdot \gamma_m(t)\, dt
$$

where $Q_{nN}^{jk}(t) = R_{nN}^j(t) R_{nN}^k(t)$ and

$$
J_l(t) = \sum_{j=n+2}^{l} K_j(0)\gamma_j(t) - \sum_{j=n+1}^{N-1} \frac{A_{jN}(0)}{A_{nN}(0)} K_{j+1}(0)\gamma_{j+1}(t).
$$

Rationale. So long as $\gamma_{nN}(t)$ is deemed to be almost deterministic we may approximate $\ln S_{nN}(T) = \ln S_{nN}(T) + \int_0^T \gamma_{nN}(t)\, dW_{nN}(t) - \frac{1}{2}\int_0^T |\gamma_{nN}(t)|^2\, dt$ by a normal variable with variance

$$
V = \int_0^T E_{nN} |\eta_{nN}(t)|^2\, dt = E_{nN} \int_0^T \sum_{j,k=n+1}^{N} Q_{nN}^{jk}(t)\gamma_j(t) \cdot \gamma_k(t)\, dt. \tag{4.30}
$$

We find using integration by parts:

$$
\int_0^T Q_{nN}^{jk}(t)\gamma_j(t) \cdot \gamma_k(t)\, dt = -\int_0^T Q_{nN}^{jk}(t)\, dC_{jk}(t,T) = Q_{nN}^{jk}(0)C_{jk}(0,T) + \int_0^T C_{jk}(t)\, dQ_{nN}^{jk}(t,T).
$$

Hence

$$E_{nN} \int_0^T Q_{nN}^{jk}(t) \gamma_j(t) \cdot \gamma_k(t)\, dt = Q_{nN}^{jk}(0) \int_0^T \gamma_j(t) \cdot \gamma_k(t)\, dt + \int_0^T C_{jk}(t, T)\, \nu_{nN}^{jk}(t)\, dt, \quad (4.31)$$

where $\nu_{nN}^{jk}(t)$ is expectation of the drift of $Q_{nN}^{jk}(t)$, namely $dE_{nN} Q_{nN}^{jk}(t) = \nu_{nN}^{jk}(t)\, dt$. Obviously

$$dQ_{nN}^{jk}(t) = \sum_{l=n+1}^{N} \frac{\partial Q_{nN}^{jk}(t)}{\partial L_l(t)} dL_l(t) + \frac{1}{2} \sum_{l,m=n+1}^{N} \frac{\partial^2 Q_{nN}^{jk}(t)}{\partial L_l(t) \partial L_m(t)} L_l(t) L_m(t) \gamma_l(t) \cdot \gamma_m(t)\, dt.$$

By (1.10) and (2.15), for $n < l \le N$

$$dL_k(t) = L_k(t) \gamma_k(t) \cdot \left[dW_{nN}(t) - \sum_{j=n+1}^{N-1} \frac{K_{j+1}(t) A_{jN}(t)}{A_{nN}(t)} \gamma_{j+1}(t) dt + \sum_{j=n+2}^{k} K_j(t) \gamma_j(t) dt \right].$$

Hence we can approximate

$$\nu_{nN}^{jk}(t) \approx \sum_{l=n+1}^{N} \frac{\partial Q_{nN}^{jk}(0)}{\partial L_l(0)} L_l(0) \gamma_l(t) \cdot J_l(t) + \frac{1}{2} \sum_{l,m=n+1}^{N} \frac{\partial^2 Q_{nN}^{jk}(0)}{\partial L_l(t) \partial L_m(0)} L_l(0) L_m(0) \gamma_l(t) \cdot \gamma_m(t).$$

Putting this into (4.31) and then to (4.30) completes the proof.

Although closed formulae for $\frac{\partial Q_{nN}^{jk}(0)}{\partial L_i(0)}$ and $\frac{\partial^2 Q_{nN}^{jk}(0)}{\partial L_i(0) \partial L_l(0)}$ in principle do exist, for practical applications their complexity deems their usage unrealistic, and we suggest numerical differentiation.

4.9 SEMILINEAR PRICING OF SWAPTIONS IN THE HJM MODEL

An analogous result may be proved in the HJM model.

Approximation 2. Let $T = T_n$. Then the distribution of shifted swap rate $1 + \delta S_{nN}(T)$ under the swap measure E_{nN} can be approximated as lognormal, with the variance of $\ln(1 + \delta S_{nN}(T))$ equal to:

$$V = \sum_{j,k=n+1}^{N} \widetilde{Q}_{nN}^{jk}(0) \int_0^T \eta_j(t) \cdot \eta_k(t)\, dt$$

$$+ \sum_{j,k,l=n+1}^{N} \frac{\partial \widetilde{Q}_{nN}^{jk}(0)}{\partial D_l(0)} D_l(0) \int_0^T F_{jk}(t, T) \eta_l(t) \cdot \widetilde{J}_l(t)\, dt$$

$$+ \sum_{j,k,l,m=n+1}^{N} \frac{1}{2} \frac{\partial^2 \widetilde{Q}_{nN}^{jk}(0)}{\partial D_l(0) \partial D_m(0)} D_l(0) D_m(0) \int_0^T F_{jk}(t, T) \eta_l(t) \cdot \eta_m(t)\, dt$$

where $\widetilde{Q}_{nN}^{jk}(t) = \widetilde{R}_{nN}^{j}(t)\widetilde{R}_{nN}^{k}(t)$ and

$$\widetilde{J}_l(t) = \sum_{j=n+2}^{l} \eta_j(t) - \sum_{j=n+1}^{N-1} \frac{A_{jN}(0)}{A_{nN}(0)} \eta_{j+1}(t).$$

Rationale. As far as $\eta_{nN}(t)$ is deemed to be almost deterministic we may approximate $\ln(1+\delta S_{nN}(T)) = \ln(1+\delta S_{nN}(T)) + \int_0^T \eta_{nN}(t)dW_{nN}(t) - \frac{1}{2}\int_0^T |\eta_{nN}(t)|^2 dt$ by a normal variable with variance

$$V = \int_0^T E_{nN} |\eta_{nN}(t)|^2 dt = E_{nN} \int_0^T \sum_{j,k=n+1}^{N} \widetilde{Q}_{nN}^{jk}(t)\eta_j(t) \cdot \eta_k(t)dt. \qquad (4.32)$$

We find using integration by parts:

$$\int_0^T \widetilde{Q}_{nN}^{jk}(t)\eta_j(t) \cdot \eta_k(t)dt = -\int_0^T \widetilde{Q}_{nN}^{jk}(t)dF_{jk}(t,T) = \widetilde{Q}_{nN}^{jk}(0)F_{jk}(0,T) + \int_0^T F_{jk}(t)d\widetilde{Q}_{nN}^{jk}(t,T).$$

Hence

$$E_{nN} \int_0^T \widetilde{Q}_{nN}^{jk}(t)\eta_j(t) \cdot \eta_k(t)dt = \widetilde{Q}_{nN}^{jk}(0)\int_0^T \eta_j(t) \cdot \eta_k(t)dt + \int_0^T F_{jk}(t,T)\widetilde{v}_{nN}^{jk}(t)dt, \quad (4.33)$$

where $\widetilde{v}_{nN}^{jk}(t)$ is expectation of the drift of $\widetilde{Q}_{nN}^{jk}(t)$, namely $dE_{nN}\widetilde{Q}_{nN}^{jk}(t) = \widetilde{v}_{nN}^{jk}(t)dt$. Obviously

$$d\widetilde{Q}_{nN}^{jk}(t) = \sum_{l=n+1}^{N} \frac{\partial \widetilde{Q}_{nN}^{jk}(t)}{\partial D_l(t)}dD_l(t) + \frac{1}{2}\sum_{l,m=n+1}^{N} \frac{\partial^2 \widetilde{Q}_{nN}^{jk}(t)}{\partial D_l(t)\partial D_m(t)}D_l(t)D_m(t)\eta_l(t) \cdot \eta_m(t)dt.$$

By (1.10) and (2.14), for $n < l \leq N$

$$dD_k(t) = D_k(t)\eta_k(t) \cdot \left[dW_{nN}(t) - \sum_{j=n+1}^{N-1} \frac{A_{jN}(t)}{A_{nN}(t)}\eta_{j+1}(t)dt + \sum_{j=n+2}^{k} \eta_j(t)dt \right].$$

Hence we can approximate

$$\widetilde{v}_{nN}^{jk}(t) \approx \sum_{l=n+1}^{N} \frac{\partial \widetilde{Q}_{nN}^{jk}(0)}{\partial D_l(0)}D_l(0)\eta_l(t) \cdot \widetilde{J}_l(t) + \frac{1}{2}\sum_{l,m=n+1}^{N} \frac{\partial^2 \widetilde{Q}_{nN}^{jk}(0)}{\partial D_l(t)\partial D_m(0)}D_l(0)D_m(0)\eta_l(t) \cdot \eta_m(t).$$

Putting this into (4.33) and then to (4.32) completes the proof.

Analogously as for the BGM case, closed formulae for $\frac{\partial \widetilde{Q}_{nN}^{jk}(0)}{\partial D_l(0)}$ and $\frac{\partial^2 \widetilde{Q}_{nN}^{jk}(0)}{\partial D_l(0)\partial D_l(0)}$ in principle do exist, but again their complexity means that numerical differentiation should be used in practice.

4.10   NONLINEAR PRICING OF SWAPTIONS

There exists an alternative formula for the swaption price. Again, after changing the reference measure:

$$Swaption_{nN}(0) = \delta E \left\{ \sum_{i=n+1}^{N} X_0^{-1}(T_i) \left(S_{nN}(T_n) - K\right)^+ \right\}$$

$$= E \left\{ X_0^{-1}(T_n) I_{\{S_{nN}(T_n)>K\}} \left(1 - B(T_n, T_N) - \delta K \sum_{i=n+1}^{N} B(T_n, T_i) \right) \right\}$$

$$= E \left\{ X_0^{-1}(T_n) I_{\{S_{nN}(T_n)>K\}} E \left(1 - \frac{X_0(T_n)}{X_0(T_N)} - \delta K \sum_{i=n+1}^{N} \frac{X_0(T_n)}{X_0(T_i)} \middle| F_{T_n} \right) \right\}. \quad (4.34)$$

$$= E \left\{ I_{\{S_{nN}(T_n)>K\}} \left(X_0^{-1}(T_n) - X_0^{-1}(T_N) - \delta K \sum_{i=n+1}^{N} X_0^{-1}(T_i) \right) \right\}$$

$$= B(0, T_n) P_n \left(S_{nN}(T_n) > K\right) - B(0, T_N) P_N \left(S_{nN}(T_n) > K\right) +$$

$$- \delta K \sum_{i=n+1}^{N} B(0, T_i) P_i \left(S_{nN}(T_n) > K\right).$$

What remains is the calculation of $P_i\left(S_{nN}(T_n) > K\right)$ for various (mutually absolutely continuous) probability measures P_i. Since $S_{nN}(T_n)$ is a function of $L_k(T_n)$, knowledge of distribution of $L_k(T_n)$ under the measure P_i is sufficient to calculate $P_i\left(S_{nN}(T_n) > K\right)$. Now – for the HJM model and for Euler, Predictor-Corrector, Brownian Bridge, modified Brownian Bridge and Lognormal approximations of the BGM model from Chapter 10, the forward swap rate is a deterministic function of the multidimensional Gaussian process $N_k(t) = \{N_k^{n+1}(t), \ldots, N_k^N(t)\}$ (in HJM case) or $M_k(t) = \{M_k^{n+1}(t), \ldots, M_k^N(t)\}$ (in BGM case), where

$$N_k^n(t) = \int_0^t \eta_n(s) \cdot dW_k(s), \quad M_k^n(t) = \int_0^t \gamma_n(s) \cdot dW_k(s).$$

Analogous algorithms are also available for nonlinear pricing – provided closed form formulae are replaced by optimizations in lower dimensions such as dimensions one and two. We still use our recursive approach – first we calculate parameters on the diagonal and the pass to the lower-left and upper-right corners.

4.11   EXAMPLES

Accuracy of the previously presented models was examined for several instruments. In order to test swap rate approximations we took a semi-annual settlement ($\delta = 0.5$) with flat initial interest rate and volatility structures: $L_i(0) = 6\%$, $\gamma_i(t) = 20\%$ with perfect correlation between the LIBOR rates (in a one factor model). We work with a 10Y payer option on a 10Y swap for three various strikes: ATM, ATM $-$ 200 bp and ATM $+$ 200 bp. We used the following pricing methods:

Monte Carlo (MC)	–	Monte Carlo simulation with 1,000,000 paths,
Semilinear lognormal (SL)	–	semilinear lognormal approximation of the swap variance under swap measure $E_{10,20}$,
Andersen-Andreasen (AA)	–	lognormal approximation $\sum_{j,k=n+1}^{N} Q_{nN}^{jk}(0) C_{jk}(0)$ of the swap variance under swap measure $E_{10,20}$ (introduced by Andersen-Andreasen, 2000),
Brace-Gatarek-Musiela (BGM)	–	nonlinear method with Euler drift approximation (introduced by Brace-Gatarek-Musiela).

The results of our various computations are shown in Table 4.2 below, where Monte-Carlo is used as a reference result.

Table 4.2 Comparison of methods

Strike	4.0 %	6.0 %	8.0 %
		Standard swaption	
MC	1017.81	609.61	368.40
		Errors w.r.t. standard swaptions	
SL	−0.49	0.37	1.57
AA	1.70	3.67	5.00
BGM	−0.49	0.39	1.62

For our knowledge, the AA method is the market standard in pricing European standard and cash-settled swaptions. The SL method outperforms the AA and seems to give very accurate and satisfactory approximations.

5
Smile Modelling in the BGM Model

Both the HJM and BGM models fit perfectly the at-the-money caps, floors and swaption volatility structures. They are different away-from-the-money: the compound factors $1 + \delta L_n(t)$ are lognormally distributed in the HJM model, while the LIBOR rates $L_n(t)$ are lognormal for the BGM model. Before the Asian crisis the BGM model seemed to fit all swaption prices perfectly but now the truth lies between: the HJM model shows a skew of swaption prices, whilst the BGM model shows no skew, and the market prices are somehow in-between HJM and BGM. The skew can be described as follows: the market swaption volatility is a function of strike prices i.e.

$$Swaption_{nN}(0, K) = \delta A_{nN}(0) BS \left(S_{nN}(0), K, 0, T_n \sigma_{nN}^2(K) \right). \tag{5.1}$$

Symmetric smiles and skews are different market phenomena and therefore there is a reason to treat them separately.

Table 5.1 Smile versus skew

Market Observations	Underlying Probability Issues	Possible Reasons	Modelling required
Symmetric smile	Kurtosis	Uncertainty, fear of illiquidity	Jumps, Stochastic volatility, Local volatility
Skew	Skewness	Fear of crises	Jumps, CEV, Local volatility, Displaced diffusion, Correlation

Therefore development of a 'model in-between' seems to be reasonable and this is a motivation to create a shifted BGM model. The direct import of methods developed in the context of equity and exchange rates may be problematic since there are different modeling problems for both asset classes as seen in the table below:

Table 5.2 Equity smile versus interest rate smile

Equity/Currency	Interest rates
One spot pricing measure	More forward pricing measures
Simple spot-forward parity	Complex spot-forward parity
Linear number of options	Nonlinear number of options
One underlying	More correlated underlyings
Liquid underlying	Most forward CMS rates non traded
Short maturities	Long maturities

5.1 THE SHIFTED BGM MODEL

In the shifted LIBOR Market Model (LMM) we assume that the LIBOR rates satisfy the following stochastic equations:

$$dL_n(t) = \left(\sum_{T_j > t+\delta}^{n} \frac{\delta \left(L_j(t) + k_j \right) \gamma_j(t)}{1 + \delta L_j(t)} \right) \gamma_n(t) \left(L_n(t) + k_n \right) dt$$

$$+ \gamma_n(t) \left(L_n(t) + k_n \right) dW(t),$$

(5.2)

where $\gamma_n(t)$ are deterministic volatility functions, $-\infty < k_n \leq \delta^{-1}$ are deterministic displacement factors and $W(t)$ is a Wiener process. Define $Z_{nN}(t)$ as

$$Z_{nN}(t) = \frac{\sum_{i=n+1}^{N} B(t, T_i) \left(L_i(t) + k_j \right)}{A_{nN}(t)} = S_{nN}(t) + \frac{\sum_{i=n+1}^{N} B(t, T_i) k_j}{A_{nN}(t)}.$$

Since $Z_{nN}(t)$ is a positive martingale with respect to the measure E_{nN}

$$dZ_{nN}(t) = \gamma_{nN}(t) Z_{nN}(t) dW(t),$$

(5.3)

where $\gamma_{nN}(t)$ is the stochastic instantaneous volatility of $Z_{nN}(t)$. On the other hand

$$dZ_{nN}(t) = \sum_{i=n+1}^{N} \frac{\partial Z_{nN}(t)}{\partial L_i(t)} \left(L_i(t) + k_i \right) \gamma_i(t) dW(t).$$

(5.4)

By the Ito formula:

$$\gamma_{nN}(t) = \sum_{k=n+1}^{N} R_{nN}^k(t) \gamma_k(t),$$

(5.5)

where

$$R_{nN}^j(t) = w_j(t) + \mu_j(t) \sum_{l=j}^{N} \left[u_j(t) - w_j(t) \right],$$

$$w_j(t) = \frac{B(t, T_j) \left(L_j(t) + k_j \right)}{\sum_{i=n+1}^{N} B(t, T_i) \left(L_i(t) + k_i \right)},$$

$$u_j(t) = \frac{B(t, T_j)}{A_{nN}(t)},$$

$$\mu_j(t) = \frac{\delta \left(L_j(t) + k_j \right)}{1 + \delta L_j(t)}.$$

If we approximate $R_{nN}^k(t)$ by $R_{nN}^k(0)$ and $Z_{nN}(t)$ by $S_{nN}(t) + k_{nN}$, where

$$k_{nN} = \sum_{i=n+1}^{N} u_i(0)k_i,$$

then the swap rate $S_{nN}(t)$ satisfies:

$$dS_{nN}(t) = \gamma_{nN}(t)(S_{nN}(t) + k_{nN})\,dW(t). \tag{5.6}$$

We denote the covariance matrix

$$\Phi^i = \begin{bmatrix} \varphi_{11}^i & \varphi_{12}^i & \cdots & \varphi_{1N}^i \\ \varphi_{21}^i & \varphi_{22}^i & \cdots & \varphi_{2N}^i \\ \cdots & \cdots & \cdots & \cdots \\ \varphi_{N1}^i & \varphi_{N2}^i & \cdots & \varphi_{NN}^i \end{bmatrix}, \tag{5.7}$$

where the elements are defined as (for $i < k$ and $i < l$)

$$\varphi_{kl}^i = \int_0^{T_i} \gamma_l(t) \cdot \gamma_k(t)\,dt.$$

In practice swap options are priced by the Black formula (e.g. for a call option, strike $= K$, option maturity $= T$)

$$Market_{nN}(K) = \delta A_{nN}(0)(S_{nN}(0)N(d_1) - KN(d_2)), \tag{5.8}$$

where

$$d_1 = \frac{\ln(S_{nN}(0)/K) + T_n\sigma_{nN}^2/2}{\sigma_{nN}\sqrt{T_n}}, \tag{5.9}$$

$$d_2 = d_1 - \sigma_{nN}\sqrt{T_n}, \tag{5.10}$$

If the shift of $S_{nN}(t)$ was equal 0, we would have direct link between market volatilities $S_{nN}(t)$ and model volatilities $S_{nN}(t)$. This however is not the case; since market volatilities are quoted in lognormal terms and they need then be transformed to their shifted form. The transformation to shifted form consists of finding sequence of market standard deviations θ_{nN} satisfying

$$Model_{nN}(K) = \delta A_{nN}(0)\left(\left(S_{nN}(0) + \sum_{i=n+1}^{N} u_i(0)k_i\right)N(d_1) - \left(K + \sum_{i=n+1}^{N} u_i(0)k_i\right)N(d_2)\right), \tag{5.11}$$

where

$$d_1 = \frac{\ln\left(S_{nN}(0) + \sum_{i=n+1}^{N} u_i(0)k_i\right) - \ln\left(K + \sum_{i=n+1}^{N} u_i(0)k_i\right) + \theta_{nN}^2/2}{\theta_{nN}}, \tag{5.12}$$

$$d_2 = d_1 - \theta_{nN}. \tag{5.13}$$

Calibrating the model consists of minimizing the square distance between model and market prices over the given set of swaptions:

$$\min \leftarrow Q\left(\Phi_{n+1}, \ldots, \Phi_N, k_{n+1}, \ldots, k_N\right) = \sum_{Swaptions} \frac{\left(Market_{nN}(K) - Model_{nN}(K)\right)^2}{Market_{nN}(K)^2}.$$

Remark 1. The family of covariance matrices $\Phi_{n+1}, \ldots, \Phi_N$ must be parameterized analogously as for the BGM model without shift.

Remark 2. For a border case, i.e. when $k_n = \delta^{-1}$, we HJM model.

The shifted BGM captures only skew. Thus it is required to incorporate a kind of stochastic volatility to model kurtosis. The most natural approach is to make the volatility functions $\gamma_n(t)$ stochastic and displacement factors $-\infty < k_n < \delta^{-1}$ random. The volatility functions $\gamma_n(t)$ may be correlated with the Wiener process W, which makes the approach impractical – the pricing of interest rate derivatives consists of calculating functionals under various forward measures, hence the dynamics of $\gamma_n(t)$ could be different for different maturities. In practice we have to assume that $\gamma_n(t)$ is independent of W – the shift k_n models skew and randomness of volatility $\gamma_n(t)$ models kurtosis. We opt for a special form of making the volatility $\gamma_n(t)$ stochastic as explained in the following sections.

5.2   STOCHASTIC VOLATILITY FOR LONG TERM OPTIONS

Let us start with the following general observation. Caps, floors and swaptions are usually options with long or very long maturity. Let $F(t)$ be the price of a forward contract maturing at T. Assume that $F(t)$ follows (under the forward measure):

$$dF(t) = \gamma(t)F(t)dW(t) \tag{5.14}$$

for $t < T$, where $W(t)$ is a Wiener process and $\gamma(t)$ is the stochastic volatility process independent of W. Let $Option(0, K)$ be the price of a call option with strike K and maturity T. By Hull (1999) it is equal to:

$$Option(0, K, T, Q(T)) = B(0, T) \int_0^\infty BS\left(\sqrt{x}, K, F(0), T\right) Q(T, dx). \tag{5.15}$$

Where the right hand side elements are given by the following:

$$Q(T, x) = P\left(\xi(T) \leq x\right) \tag{5.16}$$

$$\xi(T) = T^{-1} \int_0^T \gamma^2(t)dt, \tag{5.17}$$

$$BS(\sigma, K, F, T) = FN(d_1) - KN(d_2), \tag{5.18}$$

with, similar to before,

$$d_1 = \frac{\ln(F/K) + T\sigma^2/2}{\sigma\sqrt{T}}, \qquad (5.19)$$

$$d_2 = d_1 - \sigma\sqrt{T}. \qquad (5.20)$$

As it was already observed, for any stochastic process $\gamma(t)$ smile effect is observed: implied volatility for options away from money is larger than for options at the money. Notice the obvious fact that the option price $Option(0, K, T, Q(T))$ depends not directly on $\gamma(t)$ but on $\xi(T)$. By Borovkov (1998), for large class of stochastic processes (including 'practically all' processes used in option pricing) $\xi(T) \to \xi(\infty)$ for certain random variable $\xi(\infty)$ and $Q(T) \to Q(\infty)$, where $Q(\infty, x) = P(\xi(\infty) \le x)$. Hence it is appropriate to conclude that $Option(0, K, T, Q(T)) \approx Option(0, K, T, Q(\infty))$ for sufficiently large T. Therefore, if we assume that $F(t)$ follows the time-homogeneous version of (5.14)

$$dF(t) = \sqrt{\xi(\infty)}F(t)dW(t) \qquad (5.21)$$

we will not observe large differences in prices of long term options compared with the original dynamics (5.14). If the random variable $\xi(\infty) = m$ is deterministic, we say that the stochastic volatility process $\gamma(t)$ is mean reverting (in the language of finance) or ergodic (in the language of mathematics Borovkov (1998)). For mean reverting stochastic volatility models $Q(\infty) = \delta_m$, therefore smiles vanish as option maturity grows. Almost all studied stochastic volatility models are mean reverting, thus this makes them less suitable for pricing long term options.

Example Let the stochastic volatility process $\gamma(t)$ follow the Ornstein-Uhlenbeck (Vasiček) dynamics

$$d\gamma(t) = a(k - \gamma(t))dt + bdV(t),$$

where V is a Wiener process independent of W. Then

$$\xi(T) \to k^2 + b^2/2a$$

and option prices satisfy:

$$Option(0, K) \approx B(0, T)BS\left(\sqrt{k^2 + b^2/2a}, K, F(0), T\right).$$

Hence smiles vanish for sufficiently large T.

The simple uncertain volatility approach Brigo, Mercurio and Rapisarda (2004) is based on the equivalence between (5.14) and (5.21). Let

$$dF(t) = \sigma F(t)dW(t), \qquad (5.22)$$

where σ is a discrete random variable independent of $W(t)$ with

$$P(\sigma = \sigma_k) = p_k, \qquad (5.23)$$

where $\sigma_{k+1} > \sigma_k$ and

$$\sum_{k=1}^{M} p_k = 1. \tag{5.24}$$

Hence

$$Option(0, K) = B(0, T) \sum_{k=1}^{M} p_k BS(\sigma_k, K, F(0), T). \tag{5.25}$$

We define the implied volatility $\gamma(K)$ as a number $\sigma_1 < \gamma(K) < \sigma_M$ such that

$$BS(\gamma(K), K, F(0), T) = \sum_{k=1}^{M} p_k BS(\sigma_k, K, F(0), T). \tag{5.26}$$

Denote

$$f_n(t) = \frac{1}{\sigma_n \sqrt{2\pi}} \exp\left\{ -\frac{t^2}{2\sigma_n^2} \right\}$$

and

$$f(t) = \sum_{k=1}^{M} p_k f_k(t).$$

Thus since

$$\frac{f_n(t)}{f(t)} \to \frac{I_{\{n=M\}}}{p_n} \quad \text{as} \quad t \to \infty,$$

we observe the following simple property:

$$\gamma(K) \to \sigma_M \text{ as } K \to \infty \text{ or } K \to 0. \tag{5.27}$$

That model reflects relatively well the market's feelings on long term options: the market is not afraid that the realized volatility may fluctuate up and down – the market is afraid that the realized volatility may be larger (for longer lime) then the currently quoted volatility.

5.3   THE UNCERTAIN VOLATILITY DISPLACED LIBOR MARKET MODEL

Uncertain volatility is an easy and attractive prescription. Some pros for the uncertain volatility approach were given in Brigo, Mercurio and Rapisarda (2004):

1. Explicit marginal density (mixture of lognormal densities).
2. Explicit option prices (mixtures of Black-Scholes prices).
3. Nice fitting to smile-shaped implied volatility curves and surfaces.

On the other hand the uncertain volatility approach is counter-intuitive and causes some paradoxes but without impact on pricing abilities. Referring to Piterbarg (2003) we note that the paradoxes described are common for all pricing methods used in practice. Derivatives pricing, although strongly mathematical, is not an academic activity. The uncertain volatility displaced LIBOR market model is constructed as follows:

$$dL_k^i(t) = \left(\sum_{T_j > t + \delta}^{n} \frac{\delta \left(L_j^i(t) + \kappa_j^i \right) \eta_j^i(t)}{1 + \delta L_j^i(t)} \right) \eta_n^i(t) \left(L_n^i(t) + \kappa_n^i \right) dt + \eta_n^i(t) \left(L_n^i(t) + \kappa_n^i \right) dW(t),$$

(5.28)

where $\left\{ \eta_n^1(t), \eta_n^2(t), \ldots, \eta_n^M(t) \right\}$ are deterministic volatilities and $\left\{ \kappa_n^1, \kappa_n^2, \ldots, \kappa_n^M \right\}$ are displacements such that $\kappa_j^i \leq \delta^{-1}$. Let Z be a discrete random variable on $\{1, 2, \ldots, M\}$, independent of $W(t)$, defined by:

$$P(Z = k) = p_k,$$

(5.29)

where the p_k satisfy (5.24). The stochastic process $L_k^Z(t)$ satisfies an equation analogous to (5.2)

$$dL_k^Z(t) = \left(\sum_{T_j > t + \delta}^{n} \frac{\delta \left(L_j^Z(t) + \kappa_j^Z \right) \eta_j^i(t)}{1 + \delta L_j^Z(t)} \right) \eta_n^Z(t) \left(L_i^Z(t) + \kappa_n^z \right) dt + \eta_n^Z(t) \left(L_n^Z(t) + \kappa_n^Z \right) dW(t).$$

(5.30)

Hence the dynamics of forward swap rates may be approximated analogously as in (5.6). The pricing of all derivatives securities is extremely easy and is just a weighted average of various prices:

$$Price = \sum_{k=1}^{M} p_k Price_k,$$

(5.31)

where $Price_k$ is the price of our derivative under the k-th scenario. Monte Carlo simulation is straightforward as well.

The uncertain volatility displaced LIBOR market model is obviously only an approximation of a 'perfect' stochastic volatility model, but a sufficiently good approximation. Let us assume that $\{L_1(T_0), \ldots, L_n(T_{n-1})\}$ follows 'perfect' stochastic volatility model. Then, consider the joint distribution of $\{L_1(T_0), \ldots, L_n(T_{n-1})\}$ on $[-\delta^{-1}, +\infty)^n$. By Daniluk and Gatarek (2005), see also section 10, the distribution of $\left\{ L_1^i(T_0) + \kappa^i, \ldots, L_n^i(T_{n-1}) + \kappa_n^i \right\}$ is very close to the joint lognormal under all forward measures. Since the displaced lognormal distributions span the set of all probability distributions on $[-\delta^{-1}, +\infty)^n$, by a proper choice of $\left\{ \eta_n^1(t), \eta_n^2(t), \ldots, \eta_n^M(t) \right\}$, $\left\{ \kappa_n^1, \kappa_n^2, \ldots, \kappa_n^M \right\}$, and $\{p_1, p_2, \ldots, p_M\}$, we may approximate any dynamics of forward LIBORs by a displaced diffusion with an uncertain volatility. Thus we have that the displacement parameters $\left\{ \kappa_n^1, \kappa_n^2, \ldots, \kappa_n^M \right\}$ are responsible for skewness of caps, floors and swaptions, while variance of Z is responsible for their kurtosis. Replacing the random variable Z by a stochastic process $Z(t)$ may bring a bit more flexibility to modelling of swaption kurtosis. Since swaptions away-from-the-money are not very liquid, the uncertain volatility approach seems to be satisfactory at current state of the market.

Definitely – mean reverting stochastic volatility is a much better recipe for a hangover, than uncertain volatility. Papers Errais and Mercurio (2004) and Jarrow, Li and Zhao (2006) show that mean reverting stochastic volatility models cannot fully capture the interest rate derivatives skew, while the uncertain volatility approach can.

5.4   MIXING THE BGM AND HJM MODELS

Since $D_n(t) = 1 + \delta L_n(t)$ the HJM model is itself a displaced BGM model. Moreover the BGM and HJM models are extreme points for the class of shifted BGM models – as normal and lognormal. Hence we may find the easiest way of dealing with the skew and smile phenomenon: If we let Z be an random variable independent of $W(t)$ on the set $\{0, 1\}$ such that $P(Z = 1) = p$ for some $0 < p < 1$. Let $L_n(t)$ satisfy the following equation:

$$dL_n(t) = \left(L_n(t) + Z\delta^{-1}\right)\left(Z\eta_n(t) + (1 - Z)\gamma_n(t)\right)\left(\sigma(t, T_n)dt + dW(t)\right), \qquad (5.32)$$

where

$$\sigma(t, T_n) = \sum_{T_j > t + \delta}^{n} \frac{\left(\delta L_j(t) + Z\right)\left(Z\eta_j(t) + (1 - Z)\gamma_j(t)\right)}{1 + \delta L_j(t)}.$$

If $Z = 0$ then the LIBORs follow BGM dynamics, and if $Z = 1$ then the LIBORs follow HJM dynamics. Moreover the model is already calibrated to ATM swaptions. Here the pricing of all derivatives securities is extremely easy and is just a weighted average of the HJM and BGM prices:

$$Price = pPrice_{HJM} + (1 - p)Price_{BGM}. \qquad (5.33)$$

Fitting to the smile consists of finding a proper proportion between HJM and BGM – i.e. finding the probability p to minimize distance between model smile and market smile. This can be done by one-dimensional optimization:

$$\min \leftarrow Q(p) = \sum_{i \in Swaptions} \frac{(Mkt_i - BGM_i + p(BGM_i - HJM_i))^2}{Mkt_i^2},$$

where Mkt_i, BGM_i, HJM_i are market prices and calibrated at the money BGM and HJM prices of the swaptions under investigation. Since the optimization problem is quadratic there exists a closed-form solution p such that $Q'(p) = 0$. Hence

$$0 = Q'(p) = 2p \sum_{i \in Swaptions} \frac{(BGM_i - HJM_i)^2}{Mkt_i^2} + 2 \sum_{i \in Swaptions} \frac{(Mkt_i - BGM_i)(BGM_i - HJM_i)}{Mkt_i^2}.$$

Therefore our solution is simply

$$
p = \frac{\displaystyle\sum_{i \in Swaptions} \frac{(BGM_i - Mkt_i)(BGM_i - HJM_i)}{Mkt_i^2}}{\displaystyle\sum_{i \in Swaptions} \frac{(BGM_i - HJM_i)^2}{Mkt_i^2}}.
$$

One can take other 'quality' functions as weighted averages. There is one final optimization that may be carried out to improve the fit; the calibration is perfect ATM and we may get much closer fit away-from-the-money at the cost by simply relaxing quality of ATM fit.

6
Simplified BGM and HJM Models

The topic of this chapter is to create the 'simplest possible term structure models' for single factor BGM and HJM – surprisingly useful in some applications. We develop a 'mixture of models' approach in order to capture the volatility smile effect. As an example we derive pricing formulae for exotic CMS swaps.

6.1 CMS RATE DYNAMICS IN SINGLE-FACTOR HJM MODEL

Assume that $\eta_n(t) = \gamma(t)$. In the single factor HJM model forward discount factors $D_n(t)$ follow the equation

$$dD_n(t) = \eta(t)D_n(t)dW_n(t) = \eta(t)D_n(t)\left(\Sigma(t, T_n)dt + dW(t)\right). \qquad (6.1)$$

Hence we have that

$$\Sigma(t, T_n) = \left[\delta^{-1}(T_n - t)\right]^+ \eta(t).$$

therefore the swap rate:

$$\delta S_{nN}(t) + 1 = \frac{\sum_{i=n+1}^{N} B(t, T_i)D_i(t)}{\sum_{i=n+1}^{N} B(t, T_i)} = \exp\left\{\int_0^t \eta(s)dW(s) - \frac{1}{2}\int_0^t \eta^2(s)ds\right\} \bar{A}(t),$$

where

$$A^i(t) = D_i(0)\exp\left\{\int_0^t \eta^2(s)\left[\delta^{-1}(T_i - s)\right]ds\right\}$$

$$\bar{A}(t) = \frac{\sum_{i=n+1}^{N} B(t, T_i)A^i(t)}{A_{nN}(t)}.$$

By the Ito formula and the forward measure paradigm:

$$d\left(1 + \delta S_{nN}(t)\right) = \left(1 + \delta S_{nN}(t)\right)\eta(t)(1 - H_{nN}(t))dW_{nN}(t)$$

$$= \left(1 + \delta S_{nN}(t)\right)\eta(t)(1 - H_{nN}(t))\left(dW(t) + \frac{\sum_{i=n+1}^{N} B(t, T_i)\Sigma(t, T_i)}{A_{nN}(t)}dt\right),$$

where

$$H_{nN}(t) = \frac{\sum\limits_{j=n+1}^{N}\sum\limits_{i=n+1}^{N} B(t,T_j)B(t,T_i)\left(A^i(t)-A^j(t)\right)(i-n)}{A_{nN}(t)^2\bar{A}(t)}$$

$$= \frac{\sum\limits_{i=n+1}^{N} B(t,T_i)\left(A^i(t)-\bar{A}(t)\right)(i-n)}{\bar{A}(t)A_{nN}(t)} = \frac{\sum\limits_{i=n+1}^{N} B(t,T_i)A^i(t)(i-n)-\bar{A}(t)\sum\limits_{i=n+1}^{N}A_{ni}(t)}{\bar{A}(t)A_{nN}(t)}.$$

If we assume that $B(t,T) \leq B(t,S)$ for $T \geq S$ (this does hold in practice)

$$\left|H_{nN}(t)\right| \leq \max_{i,j}\left(A^i(t)-A^j(t)\right)\frac{N-n+1}{2}.$$

For a flat initial yield curve $H_{nN}(t)$ is close to 0. Hence the forward swap rate $S_{nN}(t)$ satisfies the approximate equation:

$$d\left(1+\delta S_{nN}(t)\right) \approx \left(1+\delta S_{nN}(t)\right)\eta_{nN}(t)dW_{n+1}(t)+\left(1+\delta S_{nN}(t)\right)\beta_{nN}(t)dt$$

$$= \left(1+\delta S_{nN}(t)\right)\gamma_{nN}(t)\left(dW_{n+1}(t)+\frac{\beta_{nN}(t)}{\gamma_{nN}(t)}dt\right),$$

where

$$\eta_{nN}(t) = \eta(t)(1-H_{nN}(0)),$$

$$H_{nN}(0) = \frac{\sum\limits_{i=n+1}^{N} B(0,T_i)\left(A^i(0)-\bar{A}(0)\right)(i-n)}{\bar{A}(0)A_{nN}(t)} = \frac{\delta\sum\limits_{i=n+1}^{N} B(0,T_i)\left(L_i(0)-S_{nN}(0)\right)(i-n)}{\left(1+\delta S_{nN}(0)\right)A_{nN}(t)}$$

$$= \frac{\delta\sum\limits_{i=n+1}^{N} B(0,T_i)L_i(0)(i-n)-\delta S_{nN}(0)\sum\limits_{i=n+1}^{N}A_{ni}(0)}{\left(1+\delta S_{nN}(0)\right)A_{nN}(t)}$$

and also

$$\beta_{nN}(t) = \eta^2(t)(1-H_{nN}(0))\frac{\sum\limits_{i+n+2}^{N} B(0,T_i)(i-n-1)}{A_{nN}(t)},$$

$$\frac{\beta_{nN}(t)}{\eta_{nN}(t)} = \gamma(t)\frac{\sum\limits_{i+n+2}^{N} B(0,T_i)(i-n-1)}{A_{nN}(t)}.$$

6.2   CMS RATE DYNAMICS IN A SINGLE FACTOR BGM MODEL

A completely analogous procedure can be performed for the single-factor BGM model, where the forward LIBOR rates satisfy:

$$dL_n(t) = \gamma(t)L_n(t)dW_n(t) = \gamma(t)L_n(t)\left(\Sigma(t, T_n)dt + dW(t)\right),$$

where

$$\Sigma(t, T_n) = \gamma(t) \sum_{T_j > t+\delta}^{n} \frac{\delta L_j(t)}{1 + \delta L_j(t)}.$$

Similarly for the swap rate:

$$S_{nN}(t) = \frac{\sum_{i=n+1}^{N} B(t, T_i)L_i(t)}{A_{nN}(t)} = \exp\left\{\int_0^t \gamma(s)dW(s) - \frac{1}{2}\int_0^t \gamma^2(s)ds\right\}\bar{C}(t),$$

where

$$C^i(t) = L_i(0)\exp\left\{\int_0^t \gamma^2(s)\left(\sum_{\frac{T_j - s}{\delta} > 1}^{n} \frac{\delta L_j(s)}{1 + \delta L_j(s)}\right)ds\right\}$$

$$\bar{C}(t) = \frac{\sum_{i=n+1}^{N} B(t, T_i)C^i(t)}{A_{nN}(t)}.$$

By the Ito formula:

$$dS_{nN}(t) = S_{nN}(t)\gamma(t)(1 - G_{nN}(t))dW_{nN}(t)$$

$$= S_{nN}(t)\gamma(t)(1 - G_{nN}(t))\left(dW(t) + \frac{\sum_{i=n+1}^{N} B(t, T_i)\Sigma(t, T_i)}{A_{nN}(t)}dt\right),$$

where

$$G_{nN}(t) = \frac{\sum_{j=n+1}^{N}\sum_{i=n+1}^{N} B(t, T_j)B(t, T_i)\left(C^i(t) - C^j(t)\right)\sum_{k=n+1}^{i} \frac{\delta L_k(t)}{1 + \delta L_k(t)}}{A_{nN}(t)^2\bar{C}(t)}$$

$$= \frac{\sum_{i=n+1}^{N} B(t, T_i)\left(C^i(t) - \bar{C}(t)\right)\sum_{k=n+1}^{i} \frac{\delta L_k(t)}{1 + \delta L_k(t)}}{\bar{C}(t)A_{nN}(t)}.$$

Hence the forward swap rate $S_{nN}(t)$ satisfies the approximate equation:

$$dS_{nN}(t) \approx S_{nN}(t)\gamma_{nN}(t)dW_{n+1}(t) + S_{nN}(t)\alpha_{nN}(t)dt$$

$$= S_{nN}(t)\eta_{nN}(t)\left(dW_{n+1}(t) + \frac{\alpha_{nN}(t)}{\eta_{nN}(t)}dt\right),$$

where

$$\gamma_{nN}(t) = \gamma(t)(1 - G_{nN}(0)),$$

$$G_{nN}(0) = \frac{\sum\limits_{i=n+1}^{N} B(0, T_i)\left(C^i(0) - \bar{C}(0)\right) \sum\limits_{k=n+1}^{i} \dfrac{\delta L_k(0)}{1 + \delta L_k(0)}}{\bar{C}(0)A_{nN}(t)},$$

$$= \frac{\sum\limits_{i=n+1}^{N} B(0, T_i)\left(L_i(0) - S_{nN}(0)\right) \sum\limits_{k=n+1}^{i} \dfrac{\delta L_k(0)}{1 + \delta L_k(0)}}{S_{nN}(0)A_{nN}(t)}$$

$$\alpha_{nN}(t) = (1 - G_{nN}(0))\gamma^2(t) \sum\limits_{i=n+2}^{N} Q_{kN}^i(0),$$

$$\frac{\alpha_{nN}(t)}{\gamma_{nN}(t)} = \gamma(t) \sum\limits_{i=n+2}^{N} Q_{kN}^i(0),$$

and

$$Q_{kN}^l(t) = \frac{\delta L_l(t)A_{l-1,N}(t)}{(1 + \delta L_l(t))A_{nN}(t)}.$$

6.3   CALIBRATION

In practice swap options are priced by the Black formula (i.e. a call option, strike $= K$, option maturity $= T$):

$$Swaption_{nN}(0) = \delta A_{nN}(0)BS\left(S_{nN}(0), K, 0, T_n\sigma_{nN}^2\right),$$

where

$$BS(S, K, U, V) = Se^U N(d_1) - KN(d_2),$$

$$d_1 = \frac{\ln(S/K) + U + V/2}{\sqrt{V}},$$

$$d_2 = d_1 - \sqrt{V},$$

$$N(x) = \frac{1}{\sqrt{2\pi}} \int_{-\infty}^{x} e^{-u^2/2} du.$$

Here the parameters σ_{nN} are given by the market and called market volatilities. The process for calibration of option models consists of determining volatilities $\eta(t)$ for the HJM model and $\gamma(t)$ for the BGM model such that market prices and model prices coincide at least for the at-the-money (ATM) swaptions. Since the market does not provide enough information to determine both $\gamma(t)$ and $\eta(t)$ completely, the determining of synthetic integral forms:

$$\sigma_n = \int_0^{T_n} \eta^2(t) dt \text{ and } \theta_n = \int_0^{T_n} \gamma^2(t) dt$$

is sufficient for most pricing purposes. A calibration to BGM model is easier – by the forward measure paradigm we clearly have

$$\theta_n = T_n \sigma_{nN}^2 (1 - G_{nN}(0))^{-2}.$$

Since the model is single-factor, the number of market volatilites must be equal to the number of model parameters, so calibration either to caps/floors or to co-terminal swaptions is straightforward. In contrast the calibration of the HJM model is slightly more complex. To make both prices for the two models consistent for at-the-money swaptions the following equality must hold:

$$
\begin{aligned}
Swaption_{nN}(0) &= \delta A_{nN}(0) BS \left(S_{nN}(0), S_{nN}(0), 0, T_n \sigma_{nN}^2 \right) \\
&= \delta A_{nN}(0) BS \left(S_{nN}(0), S_{nN}(0), 0, \theta_n (1 - G_{nN}(0))^2 \right) \qquad (6.2) \\
&= A_{nN}(0) BS \left(1 + \delta S_{nN}(0), 1 + \delta S_{nN}(0), 0, \sigma_n ((1 - F_{nN}(0))^2 \right).
\end{aligned}
$$

Since $BS(S, S, 0, V) = 2SN\left(\frac{\sqrt{V}}{2}\right) - S$, (2) reduces to

$$(1 + \delta S_{nN}(0)) N \left(\frac{(1 - F_{nN}(0)) \sqrt{\sigma_n}}{2} \right) = \delta S_{nN}(0) N \left(\frac{\sigma_{nN} \sqrt{T_n}}{2} \right) + \frac{1}{2}.$$

Since $\sigma_{n-1} \leq \sigma_n \leq \theta_n$ and $N'(x) = \frac{1}{\sqrt{2\pi}} e^{-x^2/2}$ the equation (6.2) can be easily solved by Newton method or bisection. Since σ_n are very small, the one-step Newton method is suitable. Taking two or three steps makes the approximation almost perfect.

6.4   SMILE

Both models now fit the market prices of ATM co-terminal swaptions. Is one better than the other? To examine this notion we should check prices away-from-the-money. The skew can be described as follows: market swaption volatility is a function of strike prices i.e.

$$Swaption_{nN}(0, K) = \delta A_{nN}(0) BS \left(S_{nN}(0), K, 0, T_n \sigma_{nN}^2(K) \right).$$

The easiest way of dealing with the skew phenomenon is by a random mixture of models: Let Z be an independent on $W(t)$ random variable on the set $\{0, 1\}$ such that $P(Z=1)=p$ for some $0 < p < 1$. Let $L_n(t)$ satisfy the following equation:

$$dL_n(t) = (Z\gamma(t) + (1 - Z)\eta(t))\left(L_n(t) + Z\delta^{-1}\right)(\Sigma(t, T_n)dt + dW(t)),$$

where

$$\Sigma(t, T_n) = (Z\gamma(t) + (1 - Z)\eta(t)) \sum_{T_j > t+\delta}^{n} \frac{Z + \delta L_j(t)}{1 + \delta L_j(t)}.$$

If $Z = 0$ then LIBORs follow BGM dynamics, and if $Z = 1$ then LIBORs follow HJM dynamics. Moreover the model is already calibrated to ATM swaptions. Then the pricing of all derivatives securities, including CMS, is extremely easy and is just a weighted average of HJM and BGM prices:

$$Price = pPrice_{HJM} + (1 - p)Price_{BGM}.$$

Fitting to the smile consists of finding a proper proportion between HJM and BGM – i.e. finding the probability p to minimize distance between model smile and market smile. This can be done by one-dimensional optimization:

$$Q(p) = \sum_{n=1}^{N-1} \sum_{i=1}^{M} (BS_{in}(Market) - BS_{in}(BGM) + p(BS_{in}(BGM) - BS_{in}(HJM)))^2 \to \min,$$

where

$$BS_{in}(Market) = \delta BS\left(S_{nN}(0), K_{in}, 0, T_n\sigma_{nN}^2(K_{in})\right),$$

$$BS_{in}(BGM) = \delta BS\left(S_{nN}(0), K_{in}, 0, \theta_n(1 - G_{nN}(0))^2\right),$$

$$BS_{in}(HJM) = BS\left(1 + \delta S_{nN}(0), 1 + \delta K_{in}, 0, \sigma_n(1 - F_{nN}(0))^2\right).$$

Since the optimization problem is quadratic there exists its closed-form solution p such that $Q'(p) = 0$. Hence

$$Q'(p) = 2\sum_{n=1}^{N-1} \sum_{i=1}^{M} (BS_{in}(BGM) - BS_{in}(HJM))(BS_{in}(Market) - BS_{in}(BGM))$$

$$+ 2p \sum_{n=1}^{N-1} \sum_{i=1}^{M} (BS_{in}(BGM) - BS_{in}(HJM))^2 = 0.$$

Therefore

$$p = \frac{\displaystyle\sum_{n=1}^{N-1} \sum_{i=1}^{M} (BS_{in}(BGM) - BS_{in}(HJM))(BS_{in}(BGM) - BS_{in}(Market))}{\displaystyle\sum_{n=1}^{N-1} \sum_{i=1}^{M} (BS_{in}(BGM) - BS_{in}(HJM))^2}.$$

One may take other quality functions as weighted averages. The fit may be improved by one more (very last) optimization: the calibration is perfect ATM and we may get much closer fit away-from-the-money at the cost of relaxing quality of ATM fit. Namely, for any $n < N$ minimize

$$\sum_{i=1}^{M} (BS_{in}(Market) - BS_{in}(Model, \theta_n, \sigma_n))^2 \to \min$$

subject to the constraints $\theta_{n-1} \le \theta_n$ and $\sigma_{n-1} \le \sigma_n$,

where

$$BS_{in}(Model, \theta_n, \sigma_n) = (1-p)\delta BS\left(S_{nN}(0), K_{in}, 0, \theta_n(1-G_{nN}(0))^2\right)$$
$$pBS\left(1+\delta S_{nN}(0), 1+\delta K_{in}, 0, \sigma_n(1-F_{nN}(0))^2\right).$$

Since the sensitivity of the function $BS(S, K, U, V)$ with respect to V is known as Vega, gradient methods can be used in optimization.

Returning to the initial problem of pricing cash flows of the form $(S_{nN}(T_n) - K)^+$, which is equivalent to the calculation of $E\left(D(T_{n+1})(S_{nN}(T_n) - K)^+\right)$. By our calculations

$$E\left(D(T_{n+1})(S_{nN}(T_n) - K)^+\right) = B(0, T_{n+1})\left(pBS(HJM) + (1-p)BS(BGM)\right),$$

where

$$BS(HJM) = BS\left(1+\delta S_{nN}(0), 1+\delta K, \sigma_n(1-F_{nN}(0)) \frac{\sum\limits_{i+n+2}^{N} B(0, T_i)(i-n-1)}{\sum\limits_{i=n+1}^{N} B(0, T_i)}, \right.$$

$$\left. \sigma_n(1-F_{nN}(0))^2 \vphantom{\frac{\sum\limits_{i+n+2}^{N}}{\sum\limits_{i=n+1}^{N}}} \right)$$

and

$$BS(BGM) = \delta BS\left(S_{nN}(0), K, \theta_n(1-G_{nN}(0)) \sum_{i=n+2}^{N} Q_{kN}^i(0), \theta_n(1-G_{nN}(0))^2\right).$$

Cash flows of CMS swaps are of the form $S_{nN}(T_n)$, which is equivalent to the calculation of $E\left(D(T_{n+1})S_{nN}(T_n)\right)$. Hence

$$E\left(D(T_{n+1})S_{nN}(T_n)\right) = B(0, T_{n+1})\left(pCMS(HJM) + (1-p)CMS(BGM)\right),$$

where

$$CMS(HJM) = (\delta S_{nN}(t) + 1) \exp\left(\sigma_n(1 - F_{nN}(0)) \frac{\sum\limits_{i+n+2}^{N} B(0, T_i)(i - n - 1)}{\sum\limits_{i=n+1}^{N} B(0, T_i)}\right) - 1$$

and

$$CMS(BGM) = \delta S_{nN}(0) \exp\left(\theta_n(1 - G_{nN}(0)) \sum\limits_{i=n+2}^{N} Q_{kN}^i(0)\right)$$

$$= \delta S_{nN}(0) \exp\left(\frac{T_n \sigma_{nN}^2}{1 - G_{nN}(0)} \sum\limits_{i=n+2}^{N} Q_{kN}^i(0)\right).$$

Part II
Calibration

Index of Notations for Part II

T_i	–	Time expressed as a dd/mm/yy
$B(0, T_i)$	–	Discount factor for the period $0 \div T_i$
$\sigma^{cap}(T_i, T_j) = \sigma_{i,j}^{cap}$	–	Volatility of cap for option maturing at T_i and length $T_i \div T_j$
N	–	Principal notional
$L(t, T_i, T_j)$	–	LIBOR forward rate at time t for period $T_i \div T_j$
$\delta_{i,j}$	–	Day count fraction for period $T_i \div T_j$
X	–	Strike price
W_i	–	Payoff at time T_i
$S_{i,j}(t) = S(t, T_i, T_j)$	–	Forward swap rate at time t for period $T_i \div T_j$
$c\left(t, T_{n-1}, T_n, \sigma_{n-1,n}^{cpl}\right)$	–	Caplet value for caplet covering period $T_{n-1} \div T_n$ with caplet volatility equal to $\sigma_{n-1,n}^{cpl}$
$\sigma^{cpl}(t, T_{n-1}, T_n) = \sigma_{n-1,n}^{cpl}$	–	Caplet volatility for a caplet covering period $T_{n-1} \div T_n$
$\sigma^{inst}(t, T_{i-1}, T_i)$	–	Instantaneous volatility of the forward rate $L(t, T_{i-1}, T_i)$
$\sigma^{inst}(t, T_{i-1,i}, T_{k,l})$	–	Piecewise constant instantaneous volatility of forward rate $L(t, T_{i-1}, T_i)$ at time interval $T_k \div T_l$, where $k < l \le i - 1$
$\boldsymbol{\Sigma}\_\mathbf{inst}$	–	Matrix of instantaneous volatilities
$\boldsymbol{\Sigma}\_\mathbf{cpl}$	–	Matrix of caplet volatilities
$\sigma^{swpt}(t, T_i, T_j) = \sigma_{i,j}^{swpt}$	–	Swaption volatility for swaption with maturity at T_i and underlying swap length $T_i \div T_j$

7
Calibration Algorithms to Caps and Floors

7.1 INTRODUCTION

There is a wide range of various calibration algorithms for the LIBOR Market Model when used in practice. A lot of them are described in books and articles (see Rebonato (2002), Brigo and Mercurio (2001)), however there is still a lack of detailed algorithms presenting the step-by-step procedure of calibration clearly.

In this chapter we describe at the beginning some preliminary theory. We present the methodology of cap valuation. We demonstrate how to price caplets, how to derive ATM strikes from caps and finally we present the full algorithm for stripping caplet volatilities from cap quotes. All the theory is enriched by detailed examples taken from the real market.

All the market data are taken from a particular working day. The data contains interest rates for EUR taken from both the deposit and IRS markets and also ATM cap volatilities.

The next part of the chapter is dedicated to the application of non-parametric calibration algorithms to caps. For that purpose we use an algorithm that utilizes the derivation of caplet volatilities from cap volatilities, what is hard to find anywhere. It may seem to be easy but in our opinion the presentation of a detailed algorithm is necessary.

Taking into account the current situation of the market, we present some procedures of calibration without the time homogeneity assumption and then afterwards with the time homogeneity assumption. We compare both algorithms and results are produced. We present the calibration algorithms first with piecewise constant instantaneous volatilities depending on the time to maturity and then with a dependency on the maturity of the underlying forward rate. Both algorithms were presented in Brigo and Mercurio (2001) but in this book we present them in a more detailed way allowing them to be understood by readers of all levels. We present examples that the time homogeneity assumption does not work properly in certain market conditions.

7.2 MARKET DATA

One of the goals of the chapter is to present detailed algorithms and results of calibration. To do this we take into account one set of market data. All the market data is taken from 21 January 2005. We take into account following rates in EUR: the discount factors bootstrapped to form par interest rates (LIBOR's, FRA, IRS), at-the-money cap volatilities and swaption volatilities. Table 7.1 presents the discount factors and cap volatilities for a set of particular days.

Table 7.1 Market data from 21 January 2005: discount factors and cap volatilities

Tenor T_i	Date	Discount factor $B(0, T_i)$	Cap volatility $\sigma^{cap}(T_0, T_i)$
$t = 0$	21-01-2005	1.0000000	N/A
T_0	25-01-2005	0.9997685	N/A
T_{SN}	26-01-2005	0.9997107	N/A
T_{SW}	01-02-2005	0.9993636	N/A
T_{2W}	08-02-2005	0.9989588	N/A
T_{1M}	25-02-2005	0.9979767	N/A
T_{2M}	25-03-2005	0.9963442	N/A
T_{3M}	25-04-2005	0.9945224	N/A
T_{6M}	25-07-2005	0.9890361	N/A
T_{9M}	25-10-2005	0.9832707	N/A
T_{1Y}	25-01-2006	0.9772395	0.1641
T_{2Y}	25-01-2007	0.9507588	0.2137
T_{3Y}	25-01-2008	0.9217704	0.2235
T_{4Y}	26-01-2009	0.8908955	0.2188
T_{5Y}	25-01-2010	0.8589736	0.2127
T_{6Y}	25-01-2011	0.8262486	0.2068
T_{7Y}	25-01-2012	0.7928704	0.2012
T_{8Y}	25-01-2013	0.7595743	0.1958
T_{9Y}	27-01-2014	0.7261153	0.1905
T_{10Y}	26-01-2015	0.6942849	0.1859
T_{12Y}	25-01-2017	0.6348348	0.1806
T_{15Y}	27-01-2020	0.5521957	0.1699
T_{20Y}	27-01-2025	0.4345583	0.1567

where

$B(0, T_i)$ – Discount factor for time period $0 \div T_i$

$\sigma^{cap}(T_0, T_i)$ – Market volatility of cap option starting at time T_0 and maturing at T_i.

The various discount factors are bootstrapped from interbank deposits and FRA quotations for short term below one year and IRS prices for long term above one year.

Some of the readers may not be familiar with nature of the cap mechanism. For that case it seems to be worth showing how to interpret the cap quotes.

Below we present the nature of caps and how to determine resets and payments. Let us start from cap covering one period. Usual periods are semiannual, however on the market there are also caps with quarterly periods. Payments from a cap are illustrated in Figure 7.1.

In Figure 7.1 $t = 0$ means the pricing day (today). Date T_1 is the first reset date where LIBOR rate covering the period $T_1 \div T_2$ will be determined. The payment associated with this LIBOR rate occurs in date T_2 and equals W_2.

$$W_2 = N \left(L \left(T_1, T_1, T_2 \right) - X \right)^+ \delta_{1,2}.$$

In general we have

$$W_n = N \left(L \left(T_{n-1}, T_{n-1}, T_n \right) - X \right)^+ \delta_{n-1,n} \tag{7.1}$$

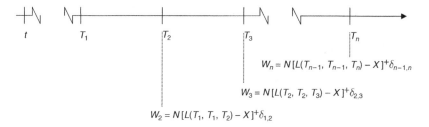

$$W_n = N[L(T_{n-1}, T_{n-1}, T_n) - X]^+\delta_{n-1,n}$$

$$W_3 = N[L(T_2, T_2, T_3) - X]^+\delta_{2,3}$$

$$W_2 = N[L(T_1, T_1, T_2) - X]^+\delta_{1,2}$$

Figure 7.1 Payments from cap option covering n periods.

where: N is notional value of the cap, $L(T_{n-1}, T_{n-1}, T_n)$ is the LIBOR rate resetting at T_{n-1} and covering the period $T_{n-1} \div T_n$, X is the strike price of the cap, symbol $()^+$ denotes value from the brackets if greater than zero and zero otherwise and finally $\delta_{n-1,n}$ denotes year fraction of period $T_{n-1} \div T_n$ computed according to one of well defined day count basis, e.g. actual/360.

It is very important that we consider at this stage cap contracts functioning in the described manner. If the payment W_2 occurs at a different moment than T_2 and the payoff function remains unchanged then we will have not a plain-vanilla instrument, but an exotic one. Analogously, payments $W_3, W_4, \ldots, W_n$ are defined accordingly.

Payments constructed as described above constitute caplets. So, we can say, that a cap option is a set of caplets. Later in the text we describe how to obtain caplet volatilities from cap volatilities, which is the first and necessary step to any calibration of cap options.

Now we can move to swaptions to present the nature of these contracts. Table 7.2 presents market quotations of at-the-money swaption volatilities. By the 'at-the-money swaption volatility' we mean such volatility for which strike price is equal to forward swap rate. The definition of the forward swap rate will be presented later in the chapter.

Table 7.2 Market data from 21 January 2005: swaption volatilities

	Underlying IRS length									
	1Y	2Y	3Y	4Y	5Y	6Y	7Y	8Y	9Y	10Y
T_{1Y}	0.2270	0.2300	0.2210	0.2090	0.1960	0.1860	0.1760	0.1690	0.1630	0.1590
T_{2Y}	0.2240	0.2150	0.2050	0.1940	0.1830	0.1740	0.1670	0.1620	0.1580	0.1540
T_{3Y}	0.2090	0.2010	0.1900	0.1800	0.1700	0.1630	0.1580	0.1550	0.1520	0.1500
T_{4Y}	0.1950	0.1870	0.1770	0.1680	0.1600	0.1550	0.1510	0.1480	0.1470	0.1450
T_{5Y}	0.1820	0.1740	0.1650	0.1580	0.1510	0.1480	0.1450	0.1430	0.1420	0.1400
T_{6Y}	0.1746	0.1674	0.1590	0.1524	0.1462	0.1436	0.1410	0.1394	0.1384	0.1368
T_{7Y}	0.1672	0.1608	0.1530	0.1468	0.1414	0.1392	0.1370	0.1358	0.1348	0.1336
T_{8Y}	0.1598	0.1542	0.1470	0.1412	0.1366	0.1348	0.1330	0.1322	0.1312	0.1304
T_{9Y}	0.1524	0.1476	0.1410	0.1356	0.1318	0.1304	0.1290	0.1286	0.1276	0.1272
T_{10Y}	0.1450	0.1410	0.1350	0.1300	0.1270	0.1260	0.1250	0.1250	0.1240	0.1240

(Option maturity)

Interpretation of ATM swaption quotes

The number 22.70 % in first column and first row means market swaption volatility with maturity equal to 1 year ($T_{1Y} = T_0$) (see column on the left) on the underlying swap starting in 1 year (T_{1Y}) and maturing in 2 years ($T_{2Y} = T_1$) from now.

We can define this volatility in the following way: $\sigma_{0,1}^{swpt} = \sigma^{swpt}(t, T_0, T_1) = 22.70\,\%$. Figure 7.2 presents a schema for payments from a swaption with maturity $T_{1Y} = T_0$ with an underlying swap period $T_0 \div T_1$.

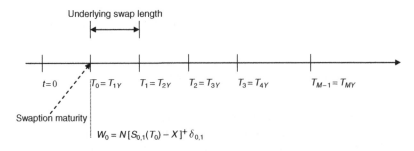

Figure 7.2   Payment from a swaption with maturity T_0 covering the period $T_0 - T_1$

Where X means strike price for the swaption and $S_{0,1}(T_0)$ is a forward swap rate that will be determined at $T_{1Y} = T_0$ and covering the period $T_0 \div T_1$.

Generally we can write $\sigma_{n,N}^{MKT}$ which means the market swaption volatility for a swaption maturing at T_n with underlying swap length $T_n \div T_N$.

We have presented in this section all necessary basic data which allows us to construct various calibration techniques. In the next section we start to present the calibration algorithms to cap options.

7.3   CALIBRATION TO CAPS

Calibration algorithms to caps are the simplest algorithms used in practice and do not require the use of optimization techniques. However, one should be careful and aware that such a calibration technique will definitely not be enough to solve the complicated pricing problems. Although the calibration is simple and almost straightforward it will be useful for later purposes to present it in a more detailed way. This is important because if one wants to obtain a good understanding of any calibration procedure for a LIBOR Market Model it is necessary to good understand how caps are quoted on the market and how to obtain caplet prices from cap quotes.

The calibration of the LIBOR Market Model requires knowing how to price caps, and more precisely, caplets in particular cap. To start with we should remember, that market prices of caplets are valued using the standard Black formula.

7.3.1   Caplet values

The LIBOR rate covering the period $T_{n-1} \div T_n$ resetting in T_{n-1} can be expressed from the perspective of today in terms of deterministic discount factors for periods $t \div T_{n-1}$ and $t \div T_n$ and year fraction $\delta_{n-1,n}$. So we have:

$$L(T_{n-1}, T_{n-1}, T_n) = F(T_0, T_{n-1}, T_n) = \left(\frac{B(T_0, T_{n-1})}{B(T_0, T_n)} - 1 \right) \frac{1}{\delta_{n-1,n}} \qquad (7.2)$$

where $F(T_0, T_{n-1}, T_n)$ is an interest rate determined at T_0 covering the period $T_{n-1} \div T_n$.

Having this we can now determine the caplet price for the period $T_{n-1} \div T_n$ with payment at T_n and strike X in the following way:

$$c\left(T_0, T_{n-1}, T_n, \sigma_{n-1,n}^{cpl}\right) = B\left(T_0, T_n\right) \delta_{n-1,n} \left[F\left(T_0, T_{n-1}, T_n\right) N\left(d_1\right) - XN\left(d_2\right)\right] \quad (7.3)$$

where:

$$N\left(d_1\right) = \frac{\ln\left(\frac{F(T_0, T_{n-1}, T_n)}{X}\right) + \frac{\sigma_{n-1,n}^{cpl\,2} \delta_{0,n-1}}{2}}{\sigma_{n-1,n}^{cpl} \sqrt{\delta_{0,n-1}}}$$

$$N\left(d_2\right) = \frac{\ln\left(\frac{F(T_0, T_{n-1}, T_n)}{X}\right) - \frac{\sigma_{n-1,n}^{cpl\,2} \delta_{0,n-1}}{2}}{\sigma_{n-1,n}^{cpl} \sqrt{\delta_{0,n-1}}}$$

and $N()$ denotes standard normal distribution function and $\sigma_{n-1,n}^{cpl}$ the market volatility of caplet covering the period $T_{n-1} \div T_n$. This is a good moment to present an example of caplet pricing.

Example 7.1 Caplet value

We compute the caplet value taking real market data from 21 January 2005. The characteristics of the caplet is presented in Table 7.3:

Table 7.3 Caplet characteristic from example 7.1

Parameter	Value
$t = 0$	21-01-2005
T_0	25-01-2005
T_{n-1}	25-01-2006
T_n	25-04-2006
$B\left(t, T_{n-1}\right)$	0.9774658
$B\left(t, T_n\right)$	0.9712884
X	2.361 %
$\sigma_{n-1,n}^{cpl}$	20.15 %

Taking the data from Table 7.3 we have caplet value for unit value of currency EUR:

$$c\left(T_0, T_{n-1}, T_n, \sigma_{n-1,n}^{cpl}\right) = 0.000733039$$

End of example 7.1

The next step is to determine ATM strikes for cap options.

7.3.2 ATM strikes for caps

Let us define the forward swap rate, the rate of fixed leg of IRS which makes the contract fair in the context of present time. For computational reasons our IRS contract has length $T_s \div T_N$. The present value of the floating leg is given by:

$$PV \text{ (Floating Leg)} = \sum_{i=s+1}^{N} B\left(T_0, T_i\right) L\left(T_{i-1}, T_{i-1}, T_i\right) \delta_{i-1,i}.$$

Analogously, the present value of the fixed leg is given by:

$$PV \text{ (Fixed Leg)} = \sum_{i=s+1}^{N} B(T_0, T_i) S(T_0, T_s, T_N) \delta_{i-1,i}.$$

Assuming that the frequency of the floating payment is the same as the frequency of the fixed payments we can write:

$$PV \text{ (Floating Leg)} = PV \text{ (Fixed Leg)} \Leftrightarrow$$

$$\sum_{i=s+1}^{N} B(T_0, T_i) L(T_{i-1}, T_{i-1}, T_i) \delta_{i-1,i} = \sum_{i=s+1}^{N} B(T_0, T_i) S(T_0, T_s, T_N) \delta_{i-1,i}.$$

So the forward swap rate can be written as

$$S(T_0, T_s, T_N) = \frac{\sum_{i=s+1}^{N} B(T_0, T_i) L(T_{i-1}, T_{i-1}, T_i) \delta_{i-1,i}}{\sum_{i=s+1}^{N} B(T_0, T_i) \delta_{i-1,i}}.$$

The LIBOR rate $L(T_{i-1}, T_{i-1}, T_i)$ in above equation can be changed to the forward LIBOR rate.

$$S(T_0, T_s, T_N) = \frac{\sum_{i=s+1}^{N} B(T_0, T_i) \left(\frac{B(T_0, T_{i-1})}{B(T_0, T_i)} - 1\right) \frac{1}{\delta_{i-1,i}} \delta_{i-1,i}}{\sum_{i=s+1}^{N} B(T_0, T_i) \delta_{i-1,i}} = \frac{B(T_0, T_s) - B(T_0, T_N)}{\sum_{i=s+1}^{N} B(T_0, T_i) \delta_{i-1,i}}. \quad (7.4)$$

For practical reasons it is important that $\delta_{i-1,i}$ denotes the year fraction of the fixed leg of given IRS. But in our particular case of calibration presented later we will use the same frequency for both the fixed and floating legs.

The forward swap rate derived above will be used to constitute the definition of an at-the-money (ATM) cap. We are saying that a particular cap is ATM if the strike price is equal to the forward swap rate. More precisely, let us consider a cap covering the period $T_s \div T_n$. Payments from that cap can be written:

$$\sum_{i=s+1}^{N} W_i = \sum_{i=s+1}^{N} N(L(T_{s-1}, T_{s-1}, T_s) - X)^+ \delta_{s-1,s}$$

If strike price X in above equation is equal to forward swap rate $S(t, T_s, T_N)$ the cap is said to be ATM. Let us move now to present an example presenting computations of ATM strikes for cap options.

Example 7.2   ATM strikes for caps

Let us compute ATM strikes for a series of caps maturing from one year up to 20 years. Having computed the discount factors (given in Table 7.1) we can determine the

ATM cap strikes taking into consideration that the ATM cap options may be constructed in two ways:

1. Cap starts at date T_0, first reset rate is on T_{3M}, first payment is on T_{6M} based on a 3-month LIBOR resetting on T_{3M} and covering the period $T_{3M} \div T_{6M}$. All the other caplet periods are based on similar three-monthly spaced intervals.
2. Cap starts at date T_0, first reset rate is on T_{3M}, first payment is on T_{6M} based on a 3-month LIBOR resetting on T_{3M} and covering the period $T_{3M} \div T_{6M}$. The caplet periods up to and including 1 year are based on similar three-monthly spaced intervals. Above one year there is change of caplet interval from three-months to six-months. So the reset moment T_{1Y} determines a 6-month LIBOR rate covering the period $T_{1Y} \div T_{18M}$ which makes the caplet payment at T_{18M}. All the other caplet periods are based on similar six-monthly spaced intervals.

In this example we will use the first case.

Table 7.4 shows the computations for ATM strikes for caps from 1 year up to 20 years.

Table 7.4   ATM strikes for caps, preliminary computations

Time T_i	Date	Year fraction ACT/360 $\delta_{i-1,i}$	Discount factor (DF) $B(T_0, T_i)$	Year fraction* DF $\delta_{i-1,i}B(T_0, T_i)$	Cumulative sum $\sum_{j=6M}^{i} \delta_{j-1,j}B(T_0, T_j)$	Difference of DF $B(T_0, T_{3M}) - B(T_0, T_i)$	Forward swap rate (ATM cap strike) $S(T_0, T_{3M}, T_i)$
3M	25-01-2005	0.25000	0.9947527				
6M	25-07-2005	0.25278	0.9892651	0.2500642	0.2500642	0.0054876	2.19 %
9M	25-10-2005	0.25556	0.9834984	0.2513385	0.5014027	0.0112543	2.24 %
1Y	25-01-2006	0.25556	0.9774658	0.2497968	0.7511995	0.0172869	2.30 %
1Y 3M	25-04-2006	0.25000	0.9712884	0.2428221	0.9940216	0.0234643	2.36 %
1Y 6M	25-07-2006	0.25278	0.9648035	0.2438809	1.2379025	0.0299492	2.42 %
1Y 9M	25-10-2006	0.25556	0.9580084	0.2448244	1.4827269	0.0367443	2.48 %
2Y	25-01-2007	0.25556	0.9509789	0.2430279	1.7257548	0.0437737	2.54 %
2Y 3M	25-04-2007	0.25000	0.9440868	0.2360217	1.9617765	0.0506659	2.58 %
2Y 6M	25-07-2007	0.25278	0.9369436	0.2368385	2.1986150	0.0578091	2.63 %
2Y 9M	25-10-2007	0.25556	0.9295484	0.2375513	2.4361663	0.0652043	2.68 %
3Y	25-01-2008	0.25556	0.9219838	0.2356181	2.6717844	0.0727689	2.72 %
3Y 3M	25-04-2008	0.25278	0.9145031	0.2311661	2.9029504	0.0802496	2.76 %
3Y 6M	25-07-2008	0.25278	0.9068886	0.2292413	3.1321917	0.0878640	2.81 %
3Y 9M	27-10-2008	0.26111	0.8990590	0.2347543	3.3669460	0.0956937	2.84 %
4Y	26-01-2009	0.25278	0.8911017	0.2252507	3.5921967	0.1036510	2.89 %
4Y 3M	27-04-2009	0.25278	0.8833709	0.2232965	3.8154933	0.1113818	2.92 %
4Y 6M	27-07-2009	0.25278	0.8754579	0.2212963	4.0367896	0.1192947	2.96 %
4Y 9M	26-10-2009	0.25278	0.8673616	0.2192497	4.2560393	0.1273911	2.99 %
5Y	25-01-2010	0.25278	0.8591725	0.2171797	4.4732190	0.1355802	3.03 %
5Y 3M	26-04-2010	0.25278	0.8512070	0.2151662	4.6883852	0.1435457	3.06 %
5Y 6M	26-07-2010	0.25278	0.8430804	0.2131120	4.9014972	0.1516723	3.09 %
5Y 9M	25-10-2010	0.25278	0.8347939	0.2110173	5.1125146	0.1599588	3.13 %
6Y	25-01-2011	0.25556	0.8264399	0.2112013	5.3237159	0.1683127	3.16 %
7Y	25-01-2012	0.25556	0.7930540	0.2026694	6.1405422	0.2016987	3.28 %
8Y	25-01-2013	0.25556	0.7597502	0.1941584	6.9256882	0.2350025	3.39 %
9Y	27-01-2014	0.26111	0.7262834	0.1896407	7.6788386	0.2684693	3.50 %
10Y	26-01-2015	0.25278	0.6944457	0.1755404	8.3930044	0.3003070	3.58 %
11Y	25-01-2016	0.25278	0.6645450	0.1679822	9.0763113	0.3302076	3.64 %
12Y	25-01-2017	0.25556	0.6349818	0.1622731	9.7331116	0.3597709	3.70 %

Table 7.4   Continued

Time T_i	Date	Year fraction ACT/360 $\delta_{i-1,i}$	Discount factor (DF) $B(T_0, T_i)$	Year fraction* DF $\delta_{i-1,i}B(T_0, T_i)$	Cumulative sum $\sum\limits_{j=6M}^{i} \delta_{j-1,j}B(T_0, T_j)$	Difference of DF $B(T_0, T_{3M}) - B(T_0, T_i)$	Forward swap rate (ATM cap strike) $S(T_0, T_{3M}, T_i)$
13Y	25-01-2018	0.25556	0.6068399	0.1550813	10.3590352	0.3879128	3.74 %
14Y	25-01-2019	0.25556	0.5792752	0.1480370	10.9567889	0.4154775	3.79 %
15Y	27-01-2020	0.26111	0.5523236	0.1442178	11.5300493	0.4424291	3.84 %
16Y	25-01-2021	0.25278	0.5273147	0.1332934	12.0726815	0.4674379	3.87 %
17Y	25-01-2022	0.25556	0.5030900	0.1285675	12.5919467	0.4916627	3.90 %
18Y	25-01-2023	0.25556	0.4795796	0.1225592	13.0870691	0.5151731	3.94 %
19Y	25-01-2024	0.25556	0.4567881	0.1167347	13.5588099	0.5379646	3.97 %
20Y	27-01-2025	0.26111	0.4346590	0.1134943	14.0115070	0.5600937	4.00 %

End of example 7.2

Having computed ATM strikes for cap options we can move to caplet bootstrapping.

7.3.3   Stripping caplet volatilities from cap quotes

The market volatility of caplets will be derived from cap volatilities quotations; to do that we need to introduce a stripping algorithm.

Let us start from a cap maturing in one year. Remembering that we have quarterly resets, so the effective date of the cap is $T_s = T_{3M}$, and payments are made at times: T_{6M}, T_{9M}, T_{1Y}. The volatility (precisely forward volatility) $\sigma^{cap}(t, T_{1Y})$ for a one year cap equals 16.41 %. The strike price $S(t, T_{3M}, T_{1Y})$ for this cap equals 2.301 %. However we need to make some assumptions if we want to compute caplet volatilities for the periods shorter than one year. To obtain this we generate two additional caps covering the periods: $T_{3M} \div T_{6M}$ and $T_{3M} \div T_{9M}$. The strike prices (ATM) for these caps equals the appropriate forward swap rates $S(t, T_{3M}, T_{6M})$ with value 2.194 % and $S(t, T_{3M}, T_{9M})$ with value 2.245 %. These strike rates can be obtained directly from yield curve. However, we have no volatilities for periods shorter than one year. To obtain these values, we use constant extrapolation, so we assume that: $\sigma^{cap}(t, T_{6M}) = \sigma^{cap}(t, T_{9M}) = \sigma^{cap}(t, T_{1Y})$. With this assumption we can compute 6-month caps using standard Black formula:

$$cap(t, T_{6M}) = B(t, T_{6M})\,\delta_{3M,6M}\lfloor F(t, T_{3M}, T_{6M})\,N\left(d_{1,6M}\right) - S(t, T_{3M}, T_{6M})\,N\left(d_{2,6M}\right)\rfloor$$

where:

$$N\left(d_{1,6M}\right) = \frac{\ln\left(\frac{F(t,T_{3M},T_{6M})}{X}\right) + \frac{\sigma^{cap}(t,T_{6M})^2 \delta_{t,3M}}{2}}{\sigma^{cap}(t, T_{6M})\sqrt{\delta_{t,3M}}}.$$

and

$$N\left(d_{2,6M}\right) = \frac{\ln\left(\frac{F(t,T_{3M},T_{6M})}{X}\right) - \frac{\sigma^{cap}(t,T_{6M})^2 \delta_{t,3M}}{2}}{\sigma^{cap}(t, T_{6M})\sqrt{\delta_{t,3M}}}.$$

Because the six month cap is built only from one caplet covering the period $T_{3M} \div T_{6M}$, the caplet volatility $\sigma^{caplet}(t, T_{3M}, T_{6M})$ for the period $T_{3M} \div T_{6M}$ is the same as the cap volatility $\sigma^{cap}(t, T_{6M})$ for the cap maturing at T_{6M} and equals 16.41 %.

Now we move to the next step, where we deal with the cap maturing at T_{9M}. We compute value of this cap again using the standard Black formula:

$$cap\left(t, T_{9M}\right) = B\left(t, T_{6M}\right) \delta_{3M,6M} \left[F\left(t, T_{3M}, T_{6M}\right) N\left(d_{1,6M}\right)\right.$$
$$- S\left(t, T_{3M}, T_{9M}\right) N\left(d_{2,6M}\right)\right] + B\left(t, T_{9M}\right) \delta_{6M,9M} \left[F\left(t, T_{6M}, T_{9M}\right) N\left(d_{1,9M}\right)\right.$$
$$\left. - S\left(t, T_{3M}, T_{9M}\right) N\left(d_{2,9M}\right)\right]$$

where:

$$N\left(d_{1,9M}\right) = \frac{\ln\left(\frac{F(t,T_{6M},T_{9M})}{X}\right) + \frac{\sigma^{cap}(t,T_{6M})^2 \delta_{t,6M}}{2}}{\sigma^{cap}\left(t, T_{9M}\right)^2 \sqrt{\delta_{t,6M}}}$$

and

$$N\left(d_{1,9M}\right) = \frac{\ln\left(\frac{F(t,T_{6M},T_{9M})}{X}\right) - \frac{\sigma^{cap}(t,T_{9M})^2 \delta_{t,6M}}{2}}{\sigma^{cap}\left(t, T_{9M}\right)^2 \sqrt{\delta_{t,6M}}}.$$

Having the value of the cap maturing at T_{9M}, we can compute the sum of the caplet values for the periods $T_{3M} \div T_{6M}$ and $T_{6M} \div T_{9M}$ in the following way:

$$caplet\left(t, T_{3M}, T_{6M}\right) = B\left(t, T_{6M}\right) \delta_{3M,6M} \left[F\left(t, T_{3M}, T_{6M}\right) N\left(d_{1,6M}\right) - S\left(t, T_{3M}, T_{9M}\right) N\left(d_{2,6M}\right)\right]$$

where

$$N\left(d_{1,6M}\right) = \frac{\ln\left(\frac{F(t,T_{3M},T_{6M})}{X}\right) + \frac{\sigma^{caplet}(t,T_{3M},T_{6M})^2 \delta_{t,3M}}{2}}{\sigma^{caplet}\left(t, T_{3M}, T_{6M}\right) \sqrt{\delta_{t,3M}}}$$

and

$$N\left(d_{2,6M}\right) = \frac{\ln\left(\frac{F(t,T_{3M},T_{6M})}{X}\right) - \frac{\sigma^{caplet}(t,T_{3M},T_{6M})^2 \delta_{t,3M}}{2}}{\sigma^{caplet}\left(t, T_{3M}, T_{6M}\right) \sqrt{\delta_{t,3M}}}.$$

In this case we input $\sigma^{caplet}\left(t, T_{3M}, T_{6M}\right)$ as the value computed in the previous step of calibration (equaling 16.41 %). Next we compute the caplet value for the second period:

$$caplet\left(t, T_{6M}, T_{9M}\right) = B\left(t, T_{9M}\right) \delta_{6M,9M} \left[F\left(t, T_{6M}, T_{9M}\right) N\left(d_{1,9M}\right) - S\left(t, T_{3M}, T_{9M}\right) N\left(d_{2,9M}\right)\right]$$

where:

$$N\left(d_{1,9M}\right) = \frac{\ln\left(\frac{F(t,T_{6M},T_{9M})}{S(t,T_{3M},T_{9M})}\right) + \frac{\sigma^{caplet}(t,T_{6M},T_{9M})^2 \delta_{t,6M}}{2}}{\sigma^{caplet}\left(t, T_{6M}, T_{9M}\right) \sqrt{\delta_{t,6M}}}$$

and

$$N\left(d_{1,9M}\right) = \frac{\ln\left(\frac{F(t,T_{6M},T_{9M})}{S(t,T_{3M},T_{9M})}\right) - \frac{\sigma^{caplet}(t,T_{6M},T_{9M})^2 \delta_{t,6M}}{2}}{\sigma^{caplet}\left(t,T_{6M},T_{9M}\right)\sqrt{\delta_{t,6M}}}.$$

The final computation in this step of calculation is solving the equation with respect to $\sigma^{caplet}\left(t,T_{6M},T_{9M}\right)$

$$cap\left(t,T_{9M}\right) = caplet\left(t,T_{3M},T_{6M}\right) + caplet\left(t,T_{6M},T_{9M}\right).$$

Next we will obtain the caplet volatilities in the same way. For the broken periods greater then one year (e.g. one year and three months) we will be obliged to interpolate (usually using the linear method) the market quotes for cap volatilities.

Now we are able to write the complete algorithm for stripping caplet volatilities having market quotes for various cap volatilities which are ATM.

Algorithm 7.1   Caplet volatilities stripping

1. Determine all resets and maturity dates of all caplets. We deduce them from the market quotes of caps. Let us denote these moments (for 3-month intervals) as: $T_s = T_{3M}, T_{6M}, T_{9M}, \ldots, T_N$.
2. Generate the artificial caps according to the determined resets and maturities

    a. Compute the appropriate forward swap rates for ATM strikes of the caps for the periods: $T_s \div T_{6M}, T_s \div T_{9M}, \ldots, T_s \div T_N$
    b. Extrapolate using an interpolation method applied to observed market cap volatilities for all generated caps to obtain volatilities: $\sigma^{cap}\left(t,T_{6M}\right), \sigma^{cap}\left(t,T_{9M}\right), \ldots, \sigma^{cap}\left(t,T_N\right)$.

3. The first caplet volatility will be equal the first cap volatility, so $\sigma^{cap}\left(t,T_{6M}\right) = \sigma^{caplet}\left(t,T_{3M},T_{6M}\right)$.
4. Compute the market value for the cap whose maturity is longer by exactly one interval then previous cap, so $\sigma^{cap}\left(t,T_{6M+i}\right) = \sigma^{cap}\left(t,T_{9M}\right)$.
5. Having computed the previous caplet volatility (for last interval) we compute the implied caplet volatility for next interval solving the equation for the appropriate cap and sum of appropriate caplets, so $cap\left(t,T_{9M}\right) = \sum_{i=1}^{N} caplet\left(t,T_i,T_{i+1}\right)$.
6. Continue up to last cap reset. Increase the index in step (5).

End of algorithm 7.1

We now present an example of the stripping algorithm using our work just completed.

Example 7.3   Stripping caplet volatilities from cap quotes

Table 7.5 presents cap volatilities for periods from one year up to 20 years. Only cap volatilities for full years are taken directly from the market. Caps before 1 year are extrapolated using one year volatility as a constant. Caps for broken periods above 1 year are linearly interpolated. Strikes for ATM caps are taken from Table 7.4.

Table 7.5 Caplet volatilities stripped from cap volatilities

Tenor T_i	Market cap volatility $\sigma^{cap}(T_0, T_i)$	Caplet volatility $\sigma^{caplet}(T_0, T_{3M}, T_i)$	Time homogeneity test[1] $\sigma^{caplet}(T_0, T_{3M}, T_i)^2 \delta_{T_0, i-1}$
6M	0.1641	0.1641	0.0067
9M	0.1641	0.1641	0.0135
1Y	0.1641	0.1641	0.0204
1Y 3M	0.1765	0.2015	0.0412
1Y 6M	0.1889	0.2189	0.0606
1Y 9M	0.2013	0.2365	0.0848
2Y	0.2137	0.2550	0.1152
2Y 3M	0.2162	0.2212	0.0992
2Y 6M	0.2186	0.2255	0.1158
2Y 9M	0.2211	0.2298	0.1336
3Y	0.2235	0.2341	0.1527
3Y 3M	0.2223	0.2097	0.1338
3Y 6M	0.2212	0.2083	0.1429
3Y 9M	0.2200	0.2077	0.1530
4Y	0.2188	0.2051	0.1602
4Y 3M	0.2173	0.2007	0.1636
4Y 6M	0.2158	0.1982	0.1695
4Y 9M	0.2142	0.1959	0.1753
5Y	0.2127	0.1938	0.1810
6Y	0.2068	0.1859	0.2015
7Y	0.2012	0.1781	0.2171
8Y	0.1958	0.1700	0.2272
9Y	0.1905	0.1622	0.2335
10Y	0.1859	0.1570	0.2439
11Y	0.1833	0.1652	0.2976
12Y	0.1806	0.1602	0.3059
13Y	0.1770	0.1451	0.2723
14Y	0.1735	0.1380	0.2656
15Y	0.1699	0.1315	0.2587
16Y	0.1673	0.1353	0.2925
17Y	0.1646	0.1300	0.2872
18Y	0.1620	0.1243	0.2782
19Y	0.1593	0.1184	0.2666
20Y	0.1567	0.1131	0.2563

Note: [1] Results of these computations will be used later in the cap calibration algorithm.

End of example 7.3

We can present our computations graphically:

Figure 7.3 shows a typical pattern for cap volatilities and caplet volatilities as a function of maturity. In the case of cap volatility the maturity is the maturity of the cap, in the case of caplet volatility it is the maturity of the caplet. The cap volatilities are akin to cumulative averages of the caplet volatilities and therefore exhibit less variability. As indicated by Figure 7.3 we usually observe a hump in the volatilities. The peak of the hump is at about the 2 to 3 year point. There is no general agreement on the reason for the existence of the hump.

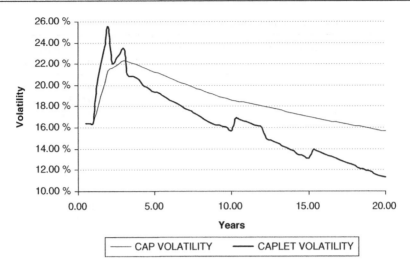

Figure 7.3   Cap and caplet volatility from 21 January 2005.

Having defined and computed caplet volatilities we can start to describe the key calibration algorithms.

7.4   NON-PARAMETRIC CALIBRATION ALGORITHMS

We have computed caplet volatility in the previous section and this is a good place to give an explanation of instantaneous volatility. The relationship between caplet volatility and instantaneous volatility of the forward rate $F(t, T_{i-1}, T_i)$ is defined as:

$$\sigma^{caplet}(t, T_{i-1}, T_i)^2 = \frac{1}{\delta_{t, T_{i-1}}} \int_t^{i-1} \sigma_i^2(t)\, dt$$

Having above equation in mind we can create many piecewise-constant instantaneous volatility structures.

Def. (Piecewise constant volatility). A volatility structure $\{\overline{\sigma}_i(.)\}_{i=1}^N$ is piecewise constant if

$$\overline{\sigma}_i(t) = (\text{const}), \ t \in (T_{i-1}, T_i)$$

Figure 7.4 below illustrates the nature of piecewise constant instantaneous volatility. We take, for example, volatility of forward rate covering the period $T_{6M} \div T_{9M}$.

The real value of forward rate $F(t, T_{6M}, T_{9M})$ will have uncertain value until time $t = T_{6M}$. Before time T_{6M} starting at T_0 we can derive the instantaneous volatility of the forward rate (e.g. from caplet volatilities). There is a practice in the market to assume, that instantaneous volatility will have constant value for a particular time period. In Figure 7.4 we assume a constant instantaneous volatility at periods $T_0 \div T_{3M}$ and $T_{3M} \div T_{6M}$.

As we will see later some of the structures can be impossible to create, because caplet volatilities may be not time-homogenous for a particular cap quotation taken from the real market.

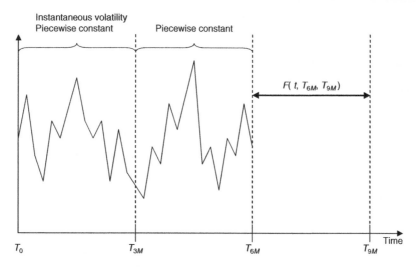

Figure 7.4 Piecewise constant instantaneous volatility.

Def. (Time homogeneity). Let us define a fixing to be one of the time points $T_1, \ldots, T_N$. Define $\vartheta : [0, T] \to \{1, \ldots, N\}$,

$$\vartheta(t) = \#\{\text{fixings in } (0, t)\}.$$

A volatility structure is said to be time homogeneous if it depends only on the index to maturity $i - \vartheta(t)$.

In our case, we can test time homogeneity in a simple way, by just multiplying the squared caplet volatilities by time. As we will see later the time homogeneity assumption does not hold for the market data used in our examples. We cannot assume that the instantaneous volatilities depend only on the time to maturity, because then some of piecewise-constant instantaneous volatilities might be negative.

We are ready to present now two approaches of LIBOR market model calibration to cap (precisely caplet) volatilities. Both are described in Brigo and Mercurio (2001), however we present more detailed algorithms and provide examples. The first of the algorithms is based upon the assumption that volatility depends only upon the time to maturity.

7.4.1 Piecewise constant instantaneous volatilities depending on the time to maturity

One possible way to determine instantaneous volatility is to assume that the piecewise constant instantaneous volatility depends only on the time to maturity. Figure 7.5 shows how piecewise constant instantaneous volatility depends on the time to maturity.

The interpretation of the Figure 7.5 is straightforward. The piecewise constant instantaneous volatility of the forward rate $F(t, T_{3M}, T_{6M})$ at the period $T_0 \div T_{3M}$ is the same as the piecewise constant instantaneous volatility of the forward rate $F(t, T_{6M}, T_{9M})$ at the period $T_{3M} \div T_{6M}$, and the same as the piecewise constant instantaneous volatility of the forward

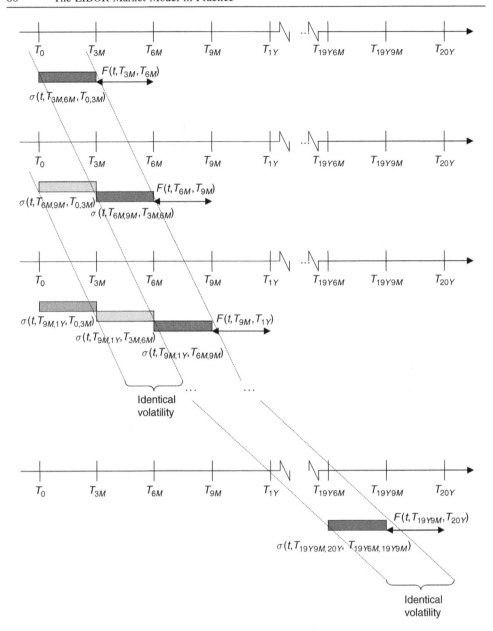

Figure 7.5 Piecewise constant instantaneous volatility dependent on time to maturity.

rate $F(t, T_{9M}, T_{1Y})$ at the period $T_{6M} \div T_{9M}$ and finally the same as the piecewise constant instantaneous volatility of the forward rate $F(t, T_{19Y9M}, T_{20Y})$ at the period $T_{19Y6M} \div T_{19Y9M}$. A similar situation exists for the other forward rates.

Our goal is to derive the instantaneous volatility matrix. So at the beginning we have to define an instantaneous volatility matrix to be computed. We present this as the lower triangular matrix below, based on a maximum caplet maturity at 20 years from now.

$$\mathbf{\Sigma\_inst} = \begin{bmatrix} \sigma^{inst}\left(t, T_{3M,6M}, T_{0,3M}\right) & - - - & - - - & \cdots & - - - \\ \sigma^{inst}\left(t, T_{6M,9M}, T_{0,3M}\right) & \sigma^{inst}\left(t, T_{6M,9M}, T_{3M,6M}\right) & - - - & \cdots & - - - \\ \sigma^{inst}\left(t, T_{9M,1Y}, T_{0,3M}\right) & \sigma^{inst}\left(t, T_{9M,1Y}, T_{3M,6M}\right) & \sigma^{inst}\left(t, T_{9M,1Y}, T_{6M,9M}\right) & \cdots & - - - \\ \cdots & \cdots & \cdots & \cdots & \cdots \\ \sigma^{inst}\left(t, T_{19.75Y,20Y}, T_{0,3M}\right) & \sigma^{inst}\left(t, T_{19.75Y,20Y}, T_{3M,6M}\right) & \sigma^{inst}\left(t, T_{19.75Y,20Y}, T_{6M,9M}\right) & \cdots & \sigma^{inst}\left(t, T_{19.75Y,20Y}, T_{19.75Y,20Y}\right) \end{bmatrix}$$

Elements of matrix $\mathbf{\Sigma\_inst}$ have the following interpretations:

$\mathbf{\Sigma\_inst}\,(1,1) = \sigma^{inst}\left(t, T_{3M,6M}, T_{0,3M}\right)$ –   instantaneous volatility related to the forward rate $F\left(t, T_{3M}, T_{6M}\right)$ for time interval $T_0 \div T_{3M}$

$\mathbf{\Sigma\_inst}\,(2,1) = \sigma^{inst}\left(t, T_{6M,9M}, T_{0,3M}\right)$ –   instantaneous volatility related to the forward rate $F\left(t, T_{6M}, T_{9M}\right)$ for time interval $T_0 \div T_{3M}$

$\mathbf{\Sigma\_inst}\,(2,2) = \sigma^{inst}\left(t, T_{6M,9M}, T_{3M,6M}\right)$ –   instantaneous volatility related to the forward rate $F\left(t, T_{6M}, T_{9M}\right)$ for time interval $T_{3M} \div T_{6M}$

$\cdots$

The elements follow exactly the same scheme.

We also need to define the matrix of caplet volatilities. This matrix is presented below

$$\mathbf{\Sigma\_cpl} = \begin{bmatrix} \sigma^{caplet}\left(t, T_{3M,6M}\right) \\ \sigma^{caplet}\left(t, T_{6M,9M}\right) \\ \sigma^{caplet}\left(t, T_{9M,1Y}\right) \\ \cdots \\ \sigma^{caplet}\left(t, T_{19.75Y,20Y}\right) \end{bmatrix}$$

Elements of the matrix $\mathbf{\Sigma\_cpl}$ have the following interpretations

$\mathbf{\Sigma\_cpl}(1) = \sigma^{caplet}(t, T_{3M,6M})$ – Market caplet volatility for time interval $T_{3M} \div T_{6M}$.

Finally we define the matrix of time $\mathbf{T}$

$$\mathbf{T} = \begin{bmatrix} 0 \\ T_{3M} \\ T_{6M} \\ \cdots \\ T_{20Y} \end{bmatrix}.$$

Having that we can then define $\delta\,(i, j) = [\mathbf{T}\,(j) - \mathbf{T}\,(i)]\,/basis$ for $j > i$.

We can move now to present the algorithm for calibration.

Algorithm 7.2 Calibration to caplets – piecewise constant instantaneous volatility depending on time to maturity

For i = 1 to N // Number of caplet volatilities

LeftSide = 0

  For j = 1 to i

       $Sum = \Sigma\_inst\,(i,\,j)^2\,\delta\,(j-1,\,j)$

       LeftSide = LeftSide + Sum

  Next j

  $RightSide = \Sigma\_cpl\,(i)^2\,\delta\,(0,\,i)$

  {Function: SolvingEquation → RightSide =   LeftSide//for $\Sigma\_inst\,(i,\,1)$}

  For k = 1 to i

      $\Sigma\_inst\,(i+1,\,k+1) = \Sigma\_inst\,(i,\,k)$ // Assignment

  Next k

  Next i

End of algorithm 7.2

Below is example for first three iterations of algorithm 7.2:

Example 7.4 Calibration to caplets – piecewise constant instantaneous volatility depending on time to maturity

Equation for **Σ_inst** (1, 1):

$$\Sigma\_cpl\,(1)^2\,\delta\,(0,\,1) = \Sigma\_inst\,(1,\,1)^2\,\delta\,(0,\,1) \Rightarrow \Sigma\_inst\,(1,\,1) = sqrt\left(\frac{\delta\,(0,\,1)}{\delta\,(0,\,1)}\Sigma\_cpl\,(1)^2\right)$$

$$= \Sigma\_cpl\,(1) = 16.41\,\%$$

$$\text{Assignments}: \Sigma\_inst\,(2,\,2) = \Sigma\_inst\,(1,\,1) = 16.41\,\%$$

Equation for **Σ_inst** (2, 1):

$$\Sigma\_cpl\,(2)^2\,\delta\,(0,\,2) = \Sigma\_inst\,(2,\,1)^2\,\delta\,(0,\,1) + \Sigma\_inst\,(2,\,2)^2\,\delta\,(1,\,2)$$

$$\Rightarrow \Sigma\_inst\,(2,\,1) = sqrt\left(\frac{\delta\,(0,\,2)}{\delta\,(0,\,1)}\Sigma\_cpl\,(2)^2 - \frac{\delta\,(1,\,2)}{\delta\,(0,\,1)}\Sigma\_inst\,(2,\,2)^2\right)$$

$$= sqrt\left(\frac{0.50277778}{0.25}16.41\,\%^2 - \frac{0.25277778}{0.25}16.41\,\%^2\right) = 16.41\,\%$$

Assignments: **Σ_inst** (3, 2) = **Σ_inst** (2, 1) = 16.41 %, **Σ_inst** (3, 3) = **Σ_inst** (2, 2) = 16.41 %

Equation for $\Sigma\_\text{inst}\,(3,1)$:

$$\Sigma\_\text{cpl}\,(3)^2\,\delta\,(0,3) = \Sigma\_\text{inst}\,(3,1)^2\,\delta\,(0,1) + \Sigma\_\text{inst}\,(3,2)^2\,\delta\,(1,2) + \Sigma\_\text{inst}\,(3,3)^2\,\delta\,(2,3)$$

$$\Rightarrow \Sigma\_\text{inst}\,(3,1) = sqrt\left(\frac{\delta\,(0,3)}{\delta\,(0,1)}\Sigma\_\text{cpl}\,(3)^2 - \frac{\delta\,(1,2)}{\delta\,(0,1)}\Sigma\_\text{inst}\,(3,2)^2 - \frac{\delta\,(2,3)}{\delta\,(0,1)}\Sigma\_\text{inst}\,(3,3)^2\right)$$

$$= sqrt\left(\frac{0.7583333}{0.25}16.41^2 - \frac{0.25277778}{0.25}16.41\%^2 - \frac{0.2599556}{0.25}16.41\%^2\right) = 16.41\%$$

Assignments: $\Sigma\_\text{inst}\,(4,2) = \Sigma\_\text{inst}\,(3,1) = 16.41\%$, $\Sigma\_\text{inst}\,(4,3) = \Sigma\_\text{inst}\,(3,2) = 16.41\%$, $\Sigma\_\text{inst}\,(4,4) = \Sigma\_\text{inst}\,(3,3) = 16.41\%$

End of example 7.4

Further computations should be done in similar way. Our results are presented in Table 7.6:

Table 7.6 Piecewise constant instantaneous volatilities depending on time to maturity

Tenor T_i	Date	Caplet volatility	Squared caplet volatility multiplied by time	Forward rate	Period 0; 3M	Period 3M; 6M	Period 6M; 9M	...	Sum of squared piecewise constant volatilities multiplied by time period
T_{6M}	25/07/2005	16.41%	0.0067322	$F_{3M,6M}(t)$	16.41%			...	0.0067322
T_{9M}	25/10/2005	16.41%	0.0135392	$F_{6M,9M}(t)$	16.41%	16.41%		...	0.0135392
T_{1Y}	25/01/2006	16.41%	0.0204210	$F_{9M,1Y}(t)$	16.41%	16.41%	16.41%	...	0.0204210
$T_{1.25Y}$	25/04/2006	20.15%	0.0411662	$F_{1Y,1.25Y}(t)$	28.71%	16.41%	16.41%	...	0.0411772
$T_{1.5Y}$	25/07/2006	21.89%	0.0605620	$F_{1.25Y,1.5Y}(t)$	27.74%	28.71%	16.41%	...	0.0605691
$T_{1.75Y}$	25/10/2006	23.65%	0.0848306	$F_{1.5Y,1.75Y}(t)$	30.92%	27.74%	28.71%	...	0.0848381
T_{2Y}	25/01/2007	25.50%	0.1152388	$F_{1.75Y,2Y}(t)$	34.60%	30.92%	27.74%	...	0.1152465
$T_{2.25Y}$	25/04/2007	22.12%	0.0992180	$F_{2Y,2.25Y}(t)$	**0.00%**	34.60%	30.92%	...	0.1155363

where:

Squared caplet volatility multiplied by time	$\sigma^{caplet}\left(T_0, T_{i,j}\right)^2\delta_{T_0,i-1}$
Sum of squared piecewise constant volatilities multiplied by time period	$\Sigma\delta_{k,l}\sigma^{inst}\left(t, T_{i,j}T_{k,l}\right)^2$

The result of the time homogeneity assumption for instantaneous volatility is visible at tenor $T_{2.25Y}$. In such case a sum of squared piecewise constant volatilities multiplied by the time period is greater than squared caplet volatility multiplied by time, even if we put zero instantaneous volatility for forward rate $F_{2Y,2.25Y}(t)$ for time period 0,3M.

We can find an alternative way of calibrating BGM to cap options. A good choice will be piecewise constant instantaneous volatility depending on the maturity of the underlying forward rate, which we present below.

7.4.2   Piecewise constant instantaneous volatilities depending on the maturity of the underlying forward rate

Another way to determine the instantaneous volatility is assuming that the piecewise constant instantaneous volatility depends only on the maturity of underlying forward rate. Figure 7.6 presents the schema of the volatility dependent only on the maturity of the underlying forward rate.

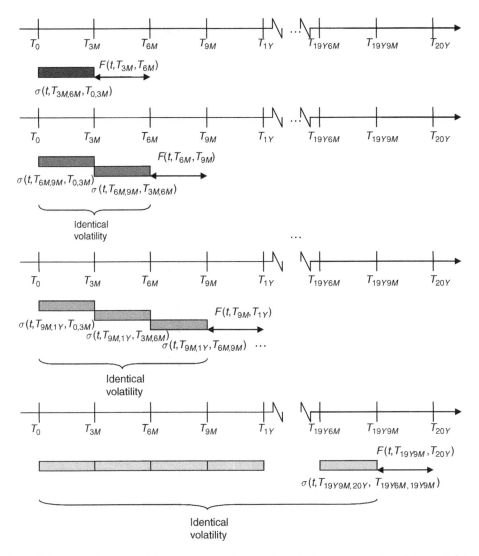

Figure 7.6   Piecewise constant instantaneous volatility dependent on the maturity of the underlying forward rate.

The piecewise constant instantaneous volatilities have identical values for all 3-month periods for a particular forward rate. For example for forward rate $F(t, T_{9Y}, T_{1Y})$ instantaneous volatility is the same in periods $T_0 \div T_{3M}, T_{3M} \div T_{6M}, T_{6M} \div T_{9M}$.

We now present our modified calibration algorithm.

Algorithm 7.3 Calibration to caplets – piecewise constant instantaneous volatility depending on the maturity of the underlying forward rate

For i = 1 to N // Number of caplet volatilities

   For j = 1 to i

           $\Sigma\_inst\,(i, j) = \Sigma\_cpl\,(i)$

   Next j

Next i

End of algorithm 7.3

Let us present an example for the first three iterations.

Example 7.5   Calibration to caplets – piecewise constant instantaneous volatility depending on the maturity of the underlying forward rate

Equation for $\Sigma\_inst\,(1, 1)$:

$$\Sigma\_cpl\,(1)^2\,\delta\,(0, 1) = \Sigma\_inst\,(1, 1)^2\,\delta\,(0, 1) \Rightarrow \Sigma\_inst\,(1, 1)$$

$$= sqrt\left(\frac{\delta\,(0, 1)}{\delta\,(0, 1)}\Sigma\_cpl\,(1)^2\right) = \Sigma\_cpl\,(1) = 16.41\%$$

Equation for $\Sigma\_inst\,(2, 1)$:

$$\Sigma\_cpl\,(2)^2\,\delta\,(0, 2) = \Sigma\_inst\,(2, 1)^2\,[\delta\,(0, 1) + \delta\,(1, 2)]$$

$$\Rightarrow \Sigma\_inst\,(2, 1) = sqrt\left(\frac{\delta\,(0, 2)}{\delta\,(0, 1) + \delta\,(1, 2)}\Sigma\_cpl\,(2)^2\right) = \Sigma\_cpl\,(2) = 16.41\%$$

Assignments: $\Sigma\_inst\,(2, 2) = \Sigma\_inst\,(2, 1) = 16.41\,\%$

Equation for $\Sigma\_inst\,(3, 1)$:

$$\Sigma\_cpl\,(3)^2\,\delta\,(0, 3) = \Sigma\_inst\,(3, 1)^2\,[\delta\,(0, 1) + \delta\,(1, 2) + \delta\,(2, 3)]$$

$$\Rightarrow \Sigma\_inst\,(3, 1) = sqrt\left(\frac{\delta\,(0, 3)}{\delta\,(0, 1) + \delta\,(1, 2) + \delta\,(2, 3)}\Sigma\_cpl\,(3)^2\right) = \Sigma\_cpl\,(3) = 16.41\%$$

Assignments: $\Sigma\_inst\,(3, 2) = \Sigma\_inst\,(3, 1) = 16.41\,\%$, $\Sigma\_inst\,(3, 3) = \Sigma\_inst\,(3, 1) = 16.41\,\%$

End of example 7.5

Further computations should be done in similar way.

   Table 7.7 presents the computed results for piecewise constant instantaneous volatilities depending on the maturity of the underlying forward rate.

   Having analysed the two approaches for BGM calibration to caps it is important to notice that the time homogeneity assumption may lead to negative instantaneous volatilities but this is not the case for every business day. Banks and financial institutions may use a calibration

Table 7.7 Piecewise constant instantaneous volatilities depending on the maturity of the underlying forward rate

Tenor T_i	Date	Caplet volatility	Squared caplet volatility multiplied by time	Forward rate	Period 0; 3M	Period 3M; 6M	Period 6M; 9M	...	Sum of squared piecewise constant volatilities multiplied by time period
T_{6M}	25/07/2005	16.41%	0.0067322	$F_{3M,6M}(t)$	16.41%			...	0.0067322
T_{9M}	25/10/2005	16.41%	0.0135392	$F_{6M,9M}(t)$	16.41%	16.41%		...	0.0135392
T_{1Y}	25/01/2006	16.41%	0.0204210	$F_{9M,1Y}(t)$	16.41%	16.41%	16.41%	...	0.0204210
$T_{1.25Y}$	25/04/2006	20.15%	0.0411662	$F_{1Y,1.25Y}(t)$	20.15%	20.15%	20.15%	...	0.0411662
$T_{1.5Y}$	25/07/2006	21.89%	0.0605620	$F_{1.25Y,1.5Y}(t)$	21.89%	21.89%	21.89%	...	0.0605620
$T_{1.75Y}$	25/10/2006	23.65%	0.0848306	$F_{1.5Y,1.75Y}(t)$	23.65%	23.65%	23.65%	...	0.0848306
T_{2Y}	25/01/2007	25.50%	0.1152388	$F_{1.75Y,2Y}(t)$	25.50%	25.50%	25.50%	...	0.1152388
$T_{2.25Y}$	25/04/2007	22.12%	0.0992180	$F_{2Y,2.25Y}(t)$	22.12%	22.12%	22.12%	...	0.0992180
...	...	...	...	...	...	...	...	...	...

to caps based on the time homogeneity assumption but under the extra condition that all instantaneous volatilities will be positive for a particular day.

7.5 CONCLUSIONS

In this chapter we have presented in a detailed way all the necessary tools which help a beginner quantitative analyst to start learning calibration algorithms for the LIBOR Market Model.

At the beginning of the chapter we have gathered market data from a particular working day, using this data in all examples in the chapter. Such an approach seems to be very useful especially in the case where someone wants to compare results generated by different algorithms. This allows one to determine which calibration algorithm is better than another. However, one should be very careful in interpreting the conclusions because what is true for one particular day may not be true for another. Nevertheless the results may be a good starting point for further research.

After presenting the market data we have showed the nature of the cap mechanism. This is due to the fact that some readers may not be familiar with this and because such knowledge is fundamental for later cases. We demonstrated how to determine resets and payments in caps. Although the chapter was intended only for calibration to caps we have also presented the mechanism for swaptions. This will be used in Chapters 8 and 9 when we present calibration algorithms to swaptions and simultaneously to caps and swaptions.

Chapter 7 should be treated as introductory tool. We have presented the most popular algorithms allowing the user to calibrate LIBOR Market Models to cap options. In some market environments that approach seems to be sufficient. These algorithms may be used if we deal with those interest rate derivatives that depend mostly on behaviour of cap movements. Additionally one should assume that instantaneous correlations of forward rates will equal to one.

Both approaches presented in the chapter require caplet volatilities to be bootstrapped from cap options. Both can be used as a base for simultaneous calibration to caps and swaptions. However, as we have seen in some market circumstances the assumption of time homogeneity may lead to obtaining negative volatilities. Much safer is using approach based on assumption that volatilities depends on the maturity of the underlying forward rate presented in section 7.4.2 than on time to maturity presented in section 7.4.1.

In the next chapter we start to introduce non parametric calibration algorithms to caps and swaptions. First we introduce a separated approach. Next we move onto locally single factor approach. We also present calibration using historical correlations and extremely useful calibration to co-terminal swaptions.

Non-Parametric Calibration Algorithms
to Caps and Swaptions

8.1 INTRODUCTION

In the previous chapter we have presented two simple calibration algorithms to cap options. It was shown how to understand the cap and swaption payments mechanism. We have showed step-by-step how to strip caplet volatilities from caps and finally presented the two most popular calibration algorithms to caps. Both were based on the piecewise constant volatility assumption. One of them has presented calibration assuming that volatilities depend only on the time to maturity, whilst the other one has assumed that volatilities depend on the maturity of the underlying forward rate.

Chapter 8 concerns non-parametric calibration algorithms of caps and swaptions. The nature of swaption quotations was presented in the previous chapter in section 7.2. The section contains also market swaption quotations taken from a particular working day, the same day for which caps and interest rate date for EUR were taken previously. Such an approach will enable comparisons between results of various calibration algorithms.

We start with a description of one of the most popular algorithm of calibration to swaptions called the separated approach. The separated approach provides a direct way of calibrating the model to the full set of swaptions. We present in detail all necessary steps allowing an implementation of the algorithm in practice. First we create a matrix of swaption volatilities and after that define the covariance matrix of the forward LIBOR rates. Next we present how to compute the elements of the covariance matrix. Additionally, that part contains intermediate calculations and intermediate results which helps the reader to fully understand the matter. As a result we obtain a variance-covariance matrix of the forward LIBOR rates. We show how to transform the obtained matrices to ensure positivity of the matrices. For this we utilize principal component analysis.

We compute matrices for each of the different variants of the separated approach. The differences arise from different specification of the parameters Λ_i used in the calibration. We see later the exact definition of these parameters. For each variant we present vectors of eigenvalues and additionally the root mean squared error between theoretical and market swaption volatilities. The two variants of calibration are then described in more detail. One can find algorithms that allow the instantaneous volatilities to be derived by a specification as orthogonal vectors. The specification is based first for the assumption of constant volatility through time and next as the piecewise constant case.

Next we develop a previously demonstrated separated approach by adding an optimization algorithm. As a target function we set a root mean squared error for the difference between the theoretical and market swaption volatilities. We minimize that function but under several restrictions for VCV. We postulate that the VCV matrix must be positive definite. For that case we implement a subalgorithm for reducing the VCV matrix by removing eigenvectors associated with negative eigenvalues. We describe all the necessary steps for that calibration routine. We present the whole calibration algorithm in Matlab code.

Another calibration algorithm presented in the chapter is the locally single factor approach. First we present all necessary assumptions and after that we move into the details of the algorithm. Based on the market reference data we show some results of the computations.

We then move into the calibration to swaptions given the exogenously computed correlations of forward LIBOR rates based on historical market data. In that part of the chapter we present how to compute historical correlations and present the final results.

The last part of the chapter is dedicated to calibration to co-terminal swaptions. We present the nature of co-terminal swaptions and the bootstrap of instantaneous volatility. Finally we present calibration results.

8.2   THE SEPARATED APPROACH

One of the popular approaches of BGM calibration is called the separated approach. This approach provides a direct way of calibrating the model to the full set of swaptions. In many situations there is more worth calibrating the model to swaptions instead of caps. This is especially true when we want to value an exotic instrument which is more dependent on swaption prices than cap volatilities. A good example will be any Bermudan type swaption.

We start our separated approach calibration by creating a matrix of swaption volatilities as below:

$$\Sigma^{SWPT} = \begin{bmatrix} \sigma_{1,2}^{swpt} & \sigma_{1,3}^{swpt} & \sigma_{1,4}^{swpt} & \cdots & \sigma_{1,m+1}^{swpt} \\ \sigma_{2,3}^{swpt} & \sigma_{2,4}^{swpt} & \sigma_{2,5}^{swpt} & \cdots & \sigma_{2,m+2}^{swpt} \\ \sigma_{3,4}^{swpt} & \sigma_{3,5}^{swpt} & \sigma_{3,6}^{swpt} & \cdots & \sigma_{3,m+3}^{swpt} \\ \cdots & \cdots & \cdots & \cdots & \cdots \\ \sigma_{m,m+1}^{swpt} & \sigma_{m,m+2}^{swpt} & \sigma_{m,m+3}^{swpt} & \cdots & \sigma_{m,M}^{swpt} \end{bmatrix}_{m \times m}$$

where in our case $m = 10$ and $M = 20$ and $\sigma_{1,2}^{swpt} = \sigma^{swpt}(t, T_1, T_2)$ is the market swaption volatility for a swaption maturing at T_1 with underlying swap period $T_1 \div T_2$. We can define the dependency of the components of Σ^{SWPT} on market swaption volatility symbols in the following way:

$$\sigma_{n,N}^{MKT} = \Sigma^{SWPT}(n, N - n)$$

Let us define the covariance matrix of forward LIBOR rates in the following way:

$$\Phi^i = \begin{bmatrix} \varphi_{1,1}^i & \varphi_{1,2}^i & \varphi_{1,3}^i & \cdots & \varphi_{1,m}^i \\ \varphi_{2,1}^i & \varphi_{2,2}^i & \varphi_{2,3}^i & \cdots & \varphi_{2,m}^i \\ \varphi_{3,1}^i & \varphi_{3,2}^i & \varphi_{3,3}^i & \cdots & \varphi_{3,m}^i \\ \cdots & \cdots & \cdots & \cdots & \cdots \\ \varphi_{m,1}^i & \varphi_{m,2}^i & \varphi_{m,3}^i & \cdots & \varphi_{m,m}^i \end{bmatrix}_{m \times m}$$

where:

$$\varphi_{kl}^i = \int_0^{T_i} \sigma^{inst}(t, T_{l-1}, T_l) \, \sigma^{inst}(t, T_{k-1}, T_k) \, dt \text{ for } i < k \text{ and } i < l$$

and $\sigma^{inst}(t, T_{l-1}, T_l)$ is the stochastic instantaneous volatility of the LIBOR rate $L_l(t, T_{l-1}, T_l)$.

We assume that

$$\varphi_{kl}^{i} = \Lambda_i \varphi_{kl}$$

where Λ_i are positive numbers and

$$\Phi = \begin{bmatrix} \varphi_{1,1} & \varphi_{1,2} & \varphi_{1,3} & \cdots & \varphi_{1,m} \\ \varphi_{2,1} & \varphi_{2,2} & \varphi_{2,3} & \cdots & \varphi_{2,m} \\ \varphi_{3,1} & \varphi_{3,2} & \varphi_{3,3} & \cdots & \varphi_{3,m} \\ \cdots & \cdots & \cdots & \cdots & \cdots \\ \varphi_{m,1} & \varphi_{m,2} & \varphi_{m,3} & \cdots & \varphi_{m,m} \end{bmatrix}_{m \times m} .$$

Parameters on diagonal can be calculated via the closed form formulae

$$\varphi_{kk} = \frac{\delta_{0,k} \sigma^{swpt}(t, T_k, T_{k+1})^2}{\Lambda_k}$$

where $k = 1, \ldots, m$.

Having that we can use the simple algorithm below to calculate the diagonal values of the matrix Φ:

Algorithm 8.1   Diagonal elements of matrix Φ

For $k = 1$ to m//number of rows in market swaption volatility matrix

$$\Phi(k, k) = \delta(0, k)\Sigma(k, 1)^2 / \Lambda(k)$$

Next k

//where $\delta(0, k)$ is a year fraction for particular day count basis between T_0 and T_k

End of algorithm 8.1

The next step is to compute the parameters $R_{i,j}^k(t)$. These parameters will be used later for determining the non-diagonal elements of the matrix Φ. We define $R_{i,j}^k(t)$ as:

$$R_{i,j}^k(0) = \frac{B(0, T_{k-1}) - B(0, T_k)}{B(0, T_i) - B(0, T_j)}$$

Now we can compute the whole matrix of parameters **R**. The form of matrix **R** is presented on the next page.

$$\mathbf{R} = \begin{bmatrix} \begin{bmatrix} R_{1,2}^2(t) \end{bmatrix} & \begin{bmatrix} R_{1,3}^2(t) \\ R_{1,3}^3(t) \end{bmatrix} & \begin{bmatrix} R_{1,4}^2(t) \\ R_{1,4}^3(t) \\ R_{1,4}^4(t) \end{bmatrix} & \cdots & \begin{bmatrix} R_{1,m+1}^2(t) \\ R_{1,m+1}^3(t) \\ R_{1,m+1}^4(t) \\ \cdots \\ R_{1,m+1}^{m+1}(t) \end{bmatrix} \\[3em] \begin{bmatrix} R_{2,3}^3(t) \end{bmatrix} & \begin{bmatrix} R_{2,4}^3(t) \\ R_{2,4}^4(t) \end{bmatrix} & \begin{bmatrix} R_{2,5}^3(t) \\ R_{2,5}^4(t) \\ R_{2,5}^5(t) \end{bmatrix} & \cdots & \begin{bmatrix} R_{2,m+2}^3(t) \\ R_{2,m+2}^4(t) \\ R_{2,m+2}^5(t) \\ \cdots \\ R_{2,m+2}^{m+2}(t) \end{bmatrix} \\[3em] \begin{bmatrix} R_{3,4}^4(t) \end{bmatrix} & \begin{bmatrix} R_{3,5}^4(t) \\ R_{3,5}^5(t) \end{bmatrix} & \begin{bmatrix} R_{3,6}^4(t) \\ R_{3,6}^5(t) \\ R_{3,6}^6(t) \end{bmatrix} & \cdots & \begin{bmatrix} R_{3,m+3}^4(t) \\ R_{3,m+3}^5(t) \\ R_{3,m+3}^6(t) \\ \cdots \\ R_{3,m+3}^{m+3}(t) \end{bmatrix} \\[3em] \cdots & \cdots & \cdots & \cdots & \cdots \\[1em] \begin{bmatrix} R_{m,11}^{m+1}(t) \end{bmatrix} & \begin{bmatrix} R_{m,12}^{m+1}(t) \\ R_{m,12}^{m+2}(t) \end{bmatrix} & \begin{bmatrix} R_{m,13}^{m+1}(t) \\ R_{m,13}^{m+2}(t) \\ R_{m,13}^{m+3}(t) \end{bmatrix} & \cdots & \begin{bmatrix} R_{m,M}^{m+1}(t) \\ R_{m,M}^{m+2}(t) \\ R_{m,M}^{m+3}(t) \\ \cdots \\ R_{m,M}^{M}(t) \end{bmatrix} \end{bmatrix}_{m \times M \times M}$$

We can treat this matrix as a three dimensional matrix. The first dimension for $R_{i,j}^k (t)$ is index i, the second j and the third k. Having that we can define assignment for the elements of matrix $\mathbf{R}$:

$$\mathbf{R} (i, j, k) = R_{i,j}^k (t)$$

And the calculation of the entries for $\mathbf{R}$ requires the algorithm presented below.

Algorithm 8.2   Elements of matrix R

For $i = 1$ to m // NumberOfSwaptionMaturities
   For $j = (i + 1)$ to $(M - m) + i$ // NumberOfSwaptionUnderlyings $+ i$
      For $k = (i + 1)$ to j
         $\mathbf{R} (i, j, k) = [\mathbf{B} (k - 1) - \mathbf{B} (k)] / [\mathbf{B} (i) - \mathbf{B} (j)]$ // $\mathbf{B}$ is a vector of discount factors
      Next k
   Next j
Next i

End of algorithm 8.2

Vector of discount factors $\mathbf{B}$ can be presented as:

$$\mathbf{B} = \begin{bmatrix} B(0, T_1) \\ B(0, T_2) \\ \ldots \\ B(0, T_M) \end{bmatrix}$$

Using algorithm 8.2 for our market data taken from 20 January 2005 gives the results presented by Table 8.1.

Table 8.1   Matrix R

R(1)	2	3	4	5	6	7	8	9	10	11
2	1									
3	0.477395	0.522605								
4	0.306688	0.335732	0.35758							
5	0.223908	0.245112	0.261063	0.269916						
6	0.175379	0.191988	0.204482	0.211416	0.216735					
7	0.143629	0.157231	0.167462	0.173141	0.177497	0.18104				
8	0.121658	0.133179	0.141846	0.146656	0.150345	0.153346	0.152969			
9	0.105449	0.115435	0.122947	0.127116	0.130314	0.132915	0.132588	0.133237		
10	0.093586	0.102449	0.109116	0.112816	0.115654	0.117963	0.117673	0.118249	0.112493	
11	0.084644	0.09266	0.09869	0.102036	0.104603	0.106691	0.106429	0.10695	0.101744	0.095553

Table 8.1   Continued

R(2)	3	4	5	6	7	8	9	10	11	12
3	1									
4	0.484244	0.515756								
5	0.315829	0.336382	0.347789							
6	0.23282	0.247971	0.25638	0.262829						
7	0.183601	0.195549	0.20218	0.207266	0.211404					
8	0.151626	0.161493	0.166969	0.171169	0.174586	0.174157				
9	0.129042	0.13744	0.1421	0.145675	0.148583	0.148218	0.148943			
10	0.113027	0.120382	0.124464	0.127596	0.130143	0.129823	0.130458	0.124107		
11	0.101228	0.107816	0.111472	0.114276	0.116557	0.116271	0.11684	0.111152	0.104389	
12	0.091758	0.097729	0.101043	0.103585	0.105653	0.105393	0.105909	0.100753	0.094623	0.093556

...

R(10)	11	12	13	14	15	16	17	18	19	20
11	1									
12	0.502837	0.497163								
13	0.341309	0.337458	0.321233							
14	0.259621	0.256691	0.24435	0.239338						
15	0.210387	0.208013	0.198012	0.193951	0.189637					
16	0.178905	0.176887	0.168382	0.164929	0.16126	0.149636				
17	0.156257	0.154494	0.147066	0.14405	0.140846	0.130693	0.126595			
18	0.139159	0.137589	0.130974	0.128288	0.125434	0.116393	0.112743	0.109419		
19	0.125814	0.124394	0.118414	0.115985	0.113405	0.10523	0.101931	0.098926	0.0959	
20	0.115097	0.113798	0.108327	0.106105	0.103745	0.096267	0.093248	0.090499	0.087731	0.085182

The representation of **R** above is explained with this small submatrix example shown below:

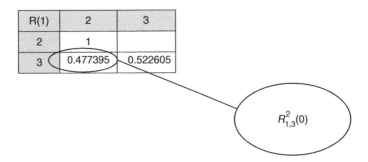

Having computed the matrix of parameters **R** we can determine the off diagonal parameters of our covariance matrix Φ. We will use the following formulae

$$\varphi_{k,N-1} = \frac{\delta_k \sigma_{kN}^2 - \Lambda_k \left(\sum_{l=k+1}^{N} \sum_{i=k+1}^{N} R_{kN}^i(0)\varphi_{i-1l-1}R_{kN}^l(0) - 2R_{kN}^{k+1}(0)\varphi_{k,N-1}R_{kN}^N(0) \right)}{2\Lambda_k R_{kN}^{k+1}(0) R_{kN}^N(0)} \tag{8.1}$$

for $k = 1, \ldots, m$ and $N = k+2, \ldots$.

The full calculation of matrix Φ requires a detailed recursive algorithm. This is presented below.

Algorithm 8.3   Matrix Φ

$s = 1$

$SumTemp = 0$

For $i = 1$ to R // NumberOfRowsInCovarianceMatrix

  For $j = i + 1$ to R // NumberOfRowsInCovarianceMatrix

    $Sum = 0$

    For $l = i + j - 2s + 1$ to $j + 1$

      For $k = i + j - 2s + 1$ to $j + 1$

        $SumTemp = R(i+j-2s, j+1, k)^*R(i+j-2s, j+1, l)^*\Phi(k-1, l-1)$

        $Sum = Sum + SumTemp$

      Next k

    Next l

    $\Phi(i+j-2s, j) =$

    $\{\delta(0, i+j-2s)^*\Sigma(i+j-2s, i+1)\char`\^2 - \Lambda(i+j-2s)^*$

    $[Sum - 2^*R(i+j-2s, j+1, i+j-2s+1)^*\Phi(i+j-2s, j)^*R(i+j-2s, j+1, j+1)]\}/$

    $[2^*D(i+j-2s)^*R(i+j-2s, j+1, i+j-2s+1)^*R(i+j-2s, j+1, j+1)]$

    $\Phi(j, i+j-2s) = \Phi(i+j-2s, j)$ // set up whole matrix

  Next j

  $s = s + 1$

Next i

End of algorithm 8.3

Below we present some of our computed matrices Φ, where elements of the matrices are expressed as $\varphi_{kl}^i = \Lambda_i \varphi_{kl}$ for several arbitrary chosen functions Λ_i. First we have assumed

Table 8.2   VCV matrix for Longstaff-Schwartz-Santa Clara string model

k/l	1	2	3	4	5	6	7	8	9	10
1	5.15%	5.50%	4.76%	3.46%	2.04%	2.76%	1.12%	1.85%	0.42%	1.66%
2	5.50%	5.02%	4.57%	3.82%	3.13%	2.19%	2.58%	2.27%	2.39%	1.23%
3	4.76%	4.57%	4.37%	4.00%	3.09%	2.61%	1.75%	2.33%	2.08%	3.15%
4	3.46%	3.82%	4.00%	3.81%	3.45%	2.73%	2.31%	1.73%	2.76%	1.59%
5	2.04%	3.13%	3.09%	3.45%	3.31%	2.88%	2.12%	1.95%	1.29%	2.83%
6	2.76%	2.19%	2.61%	2.73%	2.88%	3.05%	2.68%	2.00%	1.82%	1.37%
7	1.12%	2.58%	1.75%	2.31%	2.12%	2.68%	2.80%	2.50%	1.86%	1.70%
8	1.85%	2.27%	2.33%	1.73%	1.95%	2.00%	2.50%	2.56%	2.31%	1.75%
9	0.42%	2.39%	2.08%	2.76%	1.29%	1.82%	1.86%	2.31%	2.33%	2.14%
10	1.66%	1.23%	3.15%	1.59%	2.83%	1.37%	1.70%	1.75%	2.14%	2.10%

Table 8.3 Vector of eigenvalues of VCV matrix for LS Santa Clara string model

i	1	2	3	4	5	6	7	8	9	10
λ_i	26.676%	5.391%	2.251%	1.908%	1.456%	0.661%	−0.028%	−0.387%	−0.934%	−2.501%

Table 8.4 Matrix of eigenvectors of VCV matrix for LS Santa Clara string model

i	e_{1i}	e_{2i}	e_{3i}	e_{4i}	e_{5i}	e_{6i}	e_{7i}	e_{8i}	e_{9i}	e_{10i}
1	37.39%	−58.77%	6.98%	5.52%	−28.58%	−18.30%	2.07%	−2.24%	49.38%	38.34%
2	40.99%	−32.58%	32.11%	−20.48%	13.40%	45.00%	0.61%	41.38%	−13.76%	−41.24%
3	40.29%	−18.27%	−35.45%	−19.65%	−9.14%	−17.76%	18.82%	−23.41%	−69.94%	14.41%
4	36.23%	1.46%	−1.63%	7.84%	65.13%	−14.67%	−8.01%	−52.92%	24.43%	−26.50%
5	31.19%	19.46%	−37.37%	44.63%	11.12%	46.81%	−36.76%	16.85%	−2.14%	36.14%
6	28.49%	18.80%	19.77%	55.79%	−11.58%	−56.38%	−0.95%	34.45%	−15.20%	−24.49%
7	24.52%	38.41%	42.62%	15.14%	−15.31%	30.86%	59.07%	−27.35%	1.82%	21.22%
8	24.40%	28.87%	23.90%	−27.40%	−47.95%	0.88%	−61.78%	−31.10%	−0.71%	−12.83%
9	22.18%	37.93%	9.17%	−52.26%	32.23%	−27.86%	−1.02%	39.85%	10.74%	41.64%
10	22.63%	25.87%	−58.32%	−16.96%	−29.13%	3.22%	30.29%	12.65%	39.10%	−40.80%

that $\Lambda_i = \delta_{0,i}$ (the year fraction between time T_0 and T_i). Choosing $\Lambda_i = \delta_{0,i}$ leads to the Longstaff-Schwartz-Santa Clara model. The results are presented below.

As we can see such a matrix Φ has negative eigenvalues. What's more, taking absolute values of eigenvalues we can see that $|\lambda_{10}|$ has third biggest value. One can see that for some market data the model may give significant mispricing of European swaptions. Let us see if this is the case for our market data.

First let us compute a modified matrix Φ^{PCA} created by removing eigenvectors associated with negative eigenvalues. For such modification we have to:

1. Create a new matrix constructed by multiplying eigenvectors by corresponding squared root of eigenvalues. We do that only for positive eigenvalues.

Table 8.5 Eigenvectors multiplied by squared root of eigenvalues

i	$e_{1i}\sqrt{\lambda_1}$	$e_{2i}\sqrt{\lambda_2}$	$e_{3i}\sqrt{\lambda_3}$	$e_{4i}\sqrt{\lambda_4}$	$e_{5i}\sqrt{\lambda_5}$	$e_{6i}\sqrt{\lambda_6}$
1	19.31%	−13.64%	1.05%	0.76%	−3.45%	−1.49%
2	21.17%	−7.56%	4.82%	−2.83%	1.62%	3.66%
3	20.81%	−4.24%	−5.32%	−2.71%	−1.10%	−1.44%
4	18.71%	0.34%	−0.24%	1.08%	7.86%	−1.19%
5	16.11%	4.52%	−5.61%	6.16%	1.34%	3.81%
6	14.72%	4.37%	2.97%	7.71%	−1.40%	−4.58%
7	12.66%	8.92%	6.39%	2.09%	−1.85%	2.51%
8	12.60%	6.70%	3.59%	−3.78%	−5.79%	0.07%
9	11.46%	8.81%	1.38%	−7.22%	3.89%	−2.27%
10	11.69%	6.01%	−8.75%	−2.34%	−3.52%	0.26%

2. Multiply the matrix created in step 1 by its transposition. In effect we obtain modified matrix Φ^{PCA}.

Table 8.6   Modified covariance matrix

VCV	1	2	3	4	5	6	7	8	9	10
1	5.75%	5.04%	4.58%	3.32%	2.38%	2.45%	1.34%	1.73%	0.87%	1.45%
2	5.04%	5.53%	4.48%	3.98%	2.79%	2.52%	2.32%	2.35%	2.01%	1.62%
3	4.58%	4.48%	4.90%	3.79%	3.22%	2.59%	1.84%	2.31%	2.12%	2.74%
4	3.32%	3.98%	3.79%	4.15%	3.17%	2.79%	2.23%	1.88%	2.43%	1.92%
5	2.38%	2.79%	3.22%	3.17%	3.66%	2.68%	2.28%	1.82%	1.69%	2.46%
6	2.45%	2.52%	2.59%	2.79%	2.68%	3.27%	2.51%	2.04%	1.60%	1.58%
7	1.34%	2.32%	1.84%	2.23%	2.28%	2.51%	2.95%	2.45%	2.04%	1.48%
8	1.73%	2.35%	2.31%	1.88%	1.82%	2.04%	2.45%	2.64%	2.13%	1.85%
9	0.87%	2.01%	2.12%	2.43%	1.69%	1.60%	2.04%	2.13%	2.83%	1.77%
10	1.45%	1.62%	2.74%	1.92%	2.46%	1.58%	1.48%	1.85%	1.77%	2.67%

Having computed the matrix of modified covariances we can compute the matrix of theoretical swaptions. The matrix will contain theoretical swaption volatilities approximated via principal component modification of the initial covariance matrix. For that purpose we use the equations:

$$\varphi^{PCA^i}_{\;\;kl} = \Lambda_i \varphi^{PCA}_{kl}$$

and

$$\delta_k \sigma^2_{kN} \cong \Lambda_k \sum_{l=k+1}^{N} \sum_{i=k+1}^{N} R^i_{kN}(0)\, \varphi^{PCA}_{i-1,l-1} R^l_{kN}(0).$$

And because $\delta_k = \Lambda_k$ (for LS Santa Clara string model), we obtain:

$$\sigma^2_{kN} \cong \sum_{l=k+1}^{N} \sum_{i=k+1}^{N} R^i_{kN}(0)\, \varphi^{PCA}_{i-1,l-1} R^l_{kN}(0)$$

Below you can see results of our approximation for theoretical swaption volatilities as well as differences between theoretical and market swaption volatilities:

Table 8.7   Theoretical and market volatilities of swaptions

Theoretical	1Y	2Y	3Y	4Y	5Y	6Y	7Y	8Y	9Y	10Y
1Y	23.98%	23.10%	22.15%	20.93%	19.62%	18.61%	17.61%	16.91%	16.32%	15.90%
2Y	23.51%	21.99%	20.79%	19.46%	18.40%	17.45%	16.75%	16.22%	15.81%	
3Y	22.14%	20.38%	19.14%	18.06%	17.06%	16.35%	15.86%	15.50%		
4Y	20.35%	18.78%	17.72%	16.81%	16.02%	15.53%	15.12%			
5Y	19.12%	17.52%	16.60%	15.82%	15.22%	14.83%				
6Y	18.07%	16.76%	15.94%	15.27%	14.64%					
7Y	17.17%	16.20%	15.52%	14.74%						
8Y	16.26%	15.59%	14.80%							
9Y	16.82%	15.05%								
10Y	16.35%									

Table 8.7 Continued

Market	1Y	2Y	3Y	4Y	5Y	6Y	7Y	8Y	9Y	10Y
1Y	22.70%	23.00%	22.10%	20.90%	19.60%	18.60%	17.60%	16.90%	16.30%	15.90%
2Y	22.40%	21.50%	20.50%	19.40%	18.30%	17.40%	16.70%	16.20%	15.80%	
3Y	20.90%	20.10%	19.00%	18.00%	17.00%	16.30%	15.80%	15.50%		
4Y	19.50%	18.70%	17.70%	16.80%	16.00%	15.50%	15.10%			
5Y	18.20%	17.40%	16.50%	15.80%	15.10%	14.80%				
6Y	17.46%	16.74%	15.90%	15.24%	14.62%					
7Y	16.72%	16.08%	15.30%	14.68%						
8Y	15.98%	15.42%	14.70%							
9Y	15.24%	14.76%								
10Y	14.50%									

Difference	1Y	2Y	3Y	4Y	5Y	6Y	7Y	8Y	9Y	10Y
1Y	1.28%	0.10%	0.05%	0.03%	0.02%	0.01%	0.01%	0.01%	0.02%	0.00%
2Y	1.11%	0.49%	0.29%	0.06%	0.10%	0.05%	0.05%	0.02%	0.01%	
3Y	1.24%	0.28%	0.14%	0.06%	0.06%	0.05%	0.06%	0.00%		
4Y	0.85%	0.08%	0.02%	0.01%	0.02%	0.03%	0.02%			
5Y	0.92%	0.12%	0.10%	0.02%	0.12%	0.03%				
6Y	0.61%	0.02%	0.04%	0.03%	0.02%					
7Y	0.45%	0.12%	0.22%	0.06%						
8Y	0.28%	0.17%	0.10%							
9Y	1.58%	0.29%								
10Y	1.85%									

The root mean squared error between theoretical and market swaptions volatilities is defined as:

$$RMSE = \sum_{i,j=1}^{10} \left(\sigma_{ij}^{THEO} - \sigma_{ij}^{MKT} \right)^2 = 0.0013$$

Having computed our modified matrix Φ^{PCA} we can also determine vectors of instantaneous volatilities for the forward rates. Below we demonstrate how to do this.

Taking into account the equation for elements of covariance matrix Φ^{PCA^i}

$$\varphi^{PCA^i}{}_{kl} = \int_0^{T_i} \gamma_l(t)^T \cdot \gamma_k(t)\, dt$$

for $i \leq k$ and $i \leq l$, we can specify vectors of instantaneous volatility in the following way:

$$\begin{bmatrix} \gamma_1^1 \\ 0 \\ 0 \\ \cdots \\ 0 \end{bmatrix} \begin{bmatrix} \gamma_2^1 \\ \gamma_2^2 \\ 0 \\ \cdots \\ 0 \end{bmatrix} \begin{bmatrix} \gamma_3^1 \\ \gamma_3^2 \\ \gamma_3^3 \\ \cdots \\ 0 \end{bmatrix} \cdots \begin{bmatrix} \gamma_N^1 \\ \gamma_N^2 \\ \gamma_N^3 \\ \cdots \\ \gamma_N^N \end{bmatrix}$$

for $\gamma_1(t), \gamma_2(t), \gamma_3(t), \ldots, \gamma_N(t)$ respectively.

For pricing purposes we can assume that we have constant instantaneous volatilities through a given period of time. Having that assumption in mind we can write:

$$\varphi^{PCA^i}{}_{kl} = \int_0^{T_i} \gamma_l(t)^T \cdot \gamma_k(t)\, dt = \left(\gamma_l(t)^T \cdot \gamma_k(t)\right)\delta_{T_i} = \Lambda_i \varphi_{kl}^{PCA}$$

and

$$\gamma_1(t) = \begin{bmatrix} \gamma_1^1(t) \\ 0 \\ 0 \\ \cdots \\ 0 \end{bmatrix} \quad \text{and} \quad \gamma_1^1(t) = \gamma_1^1 \quad \text{for } 0 < t \leq T_1$$

$$\gamma_2(t) = \begin{bmatrix} \gamma_2^1(t) \\ \gamma_2^2(t) \\ 0 \\ \cdots \\ 0 \end{bmatrix} \quad \text{and} \quad \begin{matrix} \gamma_2^1(t) = \gamma_2^1 \\ \gamma_2^2(t) = \gamma_2^2 \end{matrix} \quad \text{for } 0 < t \leq T_2$$

$\cdots$

$$\gamma_N(t) = \begin{bmatrix} \gamma_N^1(t) \\ \gamma_N^2(t) \\ \gamma_N^3(t) \\ \cdots \\ \gamma_N^N(t) \end{bmatrix} \quad \text{and} \quad \begin{matrix} \gamma_N^1(t) = \gamma_N^1 \\ \gamma_N^2(t) = \gamma_N^2 \\ \gamma_N^3(t) = \gamma_N^2 \\ \cdots \\ \gamma_N^N(t) = \gamma_N^N \end{matrix} \quad \text{for } 0 < t \leq T_N$$

We present an example of the determination of vector components $\gamma_i(t)$ for $i = 1, 2, \ldots, 10$.

Example 8.1   Components of vectors $\gamma_i(t)$

First we take into consideration the elements of the matrix Φ^{PCA} from upper left corner $\varphi_{11}^{PCA} = 5.75\,\%$ and Λ_1 obtaining:

$$\Lambda_1 \varphi_{11}^{PCA} = \left(\gamma_1(t)^T \cdot \gamma_1(t)\right)\delta_{T_1}$$

Because $\Lambda_1 = \delta_{T_1}$, we can write:

$$\varphi_{11}^{PCA} = \begin{bmatrix} \gamma_1^1 \\ 0 \\ 0 \\ \cdots \\ 0 \end{bmatrix}^T \begin{bmatrix} \gamma_1^1 \\ 0 \\ 0 \\ \cdots \\ 0 \end{bmatrix} = \left(\gamma_1^1\right)^2 \Rightarrow \gamma_1^1 = \sqrt{\varphi_{11}^{PCA}} = \sqrt{5.75\%} = 23.98\,\%$$

For elements $\varphi_{21}^{PCA} = 5.04\%$ and Λ_1 we obtain:

$$\Lambda_1 \varphi_{21}^{PCA} = \left(\gamma_1 \left(t \right)^T \cdot \gamma_2 \left(t \right) \right) \delta_{T_1} \Leftrightarrow$$

$$\varphi_{21}^{PCA} = \gamma_1 \left(t \right)^T \cdot \gamma_2 \left(t \right) \Leftrightarrow$$

$$\varphi_{21}^{PCA} = \begin{bmatrix} \gamma_1^1 \\ 0 \\ 0 \\ \cdots \\ 0 \end{bmatrix}^T \begin{bmatrix} \gamma_2^1 \\ \gamma_2^2 \\ 0 \\ \cdots \\ 0 \end{bmatrix} = \gamma_1^1 \gamma_2^1 \Rightarrow \gamma_2^1 = \frac{\varphi_{21}^{PCA}}{\gamma_1^1} = \frac{5.04\%}{23.98\%} = 21.02\%$$

Similarly for elements φ_{k1}^{PCA} where $k = 3, 4, \ldots, 10$ and Λ_1 we obtain:

$$\Lambda_1 \varphi_{k1}^{PCA} = \left(\gamma_1 \left(t \right)^T \cdot \gamma_k \left(t \right) \right) \delta_{T_1} \Leftrightarrow$$

$$\varphi_{k1}^{PCA} = \gamma_1 \left(t \right)^T \cdot \gamma_k \left(t \right) \Leftrightarrow$$

$$\varphi_{k1}^{PCA} = \begin{bmatrix} \gamma_1^1 \\ 0 \\ 0 \\ \cdots \\ 0 \end{bmatrix}^T \begin{bmatrix} \gamma_k^1 \\ \gamma_k^2 \\ \gamma_k^3 \\ \cdots \\ \cdots \end{bmatrix} = \gamma_1^1 \gamma_k^1 \Rightarrow \gamma_k^1 = \frac{\varphi_{k1}^{PCA}}{\gamma_1^1}$$

Taking values for φ_{k1}^{PCA} for $k = 3, 4, \ldots, 10$

K	3	4	5	6	7	8	9	10
φ_{k1}^{PCA}	4.58%	3.32%	2.38%	2.45%	1.34%	1.73%	0.87%	1.45%

We obtain:

K	3	4	5	6	7	8	9	10
γ_k^1	19.10%	13.85%	9.92%	10.23%	5.58%	7.20%	3.63%	6.03%

Now we choose element $\varphi_{22}^{PCA} = 5.53\%$ and Λ_1 or Λ_2 obtaining:

$$\Lambda_1 \varphi_{22}^{PCA} = \left(\gamma_2 \left(t \right)^T \cdot \gamma_2 \left(t \right) \right) \delta_{T_1}$$

or

$$\Lambda_2 \varphi_{22}^{PCA} = \left(\gamma_2 \left(t \right)^T \cdot \gamma_2 \left(t \right) \right) \delta_{T_2}$$

We assume that the instantaneous volatilities are constant through a given period. Having that in mind we can write:

$$\varphi_{22}^{PCA} = \gamma_2(t)^T \cdot \gamma_2(t) \Leftrightarrow$$

$$\varphi_{22}^{PCA} = \begin{bmatrix} \gamma_2^1 \\ \gamma_2^2 \\ 0 \\ \cdots \\ 0 \end{bmatrix}^T \cdot \begin{bmatrix} \gamma_2^1 \\ \gamma_2^2 \\ 0 \\ \cdots \\ 0 \end{bmatrix} = (\gamma_2^1)^2 + (\gamma_2^2)^2 \Rightarrow \gamma_2^2 = \sqrt{\varphi_{22}^{PCA} - (\gamma_2^1)^2} \Rightarrow$$

$$\gamma_2 = \sqrt{5.53\% - (21.02)^2} = 10.53\%$$

For element $\varphi_{32}^{PCA} = 4.48\%$ and Λ_1 or Λ_2 we obtain:

$$\Lambda_1 \varphi_{32}^{PCA} = \left(\gamma_3(t)^T \cdot \gamma_2(t)\right) \delta_{T_1}$$

or

$$\Lambda_2 \varphi_{32}^{PCA} = \left(\gamma_3(t)^T \cdot \gamma_2(t)\right) \delta_{T_2}$$

Once again we have assumed that the instantaneous volatilities are constant through a given period. Having that in mind we can write:

$$\varphi_{32}^{PCA} = \gamma_3(t)^T \cdot \gamma_2(t) \Leftrightarrow$$

$$\varphi_{32}^{PCA} = \begin{bmatrix} \gamma_3^1 \\ \gamma_3^2 \\ \gamma_3^2 \\ \cdots \\ 0 \end{bmatrix}^T \cdot \begin{bmatrix} \gamma_2^1 \\ \gamma_2^2 \\ 0 \\ \cdots \\ 0 \end{bmatrix} = \gamma_3^1 \gamma_2^1 + \gamma_3^2 \gamma_2^2 \Rightarrow \gamma_3^2 = \frac{1}{\gamma_2^2}\left(\varphi_{32}^{PCA} - \gamma_3^1 \gamma_2^1\right) \Rightarrow$$

$$\gamma_3^2 = \frac{1}{10.53\%}(4.48\% - 19.10\% \cdot 21.02\%) = 4.38\%$$

Similarly for φ_{k2}^{PCA} for $k = 4, 5, \ldots, 10$ and Λ_1 or Λ_2 assuming constant instantaneous volatilities we obtain:

$$\varphi_{k2}^{PCA} = \gamma_k(t)^T \cdot \gamma_2(t) \Leftrightarrow$$

$$\varphi_{k2}^{PCA} = \begin{bmatrix} \gamma_k^1 \\ \gamma_k^2 \\ \gamma_k^2 \\ \cdots \\ \cdots \end{bmatrix}^T \cdot \begin{bmatrix} \gamma_2^1 \\ \gamma_2^2 \\ 0 \\ \cdots \\ 0 \end{bmatrix} = \gamma_k^1 \gamma_2^1 + \gamma_k^2 \gamma_2^2 \Rightarrow \gamma_k^2 = \frac{1}{\gamma_2^2}\left(\varphi_{k2}^{PCA} - \gamma_k^1 \gamma_2^1\right)$$

Taking values for φ_{k2}^{PCA} for $k = 4, 5, \ldots, 10$.

k	4	5	6	7	8	9	10
φ_{k2}^{PCA}	3.98 %	2.79 %	2.52 %	2.32 %	2.35 %	2.01 %	1.62 %

We obtain:

k	4	5	6	7	8	9	10
γ_k^2	10.13 %	6.64 %	3.52 %	10.87 %	7.95 %	11.85 %	3.33 %

Going further and generalizing the algorithm for elements φ_{kk}^{PCA}, for $k = 2, 3, 4, \ldots, 10$ for each Λ_i where $i \leq k$ instantaneous volatilities will be obtained via:

$$\varphi_{kk}^{PCA} = \gamma_k(t)^T \cdot \gamma_k(t) \Leftrightarrow$$

$$\varphi_{kk}^{PCA} = \begin{bmatrix} \gamma_k^1 \\ \gamma_k^2 \\ \gamma_k^3 \\ \cdots \\ \gamma_k^k \end{bmatrix}^T \cdot \begin{bmatrix} \gamma_k^1 \\ \gamma_k^2 \\ \gamma_k^3 \\ \cdots \\ \gamma_k^k \end{bmatrix} = \left(\gamma_k^1\right)^2 + \left(\gamma_k^2\right)^2 + \ldots + \left(\gamma_k^k\right)^2 \Rightarrow$$

$$\gamma_k^k = \sqrt{\varphi_{kk}^{PCA} - \left(\gamma_k^1\right)^2 - \left(\gamma_k^2\right)^2 + \ldots - \left(\gamma_k^{k-1}\right)^2}$$

Similarly, for elements φ_{kl}^{PCA}, for $l = 2, 3, 4, \ldots, 10$ and $l < k < 10$ for each Λ_i where $i \leq k$ and $i \leq l$ instantaneous volatilities will be obtained via:

$$\varphi_{kl}^{PCA} = \gamma_k(t)^T \cdot \gamma_l(t) \Leftrightarrow$$

$$\varphi_{kl}^{PCA} = \begin{bmatrix} \gamma_k^1 \\ \gamma_k^2 \\ \gamma_k^2 \\ \cdots \\ \gamma_k^2 \end{bmatrix}^T \cdot \begin{bmatrix} \gamma_l^1 \\ \gamma_l^2 \\ \gamma_l^2 \\ \cdots \\ \gamma_l^2 \end{bmatrix} = \gamma_k^1\gamma_l^1 + \gamma_k^2\gamma_l^2 + \ldots + \gamma_k^l\gamma_l^l \Rightarrow$$

$$\gamma_k^l = \frac{1}{\gamma_l^l} \left(\varphi_{kl}^{PCA} - \gamma_k^1\gamma_l^1 - \gamma_k^2\gamma_l^2 + \ldots - \gamma_k^{l-1}\gamma_l^{l-1}\right)$$

End of example 8.1

Having that we can present the full results of computations for the instantaneous volatility vectors:

Table 8.8   Vectors of instantaneous volatilities

Index	$\gamma_1(t)$	$\gamma_2(t)$	$\gamma_3(t)$	$\gamma_4(t)$	$\gamma_5(t)$	$\gamma_6(t)$	$\gamma_7(t)$	$\gamma_8(t)$	$\gamma_9(t)$	$\gamma_{10}(t)$
1	23.98%	21.02%	19.10%	13.85%	9.92%	10.23%	5.58%	7.20%	3.63%	6.03%
2		10.53%	4.38%	10.13%	6.64%	3.52%	10.87%	7.95%	11.85%	3.33%
3			10.29%	6.85%	10.06%	4.70%	2.94%	5.73%	8.86%	14.04%
4				8.57%	5.07%	8.11%	1.83%	−3.72%	1.35%	−2.45%
5					9.81%	5.61%	6.33%	1.98%	−4.27%	3.63%
6						9.51%	9.68%	9.94%	5.58%	1.89%
7							0.00%	0.00%	0.00%	0.00%
8								0.00%	0.00%	0.00%
9									0.00%	0.00%
10										0.00%

The structure of the matrix confirms that our computations were done properly. This is because during PCA modification of the VCV matrix we have removed four eigenvectors with associated negative eigenvalues.

One additional remark is very important. The presented algorithm is very sensitive to the precision of the computed elements of the VCV matrix. In the case of too much approximation in the values in the matrix the algorithm may fail.

We can do the same computations for VCV matrix reduced to two factors. Figure below shows two eigenvectors with the biggest eigenvalues:

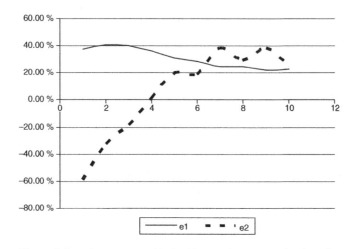

Figure 8.1   Eigenvectors with the biggest eigenvalues for $\Lambda_i = \delta_i$.

Using only two factors we obtain the following results for the theoretical swaptions:

Reducing number of factors to only the two biggest gives slightly worse results. The root mean squared error equals:

$$RMSE = \sum_{i,j=1}^{10} \left(\sigma_{ij}^{THEO} - \sigma_{ij}^{MKT}\right)^2 = 0.0030$$

Table 8.9 Theoretical and market volatilities of swaptions

Theoretical	1Y	2Y	3Y	4Y	5Y	6Y	7Y	8Y	9Y	10Y
1Y	23.65%	22.83%	22.07%	20.86%	19.50%	18.48%	17.49%	16.84%	16.29%	15.90%
2Y	22.48%	21.79%	20.53%	19.18%	18.19%	17.28%	16.67%	16.18%	15.81%	
3Y	21.24%	19.84%	18.50%	17.57%	16.77%	16.24%	15.83%	15.49%		
4Y	18.70%	17.55%	16.76%	16.16%	15.73%	15.41%	15.11%			
5Y	16.72%	16.03%	15.65%	15.29%	15.06%	14.77%				
6Y	15.34%	15.21%	14.89%	14.74%	14.44%					
7Y	15.48%	14.85%	14.70%	14.33%						
8Y	14.27%	14.31%	13.93%							
9Y	14.44%	13.76%								
10Y	13.14%									

Market	1Y	2Y	3Y	4Y	5Y	6Y	7Y	8Y	9Y	10Y
1Y	22.70%	23.00%	22.10%	20.90%	19.60%	18.60%	17.60%	16.90%	16.30%	15.90%
2Y	22.40%	21.50%	20.50%	19.40%	18.30%	17.40%	16.70%	16.20%	15.80%	
3Y	20.90%	20.10%	19.00%	18.00%	17.00%	16.30%	15.80%	15.50%		
4Y	19.50%	18.70%	17.70%	16.80%	16.00%	15.50%	15.10%			
5Y	18.20%	17.40%	16.50%	15.80%	15.10%	14.80%				
6Y	17.46%	16.74%	15.90%	15.24%	14.62%					
7Y	16.72%	16.08%	15.30%	14.68%						
8Y	15.98%	15.42%	14.70%							
9Y	15.24%	14.76%								
10Y	14.50%									

Difference	1Y	2Y	3Y	4Y	5Y	6Y	7Y	8Y	9Y	10Y
1Y	0.95%	−0.17%	−0.03%	−0.04%	−0.10%	−0.12%	−0.11%	−0.06%	−0.01%	0.00%
2Y	0.08%	0.29%	0.03%	−0.22%	−0.11%	−0.12%	−0.03%	−0.02%	0.01%	
3Y	0.34%	−0.26%	−0.50%	−0.43%	−0.23%	−0.06%	0.03%	−0.01%		
4Y	−0.80%	−1.15%	−0.94%	−0.64%	−0.27%	−0.09%	0.01%			
5Y	−1.48%	−1.37%	−0.85%	−0.51%	−0.04%	−0.03%				
6Y	−2.12%	−1.53%	−1.01%	−0.50%	−0.18%					
7Y	−1.24%	−1.23%	−0.60%	−0.35%						
8Y	−1.71%	−1.11%	−0.77%							
9Y	−0.80%	−1.00%								
10Y	−1.36%									

Let us move to analyse further the specifications for the functions Λ_i. A popular choice of function is $\Lambda_i = \sqrt{\delta_i}$. For such a specification we obtain the following eigenvalues and eigenvectors:

Table 8.10 Vector of eigenvalues of VCV matrix

i	1	2	3	4	5	6	7	8	9	10
λ_i	37.82%	21.19%	6.90%	6.07%	3.06%	1.39%	0.50%	0.16%	−2.49%	−4.03%

Comparing the results to the LS Santa Clara string model we can see that we have obtained only two negative eigenvalues with modulus smaller than the fourth biggest positive eigenvalue. Creating a modified VCV matrix by removing the two eigenvectors associated with negative eigenvalues gives result presented below.

Table 8.11 Matrix of eigenvectors of VCV matrix

i	e_{1i}	e_{2i}	e_{3i}	e_{4i}	e_{5i}	e_{6i}	e_{7i}	e_{8i}	e_{9i}	e_{10i}
1	−35.25%	−30.68%	−11.64%	−6.32%	−14.40%	23.03%	10.27%	−4.63%	77.71%	−27.16%
2	−4.81%	−51.76%	4.66%	−45.55%	−13.49%	−44.29%	−15.86%	44.99%	−0.44%	27.97%
3	15.41%	−51.06%	39.68%	−6.17%	−28.87%	46.23%	−17.41%	−21.68%	−34.42%	−24.77%
4	27.22%	−43.54%	8.69%	10.22%	62.04%	−5.41%	16.66%	−39.52%	17.69%	33.94%
5	34.04%	−26.60%	−6.61%	53.98%	−19.46%	−41.73%	31.98%	18.34%	−0.43%	−41.19%
6	35.23%	−13.56%	−53.23%	17.16%	5.30%	51.86%	−16.68%	44.86%	1.83%	20.87%
7	37.87%	3.33%	−45.32%	−26.49%	−15.69%	−26.26%	−45.24%	−47.74%	10.30%	−20.78%
8	37.00%	12.38%	−5.79%	−44.98%	−32.17%	13.51%	69.67%	−8.63%	3.16%	16.30%
9	37.16%	19.07%	31.92%	−34.13%	44.56%	5.62%	−8.06%	34.84%	18.95%	−49.16%
10	34.23%	21.38%	47.00%	25.39%	−35.42%	−2.55%	−28.20%	2.64%	44.55%	38.34%

Table 8.12 Modified covariance matrix

VCV	1	2	3	4	5	6	7	8	9	10
1	6.95%	4.06%	1.25%	−1.20%	−3.01%	−3.31%	−4.81%	−5.33%	−6.50%	−6.28%
2	4.06%	7.37%	5.45%	3.80%	1.12%	−0.14%	−0.24%	−0.76%	−1.94%	−3.36%
3	1.25%	5.45%	8.09%	5.91%	4.38%	2.28%	0.67%	1.20%	0.75%	1.17%
4	−1.20%	3.80%	5.91%	8.12%	5.92%	4.73%	2.88%	1.73%	2.89%	1.32%
5	−3.01%	1.12%	4.38%	5.92%	8.04%	5.77%	4.27%	2.73%	2.15%	4.04%
6	−3.31%	−0.14%	2.28%	4.73%	5.77%	7.60%	6.13%	4.36%	2.99%	2.41%
7	−4.81%	−0.24%	0.67%	2.88%	4.27%	6.13%	7.46%	6.40%	4.77%	3.35%
8	−5.33%	−0.76%	1.20%	1.73%	2.73%	4.36%	6.40%	7.09%	6.08%	4.81%
9	−6.50%	−1.94%	0.75%	2.89%	2.15%	2.99%	4.77%	6.08%	8.02%	5.70%
10	−6.28%	−3.36%	1.17%	1.32%	4.04%	2.41%	3.35%	4.81%	5.70%	7.70%

Having that we can compute the matrix of theoretical swaption volatilities and compare it to observed market swaption volatilities:

Table 8.13 Theoretical and market volatilities of swaptions

Theoretical	1Y	2Y	3Y	4Y	5Y	6Y	7Y	8Y	9Y	10Y
1Y	23.68%	23.73%	22.23%	21.01%	19.71%	18.65%	17.68%	16.95%	16.43%	16.04%
2Y	22.89%	21.63%	20.62%	19.41%	18.31%	17.40%	16.70%	16.22%	15.83%	
3Y	21.64%	20.14%	19.18%	18.01%	17.03%	16.30%	15.86%	15.54%		
4Y	20.18%	18.73%	17.73%	16.82%	16.02%	15.56%	15.17%			
5Y	19.02%	17.45%	16.60%	15.83%	15.24%	14.88%				
6Y	17.67%	16.75%	15.92%	15.30%	14.70%					
7Y	16.94%	16.10%	15.48%	14.80%						
8Y	16.10%	15.57%	14.84%							
9Y	16.36%	15.06%								
10Y	15.64%									

Market	1Y	2Y	3Y	4Y	5Y	6Y	7Y	8Y	9Y	10Y
1Y	22.70%	23.00%	22.10%	20.90%	19.60%	18.60%	17.60%	16.90%	16.30%	15.90%
2Y	22.40%	21.50%	20.50%	19.40%	18.30%	17.40%	16.70%	16.20%	15.80%	
3Y	20.90%	20.10%	19.00%	18.00%	17.00%	16.30%	15.80%	15.50%		
4Y	19.50%	18.70%	17.70%	16.80%	16.00%	15.50%	15.10%			
5Y	18.20%	17.40%	16.50%	15.80%	15.10%	14.80%				
6Y	17.46%	16.74%	15.90%	15.24%	14.62%					
7Y	16.72%	16.08%	15.30%	14.68%						
8Y	15.98%	15.42%	14.70%							
9Y	15.24%	14.76%								
10Y	14.50%									

Table 8.13 Continued

Difference	1Y	2Y	3Y	4Y	5Y	6Y	7Y	8Y	9Y	10Y
1Y	0.98%	0.73%	0.13%	0.11%	0.11%	0.05%	0.08%	0.05%	0.13%	0.14%
2Y	0.49%	0.13%	0.12%	0.01%	0.01%	0.00%	0.00%	0.02%	0.03%	
3Y	0.74%	0.04%	0.18%	0.01%	0.03%	0.00%	0.06%	0.04%		
4Y	0.68%	0.03%	0.03%	0.02%	0.02%	0.06%	0.07%			
5Y	0.82%	0.05%	0.10%	0.03%	0.14%	0.08%				
6Y	0.21%	0.01%	0.02%	0.06%	0.08%					
7Y	0.22%	0.02%	0.18%	0.12%						
8Y	0.12%	0.15%	0.14%							
9Y	1.12%	0.30%								
10Y	1.14%									

The root mean squared error equals:

$$RMSE = \sum_{i,j=1}^{10} \left(\sigma_{ij}^{THEO} - \sigma_{ij}^{MKT} \right)^2 = 0.0019$$

The instantaneous volatilities cannot be specified as a constant through time for this specification of the parameters Λ_i. Instead we deal with piecewise constant instantaneous volatilities. We describe this is more detail below.

Having the components of instantaneous volatility vectors as

$$\begin{bmatrix} \gamma_1^1(t) \\ 0 \\ 0 \\ \cdots \\ 0 \end{bmatrix} \begin{bmatrix} \gamma_2^1(t) \\ \gamma_2^2(t) \\ 0 \\ \cdots \\ 0 \end{bmatrix} \begin{bmatrix} \gamma_3^1(t) \\ \gamma_3^2(t) \\ \gamma_3^3(t) \\ \cdots \\ 0 \end{bmatrix} \cdots \begin{bmatrix} \gamma_N^1(t) \\ \gamma_N^2(t) \\ \gamma_N^3(t) \\ \cdots \\ \gamma_N^N(t) \end{bmatrix}$$

Then, respectively for $\gamma_1(t), \gamma_2(t), \gamma_3(t), \ldots, \gamma_N(t)$, we can write:

$$\gamma_1(t) = \begin{bmatrix} \gamma_1^1(t) \\ 0 \\ 0 \\ \cdots \\ 0 \end{bmatrix} \quad \text{and} \quad \gamma_1^1(t) = \gamma_{1,0 \div T_1}^1 \quad \text{for } 0 < t \leq T_1$$

$$\gamma_2(t) = \begin{bmatrix} \gamma_2^1(t) \\ \gamma_2^2(t) \\ 0 \\ \cdots \\ 0 \end{bmatrix} \quad \text{and} \quad \begin{aligned} \gamma_2^1(t) &= \begin{cases} \gamma_{2,0 \div T_1}^1 & \text{for } 0 < t \leq T_1 \\ \gamma_{2,T_1 \div T_2}^1 & \text{for } T_1 < t \leq T_2 \end{cases} \\ \gamma_2^2(t) &= \begin{cases} \gamma_{2,0 \div T_1}^2 & \text{for } 0 < t \leq T_1 \\ \gamma_{2,T_1 \div T_2}^2 & \text{for } T_1 < t \leq T_2 \end{cases} \end{aligned}$$

$\ldots$

$$\gamma_N(t) = \begin{bmatrix} \gamma_N^1(t) \\ \gamma_N^2(t) \\ \gamma_N^3(t) \\ \cdots \\ \gamma_N^N(t) \end{bmatrix} \quad \text{and}$$

$$\gamma_N^1(t) = \begin{cases} \gamma_{N,0 \div T_1}^1 & \text{for} \quad 0 < t \le T_1 \\ \gamma_{N,T_1 \div T_2}^1 & \text{for} \quad T_1 < t \le T_2 \\ \gamma_{N,T_2 \div T_3}^1 & \text{for} \quad T_2 < t \le T_3 \\ \cdots \\ \gamma_{N,T_{N-1} \div T_N}^1 & \text{for} \quad T_{N-1} < t \le T_N \end{cases}$$

$$\gamma_N^2(t) = \begin{cases} \gamma_{N,0 \div T_1}^2 & \text{for} \quad 0 < t \le T_1 \\ \gamma_{N,T_1 \div T_2}^2 & \text{for} \quad T_1 < t \le T_2 \\ \gamma_{N,T_2 \div T_3}^2 & \text{for} \quad T_2 < t \le T_3 \\ \cdots \\ \gamma_{N,T_{N-1} \div T_N}^2 & \text{for} \quad T_{N-1} < t \le T_N \end{cases}$$

$$\gamma_N^3(t) = \begin{cases} \gamma_{N,0 \div T_1}^3 & \text{for} \quad 0 < t \le T_1 \\ \gamma_{N,T_1 \div T_2}^3 & \text{for} \quad T_1 < t \le T_2 \\ \gamma_{N,T_2 \div T_3}^3 & \text{for} \quad T_2 < t \le T_3 \\ \cdots \\ \gamma_{N,T_{N-1} \div T_N}^3 & \text{for} \quad T_{N-1} < t \le T_N \end{cases}$$

$$\cdots$$

$$\gamma_N^N(t) = \begin{cases} \gamma_{N,0 \div T_1}^N & \text{for} \quad 0 < t \le T_1 \\ \gamma_{N,T_1 \div T_2}^N & \text{for} \quad T_1 < t \le T_2 \\ \gamma_{N,T_2 \div T_3}^N & \text{for} \quad T_2 < t \le T_3 \\ \cdots \\ \gamma_{N,T_{N-1} \div T_N}^N & \text{for} \quad T_{N-1} < t \le T_N \end{cases}$$

Therefore we can see that the generation of the instantaneous volatilities is quite similar to the previous example and thus we do not repeat that example again.

On the other hand we may reduce VCV only to three factors. The figure below shows the three eigenvectors with the biggest eigenvalues:

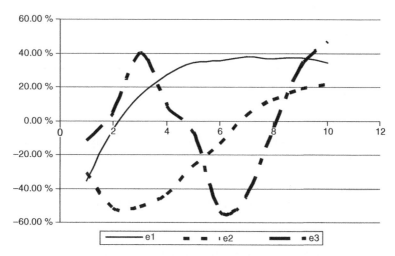

Figure 8.2   Eigenvectors with the biggest eigenvalues for $\Lambda_i = \sqrt{\delta_i}$.

Using only three factors we obtain the following results for the theoretical swaptions:

Table 8.14   Theoretical and market volatilities of swaptions

Theoretical	1Y	2Y	3Y	4Y	5Y	6Y	7Y	8Y	9Y	10Y
1Y	26.06%	22.60%	21.41%	20.81%	19.68%	18.59%	17.66%	16.85%	16.28%	15.96%
2Y	20.22%	20.73%	20.41%	19.35%	18.24%	17.39%	16.64%	16.11%	15.78%	
3Y	20.83%	19.90%	18.69%	17.60%	16.92%	16.28%	15.83%	15.52%		
4Y	18.52%	17.52%	16.96%	16.62%	16.00%	15.51%	15.17%			
5Y	16.25%	16.40%	16.83%	15.71%	15.18%	14.84%				
6Y	16.95%	16.64%	15.55%	14.87%	14.52%					
7Y	16.10%	14.90%	14.53%	14.41%						
8Y	13.97%	14.35%	14.53%							
9Y	14.94%	15.00%								
10Y	14.79%									

Market	1Y	2Y	3Y	4Y	5Y	6Y	7Y	8Y	9Y	10Y
1Y	22.70%	23.00%	22.10%	20.90%	19.60%	18.60%	17.60%	16.90%	16.30%	15.90%
2Y	22.40%	21.50%	20.50%	19.40%	18.30%	17.40%	16.70%	16.20%	15.80%	
3Y	20.90%	20.10%	19.00%	18.00%	17.00%	16.30%	15.80%	15.50%		
4Y	19.50%	18.70%	17.70%	16.80%	16.00%	15.50%	15.10%			
5Y	18.20%	17.40%	16.50%	15.80%	15.10%	14.80%				
6Y	17.46%	16.74%	15.90%	15.24%	14.62%					
7Y	16.72%	16.08%	15.30%	14.68%						
8Y	15.98%	15.42%	14.70%							
9Y	15.24%	14.76%								
10Y	14.50%									

Difference	1Y	2Y	3Y	4Y	5Y	6Y	7Y	8Y	9Y	10Y
1Y	3.36%	−0.40%	−0.69%	−0.09%	0.08%	−0.01%	0.06%	−0.05%	−0.02%	0.06%
2Y	−2.18%	−0.77%	−0.09%	−0.05%	−0.06%	−0.01%	−0.06%	−0.09%	−0.02%	
3Y	−0.07%	−0.20%	−0.31%	−0.40%	−0.08%	−0.02%	0.03%	0.02%		
4Y	−0.98%	−1.18%	−0.74%	−0.18%	0.00%	0.01%	0.07%			
5Y	−1.95%	−1.00%	0.33%	−0.09%	0.08%	0.04%				
6Y	−0.51%	−0.10%	−0.35%	−0.37%	−0.10%					
7Y	−0.62%	−1.18%	−0.77%	−0.27%						
8Y	−2.01%	−1.07%	−0.17%							
9Y	−0.30%	0.24%								
10Y	0.29%									

Reducing the number of factors to the three biggest gives slightly worse results. The root mean squared error equals:

$$RMSE = \sum_{i,j=1}^{10} \left(\sigma_{ij}^{THEO} - \sigma_{ij}^{MKT} \right)^2 = 0.0034$$

We can also specify another form for the functions Λ_i. Below we present for each specification the matching vectors of eigenvalues and root mean squared errors.

Table 8.15   Vectors of eigenvalues and root mean squared errors

Λ_i	λ_1	λ_2	λ_3	λ_4	λ_5	λ_6	λ_7	λ_8	λ_9	λ_{10}	RMSE
1)	12.21%	0.31%	0.05%	0.01%	−0.01%	−0.08%	−0.18%	−0.47%	−1.63%	−5.85%	41.527
2)	18.53%	5.67%	0.91%	0.16%	−0.08%	−0.26%	−0.51%	−0.80%	−1.67%	−6.54%	0.3578
3)	40.09%	16.56%	3.21%	2.27%	1.38%	0.59%	−0.16%	−0.81%	−3.27%	−11.94%	0.0239
4)	55.37%	24.26%	7.99%	6.90%	3.42%	1.51%	0.48%	0.06%	−4.83%	−11.67%	0.0226
5)	91.10%	42.12%	20.77%	14.79%	6.92%	3.28%	2.84%	1.80%	−7.36%	−15.88%	0.0435

1) $\Lambda_i = e^{\delta_i}$
2) $\Lambda_i = \sqrt{e^{\delta_i}}$
3) $\Lambda_i = \delta_i - \ln \delta_i$
4) $\Lambda_i = \sqrt{\delta_i - \ln \delta_i}$
5) $\Lambda_i = 1$

As an alternative calibration algorithm one can use a separated approach with an optimization algorithm, where the target function will minimize the differences between the theoretical and market swaption volatilities. In that case some restrictions for the VCV matrix must be added. First of all the VCV matrix must be positive definite. If that is not the case the algorithm must first reduce VCV matrix by removing eigenvectors associated with negative eigenvalues.

8.3   THE SEPARATED APPROACH WITH OPTIMIZATION

In this section we develop the previously demonstrated separated approach by adding an optimization algorithm. As a target function we set the root mean squared error for the differences between theoretical and market swaption volatilities. We would like to minimize that function but under several restrictions for VCV. We show that the VCV matrix must be positive definite. For that case we have to implement a subalgorithm for reducing the VCV matrix by removing eigenvectors associated with negative eigenvalues. Below we present all the necessary steps for the calibration algorithm, using code consistent with Matlab.

Step 0: Loading initial data and naming the minimization function

Minimization function:
function f = CalibrationObjectiveFunction_SeparatedOptim(Lambda);
% Definition of minimization function will be provided after step 6
% Vector of parameters [Lambda] will contain first initial data
% and after that the parameters will be subject to change during optimization

Initial data will contain:

1) Matrix of market swaption volatilities [Sig]

```
Sig = ...
[0.227      0.23       0.221      0.209      0.196      0.186      0.176      0.169      0.163      0.159;
 0.224      0.215      0.205      0.194      0.183      0.174      0.167      0.162      0.158      0.154;
 0.209      0.201      0.19       0.18       0.17       0.163      0.158      0.155      0.152      0.15;
 0.195      0.187      0.177      0.168      0.16       0.155      0.151      0.148      0.147      0.145;
 0.182      0.174      0.165      0.158      0.151      0.148      0.145      0.143      0.142      0.14;
```

0.1746	0.1674	0.159	0.1524	0.1462	0.1436	0.141	0.1394	0.1384	0.1368;
0.1672	0.1608	0.153	0.1468	0.1414	0.1392	0.137	0.1358	0.1348	0.1336;
0.1598	0.1542	0.147	0.1412	0.1366	0.1348	0.133	0.1322	0.1312	0.1304;
0.1524	0.1476	0.141	0.1356	0.1318	0.1304	0.129	0.1286	0.1276	0.1272;
0.145	0.141	0.135	0.13	0.127	0.1260	0.125	0.125	0.124	0.124;]

2) Date for computations

Today = '25-Jan-2005';

3) Vector of dates [T_Num] and vector of discount factors [B]

VectorOfDates = ...	B = ...
['25-Jan-2006';	[0.9774658
'25-Jan-2007';	0.9509789
'25-Jan-2008';	0.9219838
'26-Jan-2009';	0.8911017
'25-Jan-2010';	0.8591725
'25-Jan-2011';	0.8264399
'25-Jan-2012';	0.7930540
'25-Jan-2013';	0.7597502
'27-Jan-2014';	0.7262834
'26-Jan-2015';	0.6944457
'25-Jan-2016';	0.6645450
'25-Jan-2017';	0.6349818
'25-Jan-2018';	0.6068399
'25-Jan-2019';	0.5792752
'27-Jan-2020';	0.5523236
'25-Jan-2021';	0.5273147
'25-Jan-2022';	0.5030900
'25-Jan-2023';	0.4795796
'25-Jan-2024';	0.4567881
'27-Jan-2025'];	0.4346590];

To be consistent with Matlab code we have to transform vector of dates according to function:

T_Num = datenum(VectorOfDates);

Having loaded all necessary initial data we can we have to compute matrix of parameters **[R]**

Step 1: The Matrix of parameters [R]

% Input: Vector of discount factors [B]
% Output: Matrix of parameters [R]

Algorithm for step 1:
m = 10; % Number of swaption maturities
M = 20; % Number of swaption maturities plus number of swaption underlyings
R = []; % Setting zeros for matrix [R] as initial values
for i = 1 : m

```
for j = i + 1 : M − m + i
    for k = i + 1 : j
        R(i, j, k) = (B(k − 1) − B(k))/(B(i) − B(j));
    end
end
end
```

Step 2: The Matrix of covariances [VCV] as a function of parameters [Lambda]

```
% Input: (1) Matrix of parameters [R]
%        (2) Vector of dates [T_Num]
%        (3) Matrix of market swaption volatilities [Sig]
%        (4) Vector of initial parameters [Lambda]
% Output: Matrix of covariances [VCV] as a function of parameters [Lambda]
```

Algorithm for step 2:

```
VCV = []; % Setting zeros for matrix [VCV] as initial values
% Diagonal elements of matrix VCV
for k = 1 : m
    VCV(k, k) = yearfrac(Today, T_Num(k))*Sig(k, 1)^2/Lambda(k);
end
s = 1;
for i = 1 : m
    for j = i + 1 : m
        Sum = 0;
        for l = i + j − 2*s + 1 : j + 1
            for k = i + j − 2*s + 1 : j + 1
                SumTemp = R(i + j − 2*s, j + 1, k)*R(i + j − 2*s, j + 1, l)*VCV(k − 1, l − 1);
                Sum = Sum + SumTemp;
            end
        end
        VCV(i + j − 2*s, j) = (yearfrac(Today, T_Num(i + j − 2*s))*Sig(i + j − 2*s, i + 1)^2 −
        Lambda(i + j − 2*s)*(Sum − 2*R(i + j − 2*s, j + 1, i + j − 2*s + 1)*VCV(i + j −
        2*s, j)*R(i + j − 2*s, j + 1, j + 1)))/(2*Lambda(i + j − 2*s)*R(i + j − 2*s, j + 1, i + j −
        2*s + 1)*R(i + j − 2*s, j + 1, j + 1));
        VCV(j, i + j − 2*s) = VCV(i + j − 2*s, j);
    end
    s = s + 1;
end
```

Step 3: The Vector of eigenvalues [L] and the Matrix of eigenvectors [E] as a function of parameters [Lambda]

% Input: Matrix of covariances [VCV] as a function of parameters [Lambda]
% Output: (1) Vector of eigenvalues [L] as a function of parameters [Lambda]
%   (2) Matrix of eigenvectors [E] as a function of parameters [Lambda]

Algorithm for step 3:
[E,X] = eig(VCV);
L = diag(X);

Step 4: The modified covariance matrix [VCV_M] as a function of parameters [Lambda]

% Input: (1) Vector of eigenvalues [L] as a function of parameters [Lambda]
%   (2) Matrix of eigenvectors [E] as a function of parameters [Lambda]
% Output: Modified covariance matrix [VCV_M] as a function of parameters [Lambda]

% Step 4 contains sub-algorithm for eliminating eigenvectors associated with negative eigenvalues

Algorithms for step 4:
for i = 1 : m
    if L(i) < 0
        L_check(i) = 1;
    else
        L_check(i) = 0;
    end
end

% Matrix [E_sqrL] constructed by multiplying eigenvectors by square root of associated positive eigenvalues
for i = 1 : m
    if L_check(i) == 0
        for j = 1 : m
            E_sqrL(j, i) = E(j, i)*sqrt(L(i));
        end
    else
        for j = 1 : m
            E_sqrL(j,i) = 0;
        end
    end
end
VCV_M = E_sqrL*E_sqrL'; % symbol' denotes transposition

Step 5: Calculation of theoretical swaption volatilities [Sig_theo]

% Input: (1) Matrix of parameters [R]
%   (2) Matrix of modified covariance [VCV_M]
% Output: Matrix of theoretical swaption volatilities [Sig_theo]

Algorithm for step 5:
Sig_theo=[];
for k = 1:m
  for N = k + 1 : m + 1
    Sum = 0;
    for l = k + 1:N
      for i = k + 1:N
        SumTemp = R(k, N, i)*VCV_M(i − 1, l − 1)*R(k, N, l);
        Sum = Sum + SumTemp;
      end
    end
    Sig_theo(k,N-k)=sqrt(Sum*Lambda(k)/yearfrac(Today,T_Num(k)));
  end
end

Step 6: RSME between theoretical and market swaption volatilities

% Input: (1) Matrix of theoretical swaption volatilities [Sig_theo]
%   (2) Matrix of market swaption volatilities [Sig]
% Output: RSME between theoretical and market swaption volatilities

Algorithm for step 6:
RSME = 0;
for i = 1:m
  for j = 1 : m − i + 1
    RSME_Temp = (Sig_theo(i, j)-Sig(i, j))^2;
    RSME = RSME+RSME_Temp;
  end
end
f = RSME; % function f will be used as a minimization function

For the purpose of optimization we set initial values of parameters [Lambda] as:
Lambda0 = [1 2 3 4 5 6 7 8 9 10];
Having that we use Matlab function @fminsearch dedicated for nonlinear optimization:
[Lambda, f] = fminsearch(@CalibrationObjectiveFunction_SeparatedOptim, Lambda0);

Results of computations:

1) Parameters [Lambda]

Lambda =

2.1848
3.4058
3.3030
2.7767
2.4863
2.5656
2.7588
2.5325
1.6783
0.4483

2) Vector of eigenvalues [L]

L =

−0.0083
0.0000
0.0070
0.0119
0.0216
0.0290
0.0706
0.1367
0.2696
0.4927

3) Matrix of eigenvectors

E =

0.3073	0.1854	0.5379	−0.1028	−0.4686	0.5464	0.1659	−0.0605	0.1412	−0.0452
−0.3571	−0.6145	−0.1988	0.3945	−0.1505	0.4219	0.1730	−0.0667	0.2305	−0.1076
0.2648	−0.4985	−0.1433	−0.6669	−0.1641	−0.1958	−0.0486	−0.2608	0.2673	−0.0944
−0.3471	−0.1183	0.6026	0.1006	0.1183	−0.1818	−0.4200	−0.5105	0.0325	−0.0846
0.4086	0.0957	−0.3578	0.4094	−0.3322	−0.0654	−0.1795	−0.5742	−0.2140	0.0769
−0.4287	0.2228	−0.2551	−0.4496	0.0612	0.4319	0.0629	−0.3769	−0.3991	0.0611
0.3816	−0.3520	0.2430	0.0668	0.5225	0.0929	0.4200	−0.1711	−0.4204	0.0541
−0.2701	−0.1437	0.1694	−0.0167	−0.5571	−0.4390	0.3956	0.0861	−0.4587	0.0009
0.1275	−0.3141	0.0304	−0.0581	−0.1240	0.2421	−0.6213	0.3915	−0.5069	−0.1030
−0.0426	−0.1531	0.0753	−0.0311	−0.0632	0.0361	−0.0936	0.0400	0.0729	0.9732

4) Matrix of covariances [VCV]

VCV =

0.0236	0.0216	0.0120	0.0014	−0.0078	−0.0058	−0.0148	−0.0135	−0.0226	−0.0187
0.0216	0.0295	0.0194	0.0020	−0.0104	−0.0218	−0.0217	−0.0292	−0.0338	−0.0483
0.0120	0.0194	0.0397	0.0259	−0.0002	−0.0163	−0.0321	−0.0325	−0.0443	−0.0408
0.0014	0.0020	0.0259	0.0548	0.0400	0.0134	−0.0034	−0.0210	−0.0102	−0.0402
−0.0078	−0.0104	−0.0002	0.0400	0.0666	0.0528	0.0289	0.0200	0.0021	0.0309
−0.0058	−0.0218	−0.0163	0.0134	0.0528	0.0713	0.0600	0.0393	0.0321	0.0192
−0.0148	−0.0217	−0.0321	−0.0034	0.0289	0.0600	0.0709	0.0554	0.0260	0.0136
−0.0135	−0.0292	−0.0325	−0.0210	0.0200	0.0393	0.0554	0.0807	0.0486	−0.0104
−0.0226	−0.0338	−0.0443	−0.0102	0.0021	0.0321	0.0260	0.0486	0.1246	−0.0526
−0.0187	−0.0483	−0.0408	−0.0402	0.0309	0.0192	0.0136	−0.0104	−0.0526	0.4691

5) Matrix of modified covariances [VCV_M]

VCV_M=

0.0244	0.0207	0.0127	0.0005	−0.0067	−0.0069	−0.0138	−0.0142	−0.0222	−0.0188
0.0207	0.0305	0.0186	0.0031	−0.0116	−0.0205	−0.0229	−0.0284	−0.0341	−0.0482
0.0127	0.0186	0.0403	0.0251	0.0007	−0.0172	−0.0313	−0.0331	−0.0441	−0.0409
0.0005	0.0031	0.0251	0.0558	0.0388	0.0146	−0.0045	−0.0202	−0.0106	−0.0400
−0.0067	−0.0116	0.0007	0.0388	0.0680	0.0513	0.0302	0.0190	0.0026	0.0308
−0.0069	−0.0205	−0.0172	0.0146	0.0513	0.0728	0.0586	0.0403	0.0316	0.0194
−0.0138	−0.0229	−0.0313	−0.0045	0.0302	0.0586	0.0721	0.0545	0.0264	0.0135
−0.0142	−0.0284	−0.0331	−0.0202	0.0190	0.0403	0.0545	0.0813	0.0484	−0.0103
−0.0222	−0.0341	−0.0441	−0.0106	0.0026	0.0316	0.0264	0.0484	0.1248	−0.0526
−0.0188	−0.0482	−0.0409	−0.0400	0.0308	0.0194	0.0135	−0.0103	−0.0526	0.4691

6) Root mean squared error for differences between theoretical and market swaption volatilities

RSME = 4.6066e-005

7) Theoretical swaptions volatilities [Sig_theo]

Sig_theo=

0.2308	0.2301	0.2212	0.2091	0.1961	0.1861	0.1760	0.1690	0.1630	0.1590
0.2280	0.2150	0.2057	0.1940	0.1833	0.1740	0.1671	0.1620	0.1580	
0.2105	0.2010	0.1903	0.1800	0.1701	0.1630	0.1580	0.1550		
0.1968	0.1870	0.1772	0.1680	0.1600	0.1550	0.1510			
0.1839	0.1740	0.1652	0.1580	0.1510	0.1480				
0.1765	0.1674	0.1591	0.1524	0.1462					
0.1686	0.1608	0.1531	0.1468						
0.1604	0.1542	0.1470							
0.1525	0.1476								
0.1450									

8) Market swaptions volatilities [Sig]

Sig =

0.2270	0.2300	0.2210	0.2090	0.1960	0.1860	0.1760	0.1690	0.1630	0.1590
0.2240	0.2150	0.2050	0.1940	0.1830	0.1740	0.1670	0.1620	0.1580	
0.2090	0.2010	0.1900	0.1800	0.1700	0.1630	0.1580	0.1550		
0.1950	0.1870	0.1770	0.1680	0.1600	0.1550	0.1510			
0.1820	0.1740	0.1650	0.1580	0.1510	0.1480				
0.1746	0.1674	0.1590	0.1524	0.1462					
0.1672	0.1608	0.1530	0.1468						
0.1598	0.1542	0.1470							
0.1524	0.1476								
0.1450									

Comments

If we analyse the eigenvalues and eigenvectors we can see that we have obtained only one negative eigenvalue and of very small absolute value. If we take the absolute values of all eigenvalues, the negative eigenvalue will have eighth biggest value from the set of ten values. What is more, the first three biggest eigenvalues (0.4927, 0.2696, 0.1367) have much bigger values than other eigenvalues. The eigenvectors associated with first three biggest eigenvalues are presented on Figure 8.3:

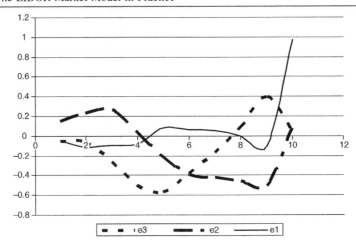

Figure 8.3 Eigenvectors associated with first three biggest eigenvalues for optimized Λ_i.

Although the eigenvectors do not have the typical humps presented in many books, these values generate very small differences between the theoretical and swaption volatilities.

The biggest differences are denoted for swaptions with one year length underlying swaps. There are practically no other significant differences in the volatilities for other maturities and underlying lengths. This suggests that this kind of calibration may be widely used in practice for valuation of various interest rate derivatives.

Let us see a graphical representation of optimized parameters Λ_i [Lambda].

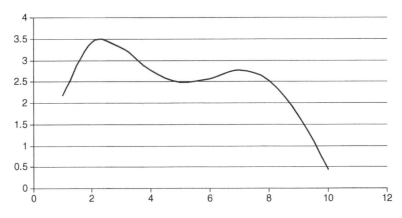

Figure 8.4 Parameters Λ_i obtained through optimization.

The values obtained through optimization are much different than for any arbitrary chosen function Λ_i presented in section 8.2. For such optimized parameters Λ_i give much a better RSME levels than previously presented. Recall that setting $\Lambda_i = \delta_i$ we had a RSME = 0.0013, setting $\Lambda_i = \sqrt{\delta_i}$ we have had a RSME = 0.0019, and in result of optimization we have obtained a RSME = 0.000046066.

Having presented the separated approach with optimization let us move on now to another widely used approach to the calibration to swaptions – which is called the locally single factor approach.

8.4   THE LOCALLY SINGLE FACTOR APPROACH

The locally single factor approach is based upon the assumption that the covariance matrices Φ^i are of single factor which means that $\varphi_{kl}^i - \varphi_{kl}^{i-1} = \varphi_k^i \varphi_l^i$ and $\varphi_{kl}^{-1} = 0$. Using this assumption we can write:

$$\varphi_{k+1}^k = \sqrt{\delta_k \sigma_{k,k+1}^2 - \sum_{j=0}^{k-1} \left(\varphi_{k+1}^j\right)^2}, \quad \varphi_N^k = \frac{\sqrt{\delta_k \sigma_{k,N}^2 - \sum_{j=0}^{k-1}\left(\sum_{i=k+1}^N R_{kN}^i(0)\varphi_i^j\right)^2} - \sum_{i=k+1}^{n-1} R_{kN}^i(0)\,\varphi_i^k}{R_{kN}^N(0)}$$

where

$$\delta_k = \delta\left(0 \div T_k\right) = \delta\left(k\right)$$

The matrix of market swaption volatilities can be arranged in a slightly different way.

$$\Sigma^{MKT} = \begin{bmatrix} \sigma_{0,1}^{MKT} & \sigma_{0,2}^{MKT} & \sigma_{0,3}^{MKT} & \cdots & \sigma_{0,m}^{MKT} & - & - & - & - \\ - & \sigma_{1,2}^{MKT} & \sigma_{1,3}^{MKT} & \cdots & \sigma_{1,m}^{MKT} & \sigma_{1,m+1}^{MKT} & - & - & - \\ - & - & \sigma_{2,3}^{MKT} & \cdots & \sigma_{2,m}^{MKT} & \sigma_{2,m+1}^{MKT} & \sigma_{2,m+2}^{MKT} & - & - \\ \cdots & \cdots & \cdots & \cdots & \cdots & \cdots & \cdots & \cdots & \cdots \\ - & - & - & \cdots & \sigma_{m-1,m}^{MKT} & \sigma_{m-1,m+1}^{MKT} & \sigma_{m-1,m+2}^{MKT} & \cdots & \sigma_{m-1,M}^{MKT} \end{bmatrix}_{m \times M}$$

Such arrangement allows us to construct a calibration algorithm in a little easier for practical implementation. The interpretation of the subscripts are presented below:

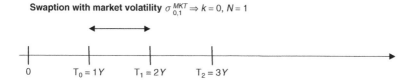

Swaption with market volatility $\sigma_{0,1}^{MKT} \Rightarrow k = 0, N = 1$

| 0 | $T_0 = 1Y$ | $T_1 = 2Y$ | $T_2 = 3Y$ |

Figure 8.5   Interpretation of swaption volatility.

Let us go to a practical example. We take market data for a swaption and appropriate discount factors only up to three years.

Example 8.2   Locally single factor calibration

Table 8.16 presents initial market data

Table 8.16   Market data – swaption volatility, discount factors

Swaption volatility		Underlying swap length		Discount factor
		1Y	2Y	
Option	T0 = 1Y	22.70 %	23.00 %	0.9774658
maturity	T1 = 2Y	22.40 %	21.50 %	0.9509789
	T2 = 3Y			0.9219838

For k = 0, N = 1 we have

$$\varphi_1^0 = \sqrt{\delta_0 \sigma_{0,1}^2 - \sum_{j=0}^{-1} \left(\varphi_1^j\right)^2} = \sqrt{\delta_0} \sigma_{0,1} = \sqrt{1} \cdot 22.70\% = 22.70\%.$$

For k = 0, N = 2 we have

$$\varphi_2^0 = \frac{\sqrt{\delta_0 \left(\sigma_{0,2}\right)^2 - \sum_{j=0}^{-1} \left(\sum_{i=1}^{2} R_{0,2}^i (0) \varphi_i^j\right)^2} - \sum_{i=1}^{1} R_{0,2}^i (0) \varphi_i^0}{R_{0,2}^2 (0)} =$$

$$= \frac{\sqrt{\delta_0 \left(\sigma_{0,2}\right)^2} - R_{0,2}^1 (0) \varphi_1^0}{R_{0,2}^2 (0)} = \frac{\sqrt{1} \cdot 23.00\% - 0.4774 \cdot 22.70\%}{0.5226} = 23.27\%.$$

For k = 1, N = 2 we have

$$\varphi_2^1 = \sqrt{\delta_1 \sigma_{1,2}^2 - \sum_{j=0}^{0} \left(\varphi_2^j\right)^2} = \sqrt{\delta_1 \left(\sigma_{1,2}\right)^2 - \left(\varphi_2^0\right)^2} = \sqrt{2 \cdot 22.40\%^2 - 23.27\%^2} = 21.49\%.$$

Finally we obtain

$$\varphi_{1,1}^0 - \varphi_{1,1}^{-1} = \varphi_1^0 \varphi_1^0 \Rightarrow \varphi_{1,1}^0 = \left(\varphi_1^0\right)^2 = 0.227^2 = 0.051529$$

$$\varphi_{1,2}^0 - \varphi_{1,2}^{-1} = \varphi_1^0 \varphi_2^0 \Rightarrow \varphi_{1,2}^0 = \varphi_1^0 \varphi_2^0 = 0.227 \cdot 0.2327 = 0.052832$$

$$\varphi_{2,2}^0 - \varphi_{2,2}^{-1} = \varphi_2^0 \varphi_2^0 \Rightarrow \varphi_{2,2}^0 = \left(\varphi_2^0\right)^2 = 0.2327^2 = 0.054168$$

$$\varphi_{2,2}^1 - \varphi_{2,2}^0 = \varphi_2^1 \varphi_2^1 \Rightarrow \varphi_{2,2}^1 = \left(\varphi_2^1\right)^2 + \varphi_{2,2}^0 = 0.2149^2 + 0.054168 = 0.100352$$

Going further we generate matrices Φ^i for the rest of the swaptions. These is shown below.

Table 8.17   Matrix with elements φ_k^i.

i/k	0	1	2	3	4	5	6	7	8	9
1	22.70%	0.00%	0.00%	0.00%	0.00%	0.00%	0.00%	0.00%	0.00%	0.00%
2	23.27%	21.49%	0.00%	0.00%	0.00%	0.00%	0.00%	0.00%	0.00%	0.00%
3	20.48%	20.85%	21.36%	0.00%	0.00%	0.00%	0.00%	0.00%	0.00%	0.00%
4	17.65%	19.60%	20.64%	20.03%	0.00%	0.00%	0.00%	0.00%	0.00%	0.00%
5	14.90%	17.69%	17.94%	20.83%	19.14%	0.00%	0.00%	0.00%	0.00%	0.00%
6	14.08%	14.32%	16.91%	17.55%	19.74%	21.05%	0.00%	0.00%	0.00%	0.00%
7	12.06%	14.16%	13.14%	16.95%	16.72%	21.51%	20.24%	0.00%	0.00%	0.00%
8	12.35%	13.04%	13.32%	12.88%	16.83%	16.53%	21.56%	18.91%	0.00%	0.00%
9	11.57%	13.72%	12.84%	13.51%	9.73%	17.39%	16.28%	21.67%	17.09%	0.00%
10	12.11%	12.62%	14.82%	10.53%	15.66%	7.05%	16.47%	15.65%	22.13%	12.92%

Table 8.18   Matrices Φ^i

i = 0	1	2	3	4	5	6	7	8	9	10
1	5.15%									
2	5.28%	5.42%								
3	4.65%	4.77%	4.20%							
4	4.01%	4.11%	3.62%	3.12%						
5	3.38%	3.47%	3.05%	2.63%	2.22%					
6	3.20%	3.28%	2.88%	2.49%	2.10%	1.98%				
7	2.74%	2.81%	2.47%	2.13%	1.80%	1.70%	1.46%			
8	2.80%	2.87%	2.53%	2.18%	1.84%	1.74%	1.49%	1.52%		
9	2.63%	2.69%	2.37%	2.04%	1.72%	1.63%	1.40%	1.43%	1.34%	
10	2.75%	2.82%	2.48%	2.14%	1.81%	1.71%	1.46%	1.50%	1.40%	1.47%

i = 1	1	2	3	4	5	6	7	8	9	10
2	10.04%									
3	9.25%	8.54%								
4	8.32%	7.70%	6.96%							
5	7.27%	6.74%	6.10%	5.35%						
6	6.35%	5.87%	5.29%	4.63%	4.03%					
7	5.85%	5.42%	4.90%	4.30%	3.73%	3.46%				
8	5.68%	5.25%	4.74%	4.15%	3.61%	3.34%	3.23%			
9	5.64%	5.23%	4.73%	4.15%	3.59%	3.34%	3.22%	3.22%		
10	5.53%	5.11%	4.61%	4.04%	3.51%	3.25%	3.14%	3.13%	3.06%	

...

i = 10	1	2	3	4	5	6	7	8	9	10
10										21.04%

Having this data, the instantaneous volatility vectors will have the following values:

Table 8.19 Instantaneous volatility vectors for locally single factor calibration

Index	$\gamma_1(t)$	$\gamma_2(t)$	$\gamma_3(t)$	$\gamma_4(t)$	$\gamma_5(t)$	$\gamma_6(t)$	$\gamma_7(t)$	$\gamma_8(t)$	$\gamma_9(t)$	$\gamma_{10}(t)$
1	22.70%	23.27%	20.48%	17.65%	14.90%	14.08%	12.06%	12.35%	11.57%	12.11%
2	0.00%	0.00%	0.00%	0.00%	0.00%	0.00%	0.00%	0.00%	0.00%	0.00%
...										
10	0.00%	0.00%	0.00%	0.00%	0.00%	0.00%	0.00%	0.00%	0.00%	0.00%

So in this case the instantaneous volatilities will be equal to the market swaption volatilities $\sigma_{i,i+1}^{MKT}$ for $i = 0, T_1, T_2, \ldots, T_9$.

Another popular way of calibration is calibration to swaptions using the historically computed correlations of forward rates.

8.5   CALIBRATION WITH HISTORICAL CORRELATIONS OF FORWARD RATES

Before we present the calibration algorithm we have to do preliminary computations. We have to compute a matrix of historical correlations.

The matrix of historical correlations will be computed using daily EUR interest rates taken from deposits and IRS (in both cases mid rates). The time series starts at 29-10-1999 and ends at 21-01-2005. Below is a graph presenting an example of historical EUR interest rates for 3 month deposit and 5Y IRS.

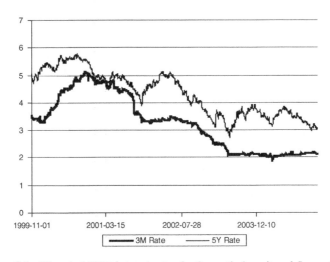

Figure 8.6 Historical EUR interest rates for 3 month deposit and 5 year IRS.

We will have to compute correlations between the rates of return from forward rates for EUR. We select the following intervals for forward rates.

3M-6M	4Y-5Y	9Y-10Y	15Y-16Y
6M-9M	5Y-6Y	10Y-11Y	16Y-17Y
9M-1Y	6Y-7Y	11Y-12Y	17Y-18Y
1Y-2Y	7Y-8Y	12Y-13Y	18Y-19Y
2Y-3Y	8Y-9Y	13Y-14Y	19Y-20Y
3Y-4Y		14Y-15Y	

All market data used in calculations was taken from Reuters.

The set of data consisted of daily-quoted closing bid and ask par rates for euro from $t = 29$ October 1999 to 20 January 2005 for the following tenors T_i

3M	2Y	6Y	10Y
6M	3Y	7Y	12Y
9M	4Y	8Y	15Y
1Y	5Y	9Y	20Y

The rates for tenors from 3M to 1Y came from the deposit market; the rates for tenors from 2Y to 20Y came from the IRS market.

Any missing records in the data, separately for bid and ask series, were interpolated using the formula

$$\widetilde{R}(t, t, T_i) = R(t - 1, t - 1, T_i)\left(1 + P_{t;t-1}\right)$$

where t indexes consecutive days, i indexes tenors T_i, $\widetilde{R}(t, t, T_i)$ is the interpolated par rate for day t and tenor T_i, $R(t - 1, t - 1, T_i)$ is the par rate taken from the previous day with the same tenor T_i and $P_{t;t-1}$ is the percentage market move, averaged across all bid or ask percentage changes for the rest of tenors

$$P_{t;t-1} = \frac{1}{n_{J^t}}\sum_{i \in J^t}^{n_{J^t}} p_{t;t-1}^i = \frac{1}{n_{J^t}}\sum_{i \in J^t}^{n_{J^t}} \frac{R(t, t, T_i) - R(t - 1, t - 1, T_i)}{R(t - 1, t - 1, T_i)} \times 100\,\%$$

In the above formula, J^t is the set of all i's for which data exists for day t, n_{J^t} is the total number of elements in set J^t and $p_{t;t-1}^i$ is the percentage change in $R(t, t, T_i)$, i.e. the change of par rate between day t and day $t - 1$ for tenor T_i.

After interpolating missing records, we obtained mid rates by averaging bid and ask rates for each tenor T_i

$$\mathbf{r}_m^i = \frac{\mathbf{r}_b^i + \mathbf{r}_a^i}{2}$$

where $\mathbf{r}_m^i$, $\mathbf{r}_b^i$ and $\mathbf{r}_a^i$ are vectors of mid, bid and ask rates, respectively.

The next step is to calculate par rates for the non-standard tenors: 11Y, 13Y, 14Y, 16Y, 17Y, 18Y and 19Y. We use linear interpolation

$$R(t, t, T_i) = \frac{R\left(t, t, T_{i_2}\right)\left(T_i - T_{i_1}\right) + R\left(t, t, T_{i_1}\right)\left(T_{i_2} - T_i\right)}{T_{i_2} - T_{i_2}}.$$

In the above expression, $R(t, t, T_i)$ is the par rate being interpolated for tenor T_i and $R\left(t, t, T_{i_1}\right)$, $R\left(t, t, T_{i_2}\right)$ are known par rates for tenor T_{i_1} and T_{i_2}, respectively. If, for example, $T_i = 17Y$, then $T_{i_1} = 15Y$ and $T_{i_2} = 20Y$.

The discount factors were calculated as follows.

As par rates for euros are quoted by Reuters in the Act/360 convention, the discount factors up to 1Y were determined using the following formula

$$B(t, T_i) = \left(1 + R(t, t, T_i) \times \frac{T^j}{360}\right)^{-1}$$

where $B(t, T_i)$ denotes the discount factor for day t and for tenor T_i. In this case we have $T_i = 90, 180, 270$ and 360.

For tenors 2Y and above, discount factors were calculated using the standard bootstrapping technique

$$B(t, T_i) = \frac{1 - R(t, t, T_i) \times \sum_{k=1}^{j-1} B(t, T_k)}{1 + B(t, T_k)}$$

The discount factors for future periods were calculated using the relationship:

$$B(i, T_i, T_{i+1}) = \frac{B(t, T_{i+1})}{B(t, T_i)}$$

where $B(t, T_i, T_{i+1})$ denotes the discount factor for future period $T_i \div T_{i+1}$.

Now that all the discount factors have been calculated for the future periods, we are able to calculate forward rates. In continuous compounding, forward rates f for tenors up to 1Y may be expressed as

$$B(t, T_i, T_{i+1}) = e^{-\frac{T_i}{360} F(t, T_i, T_{i+1})} \Rightarrow L(t, T_i, T_{i+1}) = -\frac{360}{T^j} \ln B(t, T_i, T_{i+1})$$

where $T_i = 90, 180, 270$ and 360. For tenors 2Y and above, we can write

$$B(t, T_i, T_{i+1}) = e^{-\frac{1Y}{360} \times F(t, T_i, T_{i+1})} \Rightarrow L(t, T_i, T_{i+1}) = -\ln B(t, T_i, T_{i+1}).$$

Next we calculate rates of return s from the forward rates. We defined the rates of return as follows

$$s_t^i = \ln \frac{L(t, T_i, T_{i+1})}{L(t-1, T_i, T_{i+1})}.$$

Finally we calculate correlations between the rates of return from the forward rates

$$Corr(s^i, s^k) = \frac{\sum_{t=1}^{N} (s_t^i - \bar{s}^i) \times (s_t^k - \bar{s}^k)}{\sqrt{\sum_{t=1}^{N} (s_t^i - \bar{s}^i)^2 \times \sum_{i=1}^{N} (s_t^k - \bar{s}^k)^2}}. \tag{8.2}$$

In the above formula $\bar{s}^i$ denotes the average of all rates of return in the series corresponding to tenor T_i.

The resulting correlation matrix is presented below.

Table 8.20 Historical correlation matrix of forward rates

	3M–6M	6M–9M	9M–1Y	1–2Y	2–3Y	3–4Y	4–5Y	5–6Y	6–7Y	7–8Y	8–9Y	9–10Y
3M–6M	1.000	0.128	0.214	0.159	0.223	0.200	0.155	0.082	0.046	0.020	0.074	−0.008
6M–9M	0.128	1.000	−0.072	0.179	0.199	0.200	0.215	0.065	0.062	0.056	0.069	−0.025
9M–1Y	0.214	−0.072	1.000	−0.016	0.202	0.164	0.126	0.050	0.041	0.115	0.023	−0.004
1Y–2Y	0.159	0.179	−0.016	1.000	0.513	0.379	0.354	0.259	0.134	0.124	0.155	−0.005
2Y–3Y	0.223	0.199	0.202	0.513	1.000	0.208	0.194	0.168	0.128	0.204	0.059	0.002
3Y–4Y	0.200	0.200	0.164	0.379	0.208	1.000	0.149	0.142	0.164	0.072	0.110	0.013
4Y–5Y	0.155	0.215	0.126	0.354	0.194	0.149	1.000	−0.176	0.133	0.019	0.161	−0.010
5Y–6Y	0.082	0.065	0.050	0.259	0.168	0.142	−0.176	1.000	−0.121	0.260	0.055	0.007
6Y–7Y	0.046	0.062	0.041	0.134	0.128	0.164	0.133	−0.121	1.000	−0.128	0.062	0.015
7Y–8Y	0.020	0.056	0.115	0.124	0.204	0.072	0.019	0.260	−0.128	1.000	−0.359	−0.011
8Y–9Y	0.074	0.069	0.023	0.155	0.059	0.110	0.161	0.055	0.062	−0.359	1.000	−0.709
9–10Y	−0.008	−0.025	−0.004	−0.005	0.002	0.013	−0.010	0.007	0.015	−0.011	−0.709	1.000
14–15Y	0.071	0.131	0.086	0.308	0.310	0.296	0.222	0.249	0.180	0.193	0.123	0.018
19–20Y	0.041	−0.003	0.066	0.126	0.113	0.167	0.114	0.128	0.199	0.126	0.075	0.023

	10Y–11Y	11Y–12Y	12Y–13Y	13Y–14Y	14Y–15Y	15Y–16Y	16Y–17Y	17Y–18Y	18Y–19Y	19Y–20Y	10Y–11Y	11Y–12Y
3M–6M	1.000	0.128	0.214	0.159	0.223	0.200	0.155	0.082	0.046	0.020	0.074	−0.008
6M–9M	0.128	1.000	−0.072	0.179	0.199	0.200	0.215	0.065	0.062	0.056	0.069	−0.025
9M–1Y	0.214	−0.072	1.000	−0.016	0.202	0.164	0.126	0.050	0.041	0.115	0.023	−0.004
1Y–2Y	0.159	0.179	−0.016	1.000	0.513	0.379	0.354	0.259	0.134	0.124	0.155	−0.005
2Y–3Y	0.223	0.199	0.202	0.513	1.000	0.208	0.194	0.168	0.128	0.204	0.059	0.002
3Y–4Y	0.200	0.200	0.164	0.379	0.208	1.000	0.149	0.142	0.164	0.072	0.110	0.013
4Y–5Y	0.155	0.215	0.126	0.354	0.194	0.149	1.000	−0.176	0.133	0.019	0.161	−0.010
5Y–6Y	0.082	0.065	0.050	0.259	0.168	0.142	−0.176	1.000	−0.121	0.260	0.055	0.007
6Y–7Y	0.046	0.062	0.041	0.134	0.128	0.164	0.133	−0.121	1.000	−0.128	0.062	0.015
7Y–8Y	0.020	0.056	0.115	0.124	0.204	0.072	0.019	0.260	−0.128	1.000	−0.359	−0.011
8Y–9Y	0.074	0.069	0.023	0.155	0.059	0.110	0.161	0.055	0.062	−0.359	1.000	−0.709
9–10Y	−0.008	−0.025	−0.004	−0.005	0.002	0.013	−0.010	0.007	0.015	−0.011	−0.709	1.000
14–15Y	0.071	0.131	0.086	0.308	0.310	0.296	0.222	0.249	0.180	0.193	0.123	0.018
19–20Y	0.041	−0.003	0.066	0.126	0.113	0.167	0.114	0.128	0.199	0.126	0.075	0.023

The results seem to be a little unexpected. We have obtained a lot of negative historical correlations. Perhaps this is due to the fact that market of forward rates is not as effective as everybody thinks. The presence of negative correlations creates a possibility of statistical arbitrage. That means one can construct instruments that will use the information about negative historical correlations and make an arbitrage opportunity if any counterparty does not have information about the presented fact.

Let us denote the computed correlation matrix by Ψ. Our goal is to obtain the VCV matrices. We may use for that universal volatility function presented in Chapter 4 'Swaption Pricing and Calibration'. Using this we specify formulae for φ_{m+1}^m:

$$\varphi_1^0 = \sigma_{01}, \quad \varphi_{k+1}^k = \sqrt{\delta_k \sigma_{k,k+1}^2 - \sum_{j=0}^{k-1}\left(\varphi_{k+1}^j\right)^2}$$

and the following quadratic equation for φ_N^m:

$$\left(\varphi_N^m R_{mN}^N(0)\right)^2 + 2\varphi_N^m R_{mN}^N(0)\sum_{i=m+1}^{N-1} R_{mN}^i(0)\psi_{iN}\varphi_i^m - \delta_m \sigma_{mN}^2 =$$

$$-\sum_{j=0}^{m-1}\sum_{l=m+1}^{N}\sum_{i=m+1}^{N} R_{mN}^i(0)\varphi_l^j\psi_{il}\varphi_i^j R_{mN}^l(0) - \sum_{l=m+1}^{N-1}\sum_{i=m+1}^{N-1} R_{mN}^i(0)\varphi_l^m\psi_{il}\varphi_i^m R_{mN}^l(0).$$

Let us present a practical example showing the necessary steps to compute the required VCV matrices:

Example 8.3   Calibration with historical correlations

Table 8.21 presents the initial market data for our example. The data is identical as for locally single factor calibration.

Table 8.21   Market data - swaption volatility, discount factors

Swaption volatility		Underlying swap length		Discount fact.
		1Y	2Y	
Option	T0 = 1Y	22.70 %	23.00 %	0.9774658
maturity	T1 = 2Y	22.40 %	21.50 %	0.9509789
	T2 = 3Y			0.9219838

For k = 0, N = 1 we have

$$\varphi_1^0 = \sqrt{\delta_0\sigma_{0,1}^2 - \sum_{j=0}^{-1}\left(\varphi_1^j\right)^2} = \sqrt{\delta_0}\sigma_{0,1} = \sqrt{1}\cdot 22.70\% = 22.70\%.$$

For k = 0, N = 2 we have

$$\left(\varphi_2^0\right)^2\left(R_{0,2}^2(0)\right)^2 + 2\varphi_2^0 R_{0,2}^2(0)\sum_{i=1}^{1} R_{0,2}^i(0)\,\psi_{i,2}\varphi_i^0 - \delta_0\left(\sigma_{0,2}\right)^2 =$$

$$\sum_{j=0}^{-1}\sum_{l=1}^{2}\sum_{i=1}^{2} R_{0,2}^i(0)\,\varphi_l^j\psi_{i,l}\varphi_i^j R_{0,2}^l(0) - \sum_{l=1}^{1}\sum_{i=1}^{1} R_{0,2}^i(0)\,\varphi_l^0\psi_{i,l}\varphi_i^0 R_{0,2}^l(0)$$

$$\left(\varphi_2^0\right)^2\left(R_{0,2}^2(0)\right)^2 + 2\varphi_2^0 R_{0,2}^2(0) R_{0,2}^1(0)\,\psi_{1,2}\varphi_1^0 - \delta_0\left(\sigma_{0,2}\right)^2 + R_{0,2}^1(0)\,\varphi_1^0\psi_{1,1}\varphi_1^0 R_{0,2}^1(0) = 0 \Rightarrow$$

$$0.5226^2\cdot\left(\varphi_2^0\right)^2 + 2\cdot 0.5226\cdot 0.4774\cdot 0.5133\cdot 22.70\%\cdot\left(\varphi_2^0\right) - 1\cdot(23.00\%)^2$$

$$+ 0.4774^2\cdot 22.70\%^2\cdot 1 = 0$$

$$0.2731\cdot\left(\varphi_2^0\right)^2 + 0.0581\cdot\left(\varphi_2^0\right) - 0.0412 = 0 \Rightarrow \varphi_2^0 = -50.90\% \text{ or } \varphi_2^0 = 29.61\%$$

For our calibration case we take the positive value $\varphi_2^0 = 29.61\%$.

For k = 1, N = 2 we have

$$\varphi_2^1 = \sqrt{\delta_1\sigma_{1,2}^2 - \sum_{j=0}^{0}\left(\varphi_2^j\right)^2} = \sqrt{\delta_1\left(\sigma_{1,2}\right)^2 - \left(\varphi_2^0\right)^2} = \sqrt{2\cdot 22.40\%^2 - 29.61\%^2} = 11.26\%$$

Finally we obtain:

$$\varphi_{1,1}^0 - \varphi_{1,1}^{-1} = \varphi_1^0 \varphi_1^0 \Rightarrow \varphi_{1,1}^0 = \left(\varphi_1^0\right)^2 = 0.227^2 = 0.051529$$

$$\varphi_{1,2}^0 - \varphi_{1,2}^{-1} = \varphi_1^0 \varphi_2^0 \Rightarrow \varphi_{1,2}^0 = \varphi_1^0 \varphi_2^0 = 0.227 \cdot 0.2961 = 0.067209$$

$$\varphi_{2,2}^0 - \varphi_{2,2}^{-1} = \varphi_2^0 \varphi_2^0 \Rightarrow \varphi_{2,2}^0 = \left(\varphi_2^0\right)^2 = 0.2961^2 = 0.087661$$

$$\varphi_{2,2}^1 - \varphi_{2,2}^0 = \varphi_2^1 \varphi_2^1 \Rightarrow \varphi_{2,2}^1 = \left(\varphi_2^1\right)^2 + \varphi_{2,2}^0 = 0.1126^2 + 0.087661 = 0.100340$$

We can go further and compute the whole matrix with elements φ_N^m. For this we can specify parameters a,b,c in the following way:

$$a = \left(R_{mN}^N(0)\right)^2$$

$$b = 2R_{mN}^N(0) \sum_{i=m+1}^{N-1} R_{mN}^i(0) \psi_{iN} \varphi_i^m$$

$$c = \sum_{j=0}^{m-1} \sum_{l=m+1}^{N} \sum_{i=m+1}^{N} R_{mN}^i(0) \varphi_l^j \psi_{il} \varphi_i^j R_{mN}^l(0) + \sum_{l=m+1}^{N-1} \sum_{i=m+1}^{n-1} R_{mN}^i(0) \varphi_l^m \psi_{il} \varphi_i^m R_{mN}^l(0) - \delta_m \sigma_{mN}^2$$

and compute

$$\Delta = b^2 - 4ac$$

$$\left(\varphi_N^m\right)_1 = \frac{-b-\sqrt{\Delta}}{2a}$$

$$\left(\varphi_N^m\right)_2 = \frac{-b-\sqrt{\Delta}}{2a}$$

i.e. solutions of a quadratic equation. However one can find that for some specific market data (swaption volatilities) and historical correlations the parameter Δ may have a negative value. This is the case for φ_3^2 for our market data taken from 25 January 2005. Let us see that $(k=2, N=3)$:

$$\varphi_3^2 = \sqrt{\delta_2 \sigma_{2,3}^2 - \sum_{j=0}^{1} \left(\varphi_3^j\right)^2} = \sqrt{\delta_2 \sigma_{2,3}^2 - \left(\varphi_3^0\right)^2 - \left(\varphi_3^1\right)^2} = \sqrt{3 \cdot 20.90\,\%^2 - 34.63\,\%^2 - 29.34\,\%^2}$$

$$= \sqrt{-7.50\,\%}$$

We have obtained square root from a negative value and the whole algorithm will collapse for that set of market data. On the other hand this situation is not a general rule which means that for another set of data the algorithm may give proper results.

We now present another calibration algorithm to co-terminal swaptions.

8.6   CALIBRATION TO CO-TERMINAL SWAPTIONS

Another widely used technique for BGM calibration is calibration to co-terminal swaptions. Figure 8.7 presents the idea of that calibration.

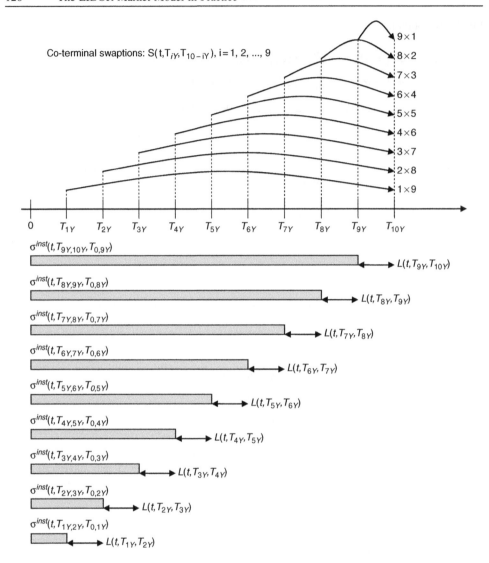

Figure 8.7   Set of co-terminal swaptions and instantaneous volatilities of forward rates.

We can see in the figure a set of nine co-terminal swaptions. Co-terminal swaptions are swaptions which expire at the same time (in our case T_{10Y}) and maturities increases through time, e.g. by one year per swaption. In our case we consider the following co-terminal swaptions: 9×1, 8×2, 7×3, 6×4, 5×5, 4×6, 3×7, 2×8, 1×9. Table 8.22 presents also a set of forward rates $L(t, T_{iY}, T_{i+1Y})$ and corresponding instantaneous volatilities of $\sigma^{inst}(t, T_{iY,i+1Y}, T_{0,iY})$ which are constant through periods $0 \div iY$.

The first step of the calibration will be deriving the forward swap rates for the considered co-terminal swaptions.

Step 1: Derivation of the forward swap rates for a co-terminal swaption

Because we have derived forward swap rates in one of our previous exercises, we present now only the results of the derivation. Table 8.22 below presents forward swap rates and additionally forward rates together with ATM swaption volatilities.

Table 8.22   Forward rates, swap rates and swaption ATM volatilities

Forward rate		Swap rate		Swaption volatility	
$L(0, T_{9Y}, T_{10Y})$	4.534 %	$S(0, T_{9Y}, T_{10Y})$	4.534 %	$\sigma^{swpt}(0, T_{9Y}, T_{10Y})$	15.24 %
$L(0, T_{8Y}, T_{9Y})$	4.520 %	$S(0, T_{8Y}, T_{10Y})$	4.527 %	$\sigma^{swpt}(0, T_{8Y}, T_{10Y})$	15.42 %
$L(0, T_{7Y}, T_{8Y})$	4.312 %	$S(0, T_{7Y}, T_{10Y})$	4.452 %	$\sigma^{swpt}(0, T_{7Y}, T_{10Y})$	15.30 %
$L(0, T_{6Y}, T_{7Y})$	4.152 %	$S(0, T_{6Y}, T_{10Y})$	4.372 %	$\sigma^{swpt}(0, T_{6Y}, T_{10Y})$	15.24 %
$L(0, T_{5Y}, T_{6Y})$	3.906 %	$S(0, T_{5Y}, T_{10Y})$	4.271 %	$\sigma^{swpt}(0, T_{5Y}, T_{10Y})$	15.10 %
$L(0, T_{4Y}, T_{5Y})$	3.675 %	$S(0, T_{4Y}, T_{10Y})$	4.161 %	$\sigma^{swpt}(0, T_{4Y}, T_{10Y})$	15.50 %
$L(0, T_{3Y}, T_{4Y})$	3.400 %	$S(0, T_{3Y}, T_{10Y})$	4.039 %	$\sigma^{swpt}(0, T_{3Y}, T_{10Y})$	15.80 %
$L(0, T_{2Y}, T_{3Y})$	3.102 %	$S(0, T_{2Y}, T_{10Y})$	3.906 %	$\sigma^{swpt}(0, T_{2Y}, T_{10Y})$	16.20 %
$L(0, T_{1Y}, T_{2Y})$	2.747 %	$S(0, T_{1Y}, T_{10Y})$	3.758 %	$\sigma^{swpt}(0, T_{1Y}, T_{10Y})$	16.30 %

Let us remember also results of the weights used for forward swap derivation that will be used in the calibration.

Table 8.23   Weights for swap rates

	2y	3y	4y	5y	6y	7y	8y	9y	10y
$9y \times 1y$									1
$8y \times 2y$								0.509736	0.490264
$7y \times 3y$							0.347558	0.332573	0.319869
$6y \times 4y$						0.266116	0.255067	0.24407	0.234747
$5y \times 5y$					0.216549	0.208489	0.199832	0.191217	0.183912
$4y \times 6y$				0.18453	0.176589	0.170017	0.162957	0.155931	0.149975
$3y \times 7y$			0.160158	0.154976	0.148307	0.142787	0.136858	0.130958	0.125955
$2y \times 8y$		0.142109	0.137398	0.132953	0.127231	0.122496	0.11741	0.112347	0.108056
$1y \times 9y$	0.127793	0.123949	0.11984	0.115962	0.110972	0.106842	0.102405	9.80E-02	0.094247

Now we are ready to move to step 2 of the co-terminal calibration. This step is very similar to the bootstrapping technique widely used in the market.

Step 2: The Bootstrapping technique for instantaneous volatility

We start our algorithm from the derivation of instantaneous volatility for the forward rate $F(t, T_{9Y}, T_{10Y})$. We assume that such volatility will be constant through all the period before our forward rate will be known, i.e. in the period: $0 \div 9Y$. We will use previously computed approximations of swaption volatility by instantaneous volatility of forward rates. For the first period the computations will be straightforward, and the volatilities for all other periods $0 \div 8Y$ for rate $F(t, T_{8Y}, T_{9Y})$, $0 \div 7Y$ for rate $F(t, T_{7Y}, T_{8Y})$ and so on, will be computed based on the results obtained in the previous steps. We also assume, that all instantaneous correlations between the forward rates are equal to one. Let us start our computations:

Period: $\underline{0 \div 9Y}$ for forward rate $F(t, T_{9Y}, T_{10Y})$

The market swaption volatility will be approximated by:

$$\sigma^{swpt}\left(t, T_{9Y}, T_{10Y}\right)^2 = \frac{w_{10Y}^{10Y,10Y}(0)^2 L\left(0, T_{9Y}, T_{10Y}\right)^2}{\delta_{0,9Y} S\left(0, T_{9Y}, T_{10Y}\right)^2} \delta_{0,9Y} \sigma^{inst}\left(0, T_{9Y,10Y}, T_{0,9Y}\right)^2$$

$$= \frac{1^2 \cdot 4.534^2 \cdot 1}{4.534^2} \cdot \sigma^{inst}\left(0, T_{9Y,10Y}, T_{0,9Y}\right)^2 = \sigma^{inst}\left(0, T_{9Y,10Y}, T_{0,9Y}\right)^2$$

$$\Rightarrow \sigma^{inst}\left(0, T_{9Y,10Y}, T_{0,9Y}\right) = 15.25\,\%$$

Period: $0 \div 8Y$ for forward rate $F\left(t, T_{8Y}, T_{9Y}\right)$

$$\sigma^{swpt}\left(t, T_{8Y}, T_{10Y}\right)^2 = \frac{w_{9Y}^{9Y,10Y}(0)^2 L\left(0, T_{8Y}, T_{9Y}\right)^2}{S\left(0, T_{8Y}, T_{10Y}\right)^2} \sigma^{inst}\left(0, T_{8Y,9Y}, T_{0,8Y}\right)^2$$

$$+ \frac{w_{10Y}^{9Y,10Y}(0)^2 L\left(0, T_{9Y}, T_{10Y}\right)^2}{S\left(0, T_{8Y}, T_{10Y}\right)^2} \sigma^{inst}\left(0, T_{9Y,10Y}, T_{0,9Y}\right)^2$$

$$+ 2 \cdot \frac{w_{9Y}^{9Y,10Y}(0)\, w_{10Y}^{9Y,10Y}(0)\, L\left(0, T_{8Y}, T_{9Y}\right) L\left(0, T_{9Y}, T_{10Y}\right)}{S\left(0, T_{8Y}, T_{10Y}\right)^2} \sigma^{inst}\left(0, T_{8Y,9Y}, T_{0,8Y}\right)$$

$$\times \sigma^{inst}\left(0, T_{9Y,10Y}, T_{0,9Y}\right).$$

We have obtained a quadratic equation with unknown $\sigma^{inst}\left(0, T_{8Y,9Y}, T_{0,8Y}\right)$. The value of instantaneous volatility $\sigma^{inst}\left(0, T_{9Y,10Y}, T_{0,9Y}\right)$ has been obtained from the previous step. We can rearrange the above equation into a classic quadratic equation. Putting in the real market data we can write:

$$A_{8Y,9Y}\sigma^{inst}\left(0, T_{8Y,9Y}, T_{0,8Y}\right)^2 + B_{8Y,9Y}\sigma^{inst}\left(0, T_{8Y,9Y}, T_{0,8Y}\right) + C_{8Y,9Y} = 0 \Leftrightarrow$$

$$\Leftrightarrow 0.0005309 \cdot \sigma^{inst}\left(0, T_{8Y,9Y}, T_{0,8Y}\right)^2 + 0.0001561 \cdot \sigma^{inst}\left(0, T_{8Y,9Y}, T_{0,8Y}\right) - 0.0000373 = 0 \Leftrightarrow$$

$$\Leftrightarrow \sigma^{inst}\left(0, T_{8Y,9Y}, T_{0,8Y}\right) = 15.06\,\% \quad \text{or} \quad \sigma^{inst}\left(0, T_{8Y,9Y}, T_{0,8Y}\right) = -75.85\,\%$$

We take into account only positive values. We show below the required computations in the next period. Other computations will be very similar.

Period: $0 \div 7Y$ for forward rate $F\left(t, T_{7Y}, T_{8Y}\right)$

$$\sigma^{swpt}\left(t, T_{7Y}, T_{10Y}\right)^2 = \frac{w_{8Y}^{8Y,10Y}(0)^2 L\left(0, T_{7Y}, T_{8Y}\right)^2}{S\left(0, T_{7Y}, T_{10Y}\right)^2} \sigma^{inst}\left(0, T_{7Y,8Y}, T_{0,7Y}\right)^2$$

$$+ \frac{w_{9Y}^{8Y,10Y}(0)^2 L\left(0, T_{8Y}, T_{9Y}\right)^2}{S\left(0, T_{7Y}, T_{10Y}\right)^2} \sigma^{inst}\left(0, T_{8Y,9Y}, T_{0,8Y}\right)^2$$

$$+ \frac{w_{10Y}^{8Y,10Y}(0)^2 L\left(0, T_{9Y}, T_{10Y}\right)^2}{S\left(0, T_{7Y}, T_{10Y}\right)^2} \sigma^{inst}\left(0, T_{9Y,10Y}, T_{0,9Y}\right)^2$$

$$+ 2 \cdot \frac{w_{8Y}^{8Y,10Y}(0)\, w_{9Y}^{8Y,10Y}(0)\, L\left(0, T_{7Y}, T_{8Y}\right) L\left(0, T_{8Y}, T_{9Y}\right)}{S\left(0, T_{8Y}, T_{10Y}\right)^2} \sigma^{inst}\left(0, T_{7Y,8Y}, T_{0,7Y}\right)$$

$$\times \sigma^{inst}\left(0, T_{8Y,9Y}, T_{0,8Y}\right) + 2 \cdot \frac{w_{8Y}^{8Y,10Y}(0)\, w_{10Y}^{8Y,10Y}(0)\, L\left(0, T_{7Y}, T_{8Y}\right) L\left(0, T_{9Y}, T_{10Y}\right)}{S\left(0, T_{8Y}, T_{10Y}\right)^2}$$

$$\times \sigma^{inst}\left(0, T_{7Y,8Y}, T_{0,7Y}\right) \sigma^{inst}\left(0, T_{9Y,10Y}, T_{0,9Y}\right)$$

$$+2 \cdot \frac{w_{9Y}^{8Y,10Y}(0)\, w_{10Y}^{8Y,10Y}(0)\, L(0,T_{8Y},T_{9Y})\, L(0,T_{9Y},T_{10Y})}{S(0,T_{8Y},T_{10Y})^2} \sigma^{inst}(0,T_{8Y,9Y},T_{0,8Y})$$

$$\times \sigma^{inst}(0,T_{9Y,10Y},T_{0,9Y})$$

Once again we have obtained a quadratic equation with unknown $\sigma^{inst}(0,T_{7Y,8Y},T_{0,7Y})$. In this step the values of the instantaneous volatilities $\sigma^{inst}(0,T_{9Y,10Y},T_{0,9Y})$ and $\sigma^{inst}(0,T_{8Y,9Y},T_{0,8Y})$ have been obtained from previous steps. We can rearrange above equation into a classic quadratic equation. Substituting in real market data we can write:

$$A_{7Y,8Y}\sigma^{inst}(0,T_{7Y,8Y},T_{0,7Y})^2 + B_{7Y,8Y}\sigma^{inst}(0,T_{7Y,8Y},T_{0,7Y}) + C_{7Y,8Y} = 0 \Leftrightarrow$$

$$\Leftrightarrow 0.0002246 \cdot \sigma^{inst}(0,T_{7Y,8Y},T_{0,7Y})^2 + 0.0001365 \cdot \sigma^{inst}(0,T_{7Y,8Y},T_{0,7Y}) - 0.0000257 = 0 \Leftrightarrow$$

$$\Leftrightarrow \sigma^{inst}(0,T_{7Y,8Y},T_{0,7Y}) = 15.06\% \text{ or } \sigma^{inst}(0,T_{7Y,8Y},T_{0,7Y}) = -105.55\%$$

Again we take into account only positive values.

The results for other periods are presented in Table 8.24.

Table 8.24 Calibration results to co-terminal swaptions

i	$A_{iY,i+1Y}$	$B_{iY,i+1Y}$	$C_{iY,i+1Y}$	$\sigma^{inst}(0,T_{iY,i+1Y},T_{0,iY})$	
9Y				15.24%	
8Y	0.0005309	0.0001561	−0.0000373	15.59%	−45.00%
7Y	0.0002246	0.0001365	−0.0000257	15.06%	−75.85%
6Y	0.0001221	0.0001105	−0.0000194	15.06%	−105.55%
5Y	0.0000716	0.0000883	−0.0000143	14.49%	−137.91%
4Y	0.0000460	0.0000713	−0.0000140	17.60%	−172.61%
3Y	0.0000296	0.0000594	−0.0000114	17.62%	−218.04%
2Y	0.0000194	0.0000482	−0.0000101	19.38%	−267.58%
1Y	0.0000123	0.0000387	−0.0000071	17.36%	−331.63%

Our results seem to be sensible. We can observe the typical hump of volatility between years 1 and 3. The result is similar to that obtained via calibration to caps.

8.7 CONCLUSIONS

This chapter was dedicated to presenting calibration algorithms to caps and swaptions. All the algorithms were non parametric. We have started with a separated approach. Based on the market data taken from particular working day we have obtained results of the calibration as a set of covariance matrices. Many of the matrices had negative eigenvalues so we have transformed them by eliminating the eigenvectors associated with the negative eigenvalues. Our results seem to be right for some of the variants of the calibration. For two parameters of Λ_i we have presented the algorithms of calibration in more detail. For these two cases we have showed how to compute instantaneous volatility vectors. We also compared the root mean squared errors between the theoretical and market swaption volatilities. The best results occurred for two forms of parameters Λ_i when equal to time δ_i specified as a day count fraction and next when equal to a squared root of time $\sqrt{\delta_i}$.

In the next section the separated approach was developed further. As a target function we have set a root mean squared error for differences between theoretical and market swaption volatilities. We have minimized that function under several restrictions for VCV. We have postulated that the VCV matrix must be positive definite. For that case we have implemented a subalgorithm for reducing VCV matrix by removing eigenvectors associated with negative eigenvalues. Results here were very good. There were much better than for any arbitrary chosen function Λ_i.

In the chapter we have also presented an approach called locally single factor. After defining initial assumptions and the constituting algorithm we have moved to results. In this simple calibration we have obtained instantaneous volatilities of forward rates equal to one year swaptions. This will be always the case as long as we are interested in obtaining instantaneous volatilities for one-year forward rates and we choose for calibration swaptions with underlying swaps length also equal to one year and paying once a year.

After that we have moved into calibration to swaptions given an exogenously instantaneous correlation matrix of forward LIBOR rates. The correlations were computed from historical data. We have presented the method of obtaining historical correlations and also computed the correlation matrix for particular working day. The results are completely unexpected. We have seen forward correlations that are close to one. Unfortunately there were a lot of negative correlations. One reason may be that the historical data is not totally accurate. The data was taken from one of most popular financial services as closing prices for LIBOR's and IRS quotations. We used a bootstrapping technique to obtain zero coupon rates and after that forward zero coupon rates. The data has daily frequency and it is possible that some marginal computation technique during interpolation caused it to have too much influence on the final results. Nevertheless one should be very careful if it was decided to use this technique in practice. It is worthy to mention that some other research obtains quite good results of historical correlations but they used data from zero coupon bonds. We still think that taking data from IRS market should be more appropriate because of the nature of LIBOR Market Model which is dedicated mainly to the money market.

The last part of the chapter was dedicated to calibration to co-terminal swaptions. Co-terminal swaptions were such swaptions which expire at the same time and maturities increased through time, e.g. by one year per swaption. We have presented all necessary steps for calibration and computed the final result. All the results seem to be very sensible. We have observed a typical hump of volatility between years 1 and 3. The results were also very similar to obtained via calibration only to caps using assumption of volatility dependency only on time to maturity.

Please be aware that the presented algorithms should be used in practice for those interest rate instruments which by nature are close to the swaption market. A classical example may be any Bermudan swaption. An example of pricing a Bermudan swaption using calibration to co-terminal swaption is presented in Chapter 10.

We have presented many variations of non-parametric calibration to swaptions. This is a good time now to move onto parametric calibration algorithms to caps and swaptions simultaneously based on optimization techniques. In the next chapter we present at the beginning non parametric calibration to caps and swaptions based on the Rebonato approach and then simultaneous parametric calibration to caps and swaptions.

9

Calibration Algorithms to Caps and Swaptions Based on Optimization Techniques

9.1 INTRODUCTION

The previous chapter was dedicated to calibration algorithms to swaptions. We have presented a separated approach, a Longstaff-Schwartz-Santa Clara approach, a locally single factor method, a calibration with historical correlations and finally a calibration to co-terminal swaptions. Some of the algorithms should be used very carefully in practice. The locally single factor may lead to negative variances and the calibration with historical correlations may lead to negative correlations.

This chapter describes simultaneous calibration approaches to caps and swaptions. The first algorithm is non-parametric, whilst the second parametric. The non-parametric calibration is based on the Rebonato approach. At the beginning we derive annual caplet volatilities driven by the dynamics of annual forward rates from the dynamics of quarterly forward rates. It is very important to notice that some market participants often forget about such a transformation. The consequence may be wrong calibration results and mispriced derivative instruments.

Next we compute forward swap rates and present an approximation of the swaption formula for LIBOR Market Model as a linear combination of forward LIBOR rates. In the calibration we use also piecewise – constant instantaneous volatilities described in Chapter 7. Finally we constitute an optimization function minimizing the difference between theoretical and market swaption volatilities. The result of the optimization is a matrix of annualized instantaneous volatilities and also instantaneous correlations. At the end we compare results of the theoretical and market caplet volatilities and the theoretical and market swaption volatilities.

The second part of the chapter is dedicated to parametric calibration to caps and swaptions. First we use caplet volatilities derived in Chapter 7 and based on that constitute some appropriate parametric functions of caplet volatilities. Next we define optimization functions minimizing differences between theoretical and market caplet prices. After that we move into calibration to swaptions. For that reason we constitute another set parametric functions and run optimizations but now to minimize the differences between the theoretical and market quotations of swaptions.

After presenting all the algorithms we move to analyse the results of such computations. Taking real market data (LIBOR rates, FRA, IRS, caps and swapations, historical correlations) from a particular working day we present in detail how the algorithms should be implemented in practice.

9.2   NON PARAMETRIC CALIBRATION TO CAPS AND SWAPTIONS

The first step before a simultaneous calibration to cap and swaptions is deriving annual caplet volatilities driven by the dynamic of annual forward rates from the dynamics of the quarterly forward rates.

Preliminary computations

We concentrate our computations on a particular case of four quarterly interest forward rates covering one particular one year period. If we do that, a generalization for all one year periods for all swaptions is straightforward.

The first step is to compute the ratios of discount factors as functions of quarterly forward rates.

$$
L\left(t, T_{k+i}, T_{k+i+1}\right) = \frac{1}{\delta_{k+i,k+i+1}} \left[\frac{B\left(t, T_{k+i}\right)}{B\left(t, T_{k+i+1}\right)} - 1 \right] \Rightarrow
$$

$$
\frac{B\left(t, T_{k+i}\right)}{B\left(t, T_{k+i+1}\right)} = \delta_{k+i,k+i+1} L\left(t, T_{k+i}, T_{k+i+1}\right) + 1
$$

for $i = 0, 1, 2, 3$.

Now we can express a one year forward rate covering the period $T_k \div T_{k+4}$ as functions of previously computed discount factor ratios

$$
L\left(t, T_k, T_{k+4}\right) = \frac{1}{\delta_{k,k+4}} \left[\frac{B\left(t, T_k\right)}{B\left(t, T_{k+4}\right)} - 1 \right]
$$

$$
= \frac{1}{\delta_{k,k+4}} \left[\frac{B\left(t, T_k\right)}{B\left(t, T_{k+1}\right)} \frac{B\left(t, T_{k+1}\right)}{B\left(t, T_{k+2}\right)} \frac{B\left(t, T_{k+2}\right)}{B\left(t, T_{k+3}\right)} \frac{B\left(t, T_{k+3}\right)}{B\left(t, T_{k+4}\right)} - 1 \right].
$$

Substituting the expression for fractions of discount factors from above expressions we obtain:

$$
L\left(t, T_k, T_{k+4}\right) = \frac{1}{\delta_{k,k+4}} \cdot
$$

$$
\left\{ \left[\delta_{k,k+1} L\left(t, T_k, T_{k+1}\right) + 1 \right] \left[\delta_{k+1,k+2} L\left(t, T_{k+1}, T_{k+2}\right) + 1 \right] \left[\delta_{k+2,k+3} L\left(t, T_{k+2}, T_{k+3}\right) + 1 \right] \right.
$$

$$
\left. \times \left[\delta_{k+3,k+4} L\left(t, T_{k+3}, T_{k+4}\right) + 1 \right] \right\}
$$

$$L\left(t, T_k, T_{k+4}\right) = \frac{1}{\delta_{k,k+4}} \cdot \tag{9.1}$$

$$
\left\{
\begin{aligned}
&1 + \delta_{k,k+1} L\left(t, T_k, T_{k+1}\right) + \delta_{k+1,k+2} L\left(t, T_{k+1}, T_{k+2}\right) + \delta_{k+2,k+3} L\left(t, T_{k+2}, T_{k+3}\right) + \delta_{k+3,k+4} L\left(t, T_{k+3}, T_{k+4}\right) \\
&+ \delta_{k,k+1} L\left(t, T_k, T_{k+1}\right) \delta_{k+1,k+2} L\left(t, T_{k+1}, T_{k+2}\right) + \delta_{k,k+1} L\left(t, T_k, T_{k+1}\right) \delta_{k+2,k+3} L\left(t, T_{k+2}, T_{k+3}\right) \\
&+ \delta_{k,k+1} L\left(t, T_k, T_{k+1}\right) \delta_{k+3,k+4} L\left(t, T_{k+3}, T_{k+4}\right) \\
&+ \delta_{k+1,k+2} L\left(t, T_{k+1}, T_{k+2}\right) \delta_{k+2,k+3} L\left(t, T_{k+2}, T_{k+3}\right) + \delta_{k+1,k+2} L\left(t, T_{k+1}, T_{k+2}\right) \delta_{k+3,k+4} L\left(t, T_{k+3}, T_{k+4}\right) \\
&+ \delta_{k+2,k+3} L\left(t, T_{k+2}, T_{k+3}\right) \delta_{k+3,k+4} L\left(t, T_{k+3}, T_{k+4}\right) \\
&+ \delta_{k,k+1} L\left(t, T_k, T_{k+1}\right) \delta_{k+1,k+2} L\left(t, T_{k+1}, T_{k+2}\right) \delta_{k+2,k+3} L\left(t, T_{k+2}, T_{k+3}\right) \\
&+ \delta_{k,k+1} L\left(t, T_k, T_{k+1}\right) \delta_{k+1,k+2} L\left(t, T_{k+1}, T_{k+2}\right) \delta_{k+3,k+4} L\left(t, T_{k+3}, T_{k+4}\right) \\
&+ \delta_{k,k+1} L\left(t, T_k, T_{k+1}\right) \delta_{k+2,k+3} L\left(t, T_{k+2}, T_{k+3}\right) \delta_{k+3,k+4} L\left(t, T_{k+3}, T_{k+4}\right) \\
&+ \delta_{k+1,k+2} L\left(t, T_{k+1}, T_{k+2}\right) \delta_{k+2,k+3} L\left(t, T_{k+2}, T_{k+3}\right) \delta_{k+3,k+4} L\left(t, T_{k+3}, T_{k+4}\right) \\
&+ \delta_{k,k+1} L\left(t, T_k, T_{k+1}\right) \delta_{k+1,k+2} L\left(t, T_{k+1}, T_{k+2}\right) \delta_{k+2,k+3} L\left(t, T_{k+2}, T_{k+3}\right) \delta_{k+3,k+4} L\left(t, T_{k+3}, T_{k+4}\right)
\end{aligned}
\right\}
$$

The dynamics of quarterly forward rates can be expressed under the measure Q^{k+4} as:

$$
\begin{aligned}
dL\left(t, T_k, T_{k+1}\right) = \\
&-\sigma_{k+i+1}^{inst}(t)\, F\left(t, T_{k+i}, T_{k+i+1}\right) \sum_{j=k+i+2}^{k+i+4} \frac{\rho_{k+i+1,j}\, \delta_{j-1,j}\, \sigma_j^{inst}(t)\, L\left(t, T_{j-1}, T_j\right)}{1 + \delta_{j-1,j} F\left(t, T_{j-1}, T_j\right)}\, dt \\
&+ \sigma_{k+i+1}^{inst}(t)\, F\left(t, T_{k+i}, T_{k+i+1}\right) dW_{k+i+1}^{k+4}(t)
\end{aligned}
\tag{9.2}
$$

for $i = 0, 1, 2, 3$

where $\rho_{k,j}$ denotes the instantaneous correlation between the forward rates $L(t, T_{k-1}, T_k)$ and $L(t, T_{j-1}, T_j)$, and $\sigma_{k+i}^{inst}(t) = \sigma^{inst}(t, T_{k+i}, T_{k+i+1})$, $i = 0, 1, 2, 3$ is the instantaneous volatility of the quarterly forward rate $L(t, T_{k+i}, T_{k+i+1})$, $i = 0, 1, 2, 3$.

The dynamic of annual the forward rate under the measure Q^{k+4} can be written:

$$dF\left(t, T_k, T_{k+4}\right) = \sigma(t)\, L\left(t, T_k, T_{k+4}\right) dW_{k+4}^{k+4}(t) \tag{9.3}$$

where $\sigma^{inst}(t) = \sigma^{inst}(t, T_k, T_{k+4})$ is the instantaneous volatility of the annual forward rate $L(t, T_k, T_{k+4})$.

Our goal is to derive an annual caplet volatility driven by the dynamic of the annual forward rate from the dynamics of quarterly forward rates. We present the algorithm based on the example for period $T_k \div T_{k+4}$ under the measure Q^{k+4}.

First we assume, that correlations between quarterly forward rates are equal to one.

Let us take logarithms of the dynamics presented by equations (9.2) and (9.3). Using Ito's lemma we have:

$$
\begin{aligned}
d\ln L\left(t, T_{k+i}, T_{k+i+1}\right) = &-\sigma_{k+i+1}^{inst}(t) \sum_{j=k+i+2}^{k+i+4} \frac{\rho_{k+i+1,j}\, \delta_{j-1,j}\, \sigma_j^{inst}(t)\, L\left(t, T_{j-1}, T_j\right)}{1 + \delta_{j-1,j} L\left(t, T_{j-1}, T_j\right)}\, dt \\
&- \frac{1}{2}\sigma_{k+i+1}^{inst}(t)^2\, dt + \sigma_{k+i+1}^{inst}(t)\, dW_{k+i+1}^{k+4}(t)
\end{aligned}
$$

for $i = 0, 1, 2, 3$ and

$$d \ln L(t, T_k, T_{k+4}) = -\frac{1}{2} \sigma^{inst}(t)^2 \, dt + \sigma^{inst}(t) \, dW_{k+4}^{k+4}(t)$$

For further computations we need the multi-dimensional Ito Lemma. In general if we have a function:

$$V(S_1, S_2, \ldots, S_n, t)$$

we can write

$$dV = \left(\frac{\partial V}{\partial t} + \frac{1}{2} \sum_{i=1}^{n} \sum_{j=1}^{n} \sigma_i \sigma_j \rho_{ij} S_i S_j \frac{\partial^2 V}{\partial S_i \partial S_j} \right) dt + \sum_{i=1}^{n} \frac{\partial V}{\partial S_i} \, dS_i. \tag{9.4}$$

In our case we need a four-dimensional version of the Ito lemma. For simplicity we can write:

$$L(t, T_k, T_{k+4}) = L_4^A(t)$$
$$L(t, T_{k+i}, T_{k+i+1}) = L_{i+1}^Q(t), \text{ for } i = 0, 1, 2, 3$$

and

$$\delta_{k,k+4} = \delta_4^A, \quad \delta_{k+i,k+i+1} = \delta_{i+1}^Q, \text{ for } i = 0, 1, 2, 3$$
$$\sigma_i^Q(t) = \sigma_{k+i}^{inst}(t), \text{ for } i = 1, 2, 3, 4.$$

So using four dimensional Ito we have:

$$L_4^A(t) = \frac{1}{\delta_4^A} \cdot$$

$$\begin{Bmatrix} \delta_1^Q L_1^Q(t) + \delta_2^Q L_2^Q(t) + \delta_3^Q L_3^Q(t) + \delta_4^Q L_4^Q(t) + \delta_1^Q L_1^Q(t) \delta_2^Q L_2^Q(t) + \delta_1^Q L_1^Q(t) \delta_3^Q L_3^Q(t) + \\ \delta_1^Q L_1^Q(t) \delta_4^Q L_4^Q(t) + \delta_2^Q L_2^Q(t) \delta_3^Q L_3^Q(t) + \delta_2^Q L_2^Q(t) \delta_4^Q L_4^Q(t) + \delta_3^Q L_3^Q(t) \delta_4^Q L_4^Q(t) + \\ \delta_1^Q L_1^Q(t) \delta_2^Q L_2^Q(t) \delta_3^Q L_3^Q(t) + \delta_1^Q L_1^Q(t) \delta_2^Q L_2^Q(t) \delta_4^Q L_4^Q(t) + \delta_1^Q L_1^Q(t) \delta_3^Q L_3^Q(t) \delta_4^Q L_4^Q(t) + \\ \delta_2^Q L_2^Q(t) \delta_3^Q L_3^Q(t) \delta_4^Q L_4^Q(t) + \delta_1^Q L_1^Q(t) \delta_2^Q L_2^Q(t) \delta_3^Q L_3^Q(t) \delta_4^Q L_4^Q(t) \end{Bmatrix}$$

and

$$\frac{\partial F_4^A(t)}{\partial F_i^Q(t)} = \frac{1}{\delta_4^A} \left[\delta_i^Q + \delta_i^Q \sum_{\substack{j=1 \\ j \neq i}}^{4} \delta_j^Q L_j^Q(t) + \delta_i^Q \sum_{\substack{j=1 \\ j \neq i}}^{3} \sum_{\substack{k=j+1 \\ k \neq i}}^{4} \delta_j^Q \delta_k^Q L_j^Q(t) L_k^Q(t) + \delta_4^A \prod_{\substack{j=1 \\ j \neq i}}^{4} L_j^Q(t) \right]$$

for $i = 0, 1, 2, 3$.

We do not need in our computations the term dt. So we can write:

$$dL_4^A(t) = (\ldots)\,dt + \frac{\partial L_4^A(t)}{\partial L_1^Q(t)}dL_1^Q(t) + \frac{\partial L_4^A(t)}{\partial L_2^Q(t)}dL_2^Q(t) + \frac{\partial L_4^A(t)}{\partial L_3^Q(t)}dL_3^Q(t) + \frac{\partial L_4^A(t)}{\partial L_4^Q(t)}dL_4^Q(t)$$

Then under the measure Q^4

$$dL_i^Q(t) = (\ldots)\,dt + \sigma_i^Q(t)\,L_i^Q(t)\,dW_i^4(t),\ \text{ for } i = 1,2,3,4$$

where:

$$dW_i^4(t)\,dW_j^4(t) = \rho_{i,j}dt,\ \text{ for } i = 0,1,2,3 \text{ and } i \neq j$$

we obtain after performing straightforward calculations:

$$
\begin{aligned}
dL_4^A(t) = (\ldots)\,dt + \sigma_1^Q(t)&\left(\frac{\delta_1^Q}{\delta_4^A}L_1^Q(t) + \frac{\delta_1^Q\delta_2^Q}{\delta_4^A}L_1^Q(t)L_2^Q(t) + \frac{\delta_1^Q\delta_3^Q}{\delta_4^A}L_1^Q(t)L_3^Q(t) \right. \\[2mm]
&+ \frac{\delta_1^Q\delta_4^Q}{\delta_4^A}L_1^Q(t)L_4^Q(t) + \frac{\delta_1^Q\delta_2^Q\delta_3^Q}{\delta_4^A}L_1^Q(t)L_2^Q(t)L_3^Q(t) + \frac{\delta_1^Q\delta_2^Q\delta_4^Q}{\delta_4^A}L_1^Q(t)L_2^Q(t)L_4^Q(t) \\[2mm]
&\left. + \frac{\delta_1^Q\delta_3^Q\delta_4^Q}{\delta_4^A}L_1^Q(t)L_3^Q(t)L_4^Q(t) + \frac{\delta_1^Q\delta_2^Q\delta_3^Q\delta_4^Q}{\delta_4^A}L_1^Q(t)L_2^Q(t)L_3^Q(t)L_4^Q(t) \right)dW_1^4(t) \\[2mm]
+ \sigma_2^Q(t)&\left(\frac{\delta_2^Q}{\delta_4^A}L_2^Q(t) + \frac{\delta_1^Q\delta_2^Q}{\delta_4^A}L_1^Q(t)L_2^Q(t) + \frac{\delta_2^Q\delta_3^Q}{\delta_4^A}L_2^Q(t)L_3^Q(t) + \frac{\delta_2^Q\delta_4^Q}{\delta_4^A}L_2^Q(t)L_4^Q(t) \right. \\[2mm]
&+ \frac{\delta_1^Q\delta_2^Q\delta_3^Q}{\delta_4^A}L_1^Q(t)L_2^Q(t)L_3^Q(t) + \frac{\delta_1^Q\delta_2^Q\delta_4^Q}{\delta_4^A}L_1^Q(t)L_2^Q(t)L_4^Q(t) + \frac{\delta_2^Q\delta_3^Q\delta_4^Q}{\delta_4^A}L_2^Q(t) \\[2mm]
&\left. \times L_3^Q(t)L_4^Q(t) + \frac{\delta_1^Q\delta_2^Q\delta_3^Q\delta_4^Q}{\delta_4^A}L_1^Q(t)L_2^Q(t)L_3^Q(t)L_4^Q(t) \right)dW_2^4(t) \\[2mm]
+ \sigma_3^Q(t)&\left(\frac{\delta_3^Q}{\delta_4^A}L_3^Q(t) + \frac{\delta_1^Q\delta_3^Q}{\delta_4^A}L_1^Q(t)L_3^Q(t) + \frac{\delta_2^Q\delta_3^Q}{\delta_4^A}L_2^Q(t)L_3^Q(t) + \frac{\delta_3^Q\delta_4^Q}{\delta_4^A}L_3^Q(t)L_4^Q(t) \right. \\[2mm]
&+ \frac{\delta_1^Q\delta_2^Q\delta_3^Q}{\delta_4^A}L_1^Q(t)L_2^Q(t)L_3^Q(t) + \frac{\delta_1^Q\delta_3^Q\delta_4^Q}{\delta_4^A}L_1^Q(t)L_3^Q(t)L_4^Q(t) \\[2mm]
&\left. + \frac{\delta_2^Q\delta_3^Q\delta_4^Q}{\delta_4^A}L_2^Q(t)L_3^Q(t)L_4^Q(t) + \frac{\delta_1^Q\delta_2^Q\delta_3^Q\delta_4^Q}{\delta_4^A}L_1^Q(t)L_2^Q(t)L_3^Q(t)L_4^Q(t) \right)dW_3^4(t) \\[2mm]
+ \sigma_4^Q(t)&\left(\frac{\delta_4^Q}{\delta_4^A}L_4^Q(t) + \frac{\delta_1^Q\delta_4^Q}{\delta_4^A}L_1^Q(t)L_4^Q(t) + \frac{\delta_2^Q\delta_4^Q}{\delta_4^A}L_2^Q(t)L_4^Q(t) + \frac{\delta_3^Q\delta_4^Q}{\delta_4^A}L_3^Q(t)L_4^Q(t) \right. \\[2mm]
&+ \frac{\delta_1^Q\delta_2^Q\delta_4^Q}{\delta_4^A}L_1^Q(t)L_2^Q(t)L_4^Q(t) + \frac{\delta_1^Q\delta_3^Q\delta_4^Q}{\delta_4^A}L_1^Q(t)L_3^Q(t)L_4^Q(t) \\[2mm]
&\left. + \frac{\delta_2^Q\delta_3^Q\delta_4^Q}{\delta_4^A}L_2^Q(t)L_3^Q(t)L_4^Q(t) + \frac{\delta_1^Q\delta_2^Q\delta_3^Q\delta_4^Q}{\delta_4^A}L_1^Q(t)L_2^Q(t)L_3^Q(t)L_4^Q(t) \right)dW_4^4(t)
\end{aligned}
\tag{9.5}
$$

Let us set:

$$a_i(t) = \frac{1}{F_4^A(t)}\left[\frac{\delta_i^Q}{\delta_4^A}F_i^Q(t) + \frac{\delta_i^Q F_i^Q(t)}{\delta_4^A}\sum_{\substack{j=1\\j\neq i}}^{4}\delta_j^Q F_j^Q(t) + \frac{\delta_i^Q F_i^Q(t)}{\delta_4^A}\sum_{\substack{j=1\\j\neq i}}^{3}\sum_{\substack{k=j+1\\k\neq i}}^{4}\delta_j^Q\delta_k^Q F_j^Q(t)F_k^Q(t) + \prod_{\substack{j=1\\j\neq i}}^{4}F_j^Q(t)\right]$$

for $i = 1, 2, 3, 4$.

Taking variance on both sides which is conditional on time t we can write:

$$\sigma^{inst}(t)^2 = \sum_{i=1}^{4}a_i(t)^2\sigma_i^Q(t)^2 + 2\sum_{i=1}^{4}\sum_{j=i}^{4}\rho_{i,j}\sigma_i^Q(t)\sigma_j^Q(t)a_i(t)a_j(t) \qquad (9.6)$$

We can freeze all F at zero time value to obtain

$$\sigma_{appr}^{inst}(t)^2 = \sum_{i=1}^{4}a_i(0)^2\sigma_i^Q(t)^2 + 2\sum_{i=1}^{4}\sum_{j=i}^{4}\rho_{i,j}\sigma_i^Q(t)\sigma_j^Q(t)a_i(0)a_j(0) \qquad (9.7)$$

We can consider F as a swap rate being the underlying of the $T_k \times 1$ swaption. In such case the squared Black's swaption volatility can be written as:

$$\sigma_{Black}^2 \approx \frac{1}{\delta_{t,T_k}}\int_0^{T_k}\sigma_{appr}(t)^2\,dt = \frac{1}{\delta_{t,T_k}}\left(\sum_{i=1}^{4}a_i(0)^2\int_0^{T_k}\sigma_i^Q(t)^2\,dt + 2\sum_{i=1}^{4}\sum_{j=i+1}^{4}\rho_{i,j}a_i(0)a_j(0)\int_0^{T_k}\sigma_i^Q(t)\sigma_j^Q(t)\,dt\right)$$
$$(9.8)$$

Considering the first integral:

$$\frac{1}{\delta_{t,T_k}}\int_0^{T_k}\sigma_1^Q(t)^2\,dt = \sigma^{cpl}(t, T_k, T_{k+1})^2$$

If we assume that the forward rates have constant volatilities, we can write:

$$\frac{1}{\delta_{t,T_k}}\int_0^{T_k}\sigma_2^Q(t)^2\,dt = \frac{1}{\delta_{t,T_k}}\int_0^{T_k}\sigma^{cpl}(t, T_{k+1}, T_{k+2})^2\,dt = \sigma^{cpl}(t, T_{k+1}, T_{k+2})^2$$

$$\frac{1}{\delta_{t,T_k}}\int_0^{T_k}\sigma_3^Q(t)^2\,dt = \frac{1}{\delta_{t,T_k}}\int_0^{T_k}\sigma^{cpl}(t, T_{k+2}, T_{k+3})^2\,dt = \sigma^{cpl}(t, T_{k+2}, T_{k+3})^2$$

$$\frac{1}{\delta_{t,T_k}}\int_0^{T_k}\sigma_4^Q(t)^2\,dt = \frac{1}{\delta_{t,T_k}}\int_0^{T_k}\sigma^{cpl}(t, T_{k+3}, T_{k+4})^2\,dt = \sigma^{cpl}(t, T_{k+3}, T_{k+4})^2$$

and

$$\frac{1}{\delta_{t,T_k}}\int_0^{T_k}\sigma_i^Q(t)\sigma_j^Q(t)\,dt = \frac{1}{\delta_{t,T_k}}\int_0^{T_k}\sigma^{cpl}(t, T_k, T_{k+i})\sigma^{cpl}(t, T_{k+i}, T_{k+j})\,dt = \sigma^{cpl}(t, T_k, T_{k+i})\sigma^{cpl}(t, T_{k+i}, T_{k+j})$$

for $i = 1, 2, 3, 4$ and $j = i + 1$.

Finally we obtain

$$\sigma_{Black}^2 \approx \left(\sum_{i=1}^{4} a_i\,(0)^2\, \sigma^{cpl}\,(t, T_k, T_{k+1})^2 + 2 \sum_{i=1}^{4} \sum_{j=i+1}^{4} \rho_{i,j} a_i\,(0)\, a_j\,(0)\, \sigma^{cpl}\,(t, T_k, T_{k+i})\, \sigma^{cpl}\,(t, T_{k+i}, T_{k+j}) \right). \quad (9.9)$$

The result is very similar to result presented in Brigo and Mercurio (2001) but here our example is for quarterly forward rates instead of annual rates. Let us present a practical example.

Example 9.1   Annualization of volatility

We will compute the annual market volatilities generated from quarterly caplet volatilities. In our computations we use market data taken from 21/01/2005 (with value date equal to 25/01/2005). We set intra-correlation of quarterly rates to one.

Let us consider period 1Y – 2Y. Table 9.1 presents data for interval with start date 25/01/2006 and end date 25/01/2007. Four quarterly sub-intervals have expiry dates 24/04/2006, 25/07/2006, 25/10/2006 and 25/01/2007. For each sub-interval we have the caplet volatility, quarterly year fraction and forward rate.

Table 9.1   Quarterly initial data

Tenor	Date	Caplet volatility	Year fraction	Forward rate (quarterly)	Discount factor	Annual forward rate
1Y	25/01/2006					
1.25Y	25/04/2006	20.15 %	0.25000	2.5440 %	0.971064	
1.50Y	25/07/2006	21.89 %	0.25278	2.6591 %	0.964580	
1.75Y	25/10/2006	23.65 %	0.25556	2.7755 %	0.957787	
2Y	25/01/2007	25.50 %	0.25556	2.8925 %	0.950759	2.7471 %

Taking data from Table 9.1 we compute the annual forward rate covering period 1Y – 2Y

$$F\,(0, T_{1Y}, T_{2Y}) = \left[\frac{B\,(0, T_{1Y})}{B\,(0, T_{2Y})} - 1 \right] \frac{360}{(T_{2Y} - T_{1Y})} = 2.7471\%.$$

Now we have to compute parameters: $a_1\,(0)$, $a_2\,(0)$, $a_3\,(0)$, $a_4\,(0)$:

$$a_1\,(0) = 0.233223$$

$$a_2\,(0) = 0.246394$$

$$a_3\,(0) = 0.259912$$

$$a_4\,(0) = 0.270786$$

Having computed parameters $a_1(0), a_2(0), a_3(0), a_4(0)$ and assuming $\rho_{ij} = 1$ we can compute the annual volatility:

$$\sigma_{Black}^2\,(0, T_{1Y}, T_{2Y}) \approx \sum_{i=1Y}^{2Y} a_i\,(0)^2\, \sigma^{cpl}\,(t, T_k, T_{k+1})^2$$

$$+ 2 \sum_{i=1Y}^{2Y} \sum_{j=i+0.25Y}^{2Y} \rho_{i,j} a_i\,(0)\, a_j\,(0)\, \sigma^{cpl}\,(0, T_k, T_{k+i})\, \sigma^{cpl}\,(0, T_{k+i}, T_{k+j})$$

$$\sigma_{Black}^2\left(0, T_{1Y}, T_{2Y}\right) \approx a_1\left(0\right)^2 \sigma^{cpl}\left(t, T_{1Y}, T_{1.25Y}\right)^2 + a_2\left(0\right)^2 \sigma^{cpl}\left(t, T_{1.25Y}, T_{1.5Y}\right)^2$$
$$+ a_3\left(0\right)^2 \sigma^{cpl}\left(t, T_{1.5Y}, T_{1.75Y}\right)^2 + a_4\left(0\right)^2 \sigma^{cpl}\left(t, T_{1.75Y}, T_{2Y}\right)^2$$
$$+ 2 \cdot a_1\left(0\right) \cdot a_2\left(0\right) \sigma^{cpl}\left(t, T_{1Y}, T_{1.25Y}\right) \sigma^{cpl}\left(t, T_{1.25Y}, T_{1.5Y}\right)$$
$$+ 2 \cdot a_1\left(0\right) \cdot a_3\left(0\right) \sigma^{cpl}\left(t, T_{1Y}, T_{1.25Y}\right) \sigma^{cpl}\left(t, T_{1.5Y}, T_{1.75Y}\right)$$
$$+ 2 \cdot a_1\left(0\right) \cdot a_4\left(0\right) \sigma^{cpl}\left(t, T_{1Y}, T_{1.25Y}\right) \sigma^{cpl}\left(t, T_{1.75Y}, T_{2Y}\right)$$
$$+ 2 \cdot a_2\left(0\right) \cdot a_3\left(0\right) \sigma^{cpl}\left(t, T_{1.25Y}, T_{1.5Y}\right) \sigma^{cpl}\left(t, T_{1.5Y}, T_{1.75Y}\right)$$
$$+ 2 \cdot a_2\left(0\right) \cdot a_4\left(0\right) \sigma^{cpl}\left(t, T_{1.25Y}, T_{1.5Y}\right) \sigma^{cpl}\left(t, T_{1.75Y}, T_{2Y}\right)$$
$$+ 2 \cdot a_3\left(0\right) \cdot a_4\left(0\right) \sigma^{cpl}\left(t, T_{1.5Y}, T_{1.75Y}\right) \sigma^{cpl}\left(t, T_{1.75Y}, T_{2Y}\right)$$

Using the real values we obtain:

$$v_{Black}^2\left(0, T_{1Y}, T_{2Y}\right) \approx 23.14\,\%$$

End of example 9.1

Table 9.2 presents the results of the computations of all annual forward volatilities:

Table 9.2   Annual forward volatilities

Tenor	Date	Caplet vol	Year fraction quarterly	Year fraction annual	Discount factor	Forward rate quarterly	Forward rate annual	a1(0) a2(0) a3(0) a4(0)	Annual volatility
1Y	25/01/2006	16.41 %	0.25556	1.0139	0.97724	2.4150 %	2.2972 %		
1.25Y	25/04/2006	20.15 %	0.25000		0.971064	2.5440 %			
1.50Y	25/07/2006	21.89 %	0.25278		0.96458	2.6591 %			
1.75Y	25/10/2006	23.65 %	0.25556		0.957787	2.7755 %			
2Y	25/01/2007	25.50 %	0.25556	1.0139	0.950759	2.8925 %	2.7471 %	0.233223	23.14 %
								0.246394	
								0.259912	
								0.270786	
2.25Y	25/04/2007	22.12 %	0.25000		0.943868	2.9201 %			
2.50Y	25/07/2007	22.55 %	0.25278		0.936727	3.0161 %			
2.75Y	25/10/2007	22.98 %	0.25556		0.929333	3.1131 %			
3Y	25/01/2008	23.41 %	0.25556	1.0139	0.92177	3.2105 %	3.1018 %	0.2377	23.05 %
								0.248157	
								0.258869	
								0.266908	
3.25Y	25/04/2008	20.97 %	0.25278		0.914291	3.2361 %			
3.50Y	25/07/2008	20.83 %	0.25278		0.906679	3.3216 %			
3.75Y	27/10/2008	20.77 %	0.26111		0.898851	3.3352 %			
4Y	26/01/2009	20.51 %	0.25278	1.0194	0.890895	3.5326 %	3.3995 %	0.242234	21.03 %
								0.248582	
								0.257753	
								0.264238	
5Y	25/01/2010	19.38 %	0.25278	1.0111	0.858974	3.7707 %	3.6754 %	0.242123	19.98 %
								0.249997	
								0.258101	
								0.263498	

10Y	26/01/2015	15.70 %	0.25278	1.0111	0.694285	4.5640 %	4.5342 %	0.247076	**16.28 %**
								0.252105	
								0.257512	
								0.260177	
20Y	27/01/2025	11.31 %	0.26111	1.0222	0.434558	4.8409 %	4.9805 %	0.2517	**11.67 %**
								0.252753	
								0.256584	
								0.25766	

Our next step in simultaneous calibration is computing forward swap rates which can be expressed as:

$$S_{sN}(t) = \frac{B(t, T_n) - B(t, T_N)}{\sum\limits_{i=n+1}^{N} \delta_{i-1,i} B(t, T_i)} \qquad (9.10)$$

The forward swap rates computed using equation (9.10) are presented below in Table 9.3.

Table 9.3 Forward swap rates

	2Y	3Y	4Y	5Y	6Y	7Y	8Y	9Y	10Y
1Y	2.92 %	3.08 %	3.22 %	3.35 %	3.47 %	3.58 %	3.68 %	3.76 %	3.81 %
2Y	3.25 %	3.39 %	3.51 %	3.63 %	3.73 %	3.83 %	3.91 %	3.96 %	4.01 %
3Y	3.54 %	3.65 %	3.77 %	3.87 %	3.97 %	4.04 %	4.08 %	4.13 %	4.17 %
4Y	3.79 %	3.90 %	4.00 %	4.10 %	4.16 %	4.20 %	4.24 %	4.27 %	4.30 %
5Y	4.03 %	4.12 %	4.21 %	4.27 %	4.30 %	4.33 %	4.36 %	4.39 %	4.42 %
7Y	4.41 %	4.45 %	4.45 %	4.47 %	4.49 %	4.51 %	4.54 %	4.56 %	4.57 %
10Y	4.51 %	4.53 %	4.57 %	4.61 %	4.62 %	4.64 %	4.66 %	4.68 %	4.71 %

The tenors in the rows represents the start dates of the forward swap rate, tenors in columns represents the end dates of the forward swap rate.

Having the forward swap rates and the ATM volatilities we can use the Black formula for swaptions to compute values of all swaptions from the tables.

$$Swaption_{nN}(0) = \sum_{i=n+1}^{N} \delta_{i-1,i} B(0, T_i) \left(S_{nN}(0)N(d_1) - KN(d_2)\right), \qquad (9.11)$$

where

$$d_1 = \frac{\ln(S_{nN}(0)/K) + \delta_{0,n}\sigma_{nN}^2/2}{\sigma_{nN}\sqrt{\delta_{0,n}}}, \quad d_2 = d_1 - \sigma_{nN}\sqrt{\delta_{0,n}},$$

Our goal is to find such instantaneous correlations of the LIBOR rates, which together with the instantaneous volatilities obtained from caplet prices will give possibly negligible difference between Black and LFM swaption prices.

The detailed algorithm of the calibration to swaption and cap prices is based on the Rebonato approach.

The LFM Black squared swaption volatility for swaptions can be approximated by

$$\left(\sigma_{n,N}^{LFM}\right)^2 = \sum_{i,j=n+1}^{N} \frac{w_i(0)\,w_j(0)\,F(0,T_{i-1},T_i)\,F(0,T_{j-1},T_j)\,\rho_{i,j}}{S_{n,N}(0)^2} \int_0^{T_n} \sigma_i(t)\,\sigma_j(t)\,dt$$

where the swap rates are expressed as a linear combination of the forward rates.

$$S_{n,N}(t) = \sum_{i=n+1}^{N} w_i(t)\,F(t,T_{i-1},T_i)$$

$$S_{n,N}(0) \overset{assumption}{=} \sum_{i=n+1}^{N} w_i(0)\,F(0,T_{i-1},T_i)$$

All $w_i(t)$ and $F(t,T_{i-1},T_i)$ are frozen at the time 0 value.

In the calibration we consider piecewise-constant instantaneous volatilities according to specification in Table 9.4.

Table 9.4 Piecewise – constant instantaneous volatilities

Time	$t \in (0, T_0)$	$t \in (T_0, T_1)$	$t \in (T_1, T_2)$	$t \in (T_{M-2}, T_{M-1})$
Forward rate				
$F(t, T_0, T_1)$	$\sigma_{1,1} = \Phi_1 \Psi_1$			
$F(t, T_1, T_2)$	$\sigma_{2,1} = \Phi_2 \Psi_2$	$\sigma_{2,2} = \Phi_2 \Psi_1$		
$F(t, T_{M-1}, T_M)$	$\sigma_{M,1} = \Phi_M \Psi_M$	$\sigma_{M,2} = \Phi_M \Psi_{M-1}$	$\sigma_{M,3} = \Phi_M \Psi_{M-2}$	$\sigma_{M,M} = \Phi_M \Psi_1$

We assume that caplet volatilities multiplied by time $\sigma^{cpl}(0, T_{i-1}, T_i)$ are read from the market. These volatilities should be annualized (an example can you find in the previous section). Then the parameters Φ can be given in terms of parameters Ψ as:

$$\Phi_i^2 = \frac{\left(\sigma^{cpl}(0, T_{i-1}, T_i)\right)^2}{\sum_{i=1}^{j} \delta_{j-2,j-1}\,\Psi_{i-j+1}^2}$$

The last approximation is

$$\rho_{i,j} = \cos\left(\theta_i - \theta_j\right).$$

Calibration is based on the algorithm of minimization for finding the best fitting parameters Ψ and θ starting from certain initial guesses and with restriction which implies that all $\rho_{i,j} > 0$.

Now we can move into some examples clarifying the theory. Let us define the Number Of Grid Points as number of annual forward rates plus one equal to the number of annual caplet rates. In our case of calibration we take Number of Grid Points equal to 21. This is because we start our calibration from period 2Y – 3Y.

Let us define vectors ε and θ. The initial values of these vectors are presented in Table 9.5 (same as in Brigo and Mercurio (2001)).

Table 9.5   Initial values of vectors ε, θ

i	$\varepsilon(i)$	$\theta(i)$
1	1.0000	$\pi/2 = 1.5708$
2	1.0000	$\pi/2 = 1.5708$
3	1.0000	$\pi/2 = 1.5708$
4	1.0000	$\pi/2 = 1.5708$
5	1.0000	$\pi/2 = 1.5708$
6	1.0000	$\pi/2 = 1.5708$
7	1.0000	$\pi/2 = 1.5708$
8	1.0000	$\pi/2 = 1.5708$
9	1.0000	$\pi/2 = 1.5708$
10	1.0000	$\pi/2 = 1.5708$
11	1.0000	$\pi/2 = 1.5708$
12	1.0000	$\pi/2 = 1.5708$
13	1.0000	$\pi/2 = 1.5708$
14	1.0000	$\pi/2 = 1.5708$
15	1.0000	$\pi/2 = 1.5708$
16	1.0000	$\pi/2 = 1.5708$
17	1.0000	$\pi/2 = 1.5708$
18	1.0000	$\pi/2 = 1.5708$
19	1.0000	$\pi/2 = 1.5708$
20	1.0000	$\pi/2 = 1.5708$
21	1.0000	$\pi/2 = 1.5708$

Now we have to generate the vector Ψ whose values are functions of parameters of vector ε. For technical reasons the first two rows of the vector Ψ will take zero values.

Algorithm 9.1   Calculation of vector Ψ

We start our loop from $i = 3$ up to [Number Of Grid Points] $= 21$

We take initial values

$SumTemp = 0$

$Sum = 0$

For each i we have to compute Sum in the following way:

Start from $j = 3$ up to current value of i and compute Sum using the loop procedure:

$SumTemp = \delta\ (j - 2, j - 1)\ \varepsilon\ (i - j + 3)^2$

$Sum = SumTemp + Sum$

Then vector Ψ will have parameters:

$$\Psi\ (i) = sqrt\left| \Sigma\text{\_cplann}\ (i)^2\ \delta\ (j - 2, j - 1)\ /Sum \right|$$

End of algorithm 9.1

In the algorithm above $\Sigma\text{\_cplann}$ is a vector of annualized caplet volatilities.

Initial values of Ψ vector for initial values of vector ε are presented in Table 9.6.

Table 9.6 Initial values of vector Ψ

i	$\Psi(i)$
1	0.0000
2	0.0000
3	0.2314
4	0.2305
5	0.2105
6	0.1997
7	0.1918
8	0.1841
9	0.1761
10	0.1676
11	0.1627
12	0.1696
13	0.1648
14	0.1499
15	0.1428
16	0.1358
17	0.1397
18	0.1342
19	0.1284
20	0.1225
21	0.1167

The next step is the generation of the matrix of weights W that will be used in further computations (e.g. for forward swap rates). This is presented by algorithm 9.2 below.

Algorithm 9.2   Generation of weights

For i = 1 To NumberOfSwaptionMaturities
If i <= 5 Then n = i
If i = 6 Then n = 7
   //due to the fact, that in our case we have no market volatilities for period 6Y,
    alternatively we may interpolate this value and skip the assignment
If i = 7 Then n = 10
   //due to the fact, that in our case we have no market volatilities
    for periods 8Y and 9Y,
    alternatively we may interpolate this values and skip the assignment
For j = 2 To NumberOfSwaptionUnderlyings
   Sum = 0
   For k = i + 1 To i + j
     Sum_1 = 0
     For l = i + 1 To i + j
       Sum_Temp = $\delta(l-1, l) \cdot \mathbf{B}(l+1)$
       Sum = Sum + Sum_Temp

Next l

$W(i, j, k - i) = \delta(k - 1, k)B(k + 1)/Sum$ // Elements of matrix of weights

Next j

Next i

End of algorithm 9.2

The structure of the matrix of weights W is thus as is presented below.

$$R = \begin{bmatrix} \begin{bmatrix} W(1,2,1) \\ W(1,2,2) \end{bmatrix} & \begin{bmatrix} W(1,3,1) \\ W(1,3,2) \\ W(1,3,3) \end{bmatrix} & \begin{bmatrix} W(1,4,1) \\ W(1,4,2) \\ W(1,4,3) \\ W(1,4,4) \end{bmatrix} & \cdots & \begin{bmatrix} W(1,10,1) \\ W(1,10,2) \\ W(1,10,3) \\ \cdots \\ W(1,10,10) \end{bmatrix} \\ \\ \begin{bmatrix} W(2,2,1) \\ W(2,2,2) \end{bmatrix} & \begin{bmatrix} W(2,3,1) \\ W(2,3,2) \\ W(2,3,3) \end{bmatrix} & \begin{bmatrix} W(2,4,1) \\ W(2,4,2) \\ W(2,4,3) \\ W(2,4,4) \end{bmatrix} & \cdots & \begin{bmatrix} W(2,10,1) \\ W(2,10,2) \\ W(2,10,3) \\ \cdots \\ W(2,10,10) \end{bmatrix} \\ \\ \cdots & \cdots & \cdots & \cdots & \cdots \\ \\ \begin{bmatrix} W(7,2,1) \\ W(7,2,2) \end{bmatrix} & \begin{bmatrix} W(7,3,1) \\ W(7,3,2) \\ W(7,3,3) \end{bmatrix} & \begin{bmatrix} W(7,4,1) \\ W(7,4,2) \\ W(7,4,3) \\ W(7,4,4) \end{bmatrix} & \cdots & \begin{bmatrix} W(7,10,1) \\ W(7,10,2) \\ W(7,10,3) \\ \cdots \\ W(7,10,10) \end{bmatrix} \end{bmatrix}$$

Figure 9.1   Structure of matrix W.

We need to create the instantaneous volatility matrix whose values are functions of the parameter ε.

Algorithm 9.3   Instantaneous volatility matrix

For i = 1 To NumberOfGridPoints-2

For j = 1 To i

$\Sigma\_inst(i, j) = \Psi(i + 1) \cdot \varepsilon(i - j + 3)$

Next j
Next i

End of algorithm 9.3

The algorithm for the theoretical LFM swaption prices is presented below. Additionally a minimization function is attached for the purpose of decreasing differences as much as possible between the theoretical and market swaption volatilities.

Algorithm 9.4   LFM theoretical swaption prices

MininizationFunction $= 0$
For i $= 1$ to NumberOfSwaptionMaturities
  if i $= 6$ then n $= 7$
    // this condition resulting from the fact
        that in our case we have no volatilities for periods 6Y, 8Y and 9Y
        elseif i $= 7$ then n $= 10$
        else n $= i$
  end
  for j $= 2$ to NumberOfSwaptionUnderlyings
    Sum_2 $= 0$
    for k $= 1$ to j
      for l $= 1$ to j
        Sum_1 $= 0$;
        for z $= 1$ to n
          Sum_1Temp $=$
          $\Sigma\_inst(n + k - 1, z) \cdot \Sigma\_inst(n + l - 1, z) \cdot \Sigma(z, z + 1)$
          Sum_1 $=$ Sum_1 $+$ Sum_1Temp
        Next z
          Sum_2Temp $=$
        Sum_1 $\cdot \mathbf{W}(i, j, k) \cdot \mathbf{W}(i, j, l) \cdot \mathbf{F}(k + n + 1) \cdot \mathbf{F}(l + n + 1) \cdot$
        $\cos(\theta(k + 2) - \theta(l + 2))/\mathbf{S}(i, j)^2 \cdot \delta(l, n + 1)$
        Sum_2 $=$ Sum_2 $+$ Sum_2Temp
        Next l
      Next k
    $\Sigma\_swaption\_LFM(i, j) =$ sort(Sum_2)
    // elements of matrix of LFM swaption volatilities
    Temp $= \Sigma\_swaption\_LFM(i, j) - \Sigma\_swaption\_mkt(i, j)$
    // difference between LFM and market swaption volatilities
    MinimizationFunction $=$ MinimizationFunction $+$ Temp;
    // creation of minimization function
  Next j
Next i

End of algorithm 9.4

In algorithm 9.4 **F** denotes a vector of forward rates with values $\mathbf{F}(i)$

Table 9.7 Forward rates

i	$\mathbf{F}(i)$	Forward rate $F(0, T_k, T_{k+1y})$ for k
1	0	0
2	0.022972	1Y
3	0.027471	2Y
4	0.031018	3Y
5	0.033995	4Y
6	0.036754	5Y
7	0.039064	6Y
8	0.041521	7Y
9	0.043117	8Y
10	0.045201	9Y
11	0.045342	10Y
12	0.044500	11Y
13	0.045794	12Y
14	0.045739	13Y
15	0.046933	14Y
16	0.047866	15Y
17	0.046906	16Y
18	0.047492	17Y
19	0.048352	18Y
20	0.049212	19Y
21	0.049805	20Y

We can write algorithm 9.4 as a function: MinimizationFunction and together with constraints for $\theta(i)$ we can define an optimization algorithm.

Target function: MinimizationFunction $\rightarrow$ MIN

Constraints : $-\dfrac{\pi}{x} \leq \theta(i) - \theta(i-1) < \dfrac{\pi}{x}$, where x are positive numbers

We now present the results of our computations for the market data from 21/01/2005. We set our restrictions for $\theta(i)$ as

$$-\frac{\pi}{2} \leq \theta(i) - \theta(i-1) < \frac{\pi}{2}.$$

Presented below are the results for vectors $\mathbf{\Psi}(i)$, $\varphi(i)$, $\varepsilon(i)$ after running the optimization algorithm.

Table 9.9 presents the theoretical and market volatilities of caps.

We show in detail how the LFM caplet volatilities were computed for periods $1Y \div 2Y$, $2Y \div 3Y, 3Y \div 4Y$.

Table 9.8 Results of optimization for vectors $\Psi(i), \varphi(i), \varepsilon(i)$

i	$\varepsilon(i)$	$\Psi(i)$	$\theta(i)$
3	1.0617	0.2180	1.4224
4	1.3808	0.1872	2.1771
5	1.6176	0.1534	1.1391
6	1.2381	0.1491	1.4950
7	0.9211	0.1513	1.5943
8	1.1882	0.1467	1.5815
9	0.4533	0.1500	1.5823
10	0.9412	0.1461	1.5712
11	1.1465	0.1418	1.5740
12	0.7785	0.1520	1.5607
13	0.5637	0.1528	1.5708
14	0.9090	0.1408	1.5708
15	0.9048	0.1357	1.5708
16	0.9387	0.1299	1.5708
17	0.9810	0.1342	1.5708
18	1.0081	0.1291	1.5708
19	1.0125	0.1237	1.5708
20	1.0162	0.1182	1.5708
21	1.0094	0.1128	1.5708

Table 9.9 Theoretical and market volatilities of caps

Tenor	Market caplet volatility	LFM caplet volatility
1Y–2Y	23.1450 %	23.1450 %
2Y–3Y	23.0510 %	23.0510 %
3Y–4Y	21.0307 %	21.0499 %
4Y–5Y	19.9772 %	19.9754 %
5Y–6Y	19.1815 %	19.1780 %
6Y–7Y	18.4074 %	18.4028 %
7Y–8Y	17.6072 %	17.6130 %
8Y–9Y	16.7570 %	16.7657 %
9Y–10Y	16.2764 %	16.2723 %
10Y–11Y	16.9667 %	16.9634 %
11Y–12Y	16.4732 %	16.4700 %
12Y–13Y	14.9914 %	14.9931 %
13Y–14Y	14.2830 %	14.2865 %
14Y–15Y	13.5744 %	13.5770 %
15Y–16Y	13.9757 %	13.9759 %
16Y–17Y	13.4165 %	13.4149 %
17Y–18Y	12.8406 %	12.8372 %
18Y–19Y	12.2463 %	12.2491 %
19Y–20Y	11.6680 %	11.6726 %

Example 9.2 LFM caplet volatilities

For the period $1Y \div 2Y$ we have:

$$\sigma_{LFM}^{cpl}(0, T_{1Y}, T_{2Y}) = \sqrt{\frac{\psi(3)^2 \, \varepsilon(3)^2}{\delta_{0,1Y}}} = \sqrt{\frac{0.2180^2 \cdot 1.0617^2}{1}} = 23.1450\%$$

For the period $2Y \div 3Y$ we have:

$$\sigma_{LFM}^{cpl}(0, T_{2Y}, T_{3Y}) = \sqrt{\frac{\psi(4)^2 \left[\varepsilon(3)^2 + \varepsilon(4)^2\right]}{\delta_{0,2Y}}} = \sqrt{\frac{0.1872^2 \cdot [1.0617^2 + 1.3808^2]}{2}} = 23.0520\%$$

For the period $3Y \div 4Y$ we have:

$$\sigma_{LFM}^{cpl}(0, T_{3Y}, T_{4Y}) = \sqrt{\frac{\psi(5)^2 \left[\varepsilon(3)^2 + \varepsilon(4)^2 + \varepsilon(5)^2\right]}{\delta_{0,3Y}}}$$

$$= \sqrt{\frac{0.1534^2 \cdot [1.0617^2 + 1.3808^2 + 1.6176^2]}{3}} = 21.0499\%$$

End of example 9.2

Table 9.10 presents the results for matrix of weights **W**

Table 9.10   Matrix of Weights

W(1,i,j) I = 1	2	3	4	5	6	7	8	9	10
j = 2	0.507635	0.492365							
3	0.343916	0.333571	0.322513						
4	0.262115	0.254231	0.245803	0.237850					
5	0.213516	0.207094	0.200228	0.193750	0.185412				
6	0.181174	0.175725	0.169899	0.164402	0.157328	0.151472			
7	0.158206	0.153447	0.148360	0.143560	0.137382	0.132269	0.126777		
8	0.141090	0.136846	0.132309	0.128029	0.122519	0.117959	0.113061	0.108187	
9	0.127793	0.123949	0.119840	0.115962	0.110972	0.106842	0.102405	0.097990	0.094247
10	0.117294	0.113766	0.109994	0.106436	0.101856	0.098064	0.093993	0.089940	0.086505	0.082152

W(2,i,j) I = 1	2	3	4	5	6	7	8	9	10
j = 2	0.508428	0.491572							
3	0.344540	0.333118	0.322341						
4	0.263316	0.254586	0.246350	0.235748					
5	0.214606	0.207491	0.200778	0.192138	0.184987				
6	0.182285	0.176242	0.170540	0.163202	0.157127	0.150603			
7	0.159325	0.154043	0.149060	0.142645	0.137336	0.131633	0.125958		
8	0.142109	0.137398	0.132953	0.127231	0.122496	0.117410	0.112347	0.108056	
9	0.128883	0.124611	0.120579	0.115390	0.111095	0.106482	0.101891	0.097999	0.093069
10	0.118353	0.114429	0.110727	0.105962	0.102018	0.097782	0.093566	0.089992	0.085464	0.081706

...

W(7,i,j) I = 1	2	3	4	5	6	7	8	9	10
j = 2	0.511016	0.488984							
3	0.347558	0.332573	0.319869						
4	0.266578	0.255085	0.245340	0.232997					
5	0.218015	0.208615	0.200646	0.190552	0.182172				

Table 9.10   Continued

W(7,i,j) I = 1	2	3	4	5	6	7	8	9	10
6	0.185584	0.177583	0.170800	0.162206	0.155073	0.148754			
7	0.162500	0.155494	0.149554	0.142030	0.135784	0.130250	0.124388		
8	0.145261	0.138998	0.133688	0.126962	0.121379	0.116432	0.111192	0.106087	
9	0.131828	0.126145	0.121326	0.115222	0.110155	0.105666	0.100910	0.096277	0.092471
10	0.121238	0.116011	0.111579	0.105966	0.101306	0.097177	0.092804	0.088543	0.085042	0.080334

The matrix of annualized instantaneous volatilities is presented by Table 9.11:

Table 9.11   Matrix of annualized instantaneous volatility

	1Y	2Y	3Y	4Y	5Y	6Y	7Y	8Y	9Y	10Y	11Y	12Y	13Y	14Y	15Y	16Y	17Y	18Y	19Y
$F(t,1Y,2Y)$	0.23																		
$F(t,2Y,3Y)$	0.26	0.20																	
$F(t,3Y,4Y)$	0.25	0.21	0.16																
$F(t,4Y,5Y)$	0.18	0.24	0.21	0.16															
$F(t,5Y,6Y)$	0.14	0.19	0.24	0.21	0.16														
$F(t,6Y,7Y)$	0.17	0.14	0.18	0.24	0.20	0.16													
$F(t,7Y,8Y)$	0.07	0.18	0.14	0.19	0.24	0.21	0.16												
$F(t,8Y,9Y)$	0.14	0.07	0.17	0.13	0.18	0.24	0.20	0.16											
$F(t,9Y,10Y)$	0.16	0.13	0.06	0.17	0.13	0.18	0.23	0.20	0.15										
$F(t,10Y,11Y)$	0.12	0.17	0.14	0.07	0.18	0.14	0.19	0.25	0.21	0.16									
$F(t,11Y,12Y)$	0.09	0.12	0.18	0.14	0.07	0.18	0.14	0.19	0.25	0.21	0.16								
$F(t,12Y,13Y)$	0.13	0.08	0.11	0.16	0.13	0.06	0.17	0.13	0.17	0.23	0.19	0.15							
$F(t,13Y,14Y)$	0.12	0.12	0.08	0.11	0.16	0.13	0.06	0.16	0.12	0.17	0.22	0.19	0.14						
$F(t,14Y,15Y)$	0.12	0.12	0.12	0.07	0.10	0.15	0.12	0.06	0.15	0.12	0.16	0.21	0.18	0.14					
$F(t,15Y,16Y)$	0.13	0.13	0.12	0.12	0.08	0.10	0.15	0.13	0.06	0.16	0.12	0.17	0.22	0.19	0.14				
$F(t,16Y,17Y)$	0.13	0.13	0.12	0.12	0.12	0.07	0.10	0.15	0.12	0.06	0.15	0.12	0.16	0.21	0.18	0.14			
$F(t,17Y,18Y)$	0.13	0.12	0.12	0.12	0.11	0.11	0.07	0.10	0.14	0.12	0.06	0.15	0.11	0.15	0.20	0.17	0.13		
$F(t,18Y,19Y)$	0.12	0.12	0.12	0.12	0.11	0.11	0.11	0.07	0.09	0.14	0.11	0.05	0.14	0.11	0.15	0.19	0.16	0.13	
$F(t,19Y,20Y)$	0.11	0.11	0.11	0.11	0.11	0.11	0.10	0.10	0.06	0.09	0.13	0.11	0.05	0.13	0.10	0.14	0.18	0.16	0.12

Let us show an example of the computation for the first six elements of the matrix represented by Table 9.9.

Example 9.3   Annualized instantaneous volatility

(a) Piecewise constant instantaneous volatility $\sigma^{inst}(0, T_{1Y,2Y}, T_{0,1Y})$ of the forward rate $F(t, T_{1Y}, T_{2Y})$ at an interval $0 \div T_{1Y}$ will be computed as:

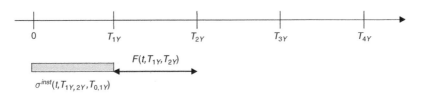

Figure 9.2   Instantaneous volatility of forward rate $F(t, T_{1Y}, T_{2Y})$ at interval $0 \div T_{1Y}$.

$$\Sigma\_\mathbf{inst}\,(1, 1) = \Sigma^{inst}\left(0, T_{1Y,2Y}, T_{0,1Y}\right) = \psi\,(3)\,\varepsilon\,(3) = 0.2180 \cdot 1.0617 = 0.2314$$

(b) Piecewise constant instantaneous volatility $\Sigma^{inst}(0, T_{2Y,3Y}, T_{0,1Y})$ of the forward rate $F(t, T_{2Y}, T_{3Y})$ at an interval $0 \div T_{1Y}$ will be computed as:

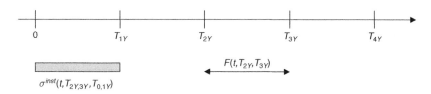

Figure 9.3 Instantaneous volatility of forward rate $F(t, T_{2Y}, T_{3Y})$ at interval $0 \div T_{1Y}$.

$$\Sigma\_inst\,(2, 1) = \Sigma^{inst}\left(0, T_{2Y,3Y}, T_{0,1Y}\right) = \psi\,(4)\,\varepsilon\,(4) = 0.1872 \cdot 1.3808 = 0.2584$$

(c) Piecewise constant instantaneous volatility $\sigma^{inst}(0, T_{2Y,3Y}, T_{1Y,2Y})$ of the forward rate $F(t, T_{2Y}, T_{3Y})$ at an interval $T_{1Y} \div T_{2Y}$ will be computed as:

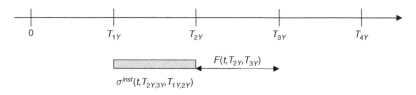

Figure 9.4 Instantaneous volatility of forward rate $F(t, T_{2Y}, T_{3Y})$ at interval $T_{1Y} \div T_{2Y}$.

$$\Sigma\_inst\,(2, 2) = \Sigma^{inst}\left(0, T_{2Y,3Y}, T_{1Y,2Y}\right) = \psi\,(4)\,\varepsilon\,(3) = 0.1872 \cdot 1.0617 = 0.1987$$

(d) Piecewise constant instantaneous volatility $\sigma^{inst}(0, T_{3Y,4Y}, T_{0,1Y})$ of the forward rate $F(t, T_{3Y}, T_{4Y})$ at an interval $0 \div T_{1Y}$ will be computed as:

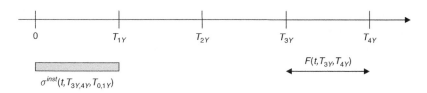

Figure 9.5 Instantaneous volatility of forward rate $F(t, T_{3Y}, T_{4Y})$ at interval $0 \div T_{1Y}$

$$\Sigma\_inst\,(3, 1) = \Sigma^{inst}\left(0, T_{3Y,4Y}, T_{0,1Y}\right) = \psi\,(5)\,\varepsilon\,(5) = 0.1534 \cdot 1.6176 = 0.2481$$

(e) Piecewise constant instantaneous volatility $\sigma^{inst}(0, T_{3Y,4Y}, T_{1Y,2Y})$ of the forward rate $F(t, T_{3Y}, T_{4Y})$ at an interval $T_{1Y} \div T_{2Y}$ will be computed as:

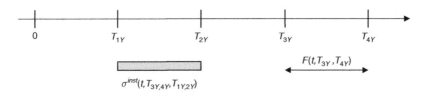

Figure 9.6   Instantaneous volatility of forward rate $F(t, T_{3Y}, T_{4Y})$ at interval $T_{1Y} \div T_{2Y}$.

$$\Sigma\_\text{inst}(3, 2) = \sigma^{inst}\left(0, T_{3Y,4Y}, T_{1Y,2Y}\right) = \psi(5)\,\varepsilon(4) = 0.1534 \cdot 1.3808 = 0.2118$$

(f) Piecewise constant instantaneous volatility $\sigma^{inst}(0, T_{3Y,4Y}, T_{2Y,3Y})$ of the forward rate $F(t, T_{3Y}, T_{4Y})$ at an interval $T_{2Y} \div T_{3Y}$ will be computed as:

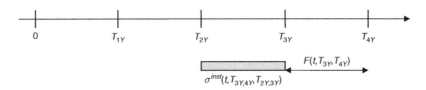

Figure 9.7   Instantaneous volatility of forward rate $F(t, T_{3Y}, T_{4Y})$ at interval $T_{2Y} \div T_{3Y}$.

$$\Sigma\_\text{inst}(3, 3) = \sigma^{inst}\left(0, T_{3Y,4Y}, T_{2Y,3Y}\right) = \psi(5)\,\varepsilon(3) = 0.1534 \cdot 1.0617 = 0.1628$$

The other volatilities would be computed in similar manner.

End of example 9.3

Let us move to present the results of the instantaneous correlations. The matrix of instantaneous correlation is presented by Table 9.12 below.

We present an example of the computation for the first three elements of the matrix presented by Table 9.10.

Example 9.4   Instantaneous correlations

(a) Instantaneous correlation $\rho^{inst}(0, T_{1Y,2Y}, T_{2Y,3Y})$ between the forward rates $F(t, T_{1Y}, T_{2Y})$ and $F(t, T_{2Y}, T_{3Y})$ will be computed as:

$$\rho^{inst}\left(t, T_{1Y,2Y}, T_{2Y,3Y}\right) = \cos[\theta(3) - \theta(4)] = \cos[1.4224 - 2.1771] = 0.728$$

Table 9.12 Matrix of instantaneous correlation

	1Y 2Y	2Y 3Y	3Y 4Y	4Y 5Y	5Y 6Y	6Y 7Y	7Y 8Y	8Y 9Y	9Y 10Y	10Y 11Y	11Y 12Y	12Y 13Y	13Y 14Y	14Y 15Y	15Y 16Y	16Y 17Y	17Y 18Y	18Y 19Y	19Y 20Y
F(t,1Y,2Y)	1.000																		
F(t,2Y,3Y)	0.728	1.000																	
F(t,3Y,4Y)	0.960	0.508	1.000																
F(t,4Y,5Y)	0.997	0.776	0.937	1.000															
F(t,5Y,6Y)	0.985	0.835	0.898	0.995	1.000														
F(t,6Y,7Y)	0.987	0.828	0.904	0.996	1.000	1.000													
F(t,7Y,8Y)	0.987	0.828	0.903	0.996	1.000	1.000	1.000												
F(t,8Y,9Y)	0.989	0.822	0.908	0.997	1.000	1.000	1.000	1.000											
F(t,9Y,10Y)	0.989	0.824	0.907	0.997	1.000	1.000	1.000	1.000	1.000										
F(t,10Y,11Y)	0.990	0.816	0.912	0.998	0.999	1.000	1.000	1.000	1.000	1.000									
F(t,11Y,12Y)	0.989	0.822	0.908	0.997	1.000	1.000	1.000	1.000	1.000	1.000	1.000								
F(t,12Y,13Y)	0.989	0.822	0.908	0.997	1.000	1.000	1.000	1.000	1.000	1.000	1.000	1.000							
F(t,13Y,14Y)	0.989	0.822	0.908	0.997	1.000	1.000	1.000	1.000	1.000	1.000	1.000	1.000	1.000						
F(t,14Y,15Y)	0.989	0.822	0.908	0.997	1.000	1.000	1.000	1.000	1.000	1.000	1.000	1.000	1.000	1.000					
F(t,15Y,16Y)	0.989	0.822	0.908	0.997	1.000	1.000	1.000	1.000	1.000	1.000	1.000	1.000	1.000	1.000	1.000				
F(t,16Y,17Y)	0.989	0.822	0.908	0.997	1.000	1.000	1.000	1.000	1.000	1.000	1.000	1.000	1.000	1.000	1.000	1.000			
F(t,17Y,18Y)	0.989	0.822	0.908	0.997	1.000	1.000	1.000	1.000	1.000	1.000	1.000	1.000	1.000	1.000	1.000	1.000	1.000		
F(t,18Y,19Y)	0.989	0.822	0.908	0.997	1.000	1.000	1.000	1.000	1.000	1.000	1.000	1.000	1.000	1.000	1.000	1.000	1.000	1.000	
F(t,19Y,20Y)	0.989	0.822	0.908	0.997	1.000	1.000	1.000	1.000	1.000	1.000	1.000	1.000	1.000	1.000	1.000	1.000	1.000	1.000	1.000

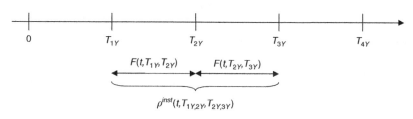

Figure 9.8 Instantaneous correlation between forward rates $F(t, T_{1Y}, T_{2Y})$ and $F(t, T_{2Y}, T_{3Y})$.

(b) Instantaneous correlation $\rho^{inst}(0, T_{1Y,2Y}, T_{3Y,4Y})$ between the forward rates $F(t, T_{1Y}, T_{2Y})$ and $F(t, T_{3Y}, T_{4Y})$ will be computed as:

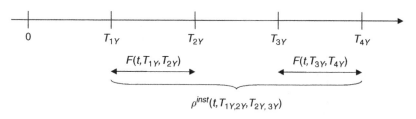

Figure 9.9 Instantaneous correlation between forward rates $F(t, T_{1Y}, T_{2Y})$ and $F(t, T_{3Y}, T_{4Y})$.

$$\rho^{inst}\left(t, T_{1Y,2Y}, T_{3Y,4Y}\right) = \cos\left[\theta\left(3\right) - \theta\left(5\right)\right] = \cos\left[1.4224 - 1.1391\right] = 0.960$$

(c) Instantaneous correlation $\rho^{inst}(0, T_{2Y,3Y}, T_{3Y,4Y})$ between the forward rates $F(t, T_{2Y}, T_{3Y})$ and $F(t, T_{3Y}, T_{4Y})$ will be computed as:

$$\rho^{inst}\left(t, T_{2Y,3Y}, T_{3Y,4Y}\right) = \cos\left[\theta\left(4\right) - \theta\left(5\right)\right] = \cos\left[2.1771 - 1.1391\right] = 0.508$$

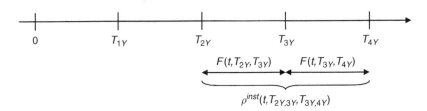

Figure 9.10   Instantaneous correlation between forward rates $F(t, T_{2Y}, T_{3Y})$ and $F(t, T_{3Y}, T_{4Y})$.

End of example 9.4

Table 9.13 presents the theoretical and market volatilities of swaptions together with differences between them after calibration has been done. The results can be regarded as a test of quality of the calibration.

Table 9.13   Theoretical and market volatilities of swaptions

Market	2Y	3Y	4Y	5Y	6Y	7Y	8Y	9Y	10Y
1Y	23.0000 %	22.1000 %	20.9000 %	19.6000 %	18.6000 %	17.6000 %	16.9000 %	16.3000 %	15.9000 %
2Y	21.5000 %	20.5000 %	19.4000 %	18.3000 %	17.4000 %	16.7000 %	16.2000 %	15.8000 %	15.4000 %
3Y	20.1000 %	19.0000 %	18.0000 %	17.0000 %	16.3000 %	15.8000 %	15.5000 %	15.2000 %	15.0000 %
4Y	18.7000 %	17.7000 %	16.8000 %	16.0000 %	15.5000 %	15.1000 %	14.8000 %	14.7000 %	14.5000 %
5Y	17.4000 %	16.5000 %	15.8000 %	15.1000 %	14.8000 %	14.5000 %	14.3000 %	14.2000 %	14.0000 %
7Y	16.0800 %	15.3000 %	14.6800 %	14.1400 %	13.9200 %	13.7000 %	13.5800 %	13.4800 %	13.3600 %
10Y	14.1000 %	13.5000 %	13.0000 %	12.7000 %	12.6000 %	12.5000 %	12.5000 %	12.4000 %	12.4000 %

Theoretical	2Y	3Y	4Y	5Y	6Y	7Y	8Y	9Y	10Y
1Y	22.8456 %	22.2082 %	21.1750 %	19.6068 %	19.2116 %	17.3138 %	16.8400 %	16.7739 %	16.3004 %
2Y	21.4321 %	20.2366 %	19.1965 %	18.4057 %	17.3602 %	16.2795 %	16.0939 %	15.9419 %	15.4138 %
3Y	19.5268 %	18.3651 %	17.8254 %	16.8311 %	16.1050 %	15.5008 %	15.3907 %	15.1239 %	14.7108 %
4Y	18.4133 %	17.4195 %	16.6899 %	15.8987 %	15.4312 %	15.0399 %	14.8372 %	14.5533 %	14.2019 %
5Y	17.6008 %	16.4634 %	15.8282 %	15.2690 %	15.0064 %	14.5916 %	14.3339 %	14.0665 %	13.7521 %
7Y	15.8337 %	14.9355 %	14.8172 %	14.4852 %	14.0973 %	13.6810 %	13.4305 %	13.2774 %	13.0863 %
10Y	15.3569 %	14.2214 %	13.7411 %	13.2651 %	13.0214 %	12.7576 %	12.5968 %	12.4248 %	12.2293 %

Difference	2Y	3Y	4Y	5Y	6Y	7Y	8Y	9Y	10Y
1Y	0.6713 %	−0.4897 %	−1.3158 %	−0.0349 %	−3.2882 %	1.6260 %	0.3549 %	−2.9076 %	−2.5183 %
2Y	0.3158 %	1.2848 %	1.0491 %	−0.5774 %	0.2289 %	2.5177 %	0.6551 %	−0.8981 %	−0.0894 %
3Y	2.8517 %	3.3415 %	0.9702 %	0.9935 %	1.1962 %	1.8937 %	0.7052 %	0.5007 %	1.9279 %
4Y	1.5331 %	1.5849 %	0.6556 %	0.6330 %	0.4437 %	0.3977 %	−0.2516 %	0.9976 %	2.0558 %
5Y	−1.1543 %	0.2218 %	−0.1786 %	−1.1190 %	−1.3944 %	−0.6319 %	−0.2368 %	0.9403 %	1.7708 %
7Y	1.5315 %	2.3825 %	−0.9349 %	−2.4417 %	−1.2738 %	0.1385 %	1.1012 %	1.5027 %	2.0486 %
10Y	−8.9138 %	−5.3435 %	−5.7007 %	−4.4495 %	−3.3444 %	−2.0610 %	−0.7740 %	−0.1998 %	1.3769 %

We present some examples of the theoretical swaption results. We will concentrate on four swaptions: $1Y \times 2Y$, $1Y \times 3Y$, $2Y \times 2Y$, $2Y \times 3Y$.

Example 9.5   LFM swaption volatilities

(a) Swaption $1Y \times 2Y$

Figure 9.11 presents graphically all components we need to compute the LFM swaption volatility.

Swaption maturity T_{1Y}

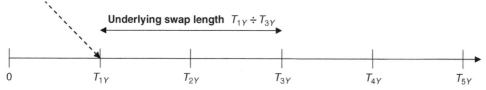

Necessary components:

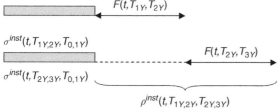

Figure 9.11   LFM swaption volatility for $T_{1Y} \div T_{3Y}$ (swaption 1Y × 2Y).

Thus the swaption volatility will be computed as:

$$\sigma_{LFM}^{swpt}(S_{1Y\times2Y}(0)) = \left\{ \left\lfloor \mathbf{W}(1,2,1)^2 F(0,T_{1Y},T_{2Y})^2 \mathbf{\Sigma\_inst}(1,1)^2 \right. \right.$$
$$+ \mathbf{W}(1,2,2)^2 F(0,T_{2Y},T_{3Y})^2 \mathbf{\Sigma\_inst}(2,1)^2$$
$$+ 2\mathbf{W}(1,2,1)\mathbf{W}(1,2,2)F(0,T_{1Y},T_{2Y})F(0,T_{2Y},T_{3Y})$$
$$\left. \cos[\theta(3)-\theta(4)]\mathbf{\Sigma\_inst}(1,1)\mathbf{\Sigma\_inst}(2,1)]/[\delta_{0,1Y}S_{1Y\times2Y}(0)] \right\}^{\frac{1}{2}}$$

Using real market data we obtain:

$$\sigma_{LFM}^{swpt}(S_{1Y\times2Y}(0)) = \left\{ \left\lfloor 0.507635^2 \cdot 0.027471^2 \cdot 0.2314^2 + 0.492365^2 \cdot 0.031018^2 \cdot 0.2584^2 \right. \right.$$
$$+ 2 \cdot 0.507635 \cdot 0.492365 \cdot 0.027471 \cdot 0.031018$$
$$\left. \cdot \cos[1.4224-2.1771] \cdot 0.2314 \cdot 0.2584]/[1 \cdot 0.0292] \right\}^{\frac{1}{2}} = 22.8456\%$$

(b) Swaption $1Y \times 3Y$

Figure 9.12 presents graphically all components we need to compute the LFM swaption volatility.

The swaption volatility will be computed as:

$$\sigma_{LFM}^{swpt}(S_{1Y\times3Y}(0)) = \left\{ \left\lfloor \mathbf{W}(1,3,1)^2 F(0,T_{1Y},T_{2Y})^2 \mathbf{\Sigma\_inst}(1,1)^2 \right. \right.$$
$$+ \mathbf{W}(1,3,2)^2 F(0,T_{2Y},T_{3Y})^2 \mathbf{\Sigma\_inst}(2,1)^2$$
$$+ \mathbf{W}(1,3,3)^2 F(0,T_{3Y},T_{4Y})^2 \mathbf{\Sigma\_inst}(3,1)^2$$
$$+ 2\mathbf{W}(1,3,1)\mathbf{W}(1,3,2)F(0,T_{1Y},T_{2Y})F(0,T_{2Y},T_{3Y})$$
$$\times \cos[\theta(3)-\theta(4)]\mathbf{\Sigma\_inst}(1,1)\mathbf{\Sigma\_inst}(2,1)$$

$$+ 2\mathbf{W}(1, 3, 1)\,\mathbf{W}(1, 3, 3)\,F(0, T_{1Y}, T_{2Y})\,F(0, T_{3Y}, T_{4Y})$$

$$\times \cos\left[\theta(3) - \theta(5)\right] \mathbf{\Sigma\_inst}(1, 1)\,\mathbf{\Sigma\_inst}(3, 1)$$

$$+ 2\mathbf{W}(1, 3, 2)\,\mathbf{W}(1, 3, 3)\,F(0, T_{2Y}, T_{3Y})\,F(0, T_{3Y}, T_{4Y})$$

$$\times \cos\left[\theta(4) - \theta(5)\right] \mathbf{\Sigma\_inst}(2, 1)\,\mathbf{\Sigma\_inst}(3, 1)\right] / \left[\delta_{0,1Y} S_{1Y \times 3Y}(0)\right]\bigg\}^{\frac{1}{2}}$$

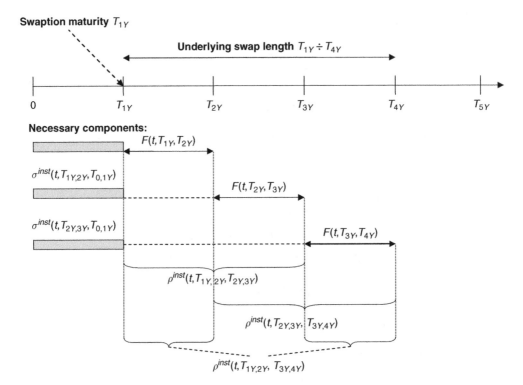

Figure 9.12　LFM swaption volatility for $T_{1Y} \div T_{4Y}$ (swaption $1Y \times 3Y$).

Using the real market data we obtain:

$$\sigma_{LFM}^{swpt}(S_{1Y \times 3Y}(0)) = \bigg\{\lfloor 0.343916^2 \cdot 0.027471^2 \cdot 0.2314^2 + 0.333571^2 \cdot 0.031018^2$$

$$\cdot 0.2584^2 + 0.322513^2 \cdot 0.033995^2 \cdot 0.2481^2 + 2 \cdot 0.343916$$

$$\cdot 0.333571 \cdot 0.027471 \cdot 0.031018 \cdot \cos\left[1.4224 - 2.1771\right] \cdot 0.2314$$

$$\cdot 0.2584 + 2 \cdot 0.343916 \cdot 0.322513 \cdot 0.027471 \cdot 0.033995$$

$$\cdot \cos\left[1.4224 - 1.1391\right] \cdot 0.2314 \cdot 0.2481 + 2 \cdot 0.333571 \cdot 0.322513$$

$$\cdot 0.031018 \cdot 0.033995 \cdot \cos\left[2.1771 - 1.1391\right] \cdot 0.2584 \cdot 0.2481]/$$

$$\left[1 \cdot 0.0308\right]\bigg\}^{\frac{1}{2}} = 22.2082\,\%$$

(c) Swaption $2Y \times 2Y$

Figure 9.13 presents graphically all components we need to compute the third LFM swaption volatility.

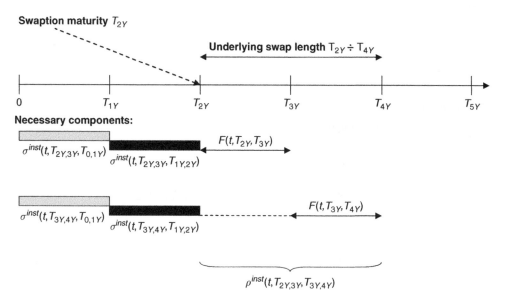

Figure 9.13   LFM swaption volatility for $T_{2Y} \div T_{4Y}$ (swaption $2Y \times 2Y$).

Thus we can compute the swaption volatility by:

$$\sigma_{LFM}^{swpt}\left(S_{2Y \times 2Y}(0)\right) = \left\{\left[\mathbf{W}\left(1,2,1\right)^2 F\left(0,T_{1Y},T_{2Y}\right)^2 \left\lfloor \mathbf{\Sigma\_inst}\left(2,1\right)^2 + \mathbf{\Sigma\_inst}\left(2,2\right)^2 \right\rfloor\right.\right.$$
$$+ \mathbf{W}\left(2,2,2\right)^2 F\left(0,T_{3Y},T_{4Y}\right)^2 \left[\mathbf{\Sigma\_inst}\left(3,1\right)^2 + \mathbf{\Sigma\_inst}\left(3,2\right)^2\right]$$
$$+ 2\mathbf{W}\left(2,2,1\right)\mathbf{W}\left(2,2,2\right)F\left(0,T_{2Y},T_{3Y}\right)F\left(0,T_{3Y},T_{4Y}\right)$$
$$\times \cos\left[\theta\left(3\right) - \theta\left(4\right)\right] \cdot \left(\mathbf{\Sigma\_inst}\left(2,1\right)\mathbf{\Sigma\_inst}\left(3,1\right)\right.$$
$$\left.+ \mathbf{\Sigma\_inst}\left(2,2\right)\mathbf{\Sigma\_inst}\left(3,2\right)\right)\right] / \left[\delta_{0,2Y}S_{2Y \times 2Y}(0)\right]\right\}^{\frac{1}{2}}$$

Finally, using the real market data we obtain:

$$\sigma_{LFM}^{swpt}\left(S_{2Y \times 2Y}(0)\right) = \left\{\left[0.508428^2 \cdot 0.031018^2 \cdot \left[0.2584^2 + 0.1987^2\right] + 0.491572^2\right.\right.$$
$$\cdot 0.033995^2 \cdot \left[0.2481^2 + 0.2118^2\right] + 2 \cdot 0.508428 \cdot 0.491572$$
$$\cdot 0.031018 \cdot 0.033995 \cdot \cos\left[1.4224 - 2.1771\right]$$
$$\left.\cdot \left(0.2584 \cdot 0.2481 + 0.1987 \cdot 0.2118\right)\right] / \left[2 \cdot 0.0325\right]\right\}^{\frac{1}{2}} = 21.4321\%$$

(d) Swaption $2Y \times 3Y$

Figure 9.14 presents graphically all components we need to compute our final LFM swaption volatility example.

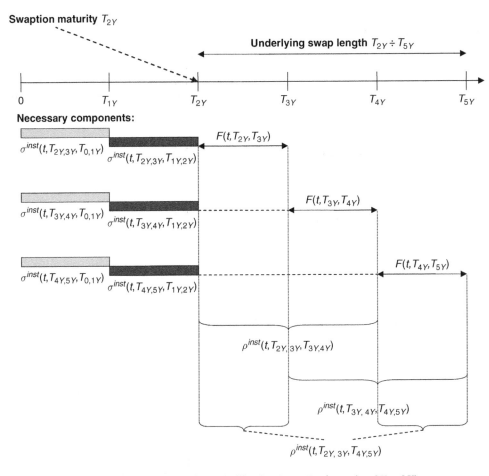

Figure 9.14   LFM swaption volatility for $T_{2Y} \div T_{5Y}$ (swaption $2Y \times 3Y$).

The final swaption volatility is given by:

$$
\begin{aligned}
\sigma_{LFM}^{swpt}\left(S_{2Y\times 3Y}(0)\right) = &\left\{ \left\lfloor \mathbf{W}(2,3,1)^2 F(0, T_{2Y}, T_{3Y})^2 \left\lfloor \mathbf{\Sigma\_inst}(2,1)^2 + \mathbf{\Sigma\_inst}(2,2)^2 \right\rfloor \right. \right. \\
&+ \mathbf{W}(2,3,2)^2 F(0, T_{3Y}, T_{4Y})^2 \left[\mathbf{\Sigma\_inst}(3,1)^2 + \mathbf{\Sigma\_inst}(3,2)^2 \right] \\
&+ \mathbf{W}(2,3,3)^2 F(0, T_{4Y}, T_{5Y})^2 \left[\mathbf{\Sigma\_inst}(4,1)^2 + \mathbf{\Sigma\_inst}(4,2)^2 \right] \\
&+ 2\mathbf{W}(2,3,1)\mathbf{W}(2,3,2) F(0, T_{2Y}, T_{3Y}) F(0, T_{3Y}, T_{4Y}) \cos\left[\theta(3) - \theta(4)\right] \\
&\cdot \left(\mathbf{\Sigma\_inst}(2,1)\mathbf{\Sigma\_inst}(3,1) + \mathbf{\Sigma\_inst}(2,2)\mathbf{\Sigma\_inst}(3,2) \right)
\end{aligned}
$$

$$+ 2\mathbf{W}(2, 3, 1)\,\mathbf{W}(2, 3, 3)\,F(0, T_{2Y}, T_{3Y})\,F(0, T_{4Y}, T_{5Y})\cos[\theta(3) - \theta(5)]$$

$$\cdot\,(\mathbf{\Sigma\_inst}(2, 1)\,\mathbf{\Sigma\_inst}(4, 1) + \mathbf{\Sigma\_inst}(2, 2)\,\mathbf{\Sigma\_inst}(4, 2))$$

$$+ 2\mathbf{W}(2, 3, 2)\,\mathbf{W}(2, 3, 3)\,F(0, T_{3Y}, T_{4Y})\,F(0, T_{4Y}, T_{5Y})\cos[\theta(4) - \theta(5)]$$

$$\cdot\,(\mathbf{\Sigma\_inst}(3, 1)\,\mathbf{\Sigma\_inst}(4, 1)$$

$$+ \mathbf{\Sigma\_inst}(3, 2)\,\mathbf{\Sigma\_inst}(4, 2))]\,/\,\big[\delta_{0,2Y} S_{2Y \times 3Y}(0)\big]\Big\}^{\frac{1}{2}}$$

Thus we obtain:

$$\begin{aligned}
\sigma_{LFM}^{swpt}(S_{2Y \times 3Y}(0)) = \Big\{&\big[0.344540^2 \cdot 0.031018^2 \cdot [0.2584^2 + 0.1987^2]\big] \\
&+ 0.333118^2 \cdot 0.033995^2 \cdot [0.2481^2 + 0.2118^2] \\
&+ 0.322341^2 \cdot 0.036754^2 \cdot [0.1846^2 + 0.2411^2] \\
&+ 2 \cdot 0.344540 \cdot 0.333118 \cdot 0.031018 \cdot 0.033995 \cdot \cos[1.4224 - 2.1771] \\
&\cdot (0.2584 \cdot 0.2481 + 0.1987 \cdot 0.2118) \\
&+ 2 \cdot 0.344540 \cdot 0.322341 \cdot 0.031018 \cdot 0.036754 \cdot \cos[1.4224 - 1.1391] \\
&\cdot (0.2584 \cdot 0.1846 + 0.1987 \cdot 0.2411) \\
&+ 2 \cdot 0.333118 \cdot 0.322341 \cdot 0.033995 \cdot 0.036754 \cdot \cos[2.1771 - 1.1391] \\
&\cdot (0.2481 \cdot 1.1846 + 0.2118 \cdot 0.2411)]\,/\,[2 \cdot 0.0339]\Big\}^{\frac{1}{2}}
\end{aligned}$$

End of example 9.5

The next part of the chapter will describe the different parametric methods for calibration to caps and swaptions.

9.3   PARAMETRIC METHOD OF CALIBRATION

This section is in two parts. The first describes the parametric calibration to caps. The second will use the results and apply them for the parametric calibration to swaptions.

9.3.1   Parametric calibration to cap prices

The purpose of this chapter is to describe a detailed algorithm allowing a calibration of the LIBOR Market Model parametric calibration to cap prices.

Step 1

Derivation of caplet prices from cap prices.

Such a derivation was done in previous sections. Thus it is not necessary to present algorithm once again. The table below presents the quarterly caplet volatilities $\sigma^{cpl}(T_0, T_{i-3M}, T_i)$ for different maturities. All maturities are expressed using day count fractions using Act/360 base convention.

Table 9.14 Caplet implied volatilities

T_i	$\dfrac{(T_i - T_0)}{360}$	$\sigma^{caplet}(T_0, T_{i-3M}, T_i)$	T_i	$\dfrac{(T_i - T_0)}{360}$	$\Sigma^{caplet}(T_0, T_{i-3M}, T_i)$
6M	0.5028	0.1641	5Y 6M	5.5778	0.1902
9M	0.7583	0.1641	5Y 9M	5.8306	0.1879
1Y	1.0139	0.1641	6Y	6.0861	0.1859
1Y 3M	1.2639	0.2015	6Y 3M	6.3361	0.1844
1Y 6M	1.5167	0.2189	6Y 6M	6.5889	0.1824
1Y 9M	1.7722	0.2365	6Y 9M	6.8444	0.1804
2Y	2.0278	0.2550	7Y	7.1000	0.1781
2Y 3M	2.2778	0.2212	7Y 3M	7.3528	0.1766
2Y 6M	2.5306	0.2255	7Y 6M	7.6056	0.1743
2Y 9M	2.7861	0.2298	7Y 9M	7.8611	0.1724
3Y	3.0417	0.2341	8Y	8.1167	0.1700
3Y 3M	3.2944	0.2097	8Y 3M	8.3667	0.1677
3Y 6M	3.5472	0.2083	8Y 6M	8.6194	0.1657
3Y 9M	3.8083	0.2077	8Y 9M	8.8750	0.1637
4Y	4.0611	0.2051	9Y	9.1361	0.1622
4Y 3M	4.3139	0.2007	9Y 3M	9.3806	0.1623
4Y 6M	4.5667	0.1982	9Y 6M	9.6333	0.1612
4Y 9M	4.8194	0.1959	9Y 9M	9.8944	0.1599
5Y	5.0722	0.1938	10Y	10.1472	0.1570
5Y 3M	5.3250	0.1925			

Step 2

Having the caplet volatilities $\sigma^{caplet}(T_0, T_{i-3M}, T_i)$ we need to multiply the time to maturities (expresses as day count fractions) by the squared implied caplet volatility. Our results are presented in Table 9.15.

Step 3

We need to find parameters v_1, v_2, v_3, v_4 using optimization algorithms. First let us define the set of functions:

$$f(T_i - t) = \left| v_1 + \left[v_2 + v_3 \frac{T_i - t}{360} \right] e^{-v_4 \frac{T_i - t}{360}} \right| \tag{9.12}$$

for $T_i = T_{3M}, T_{9M}, T_{1Y}, \ldots, T_{10Y}$ respectively.

Having that we will compute integrals of $f(T_i - t)^2$ as:

$$I(T_i - t)^2 = \int_0^{T_i} \left| v_1 + \left[v_2 + v_3 \frac{T_i - t}{360} \right] e^{-v_4 \frac{T_i - t}{360}} \right|^2 dt - \int_0^{T_{i-1}} \left| v_1 + \left[v_2 + v_3 \frac{T_i - t}{360} \right] e^{-v_4 \frac{T_i - t}{360}} \right|^2 dt \tag{9.13}$$

for $T_i = T_{6M}, T_{9M}, T_{1Y}, \ldots, T_{10Y}$ respectively.

Next let us define:

$$f_{FO}(T_i) = \sum_{T_i} I(T_i - t)^2 \tag{9.14}$$

Table 9.15 Squared caplet implied volatilities multiplied by time to maturity

T_i	$\dfrac{(T_i - T_0)}{360} \sigma^{caplet} (T_0, T_{i-3M}, T_i)^2$	T_i	$\dfrac{T_i - T_0}{360} \Sigma^{caplet} (T_0, T_{i-3M}, T_i)^2$
6M	0.0135392	5Y 6M	0.2017819
9M	0.0204210	5Y 9M	0.2058560
1Y	0.0273028	6Y	0.2103288
1Y 3M	0.0513167	6Y 3M	0.2154491
1Y 6M	0.0726744	6Y 6M	0.2192108
1Y 9M	0.0991244	6Y 9M	0.2227467
2Y	0.1318563	7Y	0.2252092
2Y 3M	0.1114504	7Y 3M	0.2293152
2Y 6M	0.1286794	7Y 6M	0.2310605
2Y 9M	0.1471291	7Y 9M	0.2336461
3Y	0.1666919	8Y	0.2345717
3Y 3M	0.1448702	8Y 3M	0.2352982
3Y 6M	0.1539100	8Y 6M	0.2366597
3Y 9M	0.1642888	8Y 9M	0.2378295
4Y	0.1708347	9Y	0.2403605
4Y 3M	0.1737656	9Y 3M	0.2470959
4Y 6M	0.1793935	9Y 6M	0.2503264
4Y 9M	0.1849549	9Y 9M	0.2529813
5Y	0.1905048	10Y	0.2501189
5Y 3M	0.1973245		

Having that our minimization function will be:

$$f_{min} = \sqrt{\sum_{T_i} \left(\left[\frac{T_i - T_0}{360} \sigma^{caplet} (T_0, T_{i-3M}, T_i)^2 \right] - [f_{FO}(T_i)] \right)^2} \to min \qquad (9.15)$$

Running the optimization starting from initial values: $v_1, v_2, v_3, v_4 = 0.1$ we obtain the values: $v_1 = 0.112346$, $v_2 = -0.441811$, $v_3 = 0.971559$, $v_4 = 1.223058$, $f_{min} = 0.0436646$. Table 9.16 presents the results of our computations.

Step 4

Let us define the function

$$\varepsilon (T_i - T_0) = g_1 + g_2 \cos \left[g_3 \frac{T_i - T_0}{360} \right] \qquad (9.16)$$

Next let us define correction factor

$$corr (T_i - T_0) = [1 + \varepsilon (T_i - T_0)] I (T_i - t)^2 \qquad (9.17)$$

And

$$f_{SO}(T_i) = \sum_{T_i} [1 + \varepsilon (T_i - T_0)] I (T_i - t)^2 =$$
$$\sum_{T_i} \left\{ [1 + g_1 + g_2 \cos (g_3 (T_i - T_0))] I (T_i - t)^2 \right\} \qquad (9.18)$$

Table 9.16 Results for step 3 of parametric calibration

T_i	$f(T_i - T_0)$	$\int_0^{T_i} f(T_i - t)^2 \, dt$	$f_{FO}(T_i)$	T_i	$f(T_i - T_0)$	$\int_0^{T_i} f(T_i - t)^2 \, dt$	$f_{FO}(T_i)$
6M	0.137578	0.010484	0.010484	5Y 6M	0.117769	0.003552	0.199307
9M	0.229015	0.009274	0.019758	5Y 9M	0.116523	0.003467	0.202775
1Y	0.269545	0.016331	0.036088	6Y	0.115547	0.003440	0.206214
1Y 3M	0.279902	0.019118	0.055207	6Y 3M	0.114809	0.003316	0.209530
1Y 6M	0.273766	0.019513	0.074720	6Y 6M	0.114231	0.003314	0.212844
1Y 9M	0.258856	0.018194	0.092914	6Y 9M	0.113783	0.003321	0.216165
2Y	0.240319	0.015946	0.108860	7Y	0.113439	0.003298	0.219463
2Y 3M	0.221586	0.013338	0.122198	7Y 3M	0.113179	0.003245	0.222708
2Y 6M	0.203654	0.011421	0.133619	7Y 6M	0.112980	0.003232	0.225940
2Y 9M	0.187368	0.009757	0.143376	7Y 9M	0.112826	0.003257	0.229198
3Y	0.173246	0.008296	0.151671	8Y	0.112709	0.003250	0.232448
3Y 3M	0.161419	0.007066	0.158737	8Y 3M	0.112622	0.003173	0.235621
3Y 6M	0.151575	0.006180	0.164918	8Y 6M	0.112555	0.003204	0.238825
3Y 9M	0.143257	0.005665	0.170583	8Y 9M	0.112504	0.003236	0.242061
4Y	0.136747	0.004947	0.175530	9Y	0.112464	0.003304	0.245365
4Y 3M	0.131513	0.004542	0.180072	9Y 3M	0.112436	0.003091	0.248456
4Y 6M	0.127338	0.004229	0.184301	9Y 6M	0.112414	0.003195	0.251651
4Y 9M	0.124027	0.003989	0.188290	9Y 9M	0.112397	0.003299	0.254950
5Y	0.121417	0.003804	0.192094	10Y	0.112384	0.003193	0.258143
5Y 3M	0.119369	0.003661	0.195755				

Having that our minimization function will then be:

$$\widetilde{f}_{\min} =$$

$$\sqrt{\sum_{T_i} \left(\left[\frac{T_i - T_0}{360} \sigma^{caplet}(T_0, T_{i-3M}, T_i)^2 \right] - \left[\sum_{T_i} [1 + g_1 + g_2 \cos(g_3(T_i - T_0))] I(T_i - t)^2 \right] \right)^2} \to \min$$

(9.19)

Running the optimization starting from initial values: $g_1, g_2, g_3 = 0.1$ we obtain values: $g_1 = -7.02054$, $g_2 = 7.027038$, $g_3 = 0.012987$, $\widetilde{f}_{\min} = 0.043502$. Table 9.17 below displays the results of our computations.

Table 9.17 Results for step 4 of parametric calibration

T_i	$\varepsilon(T_i - T_0)$	$corr(T_i - T_0)$	$f_{SO}(T_i)$	T_i	$\varepsilon(T_i - T_0)$	$corr(T_i - T_0)$	$f_{SO}(T_i)$
6M	0.006343	0.010551	0.010551	5Y 6M	-0.011935	0.003509	0.199764
9M	0.006152	0.009331	0.019881	5Y 9M	-0.013643	0.003420	0.203184
1Y	0.005884	0.016427	0.036308	6Y	-0.015445	0.003387	0.206570
1Y 3M	0.005546	0.019225	0.055533	6Y 3M	-0.017284	0.003258	0.209829
1Y 6M	0.005130	0.019613	0.075145	6Y 6M	-0.019218	0.003251	0.213079
1Y 9M	0.004632	0.018278	0.093424	6Y 9M	-0.021249	0.003250	0.216330
2Y	0.004057	0.016011	0.109435	7Y	-0.023358	0.003221	0.219551
2Y 3M	0.003419	0.013384	0.122819	7Y 3M	-0.025520	0.003162	0.222713
2Y 6M	0.002699	0.011451	0.134270	7Y 6M	-0.027757	0.003142	0.225856
2Y 9M	0.001894	0.009775	0.144045	7Y 9M	-0.030095	0.003159	0.229015
3Y	0.001011	0.008304	0.152349	8Y	-0.032511	0.003144	0.232159
3Y 3M	0.000062	0.007067	0.159416	8Y 3M	-0.034948	0.003062	0.235221
3Y 6M	-0.000962	0.006175	0.165590	8Y 6M	-0.037487	0.003084	0.238305
3Y 9M	-0.002100	0.005653	0.171243	8Y 9M	-0.040131	0.003106	0.241412
4Y	-0.003278	0.004931	0.176174	9Y	-0.042911	0.003162	0.244573
4Y 3M	-0.004532	0.004521	0.180695	9Y 3M	-0.045587	0.002950	0.247524
4Y 6M	-0.005861	0.004205	0.184900	9Y 6M	-0.048428	0.003040	0.250564
4Y 9M	-0.007267	0.003960	0.188860	9Y 9M	-0.051442	0.003129	0.253693
5Y	-0.008747	0.003771	0.192631	10Y	-0.054435	0.003019	0.256712
5Y 3M	-0.010303	0.003624	0.196254				

Step 5

In the calibration to swaptions the delta function will be used. The function will be defined as:

$$\Delta\left(T_i\right) = \frac{\frac{T_i - T_0}{360}\sigma^{caplet}\left(T_0, T_{i-3M}, T_i\right)^2}{f_{SO}\left(T_i\right)} - 1 \qquad (9.20)$$

Table 9.18 presents the results of our computations of step 5.

Table 9.18   Results for step 5 of parametric calibration

T_i	$\Delta(T_i)$	T_i	$\Delta(T_i)$
6M	0.283266	5Y 6M	0.010102
9M	0.027149	5Y 9M	0.013151
1Y	−0.248024	6Y	0.018194
1Y 3M	−0.075917	6Y 3M	0.026785
1Y 6M	−0.032884	6Y 6M	0.028775
1Y 9M	0.061017	6Y 9M	0.029662
2Y	0.204885	7Y	0.025772
2Y 3M	−0.092562	7Y 3M	0.029643
2Y 6M	−0.041638	7Y 6M	0.023045
2Y 9M	0.021408	7Y 9M	0.020222
3Y	0.094142	8Y	0.010393
3Y 3M	−0.091244	8Y 3M	0.000327
3Y 6M	−0.070538	8Y 6M	−0.006906
3Y 9M	−0.040611	8Y 9M	−0.014838
4Y	−0.030308	9Y	−0.017226
4Y 3M	−0.038351	9Y 3M	−0.001728
4Y 6M	−0.029781	9Y 6M	−0.000947
4Y 9M	−0.020677	9Y 9M	−0.002806
5Y	−0.011036	10Y	−0.025684
5Y 3M	0.005453		

Now we can extend the calibration scheme to swaptions.

9.3.2   Parametric calibration to swaptions

Parametric calibration to swaptions will be done using the previously computed parameters. Algorithm 9.5 presents our parametric calibration to swaptions.

Algorithm 9.5   Parametric calibration to swaptions

SwaptionImpliedVolatility=0; Counter=0 // Setting initial values
$\theta_1 = \theta_2 = \theta_3 = \theta_4 = 1$
// Setting the initial values of parameters used in parametric swaption calibration
$\phi_1 = \phi_2 = \phi_3 = \phi_4 = 1$
// Setting the initial values of parameters used in parametric swaption calibration
$\nu_i = \text{Algorithmx.x} \rightarrow \nu_i, i = 1, 2, 3, 4$
// Taking values computed in caplet calibration

Step 1 of calibration

For i = 1 to NumberOfCapletPeriods

$$\delta_0(i) = (T_i - T_0)/basis, \ (T_i = T_{3M}, T_{6M}, \ldots, T_{10y}) \ // \ basis = 365$$
$$\Theta(i) = \theta_1 + (\theta_2 + \theta_3\delta_0(i))e^{-\theta_4\delta_0(i)}$$
$$\Phi(i) = \phi_1 + (\phi_2 + \phi_2\delta_0(i))e^{-\phi_1\delta_0(i)}$$
$$f(i) = |v_1 + (v_2 + v_2\delta_0(i))e^{-v_1\delta_0(i)}| \ // \ \text{values taken form caplet calibration}$$
$$\Delta(i) = \text{Algorithmx.x} \rightarrow \Delta(i), i = 1, 2, \ldots, \text{Number of caplet periods}$$
$$// \ \text{values taken form caplet calibration}$$
$$\varepsilon(i) = \text{Algorithmx.x} \rightarrow \varepsilon(i), i = 1, 2, \ldots, \text{Number of caplet periods}$$
$$// \ \text{values taken form caplet calibration}$$
$$\delta_{3M}(i) = (T_i - T_{i-3M})/basis$$
$$\psi(i) = \delta_{3M}(i)L(T_0, T_{i-3M}, T_{3M})^2$$
$$// \ \text{where } L(T_0, T_{i-3M}, T_i) \text{ is a forward LIBOR for period } T_{i-3M} \div T_i$$

Next i

Step 2 of calibration

For i = 1 to NumberOfCaplet Periods
  For j = 1 to NumberOfCaplet Periods
  $$\rho(i, j) = \cos[\Phi(i) - \Phi(j)] - \sin[\Phi(i)]\sin[\Phi(j)]\{1 - \cos[\Theta(i) - \Theta(j)]\}$$
  // instantaneous correlations

  Next j

Next i

For a_1 = 1 to 6
  For b_1 = 1 to 6
  $$i = 1 + 4x, x = 1, 2, 3, 4, 5, 7 \Rightarrow i = 5, 9, 13, 17, 21, 29$$
  // Index allowing to choose time to maturity for swaptions
  $$j = 4x, x = 1, 2, 3, 4, 5, 7 \Rightarrow j = 4, 8, 12, 16, 20, 28$$
  // Index allowing to choose length of underlying swap
  $$j = i + j - 1 \Rightarrow j = 8, 16, 24, 32, 40, 56$$
  If j <=NumberOfCapletPeriods // NumberOfCapletPeriods = 40 in our case
    counter = counter +1
    $$\Psi = 0$$
    For i_1 = i to j
      $$\Psi = \Psi + \psi(i\_1)$$

  Next i

  $$\sigma^{swaption} = 0 \ // \ \text{Setting initial swaption volatility to zero}$$

  For k = i to j

    For l = i to j

    $$\psi\_k = \psi(k)/\Psi, \ \psi\_l = \psi(l)/\Psi$$
    $$\rho\_kl = 0$$

    For i_1 = 1 to i − 1

      $$f\_k = f(k - i\_1)[1 + \varepsilon(i\_1)][1 + \Delta(k)]$$
      $$f\_l = f(l - i\_1)[1 + \varepsilon(i\_1)][1 + \Delta(l)]$$

$$\rho\_kl = \rho\_kl + f\_k \cdot f\_l \cdot \delta(i\_1)$$

Next i_1

$$\sigma^{swaption} = \sigma^{swaption} + \psi\_k \cdot \psi\_l \cdot \rho(k, l) \cdot \rho\_kl$$

Next l

Next k

$$T\_i = \delta_0(i)$$
$$\sigma^{swaption} = \sqrt{\sigma^{swaption}/T\_i}$$
$$err = \sigma^{swaption} - \sigma^{swaption}()$$
// difference between theoretical and market swaption volatilities
$$rsme = rsme + err^2$$ // root mean squared error

End If

Next b_1

Next a_1

End of algorithm 9.5

Results of the calibration

Step 1

Preliminary computations

Table 9.19 presents the preliminary computation results for swaption calibration (step 1)

Table 9.19   Results for step 1 of parametric swaption calibration

T_i	$\delta_0(i)$	$\delta_{3M}(i)$	$L(T_0, T_{i-3M}, T_i)$	$\delta_{3M}(i) \cdot L(T_0, T_{i-3M}, T_i)^2$
3M	0.2466	0.2528		
6M	0.4959	0.2556	0.02194	0.00012173
9M	0.7479	0.2556	0.02294	0.00013453
1Y	1.0000	0.2500	0.02415	0.00014905
1Y 3M	1.2466	0.2528	0.02544	0.00016180
1Y 6M	1.4959	0.2556	0.02659	0.00017873
1Y 9M	1.7479	0.2556	0.02775	0.00019686
2Y	2.0000	0.2500	0.02892	0.00021381
2Y 3M	2.2466	0.2528	0.02920	0.00021318
2Y 6M	2.4959	0.2556	0.03016	0.00022994
2Y 9M	2.7479	0.2556	0.03113	0.00024767
3Y	3.0000	0.2528	0.03211	0.00026342
3Y 3M	3.2493	0.2528	0.03236	0.00026471
3Y 6M	3.4986	0.2611	0.03322	0.00027889
3Y 9M	3.7562	0.2528	0.03335	0.00029046
4Y	4.0055	0.2528	0.03533	0.00031546
4Y 3M	4.2548	0.2528	0.03462	0.00030299
4Y 6M	4.5041	02528	0.03576	0.00032320
4Y 9M	4.7534	0.2528	0.03693	0.00034470
5Y	5.0027	0.2528	0.03771	0.00035940
5Y 3M	5.2521	0.3302	0.03702	0.00034643
5Y 6M	5.5778	0.1753	0.02919	0.00028135

Table 9.19   Continued

T_i	$\delta_0(i)$	$\delta_{3M}(i)$	$L(T_0, T_{i-3M}, T_i)$	$\delta_{3M}(i) \cdot L(T_0, T_{i-3M}, T_i)^2$
5Y 9M	5.7507	0.2556	0.05662	0.00056206
6Y	6.0027	0.2500	0.03955	0.00039983
6Y 3M	6.2493	0.2528	0.03986	0.00039724
6Y 6M	6.4986	0.2556	0.04053	0.00041530
6Y 9M	6.7507	0.2556	0.04121	0.00043405
7Y	7.0027	0.2528	0.04189	0.00044850
7Y 3M	7.2521	0.2528	0.04152	0.00043569
7Y 6M	7.5014	0.2556	0.04212	0.00044839
7Y 9M	7.7534	0.2556	0.04272	0.00046647
8Y	8.0055	0.2500	0.04333	0.00047984
8Y 3M	8.2521	0.2528	0.04378	0.00047927
8Y 6M	8.5014	0.2556	0.04438	0.00049779
8Y 9M	8.7534	0.2611	0.04498	0.00051693
9Y	9.0110	0.2444	0.04461	0.00051951
9Y 3M	9.2521	0.2528	0.04479	0.00049047
9Y 6M	9.5014	0.2611	0.04421	0.00049402
9Y 9M	9.7589	0.2528	0.04373	0.00049923
10Y	10.008	0.2493	0.04564	0.00052654

Step 2 of the algorithm is the running an optimization process where the goal is to minimize the difference between the theoretical and market prices of swaptions where the optimization is over the correlation parameters.

Starting from initial values $\theta_1 = \theta_2 = \theta_3 = \theta_4 = 1$ and $\phi_1 = \phi_2 = \phi_3 = \phi_4 = 1$ after the optimization we obtain the following values:

Table 9.20   Final values of parameters θ, ϕ

θ_1	0.1000000	ϕ_1	0.0404450
θ_2	0.1354474	ϕ_2	−0.0404486
θ_3	−0.0796023	ϕ_3	−0.0000264
θ_4	0.2899784	ϕ_4	0.0006514

We can now calculate the following parameters of $\Theta(i) = \theta_1 + (\theta_2 + \theta_3 \delta_0(i))e^{-\theta_4 \delta_0(i)}$ and $\Phi(i) = \phi_1 + (\phi_2 + \phi_2 \delta_0(i))e^{-\phi_1 \delta_0(i)}$ which are then presented in Table 9.21.

We can compare the theoretical and market swaption volatilities. Table 9.22 presents these results.

The instantaneous correlations are almost equal to one. The results seem to be much worse than when obtained via non-parametric calibration algorithms. There is the possibility to improve the results by manipulating the functional forms of functions $\Theta(i) = \theta_1 + (\theta_2 + \theta_3 \delta_0(i))e^{-\theta_4 \delta_0(i)}$ and $\Phi(i) = \phi_1 + (\phi_2 + \phi_2 \delta_0(i))e^{-\phi_1 \delta_0(i)}$. Another way to improve results may be by the use of more effective optimization algorithms allowing the minimization of the differences between theoretical and market swaption volatilities further.

Table 9.21 Final values of parameters Θ, Φ

T_i	$\Theta(i)$	$\Phi(i)$	T_i	$\Theta(i)$	$\Phi(i)$
3M	0.20782734	−0.000003618	5Y 3M	0.03836996	−0.000003828
6M	0.18311905	−0.000003639	5Y 6M	0.03878027	−0.000003827
9M	0.16110851	−0.000003659	5Y 9M	0.03917682	−0.000003825
1Y	0.14178780	−0.000003678	6Y	0.03994451	−0.000003822
1Y 3M	0.12523052	−0.000003695	6Y 3M	0.04088341	−0.000003818
1Y 6M	0.11060945	−0.000003711	6Y 6M	0.04199164	−0.000003813
1Y 9M	0.09777542	−0.000003727	6Y 9M	0.04324713	−0.000003807
2Y	0.08669785	−0.000003741	7Y	0.04461381	−0.000003800
2Y 3M	0.07738401	−0.000003754	7Y 3M	0.04605355	−0.000003791
2Y 6M	0.06933744	−0.000003766	7Y 6M	0.04756188	−0.000003782
2Y 9M	0.06245475	−0.000003777	7Y 9M	0.04913960	−0.000003771
3Y	0.05669461	−0.000003787	8Y	0.05075542	−0.000003760
3Y 3M	0.05197979	−0.000003796	8Y 3M	0.05236029	−0.000003747
3Y 6M	0.04813327	−0.000003804	8Y 6M	0.05399617	−0.000003734
3Y 9M	0.04496754	−0.000003811	8Y 9M	0.05565359	−0.000003719
4Y	0.04259363	−0.000003816	9Y	0.05734173	−0.000003702
4Y 3M	0.04081855	−0.000003821	9Y 3M	0.05891017	−0.000003686
4Y 6M	0.03957031	−0.000003824	9Y 6M	0.06051381	−0.000003668
4Y 9M	0.03878407	−0.000003826	9Y 9M	0.06214526	−0.000003649
5Y	0.03840144	−0.000003828	10Y	0.06369579	−0.000003628

Table 9.22 Theoretical and market swaption volatilities

Market	1Y	2Y	3Y	4Y	5Y	7Y
1Y	22.7000 %	23.0000 %	22.1000 %	20.9000 %	19.6000 %	17.6000 %
2Y	22.4000 %	21.5000 %	20.5000 %	19.4000 %	18.3000 %	16.7000 %
3Y	20.9000 %	20.1000 %	19.0000 %	18.0000 %	17.0000 %	15.8000 %
4Y	19.5000 %	18.7000 %	17.7000 %	16.8000 %	16.0000 %	
5Y	18.2000 %	17.4000 %	16.5000 %	15.8000 %	15.1000 %	
7Y	16.7200 %	16.0800 %	15.3000 %			

Theoretical	1Y	2Y	3Y	4Y	5Y	7Y
1Y	22.8165 %	22.0415 %	19.2960 %	17.1058 %	15.5043 %	13.6844 %
2Y	22.8386 %	20.6389 %	18.4044 %	16.5967 %	15.3733 %	13.7711 %
3Y	20.1999 %	18.9490 %	17.2257 %	15.8731 %	14.8469 %	13.6224 %
4Y	19.4248 %	18.2455 %	16.7513 %	15.4790 %	14.4750 %	
5Y	18.9177 %	17.7192 %	16.2348 %	14.9735 %	14.3294 %	
7Y	17.1656 %	15.8917 %	15.0285 %			

Difference	1Y	2Y	3Y	4Y	5Y	7Y
1Y	0.1165 %	−0.9585 %	−2.8040 %	−3.7942 %	−4.0957 %	−3.9156 %
2Y	0.4386 %	−0.8611 %	−2.0956 %	−2.8033 %	−2.9267 %	−2.9289 %
3Y	−0.7001 %	−1.1510 %	−1.7743 %	−2.1269 %	−2.1531 %	−2.1776 %
4Y	−0.0752 %	−0.4545 %	−0.9487 %	−1.3210 %	−1.5250 %	
5Y	0.7177 %	0.3192 %	−0.2652 %	−0.8265 %	−0.7706 %	
7Y	0.4456 %	−0.1883 %	−0.2715 %			

9.4 CONCLUSIONS

In this chapter we have presented two expanded calibration algorithms to caps and swaptions simultaneously. Both algorithms have used optimization techniques. The first algorithm, based on the Rebonato approach, resulted in some quite good results. The market and theoretical caplet volatilities are practically the same – all the differences are negligible. The obtained piecewise constant matrix of instantaneous volatilities also seems to be logical with values in the matrix close to untransformed market data. The outstanding values are rare and have small impact in real derivatives valuation.

The matrix of instantaneous correlations is also quite good. Correlations are close to one and there are no outstanding values as in the case of historical correlations. Based on instantaneous volatilities and implied correlations the table comparing differences between the theoretical and market swaption volatilities seems to be correct. Differences are relatively small and thus such results may be used in practice for valuation purposes.

The second algorithm was based on parametric functions approximating the market quotations of caps and swaptions. First we have to compute the parametric approximations of the caplet prices. Next we have to run an optimization to minimize the differences between the theoretical and market quotations of caps. We see that the results of calibration are acceptable but definitely worse than those obtained during non parametric calibration.

Having calibrated the approximating functions to caps we have moved into the calibration to swaptions. As a result we have obtained a matrix of instantaneous correlations. However the results are not as good as for non-parametric calibration. Almost all instantaneous correlations are equal to one. The reason for that may be in the wrong form of the widely used approximation functions. The other reason for wrong results may by using ineffective optimization algorithms when minimizing differences between the theoretical and market swaption volatilities. Definitely there is a place for further research in order to find more accurate optimization routines.

It is worth noting that in this chapter there are many of intermediate results. The reason for that is to help the reader fully understand the theory of calibration and the practical algorithms for implementation of the techniques in practice.

Both algorithms are frequently used in the market. However as we have seen in some market circumstances the results may be not satisfactory. This was especially evident in the case for parametric calibration. For that reason there is a clear visible trend in the market to use non-parametric calibration algorithms. Most of them are based on the piecewise constant volatility assumption which helps to price exotic interest derivatives in practice.

Part III
Simulation

Index of Notations for Part III

$Bound_n = Cont_n \cap Stop_n$ — free boundary

$C_n(x)$ — payoff

$Cont_n = \{x \in R^d : V_n(x) = U_n(x)\}$ — continuation set

$L_n^A(t)$ — combined predictor-corrector approximation of Libor rates

$L_n^B(t)$ — Brownian bridge approximation of Libor rates

$L_n^C(t)$ — predictor-corrector approximation of Libor rates

$L_n^D(t)$ — lognormal approximation of Libor rates

$L_n^E(t)$ — Euler approximation of Libor rates

$\hat{L}_n^A(l, m)$ — numerical approximation of $L_n^A(t)$ on the tree

$\hat{L}_n^D(l, m)$ — numerical approximation of $L_n^D(t)$ on the tree

$Stop_n = \{x \in R^d : V_n(x) = C_n(x)\}$ — stopping set

$U_n(x)$ — deferred Bellman function

$\hat{U}_n^1(x), \hat{U}_n^2(x)$ — estimators of $U_n(x)$

$V_n(x)$ — Bellman function

$\tilde{V}_n(x), \hat{V}_n(x)$ — estimators of $V_n(x)$

10

Approximations of the BGM Model

In the case of the HJM model all forward rates are represented as deterministic functions of the diffusion term – a property which does not hold for the BGM model. In this chapter we will present several formulae extending this property to the BGM model, however we can only achieve this in an approximate way.

10.1   EULER APPROXIMATION

This is a very simple approximation, also called 'freezing the drift.' It just consists of freezing random term in the drift, namely:

$$L_n^E(t) = L_n(0) \exp\left(-\sum_{j=n+1}^{k} K_j(0)C_{jn}(0, t) - \frac{1}{2}C_{nn}(0, t) + M_k^n(t)\right). \qquad (10.1)$$

Define also

$$K_n^E(t) = \frac{\delta L_n^E(t)}{1 + \delta L_n^E(t)}.$$

10.2   PREDICTOR-CORRECTOR APPROXIMATION

This approximation Hunter, Jaeckel and Joshi (2001); Joshi and Stacey (2006) is based on simplest possible approximation of integrals – we take value in the left end, add to the value in the right end, multiply by length of the interval and divide by two. Length of the interval is taken as a measure of $C_{nn}(0, t)$.

$$L_n^C(t) = L_n(0) \exp\left(-\frac{1}{2}\sum_{j=n+1}^{k} C_{jn}(0, t)\left(K_j(0) + \frac{\delta L_j^C(t)}{1 + \delta L_j^C(t)}\right) - \frac{1}{2}C_{nn}(0, t) + M_k^n(t)\right).$$
$$(10.2)$$

If $n < k$, the formula (10.2) is a recursive definition of $L_n^C(t)$. If $n > k$, the formula (10.2) is not a definition but a set of equations giving unique solutions of $L_n^C(t)$, which may be solved by approximations. Taking first step in the approximations is also acceptable:

$$L_n^C(t) = L_n(0) \exp\left(\frac{1}{2}\sum_{j=k+1}^{n} C_{jn}(0, t)\left(K_j(0) + K_j^E(t)\right) - \frac{1}{2}C_{nn}(0, t) + M_k^n(t)\right). \qquad (10.3)$$

10.3   BROWNIAN BRIDGE APPROXIMATION

This approximation is due to Pietersz, Pelsser and Van Regenmortel (2004). Define a new Gaussian process

$$\hat{M}_k^n(t) = M_k^n(t) - \frac{C_{nn}(0, t)}{C_{nn}(0, T)} M_k^n(T)$$

Lemma. The process $\hat{M}_k^n(t)$ is Gaussian with mean zero, independent of $M_k^n(T)$ and its variance is equal to

$$E_k \hat{M}_k^n(t)^2 = \frac{C_{nn}(0, t) C_{nn}(t, T)}{C_{nn}(0, T)}.$$

Proof. We can clearly see that

$$E_k \hat{M}_k^n(t)^2 = E_k \left(M_k^n(t) - \frac{C_{nn}(0, t)}{C_{nn}(0, T)} M_k^n(T) \right)^2$$

$$= E_k \left(\frac{C_{nn}(t, T)}{C_{nn}(0, T)} M_k^n(t) + \frac{C_{nn}(0, t)}{C_{nn}(0, T)} (M_k^n(t) - M_k^n(T)) \right)^2 = \frac{C_{nn}(0, t) C_{nn}(t, T)}{C_{nn}(0, T)}$$

and

$$E_k \hat{M}_k^n(t) M_k^n(T) = E_k \left(M_k^n(t) M_k^n(T) - \frac{C_{nn}(0, t)}{C_{nn}(0, T)} M_k^n(T)^2 \right) = 0.$$

As uncorrelated Gaussian processes are also independent, the Lemma is proven. Hence we have

$$E_k \left(\exp(M_k^n(t)) \,|\, M_k^n(T) \right) = E_k \left(\exp \left(\hat{M}_k^n(t) + \frac{C_{nn}(0, t)}{C_{nn}(0, T)} M_k^n(T) \right) \,\Big|\, M_k^n(T) \right)$$

$$= \exp \left(\frac{C_{nn}(0, t)}{C_{nn}(0, T)} \left(M_k^n(T) + \frac{1}{2} C_{nn}(t, T) \right) \right)$$

and therefore

$$\tilde{L}_n(t, T) = E_k \left(L_n^E(t) \,|\, L_n^E(T) \right)$$

$$= L_n(0) \exp \left(\frac{C_{nn}(0, t)}{C_{nn}(0, T)} \left(M_k^n(T) - \frac{1}{2} C_{nn}(0, t) \right) - \sum_{i=n+1}^{k} K_i(0) C_{ni}(0, t) \right). \quad (10.4)$$

Thus we can define

$$L_n^B(T) = L_n(0) \exp \left(M_k^n(T) - \frac{1}{2} C_{nn}(0, T) - \int_0^t \sum_{i=n+1}^{k} \frac{\delta \tilde{L}_i(s, T) \gamma_n(s) \cdot \gamma_i(s)}{1 + \delta \tilde{L}_i(s, T)} ds \right). \quad (10.5)$$

10.4 COMBINED PREDICTOR-CORRECTOR-BROWNIAN BRIDGE

A combination of the Predictor-Corrector and Brownian bridge approaches seems to be most suitable. We make use of the approximation:

$$
L_n^A(T) = L_n(0) \exp \left(M_k^n(T) - \frac{1}{2} C_{nn}(0, T) - \sum_{i=n+1}^{k} E_k \left(\int_0^T K_i^E(s) \gamma_n(s) \cdot \gamma_i(s) ds \,\bigg|\, M_k^i(T) \right) \right),
$$

(10.6)

what is more accurate than (10.5). Calculate the auxiliary variable $Y_k^{in}(M_k^i(T), T)$

$$
Y_k^{in}(M_k^i(T), T) = E_k \left(\int_0^T K_i^E(s) \gamma_n(s) \cdot \gamma_i(s) ds \,\bigg|\, M_k^i(T) \right)
$$

$$
= E_k \left(E_k \left(\int_0^T K_i^E(s) \gamma_n(s) \cdot \gamma_i(s) ds \,\bigg|\, M_k^i(t), S \le t \le T \right) \,\bigg|\, M_k^i(T) \right)
$$

$$
= E_k \left(E_k \left(\int_0^S K_i^E(s) \gamma_n(s) \cdot \gamma_i(s) ds \,\bigg|\, M_k^i(S) \right) + \int_S^T K_i^E(s) \gamma_n(s) \cdot \gamma_i(s) ds \,\bigg|\, M_k^i(T) \right)
$$

$$
= E_k \left(Y_k^{in}(M_k^i(S), S) + \int_S^T K_i^E(s) \gamma_n(s) \cdot \gamma_i(s) ds \,\bigg|\, M_k^i(T) \right)
$$

$$
\cong E_k \left(Y_k^{in}(M_k^i(S), S) + \frac{1}{2} \left(K_i^E(S) + K_i^E(T) \right) C_{in}(S, T) \,\bigg|\, M_k^i(T) \right),
$$

where the distribution of $M_k^i(S) | M_k^i(T)$ is normal with mean $\mu = C_{ii}(0, S) M_k^i(T) / C_{ii}(0, T)$ and variance $\sigma^2 = C_{ii}(0, S) C_{ii}(t, T) / C_{ii}(0, T)$.

Hence

$$
Y_k^{in}(M_k^i(T), T) = \frac{1}{\sigma \sqrt{2\pi}} \int_{-\infty}^{\infty} \left(Y_k^{in}(x, S) + \frac{1}{2} \frac{\delta L_i^k(S, x) C_{in}(S, T)}{1 + \delta L_i^k(S, x)} \right) \exp \left(\frac{(x - \mu)^2}{2\sigma^2} \right) dx
$$

$$
+ \frac{1}{2} K_i^E(T) C_{in}(S, T),
$$

(10.7)

where

$$
L_i^k(t, x) = L_i(0) \exp \left(- \sum_{j=i+1}^{k} K_j(0) C_{jn}(0, t) - \frac{1}{2} C_{ii}(0, t) + x \right).
$$

Alternatively, if we resign from Predictor-Corrector adjustment

$$Y_k^{in}(M_k^i(T), T) \cong E_k\left(Y_k^{in}(M_k^i(S), S) + K_i^E(S)C_{in}(S, T)\,\big|\,M_k^i(T)\right)$$

and

$$Y_k^{in}(M_k^i(T), T) = \frac{1}{\sigma\sqrt{2\pi}}\int_{-\infty}^{\infty}\left(Y_k^{in}(x, S) + \frac{\delta L_i^k(S, x)C_{in}(S, T)}{1 + \delta L_i^k(S, x)}\right)\exp\left(\frac{(x-\mu)^2}{2\sigma^2}\right)dx.$$

where the integral with respect to time was replaced by a space integral and both may be calculated by numerical methods. While pricing on trees, $M_k^i(S)\big|M_k^i(T)$ is naturally calculated via the Bayes formula and backward trees. We can then finally define

$$L_n^A(T) = L_n(0)\exp\left(M_k^n(T) - \frac{1}{2}C_{nn}(0, T) - \sum_{i=n+1}^{k} Y_k^{in}(M_k^i(T), T)\right). \tag{10.8}$$

10.5 SINGLE-DIMENSIONAL CASE

In the single dimensional case we have the following properties:

$$\gamma_n(t) = \beta_n\gamma(t) \tag{10.9}$$

Where $\gamma_n(t)$ is the BGM volatility,

$$M_k^n(t) = \beta_n M_k(t), \text{ where } M_k(t) = \int_0^t \gamma(s)dW_k(s), \tag{10.10}$$

$$C_{mn}(t, T) = \beta_n\beta_m C(t, T), \text{ where } C(t, T) = \int_t^T \left|\gamma(s)\right|^2 ds. \tag{10.11}$$

It is possible to slightly improve our approximation in this case:

$$L_n^A(T) = L_n(0)\exp\left(M_k^n(T) - \frac{1}{2}C_{nn}(0, T) - \sum_{i=n+1}^{k} E_k\left(\int_0^T \frac{\delta L_i^A(s)\gamma_n(s)\cdot\gamma_i(s)}{1 + \delta L_i^A(s)}ds\,\bigg|\,M_k(T)\right)\right) \tag{10.12}$$

Thus we now have

$$Y_k^{in}(M_k(T), T) = E_k\left(\int_0^T \frac{\delta L_i^A(s)\gamma_n(s)\cdot\gamma_i(s)}{1 + \delta L_i^A(s)}ds\,\bigg|\,M_k(T)\right)$$

And we may calculate that

$$Y_k^{in}(M_k(T), T) \cong E_k\left(Y_k^{in}(M_k(S), S) + \frac{1}{2}\left(\frac{\delta L_i^A(S)}{1 + \delta L_i^A(S)} + \frac{\delta L_i^A(T)}{1 + \delta L_i^A(T)}\right)C_{in}(S, T)\,\bigg|\,M_k(T)\right), \tag{10.13}$$

Or alternatively

$$Y_k^{in}(M_k(T), T) \cong E_k \left(Y_k^{in}(M_k(S), S) + \frac{\delta L_i^A(S)}{1 + \delta L_i^A(S)} C_{in}(S, T) \middle| M_k(T) \right), \tag{10.14}$$

where the distribution of $M_k(S) \middle| M_k(T)$ is normal with mean $\mu = C(0, S)M_k(T)/C(0, T)$ and variance $\sigma^2 = C(0, S)C(S, T)/C(0, T)$. Hence from (10.14) we see that

$$Y_k^{in}(M_k(T), T) = \frac{1}{\sigma\sqrt{2\pi}} \int_{-\infty}^{\infty} \left(Y_k^{in}(x, S) + \frac{1}{2} \frac{\delta L_i^k(S, x) C_{in}(S, T)}{1 + \delta L_i^k(S, x)} \right) \exp\left(-\frac{(x - \mu)^2}{2\sigma^2} \right) dx$$

$$+ \frac{1}{2} \frac{L_i^A(T)}{1 + \delta L_i^A(T)} C_{in}(S, T), \tag{10.15}$$

where

$$L_i^k(t, x) = L_i(0) \exp\left(-\sum_{j=i+1}^{k} Y_i^{jn}(x, t) - \frac{1}{2} C_{ii}(0, t) + x \right). \tag{10.16}$$

Finally we obtain

$$L_n^A(T) = L_n(0) \exp\left(M_k^n(T) - \frac{1}{2} C_{nn}(0, T) - \sum_{i=n+1}^{k} Y_k^{in}(M_k^i(T), T) \right). \tag{10.17}$$

Where, as before, if $n < k$, the formula (10.17) is a recursive definition of $L_n^A(t)$. If $n > k$, the formula (10.17) is a set of equations giving unique solutions of $L_n^A(t)$, which may be solved by approximations.

10.6 SINGLE-DIMENSIONAL COMPLETE CASE

An analogous approximation may be performed in the multiplicative form:

$$L_n^D(T) = L_n(0) \exp\left(M_k^n(T) - \frac{1}{2} C_{nn}(0, T) \right) Z_k^n(M_k(T), T), \tag{10.18}$$

where $Z_k^n(M_k(T), T) = E_k \left(A_n^k(0, T) \middle| M_k(T) \right)$ and

$$A_k^n(t, T) = \exp\left(-\int_t^T \sum_{j=n+1}^{k} \frac{\delta L_j^D(s) \gamma_k(s) \cdot \gamma_j(s)}{1 + \delta L_j^D(s)} ds \right).$$

Calculate

$$Z_k^n(M_k(T), T) = E_k \left(E_k \left(A_k^n(0, T) \middle| M_k(s), S \leq s \leq T \right) \middle| M_k(T) \right)$$

$$= E_k \left(E_k \left(A_k^n(0, S) \middle| M_k(s), S \leq s \leq T \right) A_k^n(S, T) \middle| M_k(T) \right) \tag{10.19}$$

$$= E_k \left(Z_k^n(M_k(S), S) A_k^n(S, T) \middle| M_k(T) \right).$$

The exponential integral $A_k^n(S, T)$ may be approximated by the Predictor-Corrector method:

$$A_k^n(S, T) \cong \exp\left(-\frac{1}{2}\sum_{i=n+1}^{k}\left(\frac{\delta L_i^D(T)}{1+\delta L_i^D(T)} + \frac{\delta L_i^D(S)}{1+\delta L_i^D(S)}\right)C_{in}(S, T)\right) \qquad (10.20)$$

or Euler method

$$A_k^n(S, T) \cong \exp\left(-\sum_{i=n+1}^{k}\frac{\delta L_i^D(S)}{1+\delta L_i^D(S)}C_{in}(S, T)\right). \qquad (10.21)$$

Therefore (by using (10.19) and (10.20))

$$Z_k^n(M_k(T), T) \cong E_k\left(Z_k^n(M_k(S), S)\exp\left(-\sum_{i=n+1}^{k}\frac{K_i^D(T)+K_i^D(S)}{2}C_{in}(S, T)\right)\middle| M_k(T)\right),$$

where we have

$$K_i^D(T) = \frac{\delta L_i^D(T)}{1+\delta L_i^D(T)}.$$

Similarly as in $L_i^A(\cdot)$ case described previously distribution of $M_k(S)\big| M_k(T)$ is normal with mean $\mu = C(0, S)M_k(T)/C(0, T)$ and variance $\sigma^2 = C(0, S)C(S, T)/C(0, T)$. Hence

$$Z_k^n(M_k(T), T) = \frac{1}{\sigma\sqrt{2\pi}}\exp\left(-\frac{1}{2}\sum_{i=n+1}^{k}\frac{\delta L_i^D(T)C_{in}(S, T)}{1+\delta L_i^D(T)}\right)$$

$$\int_{-\infty}^{+\infty} Z_k^n(x, S)\cdot\exp\left(-\frac{1}{2}\frac{\delta L_i^k(S, x)C_{in}(S, T)}{1+\delta L_i^k(S, x)} - \frac{(x-\mu)^2}{2\sigma^2}\right)dx,$$

where

$$L_i^k(S, x) = L_i(0)Z_k^i(x, S)\exp\left(-\frac{1}{2}C_{ii}(0, t) + \beta_i x\right).$$

Finally

$$L_n^D(T) = L_n(0)Z_k^n(M_k(T), T)\exp\left(-\frac{1}{2}C_{nn}(0, t) + M_k^n(T)\right). \qquad (10.22)$$

Once again we have the situation that if $n < k$, the formula (10.22) is a recursive definition of $L_n^D(t)$. If $n > k$, the formula (10.22) is a set of equations giving unique solutions of $L_n^D(t)$, which may be solved by approximations.

10.7   BINOMIAL TREE CONSTRUCTION FOR $L_n^A(t)$

In the next sections we deal with numerical construction of binomial and trinomial trees. We assume that

$$\gamma(t) \equiv 1 \qquad (10.23)$$

(See (10.9))
By equations (10.23), (10.9), (10.10), (10.11) and (10.17)

$$L_n^A(t) = L_n(0) \cdot \exp\left(-\sum_{j=n+1}^{N} Y_N^{jn}\left(\beta_j W_N(t), t\right) - \frac{1}{2} \cdot \beta_n^2 \cdot t + \beta_n \cdot W_N(t)\right) \qquad (10.24)$$

where, following (10.6)

$$Y_N^{jn}\left(\beta_j W_N(t), t\right) = E_N\left(Y_N^{jn}\left(\beta_j W_N(t - \Delta t), t - \Delta t\right) + \frac{\delta L_j^A(t - \Delta t)\beta_n\beta_j}{1 + \delta L_j^A(t - \Delta t)}\Delta t\, \middle|\, W_N(t)\right) \qquad (10.25)$$

where Δt is the size of a time step inside the constructed tree.

The processes $L_n^A(t)$ depend only on the one dimensional Brownian Motion $W_N(t)$ and therefore can be modelled by binomial tree. At each node of constructed tree the values of the forward LIBORs are approximated by:

$$\hat{L}_n^A(l, m) = L_n(0) \cdot \exp\left(-\sum_{j=n+1}^{N} \hat{Y}^{jn}(l, m) - \frac{1}{2} \cdot \beta_n^2 \cdot m \cdot \Delta t + \beta_n \cdot \hat{W}(m, l)\right), \qquad (10.26)$$

where the Markov chain $\hat{W}(m)$ approximates a Brownian motion and is defined as

$$\hat{W}(0) = 0$$

$$\hat{W}(m) = \begin{cases} \hat{W}(m-1) + \sqrt{\Delta t} & \text{with probability} = 0.5 \\ \hat{W}(m-1) - \sqrt{\Delta t} & \text{with probability} = 0.5 \end{cases}$$

$$\hat{W}(m, l) = l\sqrt{\Delta t}.$$

The numbers m and l are horizontal and vertical coordinates of the tree respectively.

The discrete process $\hat{Y}^{jn}(l, m)$ approximates $Y^{jn}\left(\beta_j W_N(t), t\right)$ and is defined recursively as

$$\hat{Y}^{jn}(l, m) = E_N\left(\hat{Y}^{jn}(\cdot, m-1) + \frac{\delta \cdot \beta_j \cdot \beta_n \cdot \hat{L}_j^A(\cdot, m-1)}{1 + \delta \cdot \hat{L}_j^A(\cdot, m-1)} \cdot \Delta t\, \middle|\, \hat{W}(m) = l\sqrt{\Delta t}\right) \qquad (10.27)$$

We can demonstrate this process by means of a detailed example.

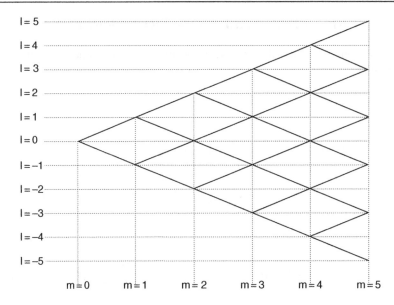

Figure 10.1   Example of a binomial tree to be used in our example.

In order to calculate $\hat{Y}^{jn}(l, m)$ let us notice that node (m, l) can be reached only from one of the two nodes (given that we are in the main part of the tree and not at an edge or at the start of the tree):

$(m - 1, l - 1)$ (let us call this node 'Low Node')

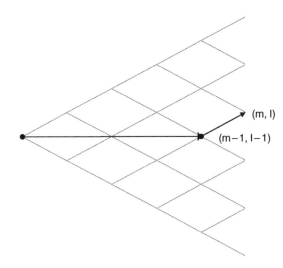

Figure 10.2   Movement up.

or $(m-1, l+1)$ (let us call this node 'Hi Node').

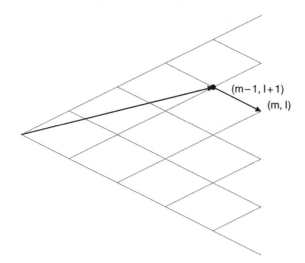

Figure 10.3 Movement down.

Following (10.27) we have

$$\hat{Y}^{jn}(l, m) = P_{Hi}(m, l) \cdot \left(\hat{Y}^{jn}(l+1, m-1) + \frac{\delta \cdot \beta_j \cdot \beta_n \cdot \hat{L}_j^A(l+1, m-1)}{1 + \hat{L}_j^A(l+1, m-1)} \cdot \Delta t \right)$$

$$+ P_{Low}(m, l) \cdot \left(\hat{Y}^{jn}(l-1, m-1) + \frac{\delta \cdot \beta_j \cdot \beta_n \cdot \hat{L}_j^A(l-1, m-1)}{1 + \hat{L}_j^A(l-1, m-1)} \cdot \Delta t \right)$$

where

$$P_{Hi}(m, l) := E_N \left(1_{\hat{W}(m-1)=(l+1)\sqrt{\Delta t}} \Big| \hat{W}(m) = l\sqrt{\Delta t} \right)$$

is a conditional probability that node (m, l) is reached from the node $(m-1, l+1)$ under condition that node (m, l) was reached at all. In addition

$$P_{Low}(m, l) := E_N \left(1_{\hat{W}(m-1)=(l-1)\sqrt{\Delta t}} \Big| \hat{W}(m) = l\sqrt{\Delta t} \right)$$

is a conditional probability that node (m, l) is reached from the node $(m-1, l-1)$ under condition that node (m, l) was reached at all.

Let us define

$$P(m, l) := E_N \left(1_{\hat{W}(m)=l\sqrt{\Delta t}} \right)$$

as the unconditional probability that node (m, l) will be reached at all, so:

$$P_{Low}(m, l) = \frac{P(m-1, l-1) \cdot 0.5}{P(m, l)} \tag{10.28}$$

The numerator of the expression above is equal to unconditional probability that node $(m-1, l-1)$ will be reached, multiplied by probability that movement from this node will be upward. So the numerator is equal to unconditional probability that both nodes $(m-1, l-1)$ and (m, l) will be reached. Analogously:

$$P_{Hi}(m, l) = \frac{P(m-1, l+1) \cdot 0.5}{P(m, l)} \tag{10.29}$$

In order to calculate $P(m, l)$ let us see that node (m, l) will be reached if and only if there are exactly $l + m/2$ movements up (out of total number of movements equal m). Hence the unconditional probability that node (m, l) will be reached is:

$$P(m, l) = \binom{m}{\frac{l+m}{2}} \cdot 2^{-m} \tag{10.30}$$

By the equation (10.28), (10.29) and (10.30) we have:

$$P_{Low}(m, l) = \frac{\binom{m-1}{\frac{l+m-2}{2}}}{\binom{m}{\frac{l+m}{2}}} \tag{10.31}$$

$$P_{Hi}(m, l) = \frac{\binom{m-1}{\frac{l+m}{2}}}{\binom{m}{\frac{l+m}{2}}} \tag{10.32}$$

Therefore we are able to calculate P_{Hi} and P_{Low} by closed formulas. Alternatively, these probabilities can be calculated numerically using the described below recursion.

$$P(1, -1) = P(1, 1) = 0.5$$

$$P(m, l) = 0.5 \cdot P(m-1, l-1) + 0.5 \cdot P(m-1, l+1)$$

10.8   BINOMIAL TREE CONSTRUCTION FOR $L_n^D(t)$

We can build our tree basing on formula (10.18). In this case forward LIBORs will be approximated by:

$$L_n^D(t) = L_n(0) \cdot Z_N^n(W_N(t), t) \exp\left(-\frac{1}{2}\beta_n^2 t + \beta_n W_N(t)\right)$$

where following (10.19) and (10.21) we have that

$$Z_N^n(W_N(t), t) = E_N\left(Z_N^n(W_N(t-\Delta t), t-\Delta t) \exp\left(-\sum_{i=n+1}^{N} \frac{\delta L_i^D(t-\Delta t)\beta_i\beta_n\Delta t}{1+\delta L_i^D(t-\Delta t)}\right)\bigg| W_N(t)\right).$$

The processes $L_n^D(t)$ can be modeled by binomial tree, analogously as processes $L_n^A(t)$. At each node of the constructed tree the $L_n^D(t)$ are approximated by

$$\hat{L}_n^D(m,l) = L_n(0)\,\hat{Z}^n(l,m)\exp\left(-\frac{1}{2}\beta_n^2 m\Delta t + \beta_n \hat{W}(m)\right),\qquad(10.33)$$

where

$$\hat{Z}^n(l,m) = E_N\left(\hat{Z}^n(\cdot,m-1)\cdot\exp\left(-\sum_{j=n+1}^{N}\frac{\delta\hat{L}_j^D(m-1,\cdot)\beta_j\beta_n\Delta t}{1+\delta\hat{L}_j^D(m-1,\cdot)}\right)\middle|\hat{W}(m)=l\sqrt{\Delta t}\right)$$

$$= P_{Hi}(m,l)\cdot\hat{Z}^n(l+1,m-1)\cdot\exp\left(-\sum_{j=n+1}^{N}\frac{\delta\hat{L}_j^D(m-1,l+1)\beta_j\beta_n\Delta t}{1+\delta\hat{L}_j^D(m-1,l+1)}\right)$$

$$(10.34)$$

$$+ P_{Low}(m,l)\cdot\hat{Z}^n(l-1,m-1)\cdot\exp\left(-\sum_{j=n+1}^{N}\frac{\delta\hat{L}_j^D(m-1,l-1)\beta_j\beta_n\Delta t}{1+\delta\hat{L}_j^D(m-1,l-1)}\right)$$

and $P_{Hi}(m,l)$ and $P_{Low}(m,l)$ are defined by formulae (10.31) and (10.32).

10.9   NUMERICAL EXAMPLE OF BINOMIAL TREE CONSTRUCTION

In this example we construct a binomial tree that models four 6M forward LIBORs L_1, L_2, L_3, L_4, so hence $N=4$. We assume that time step of the tree $\Delta t = 0.25$. It means that there are two time steps within each LIBOR period. Initial values of forward LIBOR are all equal 5%. Volatility of each forward LIBOR is assumed to be 20%, so $\beta_1 = \beta_2 = \beta_3 = \beta_4 = 0.2$. We describe the calculation of $\hat{L}_1^D, \hat{L}_2^D, \hat{L}_3^D, \hat{L}_4^D$ via this tree method. A reference tree for this example is shown on the next page.

We now work in detail through this numerical example:
At node $m=0$, $l=0$ we have

$$\hat{L}_1^D(0,0) = \hat{L}_2^D(0,0) = \hat{L}_3^D(0,0) = \hat{L}_4^D(0,0) = 0.05,\qquad(10.35)$$

$$\hat{Z}^1(0,0) = \hat{Z}^2(0,0) = \hat{Z}^3(0,0) = \hat{Z}^4(0,0) = 1.\qquad(10.36)$$

At node $m=1$, $l=-1$ following (10.31) and (10.32)

$$P_{Low}(1,-1) = 0$$

$$P_{Hi}(1,-1) = 1.$$

Then from (10.34), (10.35) and (10.36)

$$\hat{Z}^2(-1,1) = 1\cdot\exp\left(-\frac{0.5\cdot0.05\cdot0.2\cdot0.2\cdot0.25}{1+0.5\cdot0.05}-\frac{0.5\cdot0.05\cdot0.2\cdot0.2\cdot0.25}{1+0.5\cdot0.05}\right) = 0.9995123$$

$$(10.37)$$

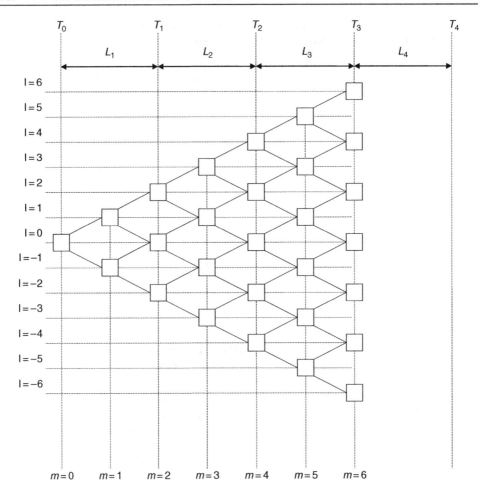

Figure 10.4   Example tree for reference.

$$\hat{Z}^3(-1,1) = 1 \cdot \exp\left(-\frac{0.5 \cdot 0.05 \cdot 0.2 \cdot 0.2 \cdot 0.25}{1 + 0.5 \cdot 0.05}\right) = 0.9997561 \tag{10.38}$$

$$\hat{Z}^4(-1,1) = 1 \tag{10.39}$$

And from (10.33), (10.37) to (10.39)

$$\hat{L}_2^D(1,-1) = 0.05 \cdot 0.9995123 \cdot \exp\left(-\frac{1}{2} \cdot 0.2^2 \cdot 1 \cdot 0.25 + 0.2 \cdot (-1) \cdot \sqrt{0.25}\right) = 0.0449943 \tag{10.40}$$

$$\hat{L}_3^D(1,-1) = 0.05 \cdot 0.9997561 \cdot \exp\left(-\frac{1}{2} \cdot 0.2^2 \cdot 1 \cdot 0.25 + 0.2 \cdot (-1) \cdot \sqrt{0.25}\right) = 0.0450052 \tag{10.41}$$

$$\hat{L}_4^D(1,-1)=0.05\cdot 1\cdot \exp\left(-\frac{1}{2}\cdot 0.2^2\cdot 1\cdot 0.25+0.2\cdot(-1)\cdot\sqrt{0.25}\right)=0.0450162 \quad (10.42)$$

At node $m=1$, $l=1$ following (10.31) and (10.32)

$$P_{Low}(1,1)=1$$

$$P_{Hi}(1,1)=0$$

Then from (10.34), (10.35) and (10.36)

$$\hat{Z}^2(1,1)=\exp\left(-\frac{0.5\cdot 0.05\cdot 0.2\cdot 0.2\cdot 0.25}{1+0.5\cdot 0.05}-\frac{0.5\cdot 0.05\cdot 0.2\cdot 0.2\cdot 0.25}{1+0.5\cdot 0.05}\right)=0.9995123$$
$$(10.43)$$

$$\hat{Z}^3(1,1)=\exp\left(-\frac{0.5\cdot 0.05\cdot 0.2\cdot 0.2\cdot 0.25}{1+0.5\cdot 0.05}\right)=0.9997561 \quad (10.44)$$

$$\hat{Z}^4(1,1)=1 \quad (10.45)$$

And from (10.33), (10.43) to (10.45)

$$\hat{L}_2^D(1,1)=0.05\cdot 0.9995123\cdot \exp\left(-\frac{1}{2}\cdot 1\cdot 0.2^2\cdot 0.25+0.2\cdot 1\cdot\sqrt{0.25}\right)=0.0549561$$
$$(10.46)$$

$$\hat{L}_3^D(1,1)=0.05\cdot 0.9997561\cdot \exp\left(-\frac{1}{2}\cdot 1\cdot 0.2^2\cdot 0.25+0.2\cdot 1\cdot\sqrt{0.25}\right)=0.0549695$$
$$(10.47)$$

$$\hat{L}_4^D(1,1)=0.05\cdot 1\cdot \exp\left(-\frac{1}{2}\cdot 0.2^2\cdot 1\cdot 0.25+0.2\cdot 1\cdot\sqrt{0.25}\right)=0.0549829 \quad (10.48)$$

At node $m=2$, $l=-2$ following (10.31) and (10.32)

$$P_{Low}(2,-2)=0$$

$$P_{Hi}(2,-2)=1$$

Then from (10.34), (10.37) to (10.42)

$$\hat{Z}^2(-2,2)=0.9995123\cdot \exp\left(-\frac{0.5\cdot 0.0450052\cdot 0.2\cdot 0.2\cdot 0.25}{1+0.5\cdot 0.0450052}-\frac{0.5\cdot 0.0450162\cdot 0.2\cdot 0.2\cdot 0.25}{1+0.5\cdot 0.0450162}\right)$$
$$(10.49)$$

$$=0.999072$$

$$\hat{Z}^3(-2,2)=0.9997561\cdot\exp\left(-\frac{0.5\cdot0.0450162\cdot0.2\cdot0.2\cdot0.25}{1+0.5\cdot0.0450162}\right)=0.999536 \quad (10.50)$$

$$\hat{Z}^4(-2,2)=1 \quad (10.51)$$

And from (10.33), (10.49) to (10.51)

$$\hat{L}_2^D(2,-2)=0.05\cdot0.999072\cdot\exp\left(-\frac{1}{2}\cdot0.2^2\cdot2\cdot0.25+0.2\cdot(-2)\cdot\sqrt{0.25}\right)=0.040492$$
$$(10.52)$$

$$\hat{L}_3^D(2,-2)=0.05\cdot0.999536\cdot\exp\left(-\frac{1}{2}\cdot0.2^2\cdot2\cdot0.25+0.2\cdot(-2)\cdot\sqrt{0.25}\right)=0.04051$$
$$(10.53)$$

$$\hat{L}_4^D(2,-2)=0.05\cdot1\cdot\exp\left(-\frac{1}{2}\cdot0.2^2\cdot2\cdot0.25+0.2\cdot(-2)\cdot\sqrt{0.25}\right)=0.040529 \quad (10.54)$$

At node $m=2$, $l=0$ following (10.31) and (10.32)

$$P_{Low}(2,0)=P_{Hi}(2,0)=0.5$$

Then from (10.34), (10.37) to (10.42), (10.43) to (10.48)

$$\hat{Z}^2(0,2)=0.5\cdot0.9995123\cdot\exp\left(-\frac{0.5\cdot0.0549695\cdot0.2\cdot0.2\cdot0.25}{1+0.5\cdot0.0549695}-\frac{0.5\cdot0.0549829\cdot0.2\cdot0.2\cdot0.25}{1+0.5\cdot0.0549829}\right)$$
$$+0.5\cdot0.9995123\cdot\exp\left(-\frac{0.5\cdot0.0450052\cdot0.2\cdot0.2\cdot0.25}{1+0.5\cdot0.0450052}-\frac{0.5\cdot0.0450162\cdot0.2\cdot0.2\cdot0.25}{1+0.5\cdot0.0450162}\right)$$
$$(10.55)$$

$$=0.999025$$

$$\hat{Z}^3(0,2)=0.5\cdot0.9997561\cdot\exp\left(-\frac{0.5\cdot0.0549829\cdot0.2\cdot0.2\cdot0.25}{1+0.5\cdot0.0549829}\right)$$
$$+0.5\cdot0.9997561\cdot\exp\left(-\frac{0.5\cdot0.0450162\cdot0.2\cdot0.2\cdot0.25}{1+0.5\cdot0.0450162}\right) \quad (10.56)$$

$$=0.999512$$

$$\hat{Z}^4(0,2)=1 \quad (10.57)$$

And from (10.33), (10.55) to (10.57)

$$\hat{L}_2^D(2,0) = 0.05 \cdot 0.999025 \cdot \exp\left(-\frac{1}{2} \cdot 0.2^2 \cdot 2 \cdot 0.25 + 0.2 \cdot 0 \cdot \sqrt{0.25}\right) = 0.049454$$

(10.58)

$$\hat{L}_3^D(2,0) = 0.05 \cdot 0.999512 \cdot \exp\left(-\frac{1}{2} \cdot 0.2^2 \cdot 2 \cdot 0.25 + 0.2 \cdot 0 \cdot \sqrt{0.25}\right) = 0.049478$$

(10.59)

$$\hat{L}_4^D(2,0) = 0.05 \cdot 1 \cdot \exp\left(-\frac{1}{2} \cdot 0.2^2 \cdot 2 \cdot 0.25 + 0.2 \cdot 0 \cdot \sqrt{0.25}\right) = 0.049502 \qquad (10.60)$$

At node $m=2$, $l=2$ following (10.31) and (10.32)

$$P_{Hi}(2,2) = 0$$
$$P_{Low}(2,2) = 1$$

Then from (10.34), (10.43) to (10.48)

$$\hat{Z}^2(2,2) = 0.9995123 \cdot \exp\left(-\frac{0.5 \cdot 0.0549695 \cdot 0.2 \cdot 0.2 \cdot 0.25}{1 + 0.5 \cdot 0.0549695} - \frac{0.5 \cdot 0.0549829 \cdot 0.2 \cdot 0.2 \cdot 0.25}{1 + 0.5 \cdot 0.0549829}\right)$$

(10.61)

$$= 0.998978$$

$$\hat{Z}^3(2,2) = 0.9997561 \cdot \exp\left(-\frac{0.5 \cdot 0.0549829 \cdot 0.2 \cdot 0.2 \cdot 0.25}{1 + 0.5 \cdot 0.0549829}\right) = 0.999489 \qquad (10.62)$$

$$\hat{Z}^4(2,2) = 1 \qquad (10.63)$$

And from (10.33), (10.61) to (10.63)

$$\hat{L}_2^D(2,2) = 0.05 \cdot 0.998978 \cdot \exp\left(-\frac{1}{2} \cdot 0.2^2 \cdot 2 \cdot 0.25 + 0.2 \cdot 2 \cdot \sqrt{0.25}\right) = 0.060401$$

(10.64)

$$\hat{L}_3^D(2,2) = 0.05 \cdot 0.999489 \cdot \exp\left(-\frac{1}{2} \cdot 0.2^2 \cdot 2 \cdot 0.25 + 0.2 \cdot 2 \cdot \sqrt{0.25}\right) = 0.060432$$

(10.65)

$$\hat{L}_4^D(2,2) = 0.05 \cdot 1 \cdot \exp\left(-\frac{1}{2} \cdot 0.2^2 \cdot 2 \cdot 0.25 + 0.2 \cdot 2 \cdot \sqrt{0.25}\right) = 0.060462 \qquad (10.66)$$

At node $m=3$, $l=-3$ From (10.31) and (10.32)

$$P_{Hi}(3,-3) = 1$$
$$P_{Low}(3,-3) = 0$$

Then from (10.34), (10.49) to (10.54)

$$\hat{Z}^3(-3,3) = 0.999536 \cdot \exp\left(\frac{-0.5 \cdot 0.040529 \cdot 0.2 \cdot 0.2 \cdot 0.25}{1 + 0.5 \cdot 0.040529}\right) = 0.999338 \qquad (10.67)$$

$$\hat{Z}^4(-3, 3) = 1 \tag{10.68}$$

And from (10.33), (10.67) and (10.68)

$$\hat{L}_3^D(-3, 3) = 0.05 \cdot 0.999338 \cdot \exp\left(-\frac{1}{2} \cdot 0.2^2 \cdot 3 \cdot 0.25 + 0.2 \cdot (-3) \cdot \sqrt{0.25}\right) = 0.036465 \tag{10.69}$$

$$\hat{L}_4^D(-3, 3) = 0.05 \cdot 1 \cdot \exp\left(-\frac{1}{2} \cdot 0.2^2 \cdot 3 \cdot 0.25 + 0.2 \cdot (-3) \cdot \sqrt{0.25}\right) = 0.036489 \tag{10.70}$$

At node $m = 3$, $l = -1$ from (10.31) and (10.32)

$$P_{Hi}(3, -1) = \frac{2}{3}$$

$$P_{Low}(3, -1) = \frac{1}{3}$$

Then from (10.34) and (10.49) to (10.54) and (10.55) to (10.60)

$$\hat{Z}^3(-1, 3) = \frac{1}{3} \cdot 0.999536 \cdot \exp\left(\frac{-0.5 \cdot 0.040529 \cdot 0.2 \cdot 0.2 \cdot 0.25}{1 + 0.5 \cdot 0.040529}\right)$$

$$+ \frac{2}{3} \cdot 0.999512 \cdot \exp\left(\frac{-0.5 \cdot 0.049502 \cdot 0.2 \cdot 0.2 \cdot 0.25}{1 + 0.5 \cdot 0.049502}\right)$$

$$= 0.999293 \tag{10.71}$$

$$\hat{Z}^4(-1, 3) = 1 \tag{10.72}$$

And from (10.33), (10.71) and (10.72)

$$\hat{L}_3^D(3, -1) = 0.05 \cdot 0.999293 \cdot \exp\left(-\frac{1}{2} \cdot 0.2^2 \cdot 3 \cdot 0.25 + 0.2 \cdot (-1) \cdot \sqrt{0.25}\right) = 0.044537 \tag{10.73}$$

$$\hat{L}_4^D(3, -1) = 0.05 \cdot 1 \cdot \exp\left(-\frac{1}{2} \cdot 0.2^2 \cdot 3 \cdot 0.25 + 0.2 \cdot (-1) \cdot \sqrt{0.25}\right) = 0.044568 \tag{10.74}$$

At node $m = 3$, $l = 1$

From (10.31) and (10.32)

$$P_{Hi}(3, 1) = \frac{1}{3}$$

$$P_{Low}(3, 1) = \frac{2}{3}$$

Then from (10.34), (10.55) to (10.60), (10.61) to (10.66)

$$\hat{Z}^3(1,3) = \frac{1}{3} \cdot 0.999489 \cdot \exp\left(-\frac{0.5 \cdot 0.060462 \cdot 0.2 \cdot 0.2 \cdot 0.25}{1 + 0.5 \cdot 0.060462}\right)$$
$$+ \frac{2}{3} \cdot 0.999512 \cdot \exp\left(-\frac{0.5 \cdot 0.049502 \cdot 0.2 \cdot 0.2 \cdot 0.25}{1 + 0.5 \cdot 0.049502}\right) \qquad (10.75)$$
$$= 0.999246$$

$$\hat{Z}^4(1,3) = 1 \qquad (10.76)$$

And from (10.33), (10.75) and (10.76)

$$\hat{L}_3^D(1,3) = 0.05 \cdot 0.999246 \cdot \exp\left(-\frac{1}{2} \cdot 0.2^2 \cdot 3 \cdot 0.25 + 0.2 \cdot 1 \cdot \sqrt{0.25}\right) = 0.054395$$
$$(10.77)$$

$$\hat{L}_4^D(1,3) = 0.05 \cdot 1 \cdot \exp\left(-\frac{1}{2} \cdot 0.2^2 \cdot 3 \cdot 0.25 + 0.2 \cdot 1 \cdot \sqrt{0.25}\right) = 0.054436 \qquad (10.78)$$

At node $m = 3$, $l = 3$

From (10.31) and (10.32)

$$P_{Hi}(3,3) = 0$$
$$P_{Low}(3,3) = 1$$

Then from (10.34) and (10.61) to (10.66)

$$\hat{Z}^3(3,3) = 0.999489 \cdot \exp\left(-\frac{0.5 \cdot 0.060462 \cdot 0.2 \cdot 0.2 \cdot 0.25}{1 + 0.5 \cdot 0.060462}\right) = 0.999195 \qquad (10.79)$$

$$\hat{Z}^4(3,3) = 1 \qquad (10.80)$$

And from (10.33), (10.79) and (10.80)

$$\hat{L}_3^D(3,3) = 0.05 \cdot 0.999195 \cdot \exp\left(-\frac{1}{2} \cdot 0.2^2 \cdot 3 \cdot 0.25 + 0.2 \cdot 3 \cdot \sqrt{0.25}\right) = 0.066435$$
$$(10.81)$$

$$\hat{L}_4^D(3,3) = 0.05 \cdot 1 \cdot \exp\left(-\frac{1}{2} \cdot 0.2^2 \cdot 3 \cdot 0.25 + 0.2 \cdot 3 \cdot \sqrt{0.25}\right) = 0.066488 \qquad (10.82)$$

Calculations for remaining nodes are left for the reader as exercises.

10.10   TRINOMIAL TREE CONSTRUCTION FOR $L_n^A(t)$

In a similar way to the above, we could use trinomial trees to construct our LIBOR rates.
This is described below.

By (10.9), (10.10), (10.11) and (10.17)

$$L_n^A(t) = L_n(0) \cdot \exp\left(\sum_{j=n+1}^{N} Y_N^{jn}\left(\beta_j M_N(t), t \right) - \frac{1}{2} \cdot \beta_n^2 \cdot \int_0^t \gamma^2(s) \cdot ds + \beta_n M_N(t) \right) \quad (10.83)$$

where, by (10.14)

$$Y^{jn}\left(\beta_j(t) M_N(t), t \right) = E_N\left(\int_0^t \frac{\delta \cdot \beta_j \cdot \beta_n \cdot \gamma^2(s) \cdot L_j^A(s)}{1 + \tau_j \cdot L_j^A(s)} \cdot ds \middle| M_N(t) \right)$$

Analogously as in binomial tree case, forward LIBORs can be approximated by

$$\hat{L}_n^A(m, l) = L_n(0) \cdot \exp\left(-\sum_{j=n+1}^{N} \hat{Y}^{jn}(l, m) - \frac{1}{2} \cdot \beta_n^2 \cdot A(m) + \beta_n \cdot \hat{M}_N(m, l) \right), \quad (10.84)$$

where m and l are horizontal and vertical coordinates of the tree respectively and Δt is
length of single time step of the tree as at Figure 10.5 below

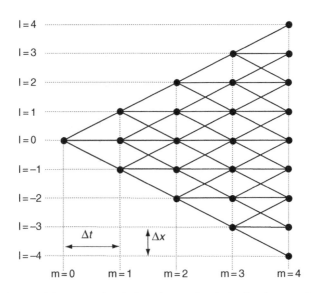

Figure 10.5   Example of trinomial tree for the basis of our work.

The discretisation of function $\gamma(t)$ is given by the formula

$$\hat{\gamma}(m) = \gamma(m \cdot \Delta t) \quad (10.85)$$

And $\hat{M}_N(m)$ is a Markov chain approximating process $M_N(t)$. It is defined by the formula

$$\hat{M}_N(0) = 0$$

$$
\hat{M}_N(m) =
\begin{cases}
\hat{M}_N(m-1) + \Delta x & \text{with prob. } \dfrac{\hat{\gamma}^2(m-1)\,\Delta t}{2\,(\Delta x)^2} \\[3mm]
\hat{M}_N(m-1) & \text{with prob. } 1 - \dfrac{\hat{\gamma}^2(m-1)\,\Delta t}{(\Delta x)^2} \\[3mm]
\hat{M}_N(m-1) - \Delta x & \text{with prob. } \dfrac{\hat{\gamma}^2(m-1)\,\Delta t}{2\,(\Delta x)^2}
\end{cases}
\qquad (10.86)
$$

The approximation of the integral $\int_0^t \gamma^2(s) \cdot ds$ for $t = m \cdot \Delta t$ is defined as

$$A(m) = \sum_{k=0}^{m-1} \hat{\gamma}^2(k) \cdot \Delta t. \qquad (10.87)$$

As in binomial tree case, $\hat{Y}^{jn}(l, m)$ will be defined recursively, basing on (10.14).

$$\hat{Y}^{jn}(l, m) = E_N\left(\hat{Y}^{jn}(\cdot, m-1) + \frac{\delta \cdot \beta_j \cdot \beta_n \cdot \hat{L}_j^A(\cdot, m-1)}{1 + \delta \cdot \hat{L}_j^A(\cdot, m-1)} \cdot \Delta t \,\middle|\, \hat{M}_N(m) = l \cdot \Delta x \right) \qquad (10.88)$$

Let us notice that given node (m,l) can be reached in one of three ways, and this is displayed on the figure below:

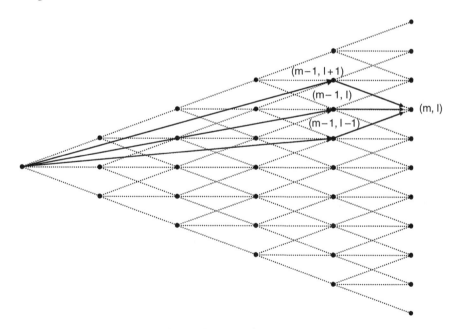

Figure 10.6 Backward tree.

- From the node $(m-1, l+1)$ (let us call it 'hi node')
- From the node $(m-1, l)$ (let us call it 'mid node')
- From the node $(m-1, l-1)$ (let us call it 'low node')

By this observation and (10.88)

$$
\begin{aligned}
\hat{Y}^{jn}(m, l) = P_{Hi}(m, l) \cdot & \left(\hat{Y}^{jn}(l+1, m-1) + \frac{\delta \cdot \beta_j \cdot \beta_n \cdot \hat{\gamma}^2(m-1) \cdot \hat{L}_j^A(m-1, l+1)}{1 + \delta \cdot \hat{L}_j^A(m-1, l+1)} \cdot \Delta t \right) \\
+ P_{Mid} \cdot & \left(\hat{Y}^{jn}(l, m-1) + \frac{\delta \cdot \beta_j \cdot \beta_n \cdot \hat{\gamma}^2(m-1) \cdot \hat{L}_j^A(m-1, l)}{1 + \delta \cdot \hat{L}_j^A(m-1, l)} \cdot \Delta t \right) \quad (10.89) \\
+ P_{Low} \cdot & \left(\hat{Y}^{jn}(l-1, m-1) + \frac{\delta \cdot \beta_j \cdot \beta_n \cdot \hat{\gamma}^2(m-1) \cdot \hat{L}_j^A(m-1, l-1)}{1 + \delta \cdot \hat{L}_j^A(m-1, l-1)} \cdot \Delta t \right)
\end{aligned}
$$

where

$$
P_{Hi}(m, l) := E_N \left(1_{\hat{M}_N(m-1)=(l+1)\cdot\Delta x} \mid \hat{M}_N(m) = l \cdot \Delta x \right) \quad (10.90)
$$

is a conditional probability that node (m,l) was reached from the node $(m-1, l+1)$ under condition that node (m,l) was reached.

$$
P_{Mid}(m, l) := E_N \left(1_{\hat{M}_N(m-1)=l\cdot\Delta x} \mid \hat{M}_N(m) = l \cdot \Delta x \right) \quad (10.91)
$$

is a conditional probability that node (m,l) was reached from the node $(m-1, l)$ under condition that node (m,l) was reached.

$$
P_{Low}(m, l) := E_N \left(1_{\hat{M}_N(m-1)=(l-1)\cdot\Delta x} \mid \hat{M}_N(m) = l \cdot \Delta x \right) \quad (10.92)
$$

is a conditional probability that node (m,l) was reached from the node $(m, l-1)$ under condition that node (m,l) was reached.

Now, let us define $P(m, l)$ as the unconditional probability that node (m,l) will be reached.

$$
P(m, l) = E_N \left(1_{\hat{M}_N(m)=l\Delta x} \right)
$$

$P(m, l)$ satisfies the following recursive formulae

$$
\begin{aligned}
P(m, l) = p_u(m-1, l-1) \cdot P(m-1, l-1) + p_m(m-1, l) \cdot P(m-1, l) \\
+ p_d(m-1, l+1) \cdot P(m-1, l+1) \quad (10.93)
\end{aligned}
$$

$$
P(0, 0) = 1
$$

where $p_u(m, l)$, $p_d(m, l)$, $p_m(m, l)$ are probabilities of up, down or flat movements from node (m, l) and are calculated as

$$p_u(m, l) = p_d(m, l) = \frac{\hat{\gamma}^2(m)\Delta t}{2(\Delta x)^2}$$

$$p_m(m, l) = 1 - \frac{\hat{\gamma}^2(m)\Delta t}{(\Delta x)^2}$$

By (10.90), (10.91) and (10.92) we can deduce that

$$P_{Hi}(m, l) = \frac{P(m-1, l+1)\cdot p_d(m-1, l+1)}{P(m, l)}$$

$$P_{Low}(m, l) = \frac{P(m-1, l-1)\cdot p_u(m-1, l-1)}{P(m, l)} \tag{10.94}$$

$$P_{Mid}(m, l) = \frac{P(m-1, l)\cdot p_m(m-1, l)}{P(m, l)}$$

By (10.89), (10.90) and (10.94) we may recursively calculate $\hat{L}_n^A$ at each node of the tree.

10.11 TRINOMIAL TREE CONSTRUCTION FOR $L_n^D(t)$

There exists an alternative approach to build a trinomial tree building based on formula (10.18):

$$L_n^D(t) = L_n(0)\exp\left(\beta_n M_N(t) - \frac{1}{2}\beta_n^2\int_0^t \gamma^2(s)\,ds\right) Z_N^n(M_N(t), t)$$

where, following (10.19) and (10.21)

$$Z_N^n(M_N(t), t) = E_N\left(Z_N^n(M_N(t-\Delta t), t-\Delta t)\exp\left(-\sum_{i=n+1}^N \frac{\delta L_i^D(t-\Delta t)\beta_i\beta_n}{1+\delta L_i^D(t-\Delta t)}\int_{t-\Delta t}^t \gamma^2(s)\,ds\right)\right)$$

The process $L_n^D(t)$ is approximated on the trinomial tree

$$\hat{L}_n^D(m, l) = L_n(0)\hat{Z}^n(l, m)\exp\left(-\frac{1}{2}\beta_n^2 A(m) + \beta_n\hat{M}_N(m, l)\right)$$

$$\hat{Z}^n(l, m) = E_N\left(\hat{Z}^n(\cdot, m-1)\exp\left(-\sum_{j=n+1}^N \frac{\delta\hat{L}_j^D(m-1, \cdot)\beta_j\beta_n\hat{\gamma}(m-1)}{1+\delta\hat{L}_j^D(m-1, \cdot)}\Delta t\right)\Bigg|\hat{M}_N(m)=l\Delta x\right)$$

$$= P_{Hi}(m, l)\hat{Z}^n(l+1, m-1)\exp\left(-\sum_{j=n+1}^N \frac{\delta\hat{L}_j^D(m-1, l+1)\beta_j\beta_n\hat{\gamma}(m-1)}{1+\delta\hat{L}_j^D(m-1, l+1)}\Delta t\right)$$

$$+P_{Mid}(m, l)\hat{Z}^n(l, m-1)\exp\left(-\sum_{j=n+1}^N \frac{\delta\hat{L}_j^D(m-1, l)\beta_j\beta_n\hat{\gamma}(m-1)}{1+\delta\hat{L}_j^D(m-1, l)}\Delta t\right)$$

$$+P_{Low}(m, l)\hat{Z}^n(l-1, m-1)\exp\left(-\sum_{j=n+1}^N \frac{\delta\hat{L}_j^D(m-1, l-1)\beta_j\beta_n\hat{\gamma}(m-1)}{1+\delta\hat{L}_j^D(m-1, l-1)}\Delta t\right)$$

10.12   NUMERICAL RESULTS

In order to verify the previously described approaches we have constructed a binomial tree
with the following parameters:

$\delta = 0.5$ (six month LIBORs)

$N = 20$ (calculations were performed under forward measure connected with a 10 year zero
coupon Bond).

We assume flat initial term structure (all forward LIBORs equal to 5 %). We have price single
caplet maturing in 4.5 years with strike K = 5 % and compare results with the analytical
results given my the Black'76 formula. The results from our calculations are shown in the
table below, followed by a chart of the errors in the two approximations when compared to
the analytical results.

Table 10.1   Caplet pricing

Volatility	Estimator $L^D(\cdot)$	Estimator $L^A(\cdot)$	Black'76
10 %	0.165 %	0.165 %	0.165 %
15 %	0.247 %	0.247 %	0.247 %
20 %	0.328 %	0.328 %	0.328 %
25 %	0.408 %	0.408 %	0.408 %
30 %	0.487 %	0.486 %	0.488 %
35 %	0.562 %	0.561 %	0.566 %
40 %	0.633 %	0.629 %	0.642 %
45 %	0.690 %	0.678 %	0.717 %
50 %	0.723 %	0.695 %	0.789 %
55 %	0.713 %	0.661 %	0.860 %
60 %	0.657 %	0.577 %	0.929 %
65 %	0.567 %	0.461 %	0.995 %
70 %	0.458 %	0.337 %	1.059 %

Chart of approximation error. Note how the errors increase dramtically after approx. 40 %
volatility.

10.13   APPROXIMATION OF ANNUITIES

In section 12 the caplet payoff (under the numeraire $B(t, T_{20})$) was defined to be

$$V(T_9) = \delta \left(L_{10}(T_9) - K\right)^+ \prod_{j=11}^{20} \left(1 + \delta L_j(T_9)\right)$$

and in the example was approximated by

$$V^A(T_9) = \delta \left(L_{10}^A(T_9) - K\right)^+ \prod_{j=11}^{20} \left(1 + \delta L_j^A(T_9)\right)$$

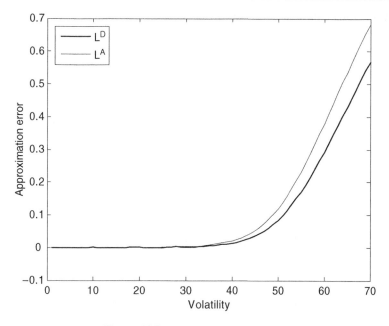

Figure 10.7   Error of caplet pricing.

or alternatively,

$$V^D (T_9) = \delta \left(L_{10}^D (T_9) - K \right)^+ \prod_{j=11}^{20} \left(1 + \delta L_j^D (T_9) \right).$$

This shows that the annuity $\prod_{j=11}^{20} (1 + \delta L_j(T_9))$ was approximated by a product of estimators. That may lead to significant approximation errors. In order to improve our approximations let us introduce two stochastic processes defined as:

$$A_n(t) = \prod_{j=n+1}^{N} \left(1 + \delta L_j (t) \right) \tag{10.95}$$

$$X_n(t) = L_n(t) A_n(t) \tag{10.96}$$

Both processes are non-Markov martingales under the measure E_N and satisfy stochastic differential equations:

$$A_n(t) = \int_0^t A_n(s) \sigma_{A_n} (s) dW_N(s) + A_n(0)$$

$$X_n(t) = \int_0^t X_n(s) \left(\sigma_{A_n} (s) + \beta_n \right) dW_N(s) + X_n(0)$$

$$\sigma_{A_n} (t) = \sum_{j=n+1}^{N} \frac{\delta L_j (t) \beta_j}{1 + \delta L_j (t)}$$

We can approximate these by the Markov processes:

$$A_n^A(t) = E_N\left(\int_0^t A_n^A(s)\,\sigma_{A_n}^A(s)\,dW_N(s)\Big|W_N(t)\right) + A_n(0)$$

$$X_n^A(t) = E_N\left(\int_0^t X_n^A(s)\,\left(\sigma_{A_n}^A(s)+\beta_n\right)\,dW_N(s)\Big|W_N(t)\right) + X_n(0)$$

$$\sigma_{A_n}^A(t) = \sum_{j=n+1}^N \frac{\delta L_j^A(t)\,\beta_j}{1+\delta L_j^A(t)}$$

or

$$A_n^D(t) = E_N\left(\int_0^t A_n^D(s)\,\sigma_{A_n}^D(s)\,dW_N(s)\Big|W_N(t)\right) + A_n(0)$$

$$X_n^D(t) = E_N\left(\int_0^t X_n^D(s)\,\left(\sigma_{A_n}^D(s)+\beta_n\right)\,dW_N(s)\Big|W_N(t)\right) + X_n(0)$$

$$\sigma_{A_n}^D(t) = \sum_{j=n+1}^N \frac{\delta L_j^D(t)\,\beta_j}{1+\delta L_j^D(t)}$$

Thus we can determine, by using these approximations, that

$$A_n^A(t) = E_N\left(A_n^A(t-\Delta t) + \int_{t-\Delta t}^t A_n^A(s)\,\sigma_{A_n}^A(s)\,dW_N(s)\Big|W_N(t)\right)$$

$$\cong E_N\left(A_n^A(t-\Delta t)\left(1+\sigma_{A_n}^A(t-\Delta t)\right)(W_N(t)-W_N(t-\Delta t))\right)\Big|W_N(t))$$

$$X_n^A(t) \cong E_N\left(X_n^A(t-\Delta t)\left(1+\left(\sigma_{A_n}^A(t-\Delta t)+\beta_n\right)(W_N(t)-W_N(t-\Delta t))\right)\Big|W_N(t)\right)$$

$$A_n^D(t) \cong E_N\left(A_n^D(t-\Delta t)\left(1+\sigma_{A_n}^D(t-\Delta t)(W_N(t)-W_N(t-\Delta t))\right)\Big|W_N(t)\right)$$

$$X_n^D(t) \cong E_N\left(X_n^D(t-\Delta t)\left(1+\sigma_{A_n}^D(t-\Delta t)+\beta_n\right)(W_N(t)-W_N(t-\Delta t))\right)\Big|W_N(t))$$

The above processes will thus be approximated by the following ones:

$$\hat{A}_n^A(m,l) = P_{Hi}(m,l)\,\hat{A}_n^A(m-1,l+1)\left(1-\hat{\sigma}_{A_n}^A(m-1,l+1)\sqrt{\Delta t}\right)$$

$$+ P_{Low}(m,l)\,\hat{A}_n^A(m-1,l-1)\left(1+\hat{\sigma}_{A_n}^A(m-1,l-1)\sqrt{\Delta t}\right)$$

$$\hat{X}_n^A(m,l) = P_{Hi}(m,l)\,\hat{X}_n^A(m-1,l+1)\left(1-\left(\hat{\sigma}_{A_n}^A(m-1,l+1)+\beta_n\right)\sqrt{\Delta t}\right)$$

$$+ P_{Low}(m,l)\,\hat{X}_n^A(m-1,l-1)\left(1+\left(\hat{\sigma}_{A_n}^A(m-1,l-1)+\beta_n\right)\sqrt{\Delta t}\right)$$

$$\hat{A}^D(m,l) = P_{Hi}(m,l)\,\hat{A}_n^D(m-1,l+1)\left(1 - \hat{\sigma}_{A_n}^D(m-1,l+1)\sqrt{\Delta t}\right)$$

$$+ P_{Low}(m,l)\,\hat{A}_n^D(m-1,l-1)\left(1 + \hat{\sigma}_{A_n}^D(m-1,l-1)\sqrt{\Delta t}\right)$$

$$\hat{X}^A(m,l) = P_{Hi}(m,l)\,\hat{X}_n^D(m-1,l+1)\left(1 - \left(\hat{\sigma}_{A_n}^D(m-1,l+1)+\beta_n\right)\sqrt{\Delta t}\right)$$

$$+ P_{Low}(m,l)\,\hat{X}_n^D(m-1,l-1)\left(1 + \left(\hat{\sigma}_{A_n}^D(m-1,l-1)+\beta_n\right)\sqrt{\Delta t}\right)$$

$$\hat{\sigma}_{A_n}^A(m,l) = \sum_{j=n+1}^{N} \frac{\delta\hat{L}_j^A(m,l)\,\beta_j}{1+\delta\hat{L}_j^A(m,l)}$$

$$\hat{\sigma}_{A_n}^D(m,l) = \sum_{j=n+1}^{N} \frac{\delta\hat{L}_j^D(m,l)\,\beta_j}{1+\delta\hat{L}_j^D(m,l)}$$

We know that the caplet payoff is equal $V(T_9) = (X_{10}(T_9) - KA_{10}(T_9))^+$ using our new processes. We approximate the payoff using $\hat{X}^A, \hat{A}^A$ or $\hat{X}^D, \hat{A}^D$ with the following results, which present a much reduced error.

Table 10.2 Improved caplet pricing

Volatility	Estimator $L^D(\cdot)$	Estimator $L^A(\cdot)$	Black'76
10 %	0.16490 %	0.16490 %	0.16500 %
15 %	0.24720 %	0.24720 %	0.24690 %
20 %	0.32820 %	0.32820 %	0.32810 %
25 %	0.40900 %	0.40900 %	0.40840 %
30 %	0.48810 %	0.48810 %	0.48760 %
35 %	0.56590 %	0.56590 %	0.56550 %
40 %	0.64260 %	0.64260 %	0.64180 %
45 %	0.71560 %	0.71560 %	0.71650 %
50 %	0.78900 %	0.78900 %	0.78920 %
55 %	0.85810 %	0.85810 %	0.86000 %
60 %	0.92450 %	0.92450 %	0.92860 %
65 %	0.98860 %	0.98860 %	0.99490 %
70 %	1.04790 %	1.04800 %	1.05890 %

10.14 SWAPTION PRICING

Our approximation was also tested on the example of an at-the-money 4.5 year option on 3 years swap under a flat yield curve equal to 5 %.

We observe a similar phenomenon as to before – the approximation is very accurate up to volatility 40 % and then the approximation error explodes. However, as swaption volatility rarely exceeds 20 % in most markets, this approximation can be used successfully. However, if the there is a need we can increase the accuracy of swaption pricing significantly if the

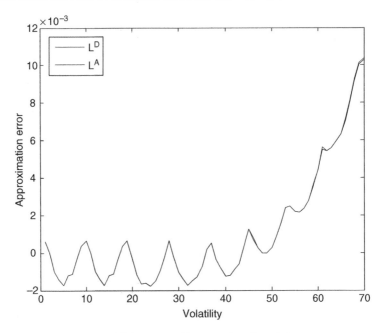

Figure 10.8   Error of improved caplet pricing.

Table 10.3   Swaption pricing

Volatility	Estimator $L^D(\cdot)$	Estimator $L^A(\cdot)$	Black'76
10 %	0.9330 %	0.9330 %	0.9314 %
15 %	1.3904 %	1.3904 %	1.3938 %
20 %	1.8549 %	1.8548 %	1.8524 %
25 %	2.3045 %	2.3041 %	2.3058 %
30 %	2.7408 %	2.7394 %	2.7529 %
35 %	3.1788 %	3.1739 %	3.1925 %
40 %	3.5784 %	3.5639 %	3.6235 %
45 %	3.9403 %	3.9027 %	4.0450 %
50 %	4.2205 %	4.1326 %	4.4559 %
55 %	4.3332 %	4.1569 %	4.8554 %
60 %	4.2809 %	3.9836 %	5.2428 %
65 %	4.0145 %	3.5722 %	5.6173 %
70 %	3.5894 %	3.0162 %	5.9784 %

annuities (defined by (10.95)) are modeled on the tree as described in section 12. The final payment of our swaption (under numeraire $B(t, T_{20})$) is

$$V(T_9) = \left(A_{10}(T_9) - A_{16}(T_9) - \delta K \sum_{j=10}^{15} A_{j+1}(T_9) \right)^+ .$$

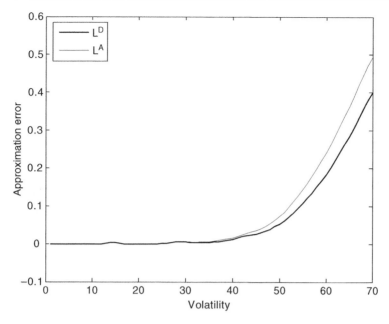

Figure 10.9   Error of swaption pricing.

Our improved results are tabulated below, and the displayed on the chart below. Notice again that the errors are somewhat oscillatory in behaviour but are now more accurate up to approx. 70 % volatility as opposed to the previous 40 % level. This approximation should cover all normal market requirements to a high level.

Table 10.4   Improved swaption pricing

Volatility	Estimator $L^D(\cdot)$	Estimator $L^A(\cdot)$	Black'76
10 %	0.9333 %	0.9333 %	0.9314 %
15 %	1.3915 %	1.3915 %	1.3938 %
20 %	1.8577 %	1.8577 %	1.8524 %
25 %	2.3107 %	2.3107 %	2.3058 %
30 %	2.7533 %	2.7532 %	2.7529 %
35 %	3.2037 %	3.2035 %	3.1925 %
40 %	3.6297 %	3.6292 %	3.6235 %
45 %	4.0524 %	4.0509 %	4.0450 %
50 %	4.4698 %	4.4669 %	4.4559 %
55 %	4.8534 %	4.8482 %	4.8554 %
60 %	5.2499 %	5.2388 %	5.2428 %
65 %	5.6156 %	5.5977 %	5.6173 %
70 %	5.9643 %	5.9304 %	5.9784 %
75 %	6.3900 %	6.3412 %	6.3255 %
80 %	7.2654 %	7.1795 %	6.6583 %

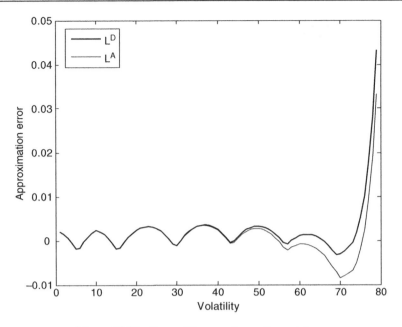

Figure 10.10 Error of improved swaption pricing.

10.15 LOGNORMAL APPROXIMATION

In the HJM model all discount factors are lognormal under all forward measures. Unfortunately we do not have this nice property for BGM model – only the relevant forward LIBOR rate is lognormal under a given forward measure. However, if street knowledge is to be believed, all LIBOR and swap rates are 'almost' lognormal. The purpose of our calculations in this section if to justify such a statement by finding an accurate lognormal approximation of the distribution of forward LIBOR rates.

Theorem. Let $T \leq \min(T_k, T_n)$. Then the distribution of LIBOR rate $L_k(T)$ under forward measure E_n can be approximated as lognormal, given by the formula:

$$L_k^D(T) = L_k(0) \exp\left(\int_0^T \gamma_{kn}(t, T)\, dW_n(t) - \frac{1}{2} C_{kk}(0, T) + \int_0^T \mu_{kn}^0(t, T)\, dt \right), \qquad (10.97)$$

where

$$\gamma_{kn}(t, T) = \gamma_k(t) - \sum_{j=k+1}^{n} C_{jk}(t, T) \frac{K_j(0)}{1 + \delta L_j(0)} \gamma_j(t) \qquad (10.98)$$

and

$$\mu_{kn}^0(t, T) = \sum_{j=k+1}^{n} K_j(0)\gamma_j(t) \cdot \left[-\gamma_k(t) + \frac{C_{jk}(t, T)}{1 + \delta L_j(0)} \sum_{i=j}^{n} K_i(0)\gamma_i(t) \right] \qquad (10.99)$$

– in case of $k < n$ or

$$\mu_{kn}^0(t) = \sum_{j=n+1}^{k} K_j(0)\gamma_j(t) \cdot \left[\gamma_k(t) + \frac{C_{jk}(t, T)}{1+\delta L_j(0)} \sum_{i=n+1}^{j-1} K_i(0)\gamma_i(t) \right] \qquad (10.100)$$

– in case of $k > n$.

Proof. Denote

$$\Sigma_{kn}(t) := \Sigma(t, T_k) - \Sigma(t, T_n) = \begin{cases} \displaystyle\sum_{j=n+1}^{k} K_j(t)\gamma_j(t), & n < k \\ 0, & n = k \\ \displaystyle-\sum_{j=k+1}^{n} K_j(t)\gamma_j(t), & n > k. \end{cases}$$

We find using integration by parts:

$$0 = C_{jk}(T, T)K_j(T) = K_j(0)C_{jk}(0, T) + \int_0^T C_{jk}(t, T)\,dK_j(t) + \int_0^T K_j(t)\,dC_{jk}(t, T),$$

hence

$$\int_0^T K_j(t)\gamma_j(t) \cdot \gamma_k(t)\,dt = -\int_0^T K_j(t)\,dC_{jk}(t, T) = K_j(0)C_{jk}(0, T) + \int_0^T C_{jk}(t, T)\,dK_j(t)$$

$$\qquad (10.101)$$

$$= \int_0^T K_j(0)\gamma_j(t) \cdot \gamma_k(t)\,dt + \int_0^T C_{jk}(t, T)\,dK_j(t)$$

With a little bit of work we can thus achieve

$$dK_j(t) = \frac{\delta dL_j(t)}{\left(1+\delta L_j(t)\right)^2} - \frac{K_j^2(t)|\gamma_j(t)|^2\,dt}{\left(1+\delta L_j(t)\right)}$$

$$= \frac{K_j(t)\gamma_j(t)}{1+\delta L_j(t)} \cdot \left(dW_n(t) + \Sigma_{jn}(t)dt\right) - \frac{K_j^2(t)|\gamma_j(t)|^2\,dt}{\left(1+\delta L_j(t)\right)}$$

$$= \frac{K_j(t)\gamma_j(t)}{1+\delta L_j(t)} \cdot \left(dW_n(t) + \left(\Sigma_{jn}(t) - K_j(t)\gamma_j(t)\right)dt\right),$$

hence 'freezing' LIBORs:

$$dK_j(t) \approx \frac{K_j(0)\gamma_j(t) \cdot}{1+\delta L_j(0)} \left[dW_n(t) - \sum_{i=j}^{n} K_j(0)\gamma_i(t)dt \right], \quad \text{for } j < n,$$

$$dK_j(t) \approx \frac{K_j(0)\gamma_j(t) \cdot}{1+\delta L_j(0)} \left[dW_n(t) + \sum_{i=n+1}^{j-1} K_j(0)\gamma_i(t)dt \right], \quad \text{for } j > n.$$

Putting this into (10.101), then using (10.99) and (10.100) and grouping integrals we obtain (10.97) which completes the proof.

10.16   COMPARISON

The presented models were examined on several instruments on basic data.

In order to test the LIBOR rate approximations we took a quarterly settlement ($\delta = 0.25$) and flat initial interest rate and volatility structures: $L_i(0) = 6\%$, $\gamma_i(t) = 21\%$ and we simulated LIBOR rates in arrears with 30Y maturity. We compared standard convexity adjustment approach (Euler method), Predictor-Corrector, Brownian bridge, combined Brownian bridge-predictor-corrector, direct Milstein method and lognormal approach (Daniluk and Gatarek (2005)). Density of approximation errors is shown in the next chart.

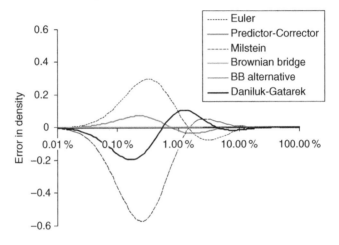

Figure 10.11   Comparison of methods.

The Brownian bridge method and then combined Brownian bridge-predictor-corrector methods seem to outperform the other approaches.

10.17   PRACTICAL EXAMPLE – CALIBRATION TO CO-TERMINAL SWAPTIONS AND SIMULATION

In this subsection we calibrate binomial tree to co-terminal swaptions and use calibrated tree to valuate Bermudian swaption. Since examples described in previous parts of this section (pricing caplets and european swaption under flat interest rate term structure) were pure theoretical and focused rather on showing accuracy of model than to be used directly in practice, the calibration to European swaption market has the significant practical importance.

Our calculations in this section were performed using estimators $L^A(\cdot)$ supported by annuities. We perform calibration with the following input data:

Table 10.5   Input data

Swaption	Forward Swap Rate	Market Volatility Swaptions
9Y × 1Y	4.534240165 %	15.24 %
8Y × 2Y	4.527014194 %	15.42 %
7Y × 3Y	4.452167050 %	15.30 %
6Y × 4Y	4.372320332 %	15.24 %
5Y × 5Y	4.271427603 %	15.10 %
4Y × 6Y	4.161450501 %	15.50 %
3Y × 7Y	4.039418324 %	15.80 %
2Y × 8Y	3.906172246 %	16.20 %
1Y × 9Y	3.758046796 %	16.30 %

Additionally 1 Y spot rate is 2.2972 %

Forward Swap Rates was calculated from IRS and interbank deposits market using standard bootstrapping algorithm, Market Volatility Swaptions is taken directly from market. Now, using an elementary algorithm we calculate forward rates, and using calibration methodology described in section 8.6 we calculate the instantaneous volatilities of these forward rates. Results are presented below.

Table 10.6   Forward rates

Period	Forward Rate	Instantaneous Volatility of The Forward Rate
9Y–10Y	4.5342 %	15.2400 %
8Y–9Y	4.5201 %	15.5937 %
7Y–8Y	4.3117 %	15.0635 %
6Y–7Y	4.1521 %	15.0626 %
5Y–6Y	3.9064 %	14.4856 %
4Y–5Y	3.6754 %	17.6026 %
3Y–4Y	3.3995 %	17.6187 %
2Y–3Y	3.1018 %	19.3789 %
1Y–2Y	2.7471 %	17.3572 %
0Y–1Y	2.2972 %	N/A

Now when we know forward rates and their instantaneous volatilities the construction of a binomial tree is straightforward. Below in Table 10.7 we compare European at the money swaption prices calculated using the binomial tree method, a binomial tree method with improvement and the closed formula for swaptions (Black). Prices are presented as percentage of the swap notional.

Our aforementioned improvement of the calibration is performed as follows:

Define σ as a vector of instantaneous volatilities of the forward rate. Let $\sigma(10)$ be the volatility of the forward rate (9Y − 10Y), $\sigma(9)$ be the volatility of the forward rate (8Y − 9Y) etc. ε is a small constant number (in our case 0.001). Then algorithm of volatility improvement is

Table 10.7   Values in tree nodes

Swaption	Value (Black)	Value (Tree)	Value (Tree with improvement)
9Y × 1Y	0.572 %	0.573 %	0.572 %
8Y × 2Y	1.116 %	1.117 %	1.116 %
7Y × 3Y	1.564 %	1.565 %	1.564 %
6Y × 4Y	1.933 %	1.930 %	1.933 %
5Y × 5Y	2.184 %	2.170 %	2.184 %
4Y × 6Y	2.396 %	2.384 %	2.396 %
3Y × 7Y	2.448 %	2.433 %	2.448 %
2Y × 8Y	2.312 %	2.299 %	2.312 %
1Y × 9Y	1.816 %	1.799 %	1.816 %

Algorithm 10.1

For i = 10 to 2 step -1

   V = Value of i –th swaption calculated on the tree using volatility vector σ

   $\widetilde{\sigma}$ is defined as follow: for j = 2 to 10: $\widetilde{\sigma}(j) = \begin{cases} \sigma(j), & \text{if } j \neq i \\ \sigma(j) + \varepsilon & \text{if } j = i \end{cases}$

   $\widetilde{V}$ = Value of i-th swaption calculated on the tree using volatility vector $\widetilde{\sigma}$

   $$Vega = \frac{\widetilde{V} - V}{\varepsilon}$$

   V76 = Value of i-th swaption calculated using Black for swaption formula (with swaption volatility taken directly from the market)

   $$\sigma(i) = \sigma(i) + \frac{V - V76}{Vega}$$

Next i

End of algorithm 10.1

After calculation $\sigma(i)$ is the improved volatility vector.

By the 'i-th swaption' we understood 9Y × 1Y for i = 10, 8Y × 2Y for i = 9 etc.

   Our accuracy of such an improved calibration is very close to perfect; the differences between the price of the European options calculated analytically and using the tree are presented in Table 10.8 below.

   Now we can use the constructed and calibrated tree to valuation a Bermudian swaption with following details:

- Right to receive floating leg and pay fixed leg
- Strike 4.25 %
- Maturity of the Swap: 10Y
- Moments when swaption can be exercised: 3Y, 4Y, 5Y, 6Y, 7Y, 8Y, 9Y

Table 10.8   Pricing errors

Swaption	Difference between tree and analytical formula (in % of swap notional)
9Y × 1Y	0.000000387 %
8Y × 2Y	0.000000385 %
7Y × 3Y	−0.000000159 %
6Y × 4Y	0.000000133 %
5Y × 5Y	0.000011210 %
4Y × 6Y	0.000000080 %
3Y × 7Y	0.000000362 %
2Y × 8Y	0.000000006 %
1Y × 9Y	−0.000000251 %

Results:

Table 10.9   Results

Calibration without improvement	2.890 %
Calibration with improvement	2.907 %

11

The One Factor LIBOR
Markov Functional Model

In this section we describe a functional market model that can be easily calibrated to market volatility and allow the pricing of derivatives effectively just like short rate models. The main characteristic of the functional market model family is that discount factors or forward LIBORs are at any time deterministic functions of a low-dimensional process being Markovian in some martingale measure – for practical reasons we focus on the terminal measure. This allows implementation of the model using standard ideas, such as binomial or trinomial trees, that is important for all valuations requiring using optimal stopping rules, e.g. American or Bermudian. Market models themselves does not possess this property and their exact implementation leads to constructing extremely inefficient non recombining trees. On the other hand there exist very reasonable approximations of market models (some of them are described in Chapter 10. Approximations of the BGM model) where approximated forward LIBORs and discount factors are deterministic functions of Markovian martingales.

Theoretically, the calibration of functional market models is more than straightforward: it is a part of model construction. However, direct implementation of the model construction can lead to significant mispricing (see subsection 'Binomial tree construction – approach 1' below).

The interesting feature of the functional market models is that, unlike the case of majority of used models, there are no closed formulas for the SDEs driving interest rates or discount factors, so users and researches can rely only on numerical calculations. This fact can reduce the understanding of the risk factor behaviour under the functional Markov models. For example, the distribution of the forward LIBOR at its reset date is known and is exactly the same as under the BGM model (approximately lognormal), but distribution of the same forward LIBOR at any time before reset is difficult to observe under a functional Markov model while under BGM it remains still more or less lognormal.

11.1 LIBOR MARKOV FUNCTIONAL MODEL CONSTRUCTION

In this section we will construct a model that:

– is arbitrage free
– is easy to calibrate with market volatilities
– has all forward LIBOR rates being (under the forward measure associated with the numeraire being a zero coupon bond maturing at T_N) deterministic functions of the stochastic process:

$$M_N(t) = \int_0^t \gamma(u)dW_N(u) \qquad (11.1)$$

and can be expressed as $L_i(t, M_N(t))$. This function is monotonically increasing in respect to second argument. Presented construction is basing on Hunt, Kennedy and Pelsser (2000). Other publications that deal with the problem are Balland and Hughston (2000) and Brigo and Mercurio (2003).

In order to calibrate to market volatilities let us calculate:

$$J_i(M^*) = B(T_0, T_N) E_N \left(1_{M_N(T_{i-1}) > M^*} \frac{1}{B(T_i, T_N)} \right)$$

$$= B(T_0, T_N) E_N \left(1_{M_N(T_{i-1}) > M^*} E_N \left(\frac{1}{B(T_i, T_N)} \middle| F_{T_{i-1}} \right) \right) \tag{11.2}$$

where $J_i(M^*)$ is a value of digital caplet with maturity T_{i-1} and strike price $L_i(T_{i-1}, M^*)$. So according to the Black formula:

$$J_i(M^*) = B(T_0, T_i) N \left(\frac{\ln\left(\frac{L_i(T_0, 0)}{L_i(T_{i-1}, M^*)} \right)}{\sigma_i \sqrt{T_{i-1} - T_0}} - \frac{1}{2} \sigma_i \sqrt{T_{i-1} - T_0} \right) \tag{11.3}$$

From (11.3) we can calculate

$$L_i(T_{i-1}, M^*) = L_i(T_0, 0) \exp\left(-\frac{1}{2}\sigma_i^2 (T_{i-1} - T_0) - \sigma_i \sqrt{T_{i-1} - T_0} N^{-1} \left(\frac{J_i(M^*)}{B(T_0, T_i)} \right) \right) \tag{11.4}$$

Formulae (11.2) and (11.4) define functions $L_i(t, x)$ in the following way:

Let us assume that all functions $L_{i+1}(t, x), L_{i+2}(t, x), \ldots, L_N(t, x)$ are defined for all x and all t where the appropriate forward LIBOR is alive. According to formulas (11.2) and (11.4) the function $L_i(t, x)$ can be calculated for each x and $t = T_{i-1}$. $L_i(t, x)$ for $t < T_{i-1}$ and can be calculated in the following way:

Let us define:

$$A_j^N(t, x) = \prod_{k=j}^{N} (1 + \delta L_k(t, x)) \tag{11.5}$$

with the note that if $j > N$ then $A_j^N(t, x) = 1$.

According to our assumption $A_{i+1}^N(t, x)$ is calculated for all x and t. Additionally $A_i^N(T_{i-1}, x)$ is also defined for all x. Since $A_i^N(t, M_N(t))$ is T_N - martingale then $A_i^N(t, x)$ can be calculated for all x and all $t < T_{i-1}$:

$$A_i^N(t, x) = E_N \left(A_i^N(T_{i-1}, M_N(T_{i-1})) \middle| M_N(t) = x \right) \tag{11.6}$$

Now, following (11.5) we achieve the following result

$$L_i(t, x) = \frac{1}{\delta}\left(\frac{A_i^N(t, x)}{A_{i+1}^N(t, x)} - 1 \right)$$ (11.7)

11.2   BINOMIAL TREE CONSTRUCTION – APPROACH 1

Let us assume that $\gamma(t) \equiv 1$. Then formula (11.1) converts into

$$M_N(t) = W_N(u)$$

and forward LIBOR can be modelled using a binomial tree. Forward LIBORs $L_i(t, W_N(t))$ will be approximated by the discrete processes:

$$\hat{L}_i\left(m, \hat{W}(m, l) \right)$$

Where $\hat{W}(m)$ is a Markov chain approximating Brownian motion. It is defined as

$$\hat{W}(0) = 0$$
$$\hat{W}(m) = \begin{cases} \hat{W}(m-1) + \sqrt{\Delta t} \text{ with probability} = 0.5 \\ \hat{W}(m-1) - \sqrt{\Delta t} \text{ with probability} = 0.5 \end{cases}$$
$$\hat{W}(m, l) = l\sqrt{\Delta t}$$

and m and l are horizontal and vertical coordinates of the tree:

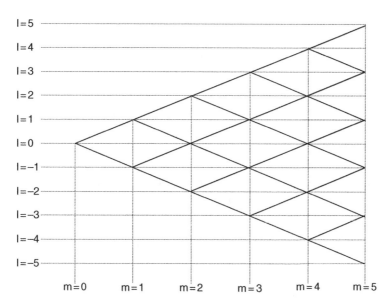

Figure 11.1   Binomial tree

For the sake of clarity and notation let us abbreviate:

$$\hat{L}(m, l) = \hat{L}\left(m, \hat{W}(m, l)\right)$$

Values $\hat{L}_i(m, l)$ will be calculated recursively using backward induction on the tree. Let us assume that all values $\hat{L}_i(m+1, \cdot)$ are known. Now we calculate all values $\hat{L}_i(m, \cdot)$. In addition let us assume that $T_{j-1} \le m\Delta t < T_j$, i.e. we have

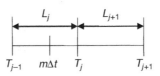

Figure 11.2   Time grid.

Now we will proceed in two steps:

1) Calculate forward LIBORs $\hat{L}_{j+1}(m, \cdot), \ldots, \hat{L}_N(m, \cdot)$ based on the values $\hat{L}_{j+1}(m+1, \cdot), \ldots, \hat{L}_N(m+1, \cdot)$ calculated during previous induction step
2) Additionally if $m\Delta t = T_{j-1}$ calculate LIBOR $\hat{L}_j(m, \cdot)$ basing on market volatility for digital caplets and forward LIBORs $\hat{L}_{j+1}(m, \cdot), \ldots, \hat{L}_N(m, \cdot)$ calculated during step 1)

<u>Part (1)</u>

Following formula (11.6) we can calculate (for $t \le T_j - \Delta t$, $i = j+1, \ldots N$)

$$
\begin{aligned}
A_i^N(t, x) &= E_N\left(A_i^N\left(T_j, M_N\left(T_j\right)\right) \middle| M_N(t) = x\right) \\
&= E_N\left(E_N\left(A_i^N\left(T_j, M_N\left(T_j\right)\right) \middle| F_{t+\Delta t}\right) \middle| M_N(t) = x\right)
\end{aligned}
\tag{11.8}
$$

Since $A_i^N(t, M_N(t))$ is T_N then martingale (11.8) converts into

$$A_i^N(t, x) = E_N\left(A_i^N(t + \Delta t, M_N(t + \Delta t)) \middle| M_N(t) = x\right) \tag{11.9}$$

The stochastic process $A_i^N(t, M_N(t))$ will be approximated on the tree by the process $\hat{A}_i^N\left(m, \hat{W}(m, \cdot)\right)$ following the equation:

$$
\begin{aligned}
\hat{A}_i^N\left(m, \hat{W}(m, l)\right) &= E_N\left(\hat{A}_i^N\left(m+1, \hat{W}(m+1, \cdot)\right) \middle| \hat{W}(m, \cdot) = l\sqrt{\Delta t}\right) \\
&= \frac{1}{2}\hat{A}_i^N\left(m+1, \hat{W}(m+1, l+1)\right) \\
&\quad + \frac{1}{2}\hat{A}_i^N\left(m+1, \hat{W}(m+1, l-1)\right)
\end{aligned}
\tag{11.10}
$$

By analogy to formula (11.5) we thus have the following result:

$$\hat{L}_i(m, l) = \frac{1}{\delta} \left(\frac{\hat{A}_i^N\left(m, \hat{W}(m, l)\right)}{\hat{A}_{i+1}^N\left(m, \hat{W}(m, l)\right)} - 1 \right) \tag{11.11}$$

Part (2)

Let us define

$$\hat{J}_i(l) = B(T_0, T_N) E_N \left(1_{\hat{W}\left(m_{T_{i-1}}, \cdot\right) \geq l\sqrt{\Delta t}} \hat{A}_{i+1}^N\left(m_{T_i}, \cdot\right) \right)$$

$$= B(T_0, T_N) E_N \left(1_{\hat{W}\left(m_{T_{i-1}}, \cdot\right) \geq l\sqrt{\Delta t}} E_N \left(\hat{A}_{i+1}^N\left(m_{T_i}, \cdot\right) \big| F_{T_{i-1}} \right) \right) \tag{11.12}$$

$$= B(T_0, T_N) E_N \left(1_{\hat{W}\left(m_{T_{i-1}}, \cdot\right) \geq l\sqrt{\Delta t}} \hat{A}_{i+1}^N\left(m_{T_{i-1}}, \cdot\right) \right)$$

where m_{T_i} is a number of time steps on the tree corresponding to time T_i. It means that

$$m_{T_i} = \frac{T_i}{\Delta t}$$

From (11.12)

$$\hat{J}_j(l) = B(T_0, T_N) E_N \left(1_{\hat{W}\left(m_{T_{j-1}}, \cdot\right) \geq l\sqrt{\Delta t}} \hat{A}_{j+1}^N\left(m_{T_{j-1}}, \cdot\right) \right) \tag{11.13}$$

Values $\hat{A}_{j+1}^N\left(m_{T_{j-1}}, \cdot\right)$ have been calculated during step 1).
From the features of the binomial tree:

$$E_N \left(1_{\hat{W}\left(m_{T_{j-1}}, \cdot\right) \geq l\sqrt{\Delta t}} \hat{A}_{j+1}^N\left(m_{T_{j-1}}, \cdot\right) \right) = 2^{-m_{T_{j-1}}} \sum_{k=\frac{m_{T_{j-1}}+l}{2}}^{m_{T_{j-1}}} \binom{m_{T_{j-1}}}{k} \hat{A}_{j+1}^N\left(m_{T_{j-1}}, k\right) \tag{11.14}$$

On the other hand $\hat{J}_j(l)$ is the price of a digital caplet with maturity T_{j-1} and strike price equal to $\hat{L}_j\left(m_{T_{j-1}}, l\right)$. From (11.13), (11.14) and the formula for the digital caplet price we obtain formula for j-th LIBOR corresponding to node $\left(m_{T_{j-1}}, l\right)$:

$$\hat{L}_j\left(m_{T_{j-1}}, l\right) = L_j(T_0) \exp \left(-\frac{1}{2}\sigma_j^2 (T_{j-1} - T_0) - \sigma_j\sqrt{T_{j-1} - T_0} N^{-1}\left(\frac{\hat{J}_j(l)}{B(T_0, T_j)}\right) \right)$$

$$\hat{J}_j(l) = 2^{-m_{T_{j-1}}} B(T_0, T_N) \sum_{k=\frac{m_{T_{j-1}}+l}{2}}^{m_{T_{j-1}}} \binom{m_{T_{j-1}}}{k} \hat{A}_{j+1}^N\left(m_{T_{j-1}}, k\right) \tag{11.15}$$

And analogically to formula (11.5)

$$\hat{A}_j^N \left(m_{T_{j-1}}, l \right) = \hat{A}_{j+1}^N \left(m_{T_{j-1}}, l \right) \left(1 + \delta L_j \left(m_{T_{j-1}}, l \right) \right) \quad \text{for } j \leq N$$

$$\hat{A}_{N+1}^N \left(m_{T_{N-1}, l} \right) = 1$$

(11.16)

Example 11.1

In this example we construct part of a binomial tree. This example tree models four forward 6M LIBORs L_1, L_2, L_3, L_4, thus we have $N = 4$. We assume that time step of the tree $\Delta t = 0.25$. It means that there are two time steps within each LIBOR period. The initial values of the forward LIBOR are all equal 5%. We assume that the market volatility of each caplet is 20%. Calculations yield

$$B_N (T_0, T_4) = \prod_{k=1}^{4} \frac{1}{1 + 0.5 L_k (T_0)} = 0.90595.$$

Now, let us focus on the upper right part of the tree (see Figures 11.3 and 11.4).

For node (m = 6, l = 6):

From formula (11.15)

$$\hat{J}_4 (6) = 2^{-6} \cdot 0.90595 \cdot \binom{6}{6} \cdot 1 = 0.014155$$

$$\hat{L}_4 (6, 6) = 0.05 \cdot \exp \left(-\frac{1}{2} \cdot 0.2^2 \cdot 1.5 - 0.2 \cdot \sqrt{1.5} \cdot N^{-1} \left(\frac{0.014155}{0.90595} \right) \right)$$

(11.17)

$$= 0.082238.$$

From (11.16) and (11.17)

$$\hat{A}_4^4 (6, 6) = \left(1 + \frac{1}{2} \cdot 0.082238 \right) = 1.041119.$$

(11.18)

For node (m = 6, l = 4)

$$\hat{J}_4 (4) = 2^{-6} \cdot 0.90595 \cdot \left(\binom{6}{6} \cdot 1 + \binom{6}{5} \cdot 1 \right) = 0.099088$$

(11.19)

$$\hat{L}_4 (6, 4) = 0.05 \cdot \exp \left(-\frac{1}{2} \cdot 0.2^2 \cdot 1.5 - 0.2 \cdot \sqrt{1.5} \cdot N^{-1} \left(\frac{0.099088}{0.90595} \right) \right) = 0.06558$$

$$\hat{A}_4^4 (6, 4) = \left(1 + \frac{1}{2} \cdot 0.06558 \right) = 1.03279$$

(11.20)

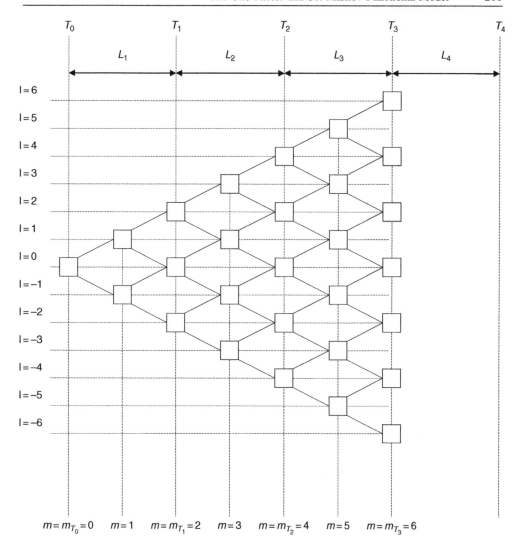

Figure 11.3   Tree for calculations

For node (m = 6, l = 2)

$$\hat{J}_4(2) = 2^{-6} \cdot 0.90595 \cdot \left(\binom{6}{6} \cdot 1 + \binom{6}{5} \cdot 1 + \binom{6}{4} \cdot 1 \right) = 0.311421$$

$$\hat{L}_4(6,2) = 0.05 \cdot \exp\left(-\frac{1}{2} \cdot 0.2^2 \cdot 1.5 - 0.2 \cdot \sqrt{1.5} \cdot N^{-1}\left(\frac{0.311421}{0.90595} \right) \right) \qquad (11.21)$$

$$= 0.053547$$

$$\hat{A}_4^4(6,2) = \left(1 + \frac{1}{2} \cdot 0.053547 \right) = 1.026773 \qquad (11.22)$$

For node (m = 6, 1 = 0)

$$\hat{J}_4(0) = 2^{-6} \cdot 0.90595 \cdot \left(\binom{6}{6} \cdot 1 + \binom{6}{5} \cdot 1 + \binom{6}{4} \cdot 1 + \binom{6}{3} \cdot 1 \right) = 0.59453$$

$$\hat{L}_4(6,0) = 0.05 \cdot \exp \left(-\frac{1}{2} \cdot 0.2^2 \cdot 1.5 - 0.2 \cdot \sqrt{1.5} \cdot N^{-1} \left(\frac{0.59453}{0.90595} \right) \right) = 0.043969 \qquad (11.23)$$

$$\hat{A}_4^4(6,0) = \left(1 + \frac{1}{2} \cdot 0.043969 \right) = 1.021985 \qquad (11.24)$$

The calculations for nodes (m = 6, 1 = −2), (m = 6, 1 = −4), (m = 6, 1 = −6) are analogous to that presented above.

Now for node (m = 5, 1 = 5):

From formulae (11.10), (11.18) and (11.20)

$$\hat{A}_4^4(5,5) = 0.5 \cdot \hat{A}_4^4(6,6) + 0.5 \cdot \hat{A}_4^4(6,4) = 0.5 \cdot 1.041119 + 0.5 \cdot 1.03279$$
$$= 1.036954 \qquad (11.25)$$

And from formulae (11.11) and (11.25)

$$\hat{L}_4(5,5) = \frac{1}{0.5} \cdot \left(\frac{\hat{A}_4^4(5,5)}{\hat{A}_5^4(5,5)} - 1 \right) = 2 \cdot \left(\frac{1.036954}{1} - 1 \right) = 0.073909 \qquad (11.26)$$

For node (m = 5, 1 = 3)

$$\hat{A}_4^4(5,3) = 0.5 \cdot \hat{A}_4^4(6,4) + 0.5 \cdot \hat{A}_4^4(6,2) = 1.029782 \qquad (11.27)$$

$$\hat{L}_4(5,3) = \frac{1}{0.5} \cdot \left(\frac{1.029782}{1} - 1 \right) = 0.059563 \qquad (11.28)$$

For node (m = 5, 1 = 1)

$$\hat{A}_4^4(5,1) = 0.5 \cdot \hat{A}_4^4(6,2) + 0.5 \cdot \hat{A}_4^4(6,0) = 1.024379 \qquad (11.29)$$

$$\hat{L}_4(5,1) = \frac{1}{0.5} \cdot \left(\frac{1.024379}{1} - 1 \right) = 0.048758 \qquad (11.30)$$

Again the calculations for the similar nodes (m = 5, 1 = −1), (m = 5, 1 = −3), (m = 5, 1 = −5) are analogous and we leave them as exercise for the reader.

Now, for node (m = 4, 1 = 4) from (11.10), (11.25) and (11.27), we calculate

$$\hat{A}_4^4(4,4) = 0.5 \cdot \hat{A}_4^4(5,5) + 0.5 \cdot \hat{A}_4^4(5,3) = 1.033368 \qquad (11.31)$$

From (11.11) and (11.31)

$$\hat{L}_4^4(4,4) = \frac{1}{0.5} \cdot \left(\frac{\hat{A}_4^4(4,4)}{\hat{A}_5^4(4,4)} - 1 \right) = 0.066736 \tag{11.32}$$

From (11.15) and (11.31)

$$\hat{J}_3(4) = 2^{-4} \cdot 0.90595 \cdot \binom{4}{4} \cdot \hat{A}_4^4(4,4) = 0.058511 \tag{11.33}$$

From (11.15) and the fact that

$$B(T_0, T_3) = \frac{1}{(1+0.5 \cdot 0.05)^3} = 0.928599 \tag{11.34}$$

$$\hat{L}_3(4,4) = 0.05 \cdot \exp\left(-\frac{1}{2} \cdot 0.2^2 \cdot 1 - 0.2 \cdot \sqrt{1} \cdot N^{-1}\left(\frac{0.058511}{0.928599} \right) \right) = 0.066554 \tag{11.35}$$

From (11.16), (11.31) and (11.35)

$$\hat{A}_3^4(4,4) = (1+0.5 \cdot 0.066554) \cdot 1.033368 = 1.067756 \tag{11.36}$$

For node $(m=4, \ 1=2)$ from (11.10), (11.27) and (11.29)

$$\hat{A}_4^4(4,2) = 0.5 \cdot \hat{A}_4^4(5,3) + 0.5 \cdot \hat{A}_4^4(5,1) = 1.02708 \tag{11.37}$$

From (11.11) and (11.37)

$$\hat{L}_4^4(4,2) = \frac{1}{0.5} \cdot \left(\frac{\hat{A}_4^4(4,2)}{\hat{A}_5^4(4,2)} - 1 \right) = 0.054161 \tag{11.38}$$

From (11.15), (11.31) and (11.37)

$$\hat{J}_3(2) = 2^{-4} \cdot 0.90595 \cdot \left(\binom{4}{4} \cdot \hat{A}_4^4(4,4) + \binom{4}{3} \cdot \hat{A}_4^4(4,2) \right) = 0.291132 \tag{11.39}$$

From (11.15), (11.34) and (11.39)

$$\hat{L}_3^4(4,2) = 0.05 \cdot \exp\left(-\frac{1}{2} \cdot 0.2^2 \cdot 1 - 0.2 \cdot \sqrt{1} \cdot N^{-1}\left(\frac{0.291132}{0.928599} \right) \right) = 0.054012 \tag{11.40}$$

From (11.16), (11.37) and (11.40)

$$\hat{A}_3^4(4,2) = (1+0.5 \cdot 0.054012) \cdot 1.02708 = 1.054818 \tag{11.41}$$

We can represent these calculations on the following diagram:

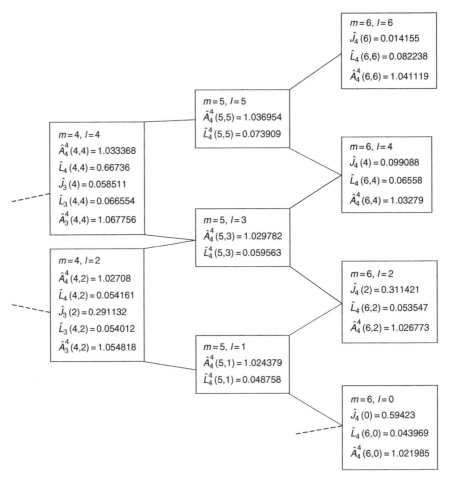

Figure 11.4 Tree with data

End of example

Numerical results

In order to test our binomial tree construction described above we construct a tree for the following input parameters:

– flat interest rate term structure (each forward 6M LIBOR equal to 5 %)
– terminal measure is associated with a 10 year zero-coupon Bond
– market volatilities for digital caplets equal to 20 % and 50 %

The constructed tree has been used to price a plain vanilla caplet with a maturity of 4.5 years for different strike prices. Results are presented below.

For volatility $= 20\%$

Table 11.1 Low volatility

Strike Price	Tree	Black'76
4.50 %	0.365 %	0.419 %
4.60 %	0.346 %	0.399 %
4.70 %	0.330 %	0.380 %
4.80 %	0.314 %	0.362 %
4.90 %	0.297 %	0.345 %
5.00 %	0.281 %	0.328 %
5.10 %	0.268 %	0.312 %
5.20 %	0.255 %	0.297 %
5.30 %	0.241 %	0.283 %
5.40 %	0.228 %	0.269 %

For volatility $= 50\%$

Table 11.2 High volatility

Strike Price	Tree	Black'76
4.50 %	0.755 %	0.851 %
4.60 %	0.743 %	0.838 %
4.70 %	0.730 %	0.825 %
4.80 %	0.720 %	0.813 %
4.90 %	0.710 %	0.801 %
5.00 %	0.700 %	0.789 %
5.10 %	0.690 %	0.778 %
5.20 %	0.680 %	0.767 %
5.30 %	0.670 %	0.755 %
5.40 %	0.660 %	0.745 %

As previously mentioned this shows that the construction of the tree leads to significant mispricing.

11.3   BINOMIAL TREE CONSTRUCTION – APPROACH 2

In order to improve the calculation accuracy we decide to provide some improvement in the tree construction. All calculations remain the same except formula (11.15). Now this formula is used to calculate auxiliary variables:

$$\hat{L}_j' \left(m_{T_{j-1}}, l \right) = L_j(T_0) \exp \left(-\frac{1}{2} \sigma_j^2 \left(T_{j-1} - T_0 \right) - \sigma_j \sqrt{T_{j-1} - T_0} N^{-1} \left(\frac{\hat{J}_j(l)}{P(T_0, T_j)} \right) \right)$$

$$\hat{J}_j(l) = 2^{-m_{T_{j-1}}} P(T_0, T_N) \sum_{k=\frac{m_{T_{j-1}}+l}{2}}^{m_{T_{j-1}}} \binom{m_{T_{j-1}}}{k} \hat{A}_{j+1}^N \left(m_{T_{j-1}}, k \right) \tag{11.42}$$

The calculations of LIBOR corresponding to a given node are performed based on results calculated using formula (11.42):

$$
\hat{L}_j\left(m_{T_{j-1}}, l\right) =
\begin{cases}
\dfrac{3}{2}\hat{L}_j{}'\left(m_{T_{j-1}}, l\right) - \dfrac{1}{2}\hat{L}_j{}'\left(m_{T_{j-1}}, l-2\right) & \text{if } m_{T_{j-1}} = l \\[2mm]
\dfrac{1}{2}\hat{L}_j{}'\left(m_{T_{j-1}}, l\right) + \dfrac{1}{2}\hat{L}_j{}'\left(m_{T_{j-1}}, l+2\right) & \text{otherwise}
\end{cases}
\tag{11.43}
$$

These changes provide a significant improvement in the accuracy of the pricing. For the same case as in approach 1 the results are:

For volatility $= 20\%$

Table 11.3 Low volatility – second approach

Strike Price	Tree	Black'76
4.50 %	0.421 %	0.419 %
4.60 %	0.402 %	0.399 %
4.70 %	0.382 %	0.380 %
4.80 %	0.363 %	0.362 %
4.90 %	0.347 %	0.345 %
5.00 %	0.331 %	0.328 %
5.10 %	0.314 %	0.312 %
5.20 %	0.298 %	0.297 %
5.30 %	0.284 %	0.283 %
5.40 %	0.271 %	0.269 %

For volatility $= 50\%$

Table 11.4 High volatility – second approach

Strike Price	Tree	Black'76
4.50 %	0.856 %	0.851 %
4.60 %	0.843 %	0.838 %
4.70 %	0.830 %	0.825 %
4.80 %	0.817 %	0.813 %
4.90 %	0.804 %	0.801 %
5.00 %	0.792 %	0.789 %
5.10 %	0.781 %	0.778 %
5.20 %	0.771 %	0.767 %
5.30 %	0.760 %	0.755 %
5.40 %	0.749 %	0.745 %

Our approximation was also tested on the example of an at-the-money 4.5 year option on 3 years swap under the flat yield curve equal to 5 % and the results are:

For volatility $= 20\%$

Table 11.5 Low volatility – second approach

Strike Price	Tree	Black'76
4.50 %	2.382 %	2.364 %
4.60 %	2.274 %	2.253 %
4.70 %	2.166 %	2.146 %
4.80 %	2.059 %	2.044 %
4.90 %	1.963 %	1.946 %
5.00 %	1.873 %	1.852 %
5.10 %	1.784 %	1.763 %
5.20 %	1.694 %	1.677 %
5.30 %	1.608 %	1.595 %
5.40 %	1.535 %	1.517 %

For volatility $= 50\%$

Table 11.6 High volatility – second approach

Strike Price	Tree	Black'76
4.50 %	4.940 %	4.803 %
4.60 %	4.872 %	4.731 %
4.70 %	4.804 %	4.660 %
4.80 %	4.736 %	4.590 %
4.90 %	4.668 %	4.522 %
5.00 %	4.600 %	4.456 %
5.10 %	4.532 %	4.391 %
5.20 %	4.468 %	4.327 %
5.30 %	4.414 %	4.265 %
5.40 %	4.359 %	4.204 %

However, although the accuracy of approach 2 is much better than the accuracy of approach 1 it is still far from the accuracy of Brownian Bridge approach described in Chapter 10.

12

Optimal Stopping and
Pricing of Bermudan Options

Pricing of Bermudan options in the interest rate market is related to the optimization problem in large dimensions because of the high number of risk factors in the interest rate world. We are going to describe briefly the most popular pricing methods. Consider option price given by the formula:

$$Option = E\left\{X_0^{-1}(T_k)\xi\right\}$$

with the intrinsic value ξ. Obviously

$$Option = B(0, T_n)E_n\left\{\frac{X_0(T_n)\xi}{X_0(T_k)}\right\} = B(0, T_n)E_n\left\{\xi \prod_{i=k+1}^{n} D_i(T_k)\right\}.$$

By Doob the optional sampling theorem the same formula holds if τ is a stopping time with values in $T_1, T_2, \ldots, T_n$

$$Option = E\left\{X_0^{-1}(\tau)\xi\right\} = B(0, T_n)E_n\left\{\xi \prod_{T_i > \tau} D_i(\tau)\right\}. \tag{12.1}$$

In conclusion – if we price options under the forward measure, discounting may be extracted from the expected value; hence all pricings of Bermudan options may be reduced to the following problem of optimal stopping in discrete time:

Let X_n be a Markov process on R_+^d. Define

$$V_n(x) = \sup_{n \leq \tau \leq N} E[C_\tau(X_\tau)|X_n = x], \tag{12.2}$$

where the supremum is taken over the set of all stopping times with values in $[n, \ldots, N]$. Then $V_n(x)$ is the value of the option at date n in state x, given that the option was not exercised at $0, 1, \ldots, n-1$. Our objective is to find $V_0(x)$. The option values satisfy the dynamic programming equations Longstaff and Schwartz (2001). Define

$$V_n(x) = \sup_{n \leq \tau \leq N} E[C_\tau(X_\tau)|X_n = x],$$

$$U_n(x) = \sup_{n < \tau \leq N} E[C_\tau(X_\tau)|X_n = x] = E[V_{n+1}(X_{n+1})|X_n = x] = T_n V_n(x).$$

Then

$$V_N(x) = C_N(x),$$
$$V_n(x) = \max\{C_n(x); U_n(x)\}. \tag{12.3}$$

Taking formula (12.1) into consideration we have not included discount factors. If, in addition, we define

$$Stop_n = \left\{x \in R^d : V_n(x) = C_n(x)\right\},$$
$$Cont_n = \left\{x \in R^d : V_n(x) = U_n(x)\right\}.$$

Then the set $Bound_n = Cont_n \cap Stop_n = \left\{x \in R^d : V_n(x) = U_n(x) = C_n(x)\right\}$ is called the *stopping boundary*. The stopping time

$$\tau_* = \min\left\{n \geq 0 : X_n \in Stop_n\right\}.$$

is the optimal stopping time to exercise the option, i.e.

$$V_0(x) = E\left[C_{N \wedge \tau_*}(X_{N \wedge \tau_*}) | X_0 = x\right].$$

The problem thus consists in fact of calculation of $U_n(x)$.

Remark 1. By (12.3), V is represented as

$$V_n(x) = \max\{C_n(x), U_n(x)\} = C_n(x) + Q_n^+(x), \tag{12.4}$$

where $Q_n(x) = U_n(x) - C_n(x)$ is called time-value of the option. In most cases

$$Q_n^+(x) \to 0 \text{ as } x \to \infty \text{ or } x \to 0. \tag{12.5}$$

12.1   TREE/LATTICE PRICING

Continuous mathematics is a proper tool for human imagination but numerical calculations require a discrete state space. Discretisation of the problem normally follows the following algorithm:

1. For every time step n define $N(n)$ grid points X_n^k.
2. Calculate transition probabilities $X_n^p \mapsto X_{n+1}^k$ as $P(X_{n+1}^k | X_n^p)$.
3. Calculate $U_n(X_n^p) = \sum_{k=1}^{N} V_{n+1}(X_{n+1}^k) P(X_{n+1}^k | X_n^p)$.

We may list several practical problems associated to discretization scheme:

- Number of $N(n)$ grid points may increase with n (trees) or be constant (lattices).
- Transition probabilities are often null for most transitions $X_n^p \mapsto X_{n+1}^k$.
- There are many methods of calculation of transition probabilities:

  - Preserving likehood ratios,
  - Preserving moments,
  - Preserving probabilities.

Tree simulation method presented in section 3 is especially useful in pricing of Bermudan products. We refer to Glasserman (2003) for detailed discretisation formulae and algorithms.

12.2   STOCHASTIC MESHES

The Stochastic mesh is described in Glasserman (2003) as a Monte Carlo counterparty to tree/lattice pricing. It is based on the concept that Monte Carlo paths are somehow 'typical' for the dynamics of the process. The Stochastic mesh algorithm is very similar to deterministic methods:

1. Generate N independent realizations X_n^k of random trajectory X_n.
2. Calculate transition probabilities $X_n^p \mapsto X_{n+1}^k$ as $P(X_{n+1}^k | X_n^p)$.
3. Calculate $U_n(X_n^p) = \sum_{k=1}^{N} V_{n+1}(X_{n+1}^k) P(X_{n+1}^k | X_n^p)$.

Point 2 forms the major problem, since the Monte Carlo simulation gives no transition probability between the simulated grid points X_n^k. The most popular is the preserved likehood ratio approach with

$$P(X_{n+1}^k | X_n^p) = \frac{f(X_{n+1}^k | X_n^p)}{\sum_{i=1}^{N} f(X_{n+1}^i | X_n^p)},$$

where $f(X_{n+1}^k | X_n^p)$ is the transition density for the continuous dynamics.

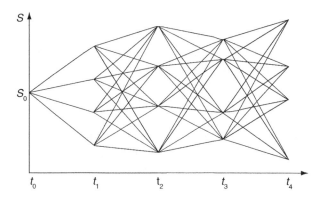

Figure 12.1   Example of a stochastic mesh that could be used for pricing

12.3   THE DIRECT METHOD

The direct method is conceptually very simple – it consists of parameterization of the stopping boundary $Stop_n(\alpha)$ with a family of parameters α and find its optimal value by optimization. For swaptions in the BGM model this is called the Andersen (1999/2000) method. Namely

$$\tau_\alpha^k = \min \left\{ n \geq 0 : X_n^k \in Stop_n(\alpha) \right\},$$

$$V(\alpha) = \frac{1}{M} \sum_{k=1}^{M} C_{N \wedge \tau_\alpha^k} \left(X_{N \wedge \tau_\alpha^k}^k \right)$$

and

$$V_0(X_0) = \min_{\alpha} V(\alpha).$$

Of course the difficulty lies in details and finding the proper parameterization thus making a nontrivial numerical problem.

12.4   THE LONGSTAFF-SCHWARTZ METHOD

The Longstaff-Schwartz method Longstaff and Schwartz (2001); Carriere (1996) is based on a completely different concept. First notice that

$$U_n(X_n) = E\left(V_{n+1}(X_{n+1}) | X_n\right).$$

Hence

$$\min_{H} E\left(V_{n+1}(X_{n+1}) - H(X_n)\right)^2 = E\left(V_{n+1}(X_{n+1}) - U_n(X_n)\right)^2.$$

Obviously, we do not know all paths of a stochastic process but via Monte Carlo simulation can create some of them. Let X_n^k be independent realizations of random variable X_n. The Longstaff-Schwartz algorithm consists of calculation of $U_n(x)$ as

$$U_n(X_n^k) = V_{n+1}(X_{n+1}^k) + \varepsilon_k = H(\alpha, X_n^k), \tag{12.6}$$

where H is deterministic function and α is a vector parameter. In the original Longstaff-Schwartz article H is a linear function of α and a family of polynomials, this assumption may be relaxed. The parameter α is calculated in the standard error minimization:

$$\sum_{k=1}^{M} \left(V_{n+1}(X_{n+1}^k) - H(\alpha, X_n^k)\right)^2 \to \min \tag{12.7}$$

In the original linear parameterization the function H is of a linear form with respect to α:

$$H(\alpha, x) = \sum_{i=1}^{d} \alpha_i H_i(x),$$

where $H_i(x)$ is a basis function. Longstaff and Schwartz propose:

- Polynomials,
- Polynomials multiplied by a decay function,
- Trigonometric series.

Then the optimization problem:

$$\sum_{k=1}^{N}\left(V_{n+1}(X_{n+1}^k) - \sum_{i=1}^{d}\alpha_i H_i\left(X_n^k\right)\right)^2 \to \min$$

is equivalent to a set of linear equations

$$\sum_{k=1}^{M} H_j(X_n^k)\left(V_{n+1}(X_{n+1}^k) - \sum_{i=1}^{d}\alpha_i H_i\left(X_n^k\right)\right) = 0$$

for all j. Hence

$$\sum_{i=1}^{d}\alpha_i \sum_{k=1}^{M} H_i\left(X_n^k\right) H_j\left(X_n^k\right) = \sum_{k=1}^{M} H_i\left(X_n^k\right) V_{n+1}\left(X_{n+1}^k\right).$$

In matrix notation: $BA = C$, where

$$A = [\alpha_1, \ldots, \alpha_d],$$

$$b_{ij} = \sum_{k=1}^{M} H_i\left(X_n^k\right) H_j\left(X_n^k\right),$$

$$c_i = \sum_{k=1}^{M} H_i\left(X_n^k\right) V_{n+1}\left(X_{n+1}^k\right).$$

Hence $A = B^{-1}C$. Longstaff-Schwartz reduce sample paths to in-the-money: $X_n^k \in Cont_n$, which will be explained later. The dimension of the problem may be reduced by introduction of synthetic explanatory variables. This is made clearer by the means of the following example:

Example. Let the payoff function be of the form:

$$C_n(x) = (g(x) - K)^+$$

for the call option and

$$C_n(x) = (K - g(x))^+$$

for the put option, where x represents the term structure of interest rates and $g(x)$ represents the underlying, e.g. swap rate, CMS spread, etc. then we may set the function H of the form:

$$H(\alpha, x) = C_n(x) + Q(g(x)).$$

We may set:

$$H(\alpha, x) = \begin{cases} K - g(x) & \text{for } g(x) < \kappa_0, \\ (K - \kappa_0)\,\exp\left(\lambda_0(\kappa_0 - g(x))\right) & \text{for } g(x) > \kappa_0 \end{cases}$$

for call options and for put options we have

$$H(\alpha, x) = \begin{cases} g(x) - K & \text{for } g(x) > \kappa_0, \\ (\kappa_0 - K) \, \exp(\lambda_0(g(x) - \kappa_0)) & \text{for } g(x) < \kappa_0 \end{cases}$$

The numbers λ_0 and κ_0 may be found by optimization. Stylized experimental facts support such choice of function. By the use of explanatory variables, optimization was reduced to a two-dimensional problem. We note that the choice of explanatory variables should follow market intuition rather than scientific methods.

The accuracy may be improved if we then calculate

$$V_0(X_0) = \frac{1}{M} \sum_{k=1}^{M} C_{N \wedge \tau_*^k} \left(X_{N \wedge \tau_*^k}^k \right).$$

Where $\tau_*^k = \min \{ n \geq 0 : X_n^k \in Stop_n \}$. This makes the Longstaff-Schwartz method a direct one in some sense. Indeed – we do not calculate the value functions V_n but only determine the stopping boundary $Bound_n$ and then calculate the initial value $V_0(X_0)$ by Monte Carlo simulation. This justifies why we may reduce sample paths to in-the-money and even more restrictive reductions are also possible. Therefore the choice of basis functions $H(x, \alpha)$ is not that important – since they are used to determine the stopping boundary only.

12.5   ADDITIVE NOISE

If we assume noise to be additive, we may calculate directly the approximate value functions for Bermudan options in a standard dynamic programming approach. The dynamics of a multidimensional financial parameter $X(n) = (X_1(n), X_2(n), \ldots, X_m(n))$ are assumed to be given by the following recursive formula:

$$X(n) = F_n(X(n-1)) + \xi_n(X(n-1)), \tag{12.8}$$

where $\xi_n(x) \in R^m$ is a sequence of independent zero mean vector normal variables with covariance matrix $\Sigma^n(x) \in R^{m \times m}$. The process X itself is not simulated. We rely strongly on recursive formula of the type (12.3), which may be considered restrictive in theory, but this is the most common practice, coming from discretization of stochastic Ito equations.

Providing the payoff function C is known, the problem reduces to calculation of

$$U(x) = E\left[V_{n+1}(X(n+1))|X(n) = x\right] = TV(x) = E\left[V(F(x) + \xi(x))\right],$$

(where we have dropped the indices from V, F and ξ for clarity).

We use the analytical properties of Hermite polynomials, Wick formula and their relations with normal variables. The Hermite polynomials are defined by the recurrence relations[1]

$$H_0(x) = 1,$$
$$H_1(x) = 2x, \tag{12.9}$$
$$H_{n+1}(x) = 2xH_n(x) - 2nH_{n-1}(x).$$

[1] http://mathworld.wolfram.com/.

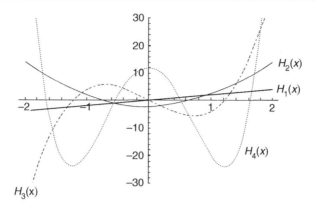

Figure 12.2 Hermite polynomials

Here are formulae for the next Hermite polynomials:

$$H_2(x) = 4x^2 - 2,$$
$$H_3(x) = 8x^3 - 12x,$$
$$H_4(x) = 16x^4 - 48x^2 + 12,$$
$$H_5(x) = 32x^5 - 160x^3 + 120x.$$

Their crucial property is that they are orthogonal in the range $(-\infty, +\infty)$ with respect to the weighting function e^{-x^2}

$$\int_{-\infty}^{+\infty} H_n(x) H_m(x) e^{-x^2} dx = \delta_{nm} 2^n n! \sqrt{\pi} = \delta_{nm} K_n. \tag{12.10}$$

Another important property is the equality:

$$H_n(x+y) = \sum_{k=0}^{n} \binom{n}{k} H_k(x)(2y)^{n-k} \tag{12.11}$$

Hermite polynomials are also defined in dimension m by

$$\mathbf{H}_n(x) = \prod_{i=1}^{m} H_{n_i}(x_i) \quad \text{with } n = (n_1, \ldots, n_m) \text{ and } x = (x_1, \ldots, x_m), \tag{12.12}$$

(where we use boldface for vector polynomials in order to avoid any confusion).

In our approach we approximate the option payoff V by a linear combination of Hermite polynomials in dimension m. Let α_i be weights such that:

$$V(x) \approx \sum_{i=0}^{n} \alpha_i \mathbf{H}_i(x). \tag{12.13}$$

Recall that both x and n are multidimensional, i.e. $n = (n_1, \ldots, n_m)$ and $x = (x_1, \ldots, x_m)$, so summation is also multidimensional. Since Hermite polynomials form an orthogonal basis in the Hilbert space of square integrable functions on R^m with weight $e^{-x^2} = \prod_{i=1}^{m} e^{-x_i^2}$ then we have

$$\alpha_i = K_i^{-1} \int_{-\infty}^{+\infty} V(x)\mathbf{H}_i(x)e^{-x^2}dx = K_i^{-1} \int_{-\infty}^{+\infty} \cdots \int_{-\infty}^{+\infty} V(x)\mathbf{H}_i(x)e^{-x^2}dx_1 \ldots dx_m, \qquad (12.14)$$

where

$$K_i = \sqrt{\pi^m} \prod_{j=1}^{m} 2^{i_j}i_j! \text{ and } i = (i_1, \ldots, i_m).$$

We know from the Hilbert space theory Maurin (1967) that

$$\int_{-\infty}^{+\infty} \left(V(x) - \sum_{i=0}^{n} \alpha_i \mathbf{H}_i(x) \right)^2 e^{-x^2}dx \to 0 \text{ as } n \to \infty$$

and

$$\int_{-\infty}^{+\infty} V^2(x)e^{-x^2}dx = \sum_{i=0}^{\infty} K_i \alpha_i^2.$$

Calculation of α_i may be performed in various ways, the easiest one is probably by Monte Carlo or quasi-Monte Carlo. Let $\xi_k \in R^m$ be a sequence of independent multidimensional normal variables with standard deviation $1/\sqrt{2}$, not related to the process $X(n)$. Then Glasserman (2003)

$$\alpha_i \approx \sqrt{\pi^m}K_i^{-1}N^{-1}\sum_{k=1}^{N} V(\xi_k)\mathbf{H}_i(\xi_k). \qquad (12.15)$$

Remark. By (12.3), V is represented as

$$V(x) = \max\{C(x), \ U(x)\} = C(x) + Q(x), \qquad (12.16)$$

where Q is called time-value of the option. In most cases $Q(x) \to 0$ as $x \to \infty$. If C remains the same for all steps in dynamic programming, separation of C and Q may accelerate calculations.

Now we may return to calculations of the expected value $U(x) = E[V(F(x) + \xi(x))]$, where $\xi(x)$ is a normal variable. By (12.13)

$$U(x) \approx \sum_{i=0}^{n} \alpha_i E[\mathbf{H}_i(F(x) + \xi(x))] = \sum_{i=0}^{n} \alpha_i U_i(x). \qquad (12.17)$$

By linearity it suffices to calculate the value of $U_i(x)$. By (12.11)

$$U_i(x) = TH_i(x) = E[H_i(F(x) + \xi(x))] \tag{12.18}$$

$$= \sum_{k_1=0}^{i_1} \cdots \sum_{k_m=0}^{i_m} \binom{i_1}{k_1} H_{k_1}(F_1(x))2^{i_1-k_1} \cdots \binom{i_m}{k_m} H_{k_m}(F_m(x))2^{i_m-k_m} E\left[\prod_{j=1}^{m} \xi_j^{i_j-k_j}(x)\right].$$

Let the covariance matrix $\Sigma(x)$ of $\xi(x)$ admit the representation

$$\Sigma(x) = \begin{bmatrix} \sigma_{11}(x) & \sigma_{12}(x) & \cdots & \sigma_{1m}(x) \\ \sigma_{21}(x) & \sigma_{22}(x) & \cdots & \sigma_{2m}(x) \\ \cdots & \cdots & \cdots & \cdots \\ \sigma_{m1}(x) & \sigma_{m2}(x) & \cdots & \sigma_{mm}(x) \end{bmatrix}. \tag{12.19}$$

We replace the term $E\left[\prod_{j=1}^{m} \xi_j^{i_j-k_j}(x)\right]$ by $E\left[\prod_{j=1}^{N} \xi_j(x)\right]$, where the variable $\xi_1(x)$ is taken $i_1 - k_1$ times, the variable $\xi_2(x)$ is taken $i_2 - k_2$ times, and so on, up to the variable $\xi_m(x)$ which is taken $i_m - k_m$ times. By the Wick formula Simon (1974), Triantafyllopoulos (2003)

$$E\left[\prod_{j=1}^{N} \xi_j(x)\right] = \begin{cases} 0 & \text{if } N \text{ is odd,} \\ \sum_{i,j} \sigma_{i_1 j_1}(x) \cdots \sigma_{i_1 j_1}(x) & \text{if } N = 2n \text{ is even.} \end{cases} \tag{12.20}$$

The sum in (12.20) runs over all pairs of increasing sequences $\{i_1 < i_2 < \ldots < i_n\}$, $\{j_1 < j_2 < \ldots < j_n\}$, such that $i_k < j_k$ for each k. The sum in (12.20) is called Hafnian and is a standard tool of calculating functionals in quantum physics Simon (1974). If the variables $\xi_i(x)$ are independent, formula (12.20) simplifies to

$$U_i(x) = E[H_i(F(x) + \xi(x))] = \prod_{j=1}^{m} \left(\sum_{k=0}^{i_j} \binom{i_j}{k} H_k(F_j(x))2^{i_j-k} E\left[\xi_j^{i_j-k}(x)\right]\right). \tag{12.21}$$

The values of $E\xi_j^k(x)$ are just central moments of normal variables. For odd powers k, $E\xi_j^k(x) = 0$ because of symmetry of normal distribution, for even powers k, we have:

$$\text{variance} = E\xi_j^2(x) = \sigma_j^2(x), \quad \text{kurtosis} = E\xi_j^4 = 3\sigma_j^4(x). \tag{12.22}$$

If $\xi_j(x) = \xi_j$ is a normal variable with standard deviation $1/\sqrt{2}$, formula (12.20) simplifies even more. Again by (12.11)

$$U_i(x) = \frac{1}{\sqrt{\pi^m}} \int_{-\infty}^{+\infty} H_i(F(x) + y)e^{-y^2} dy$$

$$= \frac{1}{\sqrt{\pi^m}} \prod_{j=1}^{m} \left(\sum_{k=0}^{i_j} \binom{i_j}{k} (2F(x)_j)^{i_j-k} \int_{-\infty}^{+\infty} H_k(y)H_0(y)e^{-y^2} dy\right).$$

Then by orthogonality from (12.10)

$$U_i(x) = T\mathbf{H}_i(x) = \prod_{j=1}^{m} \left(2F(x)_j\right)^{i_j}, \tag{12.23}$$

which leads to the following nice interpretation: the Hermite expansion of $V(x)$ gives a Taylor-like expansion of $U(x)$ with the same coefficients.

The described procedure can be repeated recursively: having calculated $U(x)$, we may set new $V(x)$ as $V(x) = \max\{C(x), U(x)\}$, approximate it as in (12.13) and so on back to the initial point.

12.6 EXAMPLE OF BGM DYNAMICS

The dynamic of LIBOR rates in the BGM model follows the recursive formula:

$$L_n(T_k) = L_n(T_{k-1}) \exp\left\{ M_k^n + \sum_{j=k+1}^{n} \frac{\delta L_j(T_{k-1})\sigma_{jn}^k}{1 + \delta L_j(T_{k-1})} - \frac{\sigma_{nn}^k}{2} \right\}, \tag{12.24}$$

where

$$\sigma_{kl}^i = \int_{T_{i-1}}^{T_i} \gamma_l(t) \cdot \gamma_k(t) dt, \quad \Sigma^i = \begin{bmatrix} \sigma_{11}^i & \sigma_{12}^i & \cdots & \sigma_{1N}^i \\ \sigma_{21}^i & \sigma_{22}^i & \cdots & \sigma_{2N}^i \\ \cdots & \cdots & \cdots & \cdots \\ \sigma_{N1}^i & \sigma_{N2}^i & \cdots & \sigma_{NN}^i \end{bmatrix} \tag{12.25}$$

and M_k^n is a Gaussian random variable with covariance matrix Σ^k. Set $X_n(k-1) = \ln L_n(T_{k-1})$ and $X(n) = (X_1(n), X_2(n), \ldots, X_m(n)) \in R^m$. Then X satisfies (12.8) with

$$F_k(x)_n = x_n + \sum_{j=k+1}^{n} \frac{\delta \exp(x_n) \sigma_{jn}^k}{1 + \delta \exp(x_n)} - \frac{\sigma_{nn}^k}{2}.$$

12.7 COMPARISON OF METHODS

Recombining trees and lattices are most popular in smaller dimensions (less than four) but are very slow for larger dimensions. The Stochastic mesh method has very good theoretical properties but is too slow for practical applications. Direct methods are good in dimension one, but are ambiguous in larger and strongly product dependent. The additive noise approach is not very accurate and not really used in practice, being more applicable to other stochastic control problems such as gas contract pricing. Methods based on PDEs are questionable in larger dimensions. The Longstaff-Schwartz method in various versions dominates the market, although we must mention that it is product dependent as well.

13

Using the LSM Approach
for Derivatives Valuation

This section is devoted to algorithms that use a Least Squares Monte Carlo (LSM) approach for pricing American/Bermudian value.

In the first part of the chapter we describe a few algorithms that use the LSM approach for the pricing of American/Bermudian derivatives.

In the second part we present detailed numerical examples of algorithms selected from the algorithms described in the first section. Our described algorithms are applied to price a Bermudian Swaption.

In the third part we present results of pricing a Bermudian swaption using the described algorithms and we compare calculated values with value calculated using a binomial tree with drift approximation (see Chapter 10, Approximations of the BGM model).

In the fourth part we focus of some theoretical features of the tested algorithms. The section focusses especially on trying to address the question about when the algorithms might cause an under- or over- estimation of the instrument value.

In the fifth and final part we try to interpret the results of the simulation described in the third section and theoretical divagation described in section four. We try to determine usability of each of described algorithms for practice purposes.

13.1   PRICING ALGORITHMS

The key point of pricing an American/Bermudian option is the recursive calculation of the option value at time n in state x basing on the expected value of the option at time $n+1$ (see Chapter 12, Optimal stopping and pricing of Bermudan options). Following (12.3) this value is:

$$V_N(x) = C_N(x)$$

$$V_n(x) = \max\{C_n(x), U_n(x)\} \tag{13.1}$$

Where

$$U_n(x) = E\left[|V_{n+1}(X_{n+1})| X_n = x\right].$$

Of course, during MC simulations, we are not able to calculate $V_n(x)$ nor $U_n(x)$ themselves. Instead of them we need to use their estimators and formula (13.1) is approximated by:

$$\hat{V}_n(x) = 1_{C_n(x) > \hat{U}_n^1(x)} C_n(x) + 1_{C_n(x) \leq \hat{U}_n^1(x)} \hat{U}_n^2(x) \tag{13.2}$$

Where $\hat{V}_n(x)$ is an estimator of $V_n(x)$ and $\hat{U}_n^1(x), \hat{U}_n^2(x)$ are estimators of $U_n(x)$.

Below we present a few algorithms that implement Bermudan/American option pricing using formula (13.2). Symbols X_n^k and $H(\cdot, \cdot)$ are defined in Chapter 12, Optimal stopping and pricing of Bermudan options in subsection 'The Longstaff-Schwarz method'. M is the number of generated scenarios.

For each of these implementation we describe recursive calculation for one time step. During this step calculations for time T_n are based on the values calculated for time T_{n+1}.

Algorithm 13.1

In this algorithm estimator $\hat{U}_n^1\left(X_n^k\right)$ is estimated using LSM while $\hat{U}_n^2\left(X_n^k\right)$ is the value of the option calculated in previous step of simulation.

Begin

   Find regression coefficient vector α that minimizes the expression (LSM algorithm) below.

   $$\sum_{k=1}^{M}\left(\hat{V}_{n+1}\left(X_{n+1}^k\right) - H\left(\alpha, X_n^k\right)\right)^2$$

   Denote this vector as $\alpha_{\min}$

   For each scenario k calculate:

   If $C_n\left(X_n^k\right) > H\left(\alpha_{\min}, X_n^k\right)$ then

   $$\hat{V}_n\left(X_n^k\right) = C_n\left(X_n^k\right) \quad /*\text{Exercise option}*/$$

   Else

   $$\hat{V}_n\left(X_n^k\right) = \hat{V}_{n+1}\left(X_{n+1}^k\right) \quad /*\text{Continue option}*/$$

   End If

   Next k

End of algorithm 13.1

Value of the derivative is calculated as the average of $\hat{V}_1\left(X_1^k\right)$ across all scenarios

Algorithm 13.2

Algorithm 13.2 is similar to Algorithm 13.1 with the exception that the regression coefficients are calculated basing on one MC scenarios set while the derivative pricing is done basing on another scenarios set (both MC scenario sets are realizations of the same stochastic process). We denote the scenario set generated for the calculation of the regression coefficients as 'Scenario Set 1' and denote the scenario set generated for the derivative pricing as 'Scenario Set 2'.

In the algorithm below:

$X_n^{k,1}$ – means realization of Markovian Process X_n for scenario k from Scenario Set 1

$X_n^{k,2}$ – means realization of Markovian Process X_n for scenario k from Scenario Set 2

Begin

   Find regression coefficient vector α that minimizes the expression (LSM algorithm).

   $$\sum_{k=1}^{M}\left(\hat{V}_{n+1}\left(X_{n+1}^{1,k}\right) - H\left(\alpha, X_n^{1,k}\right)\right)^2$$

Denote this vector as α_{min}

For each scenario k from Scenario Set 1 calculate:

> **If** $C_n\left(X_n^{1,k}\right) > H\left(\alpha_{min}, X_n^{1,k}\right)$ **then**
>
> > $\hat{V}_n\left(X_n^{1,k}\right) = C_n\left(X_n^{1,k}\right)$ / * **Exercise option** * /
>
> **Else**
>
> > $\hat{V}_n\left(X_n^{1,k}\right) = \hat{V}_{n+1}\left(X_{n+1}^{1,k}\right)$ / * **Continue option** * /
>
> **End If**

Next k

For each scenario k from Scenario Set 2 calculate:

> **If** $C_n\left(X_n^{2,k}\right) > H\left(\alpha_{min}, X_n^{2,k}\right)$ **then**
>
> > $\hat{V}_n\left(X_n^{2,k}\right) = C_n\left(X_n^{2,k}\right)$ / * **Exercise option** * /
>
> **Else**
>
> > $\hat{V}_n\left(X_n^{2,k}\right) = \hat{V}_{n+1}\left(X_{n+1}^{2,k}\right)$ / * **Continue option** * /
>
> **End If**

Next k

End of algorithm 13.2

In the algorithm above values $\hat{V}_n\left(X_n^{1,k}\right)$ are calculated only for regression purposes. The final value of the priced financial instrument is calculated as the average of $\hat{V}_1\left(X_1^{2,k}\right)$ across all scenarios.

Algorithm 13.3

We use only one set of MC Scenarios. $\hat{U}_n^1(x) \equiv \hat{U}_n^2(x)$ and it is calculated by LSM

Begin

Find regression coefficient vector α **that minimizes the expression (LSM algorithm).**
Denote this vector as α_{min}

$$\sum_{k=1}^{M}\left(\hat{V}_{n+1}\left(X_{n+1}^{k}\right) - H\left(\alpha, X_n^k\right)\right)^2$$

For each scenario k calculate:

> **If** $C_n\left(X_n^k\right) > H\left(\alpha_{min}, X_n^k\right)$ **then**
>
> > $\hat{V}_n\left(X_n^k\right) = C_n\left(X_n^k\right)$ / * **Exercise option** * /
>
> **Else**
>
> > $\hat{V}_n\left(X_n^k\right) = H\left(\alpha_{min}, X_n^k\right)$ / * **Continue option** * /
>
> **End If**

Next k

End of algorithm 13.3

The final value of the priced derivative is calculated as an average of $\hat{V}_1\left(X_1^k\right)$ across all scenarios.

Algorithm 13.4

Algorithm 13.4 is similar to algorithm 13.3 with exception that regression coefficients are calculated based on a generated scenario set while values $\hat{V}_n\left(X_n^k\right)$ are calculated based on a modification of this scenario set.

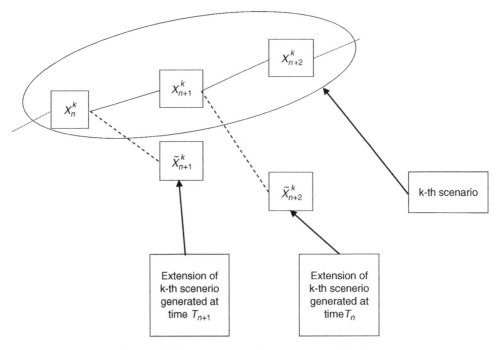

Figure 13.1   Generation of the scenario modification

Find regression coefficient vector α that minimizes the expression (LSM algorithm). Denote this vector as α_{min}^n

$$\sum_{k=1}^{M}\left(V_{n+1}\left(X_{n+1}^k\right) - H\left(\alpha, X_n^k\right)\right)^2$$

For each scenario k from set 1 calculate:

Generate a new realization of the random variable $\widetilde{X}_{n+1}^k$ starting at X_n^k.

/*See Figure 13.1 above*/

If $n+1$ is the maturity of valued instrument then

$$\widetilde{V}_{n+1}\left(\widetilde{X}_{n+1}^k\right) = C_{n+1}\left(\widetilde{X}_{n+1}^k\right)$$

Else

$$\widetilde{V}_{n+1}\left(\widetilde{X}_{n+1}^k\right) = \max\left(C_{n+1}\left(\widetilde{X}_{n+1}^k\right), H\left(\alpha_{min}^{n+1}, \widetilde{X}_{n+1}^k\right)\right)$$

End If

If $C_n\left(X_n^k\right) > \widetilde{V}_{n+1}\left(\widetilde{X}_{n+1}^k\right)$ then

$$\hat{V}_n\left(X_n^k\right) = C_n\left(X_n^k\right) \quad /*\text{Exercise option}*/$$

Else

$$\hat{V}_n\left(X_n^k\right) = \tilde{V}_{n+1}\left(\tilde{X}_{n+1}^k\right) \quad /*\textbf{Continue option}*/$$

End If

Next k

End of algorithm 13.4

Again, the final value of the priced derivative is calculated as an average of $\hat{V}_1\left(X_1^k\right)$ across all scenarios.

Algorithm 13.5

Algorithm 13.5 is a modification of Algorithm 13.4. The difference between these two algorithms is that in case of Algorithm 13.4

$$\hat{U}_n^1\left(X_n^k\right) = \hat{U}_n^2\left(X_n^k\right) = \tilde{V}_{n+1}\left(\tilde{X}_{n+1}^k\right),$$

while in the case of Algorithm 13.5

$$\hat{U}_n^1\left(X_n^k\right) = \tilde{V}_{n+1}\left(\tilde{X}_{n+1}^k\right)$$

$$\hat{U}_n^2\left(X_n^k\right) = \hat{V}_{n+1}\left(X_{n+1}^k\right)$$

Begin

 Find regression coefficient vector α that minimizes the expression (LSM algorithm). Denote this vector as $\alpha_{\min}^n$

$$\sum_{k=1}^{M}\left(\hat{V}_{n+1}\left(X_{n+1}^k\right) - H\left(\alpha, X_n^k\right)\right)^2$$

 For each scenario k from set 1 calculate:

  Generate a new realization of the random variable $\tilde{X}_{n+1}^k$ starting at X_n^k.

  If n + 1 is the maturity of instrument then

$$\tilde{V}_{n+1}\left(\tilde{X}_{n+1}^k\right) = C_{n+1}\left(\tilde{X}_{n+1}^k\right)$$

  Else

$$\tilde{V}_{n+1}\left(\tilde{X}_{n+1}^k\right) = \max\left(C_{n+1}\left(\tilde{X}_{n+1}^k\right), H\left(\alpha_{\min}^{n+1}, \tilde{X}_{n+1}^k\right)\right)$$

  End If

  If $C_n\left(X_n^k\right) > \tilde{V}_{n+1}\left(\tilde{X}_{n+1}^k\right)$ then

$$\hat{V}_n\left(X_n^k\right) = C_n\left(X_n^k\right) \quad /*\textbf{Exercise option}*/$$

  Else

$$\hat{V}_n\left(X_n^k\right) = \hat{V}_{n+1}\left(X_{n+1}^k\right) \quad /*\textbf{Continue option} - \textbf{instead of}$$
$$\hat{V}_n(X_n^k) = \tilde{V}_{n+1}\left(\tilde{X}_{n+1}^k\right) \textbf{ in Algorithm 13.4 }*/$$

  End If

 Next k

End of algorithm 13.5

The final value of the priced derivative is calculated as an average of $\hat{V}_1\left(X_1^k\right)$ across all scenarios.

13.2 NUMERICAL EXAMPLES OF ALGORITHMS 13.1–13.4

In these part we present detailed numerical examples of the application of Algorithms 13.1–13.4 described above to pricing a Bermudian swaption. Let us assume that the swaption gives its holder right to enter into a swap paying float and receiving fix. Let the fixed payment frequency be 6 months. The swaption can be exercised at three time points:

$T_1 = 0.5$	Gives right to enter into IRS starting at T_1 and maturing at T_4
$T_2 = 1$	Gives right to enter into IRS starting at T_2 and maturing at T_4
$T_3 = 1.5$	Gives right to enter into IRS starting at T_3 and maturing at T_4. This swaption is degenerate to the caplet

The fixed rate of the swap is $K = 5\%$. Maturity of the swap is $T_4 = 2$

The simulation will be performed under the terminal measure, i.e. the forward measure associated with the zero coupon bond maturing at time $T_4 = 2$. There are two time steps of simulation within each forward LIBOR period so time step of the simulation is $\Delta t = 0.25$. The Markovian process X_n will be defined as a multidimensional process:

$$X_n = \begin{bmatrix} L_1\left(T_n\right) \\ L_2\left(T_n\right) \\ L_3\left(T_n\right) \\ L_4\left(T_n\right) \\ W_{T_n} \end{bmatrix} \tag{13.3}$$

This process as a whole vector is Markovian under the forward measure associated with a zero coupon bond maturing at T_4. However, it is not necessarily true for each of its components.

In order to perform the calculations we need to model three forward LIBORs: L_2, L_3, L_4 driven by following stochastic processes consistent with standard LMM:

$$dL_i = L_i\left(-\sum_{j=i+1}^{4} \frac{\delta L_j \sigma_i \sigma_j}{1 + \delta L_j} dt + \sigma_i dW_t\right)$$

In our example W_t is a one dimensional Brownian Motion. We set the volatilities to be $\sigma_i = 0.3$. In order to describe algorithm easily we will only generate ten scenarios of the LIBOR. We use the Euler schema:

$$L_i\left(t + \Delta t\right) = L_i\left(t\right) + L_i\left(t\right)\left(-\sum_{j=i+1}^{4} \frac{\delta L_j\left(t\right) \sigma_i \sigma_j}{1 + \delta L_j\left(t\right)} \Delta t + \sigma_i\left(W_{t+\Delta t} - W_t\right)\right) \tag{13.4}$$

The results of our simulations are given below:

Example of Algorithm 13.1

Scenario Set 1

	$T_0=0$	$T_0^1=0.25$	$T_1=0.5$	$T_1^1=0.75$	$T_2=1$	$T_2^1=1.25$	$T_3=1.5$
Scenario 1							
W	0	−0.62556	0.142542	−0.47478	−0.78972	−0.46497	−0.86703
L 1	5.0000 %	Expired	Expired	Expired	Expired	Expired	Expired
L 2	5.0000 %	4.0562 %	4.9872 %	Expired	Expired	Expired	Expired
L 3	5.0000 %	4.0589 %	4.9924 %	4.0651 %	3.6792 %	Expired	Expired
L 4	5.0000 %	4.0617 %	4.9976 %	4.0720 %	3.6873 %	4.0466 %	3.5585 %
Scenario 2							
W	0	0.62556	−0.14254	0.474783	0.789724	0.464967	0.867028
L 1	5.0000 %	Expired	Expired	Expired	Expired	Expired	Expired
L 2	5.0000 %	5.9329 %	4.5580 %	Expired	Expired	Expired	Expired
L 3	5.0000 %	5.9356 %	4.5640 %	5.4069 %	5.9146 %	Expired	Expired
L 4	5.0000 %	5.9383 %	4.5700 %	5.4163 %	5.9281 %	5.3505 %	5.9959 %
Scenario 3							
W	0	−0.05002	−0.06374	−0.32575	−1.10699	−1.07849	−0.45718
L 1	5.0000 %	Expired	Expired	Expired	Expired	Expired	Expired
L 2	5.0000 %	4.9195 %	4.8939 %	Expired	Expired	Expired	Expired
L 3	5.0000 %	4.9222 %	4.8993 %	4.5116 %	3.4519 %	Expired	Expired
L 4	5.0000 %	4.9250 %	4.9047 %	4.5192 %	3.4600 %	3.4896 %	4.1400 %
Scenario 4							
W	0	0.050018	0.06374	0.325749	1.10699	1.078491	0.457183
L 1	5.0000 %	Expired	Expired	Expired	Expired	Expired	Expired
L 2	5.0000 %	5.0695 %	5.0848 %	Expired	Expired	Expired	Expired
L 3	5.0000 %	5.0723 %	5.0903 %	5.4876 %	6.7704 %	Expired	Expired
L 4	5.0000 %	5.0750 %	5.0959 %	5.4965 %	6.7847 %	6.7267 %	5.4729 %
Scenario 5							
W	0	0.003759	1.193405	1.758721	1.949461	2.595586	3.527374
L 1	5.0000 %	Expired	Expired	Expired	Expired	Expired	Expired
L 2	5.0000 %	5.0002 %	6.7792 %	Expired	Expired	Expired	Expired
L 3	5.0000 %	5.0029 %	6.7856 %	7.9314 %	8.3785 %	Expired	Expired
L 4	5.0000 %	5.0056 %	6.7921 %	7.9440 %	8.3986 %	10.0266 %	12.8294 %
Scenario 6							
W	0	−0.00376	−1.19341	−1.75872	−1.94946	−2.59559	−3.52737
L 1	5.0000 %	Expired	Expired	Expired	Expired	Expired	Expired
L 2	5.0000 %	4.9889 %	3.2029 %	Expired	Expired	Expired	Expired
L 3	5.0000 %	4.9916 %	3.2074 %	2.6623 %	2.5092 %	Expired	Expired
L 4	5.0000 %	4.9944 %	3.2119 %	2.6672 %	2.5146 %	2.0271 %	1.4605 %
Scenario 7							
W	0	−0.50241	−0.33478	−0.49262	0.165897	0.310097	1.011739
L 1	5.0000 %	Expired	Expired	Expired	Expired	Expired	Expired
L 2	5.0000 %	4.2409 %	4.4502 %	Expired	Expired	Expired	Expired
L 3	5.0000 %	4.2436 %	4.4551 %	4.2419 %	5.0780 %	Expired	Expired
L 4	5.0000 %	4.2464 %	4.4599 %	4.2488 %	5.0881 %	5.3082 %	6.4256 %
Scenario 8							
W	0	0.502406	0.334777	0.492616	−0.1659	−0.3101	−1.01174
L 1	5.0000 %	Expired	Expired	Expired	Expired	Expired	Expired
L 2	5.0000 %	5.7481 %	5.4518 %	Expired	Expired	Expired	Expired
L 3	5.0000 %	5.7509 %	5.4580 %	5.7132 %	4.5810 %	Expired	Expired
L 4	5.0000 %	5.7536 %	5.4643 %	5.7230 %	4.5924 %	4.3937 %	3.4689 %

	$T_0=0$	$T_0^1=0.25$	$T_1=0.5$	$T_1^1=0.75$	$T_2=1$	$T_2^1=1.25$	$T_3=1.5$
Scenario 9							
W	0	0.170297	−0.30515	−0.24493	−0.51339	−0.23812	−0.92795
L 1	5.0000 %	Expired	Expired	Expired	Expired	Expired	Expired
L 2	5.0000 %	5.2500 %	4.4951 %	Expired	Expired	Expired	Expired
L 3	5.0000 %	5.2527 %	4.5005 %	4.5795 %	4.2084 %	Expired	Expired
L 4	5.0000 %	5.2554 %	4.5058 %	4.5872 %	4.2178 %	4.5661 %	3.6211 %
Scenario 10							
W	0	−0.1703	0.30515	0.244925	0.513385	0.238115	0.927954
L 1	5.0000 %	Expired	Expired	Expired	Expired	Expired	Expired
L 2	5.0000 %	4.7391 %	5.4101 %	Expired	Expired	Expired	Expired
L 3	5.0000 %	4.7418 %	5.4157 %	5.3146 %	5.7395 %	Expired	Expired
L 4	5.0000 %	4.7446 %	5.4213 %	5.3233 %	5.7521 %	5.2771 %	6.3692 %

The final payment at time $T_3 = 1.5$ expressed with the numeraire being a zero coupon bond maturing at time $T_4 = 2$ (assuming that swaption has not been exercised previously) is:

$$\hat{V}_3\left(X_3^k\right) = \delta\left(L_4 - K\right)^+ \tag{13.5}$$

The final payments for each scenario is listed in Table 13.1 below.

Table 13.1

Scenario Number	L_4	$\hat{V}_3\left(X_3^k\right)$
1	3.5585 %	0.0000 %
2	5.9959 %	0.4980 %
3	4.1400 %	0.0000 %
4	5.4729 %	0.2365 %
5	12.8294 %	3.9147 %
6	1.4605 %	0.0000 %
7	6.4256 %	0.7128 %
8	3.4689 %	0.0000 %
9	3.6211 %	0.0000 %
10	6.3692 %	0.6846 %

During the calculations for the time T_2 we need to compare two values:

1) Intrinsic value of the swaption. This value at T_2 is

$$C_2\left(X_2^k\right) = \left[(1 + \delta L_3)(1 + \delta L_4) - 1 - \delta k\left[(1 + \delta L_4) + 1\right]\right]^+ \tag{13.6}$$

2) Value of the swaption under assumption that it is not exercised at T_2. For this comparison the value of continuation is estimated by

$$\hat{U}_2^1\left(X_n^k\right) = H\left(\alpha_{\min}, X_n^k\right) = a_0 + a_1 W_{T_2} + a_2 W_{T_2}. \tag{13.7}$$

Where

$$\alpha_{min} = \begin{bmatrix} a_0 \\ a_1 \\ a_2 \end{bmatrix}$$

Coefficients a_0, a_1, a_2 will be estimated using an LSM approach across all scenarios in order to minimize the expression

$$\sum_{k=1}^{10} \left(H\left(\alpha, W_{T_2}^k\right) - \hat{V}_3\left(X_3^k\right) \right)^2.$$

Where $W_{T_2}^k$ is a realization of random variable W_{T_2} in k-th scenario

In Table 13.2 below we have value of Brownian motion at time T_2 and value that swaption holder receive under given scenario if decide not to exercise swaption at T_2. This value is equal to swaption payoff at T_3 and it is rewritten from Table 13.1.

Table 13.2

Scenario Number	W_{T_2}	$\hat{V}_3\left(X_3^k\right)$
1	−0.78972	0.0000 %
2	0.78972	0.4980 %
3	−1.10699	0.0000 %
4	1.10699	0.2365 %
5	1.949461	3.9147 %
6	−1.949461	0.0000 %
7	0.165897	0.7128 %
8	−0.165897	0.0000 %
9	−0.51339	0.0000 %
10	0.51339	0.6846 %

Now we regress the last column of the Table 13.2 on 1, W_{T_2}, $W_{T_2}^2$ across all scenarios. We obtain following values of regression coefficients:

$$\begin{aligned} a_0 &= 0.0006473 \\ a_1 &= 0.007370 \\ a_2 &= 0.004544 \end{aligned} \qquad (13.8)$$

Now, using formula (13.7) with calculated coefficients (13.8) we calculate the values of the estimator $\hat{U}_2^1\left(X_2^1\right)$ for each scenario. For example for the scenario 1 this value is:

$$\hat{U}_2^1\left(X_2^1\right) = 0.0006473 + 0.007370 \cdot W_{T_2} \cdot 0.004544 \cdot \left(W_{T_2}\right)^2$$

$$= 0.0006473 + 0.007370 \cdot (-0.78972) + 0.004544 \cdot (-0.78972)^2$$

$$= -0.002339$$

And using formula (13.6) we can calculate the value of exercising at time T_2 which is $C_2\left(X_2^k\right)$ for each of generated scenarios. For example for the scenario 2 value of exercising will be calculated as

$$C_2\left(X_2^2\right) = [(1+0.5\cdot0.059146)\cdot(1+0.5\cdot0.059281) - 1 - 0.5\cdot0.05$$
$$\cdot(1+0.5\cdot0.059281 + 1)]^+ = 0.009349$$

The results of calculation are presented in Table 13.3 below.

Table 13.3

Scenario Number	W_{T_2}	L_3	L_4	$C_2\left(X_2^k\right)$	$\hat{U}_2^1\left(X_2^k\right)$	Optimal Decision
1	−0.78972	3.6792 %	3.6873 %	0.0000 %	−0.2339 %	Exercise
2	0.78972	5.9146 %	5.9281 %	0.9349 %	0.9301 %	Exercise
3	−1.10699	3.4519 %	3.4600 %	0.0000 %	−0.1942 %	Exercise
4	1.10699	6.7704 %	6.7847 %	1.8076 %	1.4370 %	Exercise
5	1.949461	8.3785 %	8.3986 %	3.4595 %	3.2280 %	Exercise
6	−1.949461	2.5092 %	2.5146 %	0.0000 %	0.3545 %	Continue
7	0.165897	5.0780 %	5.0881 %	0.0840 %	0.1995 %	Continue
8	−0.165897	4.5810 %	4.5924 %	0.0000 %	−0.0450 %	Exercise
9	−0.51339	4.2084 %	4.2178 %	0.0000 %	−0.1938 %	Exercise
10	0.51339	5.7395 %	5.7521 %	0.7564 %	0.5628 %	Exercise

In some cases continuation value $\hat{U}_2^1\left(X_2^k\right)$ is less than zero. It is possible since the regression gives only an approximation of the continuation value not its exact value. It causes strange situations: option may be expired although it is out of the money. We decide to not improve this feature of the algorithm in order to preserve its generality (in cases of exotics instruments it can be not possible to determine if they are out of the money or in the money).

Now according to our simulation for all scenarios except scenarios 6 and 7 the swaption should be exercised at time T_2 (of course if it has not been exercised earlier). Below in Table 13.4 we present the value of swaption at time T_2 across all ten scenarios. This value is calculated as:

1) If according to regression results the option should be exercised (column 'Optimal Decision' in Table 13.4) then the value is equal to the intrinsic value

$$\hat{V}_2\left(X_2^k\right) = C_2\left(X_2^k\right)$$

2) If according to the regression results the option should be continued then the value is equal to continuation value. But now continuation value is estimated by $\hat{U}_2^2\left(X_2^k\right) = \hat{V}_3\left(X_3^k\right)$, (instead of $\hat{U}_2^1\left(X_n^k\right)$ that is used to check if option should be continued or exercised), so

$$\hat{V}_2\left(X_2^k\right) = \hat{U}_2^2\left(X_2^k\right) = \hat{V}_3\left(X_3^k\right)$$

Table 13.4

Scenario Number	Optimal Decision	$\hat{V}_3\left(X_3^k\right)$	$C_2\left(X_2^k\right)$	$\hat{V}_2\left(X_2^k\right)$
1	Exercise	0.0000 %	**0.0000 %**	0.0000 %
2	Exercise	0.4980 %	**0.9349 %**	0.9349 %
3	Exercise	0.0000 %	**0.0000 %**	0.0000 %
4	Exercise	0.2365 %	**1.8076 %**	1.8076 %
5	Exercise	3.9147 %	**3.4595 %**	3.4595 %
6	Continue	**0.0000 %**	0.0000 %	0.0000 %
7	Continue	**0.7128 %**	0.0840 %	0.7128 %
8	Exercise	0.0000 %	**0.0000 %**	0.0000 %
9	Exercise	0.0000 %	**0.0000 %**	0.0000 %
10	Exercise	0.6846 %	**0.7564 %**	0.7564 %

The result of this calculation is presented in Table 13.4 below. $C_2\left(X_2^k\right)$ is rewritten from Table 13.3 and $\hat{V}_3\left(X_3^k\right)$ is rewritten from Table 13.1.

Now, basing on the calculated value of the swaption at time T_2 which is $\hat{V}_2\left(X_2^k\right)$ (Table 13.4 above) we can calculate the value of the swaption at time T_1. Similarly as before at time T_2 we have to compare:

1) Intrinsic value of the swaption. This value at T_1 is

$$C_1\left(X_1^k\right)=\left[(1+\delta L_2)\,(1+\delta L_3)\,(1+\delta L_4)-1-\delta k\left[(1+\delta L_3)\,(1+\delta L_4)+(1+\delta L_4)+1\right]\right]^+$$

(13.9)

2) Value of the swaption under the condition that option is not exercised, estimated by

$$\hat{U}_1^1\left(X_1^k\right)=a_0+a_1 W_{T_1}+a_2 W_{T_1}^2$$

(13.10)

The coefficients a_0, a_1, a_2 are calculated by the LSM algorithm using the data listed in Table 13.5 below.

Table 13.5

Scenario number	W_{T_1}	$\hat{V}_2\left(X_2^k\right)$
1	0.142542	0.0000 %
2	−0.142542	0.9349 %
3	−0.06374	0.0000 %
4	0.06374	1.8076 %
5	1.193405	3.4595 %
6	−1.193405	0.0000 %
7	−0.33478	0.7128 %
8	0.33478	0.0000 %
9	−0.30515	0.0000 %
10	0.30515	0.7564 %

We regress the last column of the table on 1, W_{T_1}, $W_{T_1}{}^2$ across all scenarios. We obtain following values of regression coefficients:

$$a_0 = 0.004847$$
$$a_1 = 0.01240 \quad\quad (13.11)$$
$$a_2 = 0.008537$$

Then we can find the optimal decision regarding continuation of the option:
If $\hat{U}_1^1 (X_1^k) > C_1 (X_1^k)$ then the optimal decision should be: Continue
Otherwise it should be: Exercise.

The optimal decisions for each scenario are listed in Table 13.6 below.

Table 13.6

Scenario Number	W_{T_1}	L_2	L_3	L_4	$C_1(X_1^k)$	$\hat{U}_{11}^1(X_1^k)$	Optimal Decision
1	0.142542	4.9872 %	4.9924 %	4.9976 %	0.0000 %	0.6788 %	Continue
2	−0.142542	4.5580 %	4.5640 %	4.5700 %	0.0000 %	0.3253 %	Continue
3	−0.06374	4.8939 %	4.8993 %	4.9047 %	0.0000 %	0.4091 %	Continue
4	0.06374	5.0848 %	5.0903 %	5.0959 %	0.1388 %	0.5672 %	Continue
5	1.193405	6.7792 %	6.7856 %	6.7921 %	2.7702 %	3.1804 %	Continue
6	−1.193405	3.2029 %	3.2074 %	3.2119 %	0.0000 %	0.2207 %	Continue
7	−0.33478	4.4502 %	4.4551 %	4.4599 %	0.0000 %	0.1653 %	Continue
8	0.33478	5.4518 %	5.4580 %	5.4643 %	0.7058 %	0.9955 %	Continue
9	−0.30515	4.4951 %	4.5005 %	4.5058 %	0.0000 %	0.1857 %	Continue
10	0.30515	5.4101 %	5.4157 %	5.4213 %	0.6404 %	9.4270 %	Continue

Now according to the performed simulation the option should be continued for all ten scenarios. Analogously as in the case of swaption value calculation for T_2 value of swaption at time T_1 is equal:

1) If according to the regression results the option should be exercised (column 'Optimal Decision' in Table 13.6) then the value is equal to the intrinsic value:

$$\hat{V}_1 (X_1^k) = C_1 (X_1^k)$$

2) If according to the regression results the option should be continued then the value is equal to the continuation value estimated by $\hat{U}_1^2(X_1^k) = \hat{V}_2(X_1^k)$, so

$$\hat{V}_1 (X_1^k) = \hat{V}_2 (X_2^k).$$

As mentioned in our particular case condition 2) held for all ten scenarios. Table 13.7 below presents results of calculations for each scenario. Columns: 'Optimal Decision' and $C_1(X_1^k)$ are rewritten from Table 13.6. Column $\hat{V}_2(X_2^k)$ is rewritten from Table 13.5.

Table 13.7

Scenario Number	Optimal Decision	$\hat{V}_2(X_2^k)$	$C_1(X_1^k)$	$\hat{V}_1(X_1^k)$
1	Continue	**0.0000 %**	0.0000 %	0.0000 %
2	Continue	**0.9349 %**	0.0000 %	0.9349 %
3	Continue	**0.0000 %**	0.0000 %	0.0000 %
4	Continue	**1.8076 %**	0.1388 %	1.8076 %
5	Continue	**3.4595 %**	2.7702 %	3.4595 %
6	Continue	**0.0000 %**	0.0000 %	0.0000 %
7	Continue	**0.7128 %**	0.0000 %	0.7128 %
8	Continue	**0.0000 %**	0.7058 %	0.0000 %
9	Continue	**0.0000 %**	0.0000 %	0.0000 %
10	Continue	**0.7564 %**	0.6404 %	0.7564 %

Now, the value of the swaption at pricing time (T_0) can be calculated as the average of 'Value at time T_1' from Table 13.7 above. This calculation gives us:

$$\widetilde{S}_{T_0} = 0.7671\,\% \tag{13.12}$$

But we should remember that this value is expressed with the numeraire being a zero coupon bond maturing at time T_4. In order to obtain value of swaption expressed in currency we need simply multiplied calculated value (13.12) by value of the numeraire. Then the value of the swaption is:

$$S_{T_0} = \widetilde{S}_{T_0} \cdot B\,(T_0, T_4) = \frac{\widetilde{S}_{T_0}}{\prod\limits_{i=1}^{4}(1+\delta L_1\,(T_0))} = \frac{0.7671\%}{(1+0.5 \cdot 0.05)^4} = 0.6949\,\% \tag{13.13}$$

Example of Algorithm 13.2

As mentioned, algorithm 13.2 requires the generation of two sets of scenarios. The first set is used only for calculating the regression coefficients, while the pricing of the derivative is done with the second set of Monte Carlo scenarios. We assume that the first set of MC scenarios is the set generated in Example of Algorithm 13.1 above (Scenario Set 1). The second set of scenarios

Scenario Set 2

	$T_0=0$	$T_0^1=0.25$	$T_1=0.5$	$T_1^1=0.75$	$T_2=1$	$T_2^1=1.25$	$T_3=1.5$
Scenario 1							
W	0	0.13659	0.997955	1.395052	1.949337	2.153192	3.011643
L 1	5.0000 %	Expired	Expired	Expired	Expired	Expired	Expired
L 2	5.0000 %	5.1994 %	6.5370 %	Expired	Expired	Expired	Expired
L 3	5.0000 %	5.2021 %	6.5435 %	7.3183 %	8.5294 %	Expired	Expired
L 4	5.0000 %	5.2049 %	6.5499 %	7.3302 %	8.5491 %	9.0719 %	11.4082 %
Scenario 2							
W	0	−0.13659	−0.99795	−1.39505	−1.94934	−2.15319	−3.01164
L 1	5.0000 %	Expired	Expired	Expired	Expired	Expired	Expired
L 2	5.0000 %	4.7896 %	3.5469 %	Expired	Expired	Expired	Expired
L 3	5.0000 %	4.7924 %	3.5515 %	3.1270 %	2.6059 %	Expired	Expired
L 4	5.0000 %	4.7951 %	3.5560 %	3.1324 %	2.6115 %	2.4518 %	1.8204 %

Continued

	$T_0 = 0$	$T_0^1 = 0.25$	$T_1 = 0.5$	$T_1^1 = 0.75$	$T_2 = 1$	$T_2^1 = 1.25$	$T_3 = 1.5$
Scenario 3							
W	0	0.22994	1.017657	1.606291	1.995752	2.031917	1.966467
L 1	5.0000 %	Expired	Expired	Expired	Expired	Expired	Expired
L 2	5.0000 %	5.3394 %	6.5950 %	Expired	Expired	Expired	Expired
L 3	5.0000 %	5.3422 %	6.6015 %	7.7625 %	8.6629 %	Expired	Expired
L 4	5.0000 %	5.3449 %	6.6080 %	7.7749 %	8.6833 %	8.7775 %	8.6052 %
Scenario 4							
W	0	−0.22994	−1.01766	−1.60629	−1.99575	−2.03192	−1.96647
L 1	5.0000 %	Expired	Expired	Expired	Expired	Expired	Expired
L 2	5.0000 %	4.6496 %	3.5461 %	Expired	Expired	Expired	Expired
L 3	5.0000 %	4.6523 %	3.5505 %	2.9222 %	2.5798 %	Expired	Expired
L 4	5.0000 %	4.6551 %	3.5550 %	2.9272 %	2.5852 %	2.5572 %	2.6074 %
Scenario 5							
W	0	1.396211	2.176931	2.866458	2.935699	3.011579	2.878209
L 1	5.0000 %	Expired	Expired	Expired	Expired	Expired	Expired
L 2	5.0000 %	7.0888 %	8.7382 %	Expired	Expired	Expired	Expired
L 3	5.0000 %	7.0916 %	8.7471 %	10.5482 %	10.7554 %	Expired	Expired
L 4	5.0000 %	7.0943 %	8.7559 %	10.5672 %	10.7867 %	11.0322 %	10.5908 %
Scenario 6							
W	0	−1.39621	−2.17693	−2.86646	−2.9357	−3.01158	−2.87821
L 1	5.0000 %	Expired	Expired	Expired	Expired	Expired	Expired
L 2	5.0000 %	2.9002 %	2.2191 %	Expired	Expired	Expired	Expired
L 3	5.0000 %	2.9029 %	2.2221 %	1.7619 %	1.7249 %	Expired	Expired
L 4	5.0000 %	2.9057 %	2.2251 %	1.7648 %	1.7282 %	1.6888 %	1.7564 %
Scenario 7							
W	0	−0.01038	−0.55202	−0.61657	−1.39958	−1.41616	−1.70855
L 1	5.0000 %	Expired	Expired	Expired	Expired	Expired	Expired
L 2	5.0000 %	4.9789 %	4.1645 %	Expired	Expired	Expired	Expired
L 3	5.0000 %	4.9817 %	4.1695 %	4.0868 %	3.1250 %	Expired	Expired
L 4	5.0000 %	4.9844 %	4.1745 %	4.0937 %	3.1320 %	3.1165 %	2.8431 %
Scenario 8							
W	0	0.010376	0.552016	0.616574	1.399581	1.416164	1.708546
L 1	5.0000 %	Expired	Expired	Expired	Expired	Expired	Expired
L 2	5.0000 %	5.0101 %	5.8187 %	Expired	Expired	Expired	Expired
L 3	5.0000 %	5.0128 %	5.8246 %	5.9337 %	7.3237 %	Expired	Expired
L 4	5.0000 %	5.0156 %	5.8306 %	5.9435 %	7.3396 %	7.3761 %	8.0231 %
Scenario 9							
W	0	−0.1661	−0.42833	−0.83104	−0.48295	−0.66263	−0.73868
L 1	5.0000 %	Expired	Expired	Expired	Expired	Expired	Expired
L 2	5.0000 %	4.7454 %	4.3671 %	Expired	Expired	Expired	Expired
L 3	5.0000 %	4.7481 %	4.3721 %	3.8418 %	4.2413 %	Expired	Expired
L 4	5.0000 %	4.7508 %	4.3771 %	3.8483 %	4.2502 %	4.0211 %	3.9293 %
Scenario 10							
W	0	0.166102	0.428331	0.831039	0.482948	0.662631	0.738679
L 1	5.0000 %	Expired	Expired	Expired	Expired	Expired	Expired
L 2	5.0000 %	5.2437 %	5.6501 %	Expired	Expired	Expired	Expired
L 3	5.0000 %	5.2464 %	5.6561 %	6.3359 %	5.6699 %	Expired	Expired
L 4	5.0000 %	5.2492 %	5.6621 %	6.3461 %	5.6834 %	5.9898 %	6.1265 %

is listed below. Both scenarios sets are realizations of the same Markovian process X_n defined by (13.3).

The final payment at time $T_3 = 1.5$ expressed with numeraire being a zero coupon bond maturing at time $T_4 = 2$ (assuming that swaption has not been exercised previously) is calculated with formula (13.5). Our results of this calculation for the scenarios from Scenario Set 2 are given in Table 13.8 below.

Table 13.8

Scenario Number	L_4	$\hat{V}_3(X_3^k)$
1	11.4082 %	3.2041 %
2	1.8204 %	0.0000 %
3	8.6052 %	1.8026 %
4	2.6074 %	0.0000 %
5	10.5908 %	2.7954 %
6	1.7564 %	0.0000 %
7	2.8431 %	0.0000 %
8	8.0231 %	1.5116 %
9	3.9293 %	0.0000 %
10	6.1265 %	0.5632 %

During the calculation for the time T_2 we need to compare two values (calculated for scenarios from Scenario Set 2)

1) Intrinsic value of the swaption – formula (13.6)
2) Value of continuation approximated by formula (13.7)

If 1) > 2) then the swaption should be exercised at time T_2, otherwise the swaption should be continued.

In the case of Algorithm 2 the regression coefficients are calculated based on one scenario set (Scenario Set 1) and then applied to values of a Brownian motion (using formula (13.7) taken from another set of scenarios (Scenario Set 2). In case of Algorithm 13.1 the regression coefficients and value of continuation (13.7) are calculated basing of the same scenario set.

Table 13.9 below presents intrinsic value (13.6) and value of continuation (13.7), both calculated for Scenario Set 2. Regression coefficients for formula (13.7) are calculated with Scenario Set 1 and therefore they are identical as regression coefficients calculated by Algorithm 13.1, so they are given by formula (13.8).

Identically as in case of previous version of the algorithm the optimal decision is assumed to be 'exercise' if $C_2(X_2^k) > \hat{U}_2^1(X_2^k)$ and 'continue' otherwise.

For each scenario

1) If according to Table 13.9 above Optimal Decision is 'exercise' – the swaption value at T_2 is equal its intrinsic value.

$$\hat{V}_2(X_2^k) = C_2(X_2^k)$$

2) Otherwise, the swaption value at T_2 is equal to continuation value estimated by $\hat{U}_2^2(X_2^k) = \hat{V}(X_3^k)$

$$\hat{V}_2(X_2^k) = \hat{V}_3(X_3^k)$$

Table 13.9

Scenario Number	W_{T_2}	L_3	L_4	$C_2(X_2^k)$	$\hat{U}_2(X_2^k)$	Optimal Decision
1	1.949337	8.5294 %	8.5491 %	3.6147 %	3.2281 %	Exercise
2	−1.949337	2.6059 %	2.6115 %	0.0000 %	0.3547 %	Continue
3	1.995752	8.6629 %	8.6833 %	3.7526 %	3.3455 %	Exercise
4	−1.995752	2.5798 %	2.5852 %	0.0000 %	0.4037 %	Continue
5	2.935699	10.7554 %	10.7867 %	5.9262 %	6.1445 %	Continue
6	−2.935699	1.7249 %	1.7282 %	0.0000 %	1.8173 %	Continue
7	−1.39958	3.1250 %	3.1320 %	0.0000 %	−0.0770 %	Exercise
8	1.39958	7.3237 %	7.3396 %	2.3743 %	1.9863 %	Exercise
9	−0.48295	4.2413 %	4.2502 %	0.0000 %	−0.1850 %	Exercise
10	0.48295	5.6699 %	5.6834 %	0.6862 %	0.5266 %	Exercise

The results of calculation are presented in Table 13.10 below. Columns 'Optimal Decision' and $C_2(X_2^k)$ are rewritten from Table 13.9. Column $\hat{V}_3(X_3^k)$ is rewritten from Table 13.8.

Table 13.10

Scenario Number	Optimal Decision	$\hat{V}_3(X_3^k)$	$C_2(X_2^k)$	$\hat{V}_2(X_2^k)$
1	Exercise	3.2041 %	**3.6147 %**	3.6147 %
2	Continue	**0.0000 %**	0.0000 %	0.0000 %
3	Exercise	1.8026 %	**3.7526 %**	3.7526 %
4	Continue	**0.0000 %**	0.0000 %	0.0000 %
5	Continue	**2.7954 %**	5.9262 %	2.7954 %
6	Continue	**0.0000 %**	0.0000 %	0.0000 %
7	Exercise	0.0000 %	**0.0000 %**	0.0000 %
8	Exercise	1.5116 %	**2.3743 %**	2.3743 %
9	Exercise	0.0000 %	**0.0000 %**	0.0000 %
10	Exercise	0.5632 %	**0.6862 %**	0.6862 %

Based on the calculations done for time T_2 we calculate the value of the swaption for each scenario at time T_1. Similarly to the calculations for time T_2 we have to compare intrinsic value of the swaption (13.9) and value of swaption continuation – formula (13.10) with regression coefficients (13.11). Identically as in the case of T_2 coefficients calculation is done using Scenario Set 1. All remaining calculations use Scenario Set 2.

The option should be continued for all ten scenarios because for each scenario $\hat{U}_1^2(X_1^k) > C_1(X_1^k)$. Therefore the swaption value at time T_1 is equal to continuation value estimated by $\hat{U}_1^2(X_1^k) = \hat{V}_2(X_2^k)$, then

$$\hat{V}_1(X_1^k) = \hat{V}_2(X_2^k).$$

The results of calculation are listed in Table 13.12 below. Columns 'Optimal Decision' and $C_1(X_1^k)$ are rewritten from Table 13.12, column $\hat{V}_2(X_2^k)$ is rewritten from Table 13.10.

Table 13.11

Scenario Number	W_{T_1}	L_2	L_3	L_4	$C_1(X_1^k)$	$\hat{U}_1(X_1^k)$	Optimal Decision
1	0.997955	6.5370 %	6.5435 %	6.5499 %	2.3916 %	2.5724 %	Continue
2	−0.99795	3.5469 %	3.5515 %	3.5560 %	0.0000 %	0.0974 %	Continue
3	1.017657	6.5950 %	6.6015 %	6.6080 %	2.4822 %	2.6307 %	Continue
4	−1.01766	3.5461 %	3.5505 %	3.5550 %	0.0000 %	0.1069 %	Continue
5	2.176931	8.7382 %	8.7471 %	8.7559 %	5.8698 %	7.2298 %	Continue
6	−2.17693	2.2191 %	2.2221 %	2.2251 %	0.0000 %	1.8310 %	Continue
7	−0.55202	4.1645 %	4.1695 %	4.1745 %	0.0000 %	0.0603 %	Continue
8	0.552016	5.8187 %	5.8246 %	5.8306 %	1.2731 %	1.4293 %	Continue
9	−0.42833	4.3671 %	4.3721 %	4.3771 %	0.0000 %	0.1102 %	Continue
10	0.428331	5.6501 %	5.6561 %	5.6621 %	1.0121 %	1.1725 %	Continue

Table 13.12

Scenario Number	Optimal Decision	$\hat{V}_2(X_2^k)$	$C_1(X_1^k)$	$\hat{V}_1(X_1^k)$
1	Continue	**3.6147 %**	2.3916 %	3.6147 %
2	Continue	**0.0000 %**	0.0000 %	0.0000 %
3	Continue	**3.7526 %**	2.4822 %	3.7526 %
4	Continue	**0.0000 %**	0.0000 %	0.0000 %
5	Continue	**2.7954 %**	5.8698 %	2.7954 %
6	Continue	**0.0000 %**	0.0000 %	0.0000 %
7	Continue	**0.0000 %**	0.0000 %	0.0000 %
8	Continue	**2.3743 %**	1.2731 %	2.3743 %
9	Continue	**0.0000 %**	0.0000 %	0.0000 %
10	Continue	**0.6862 %**	1.0121 %	0.6862 %

Now the value of the swaption (expressed in assumed numeraire – a zero coupon bond) at pricing time (T_0) is calculated as the average of 'Value at $T_1 - \hat{V}_1(X_1^k)$' from Table 13.12 above across all ten scenarios and it is:

$$\tilde{S}_{T_0} = 1.3223 \% \tag{13.14}$$

Finally we can express the swaption in currency as:

$$S_{T_0} = \frac{\tilde{S}_{T_0}}{\prod_{i=1}^{4}(1+\delta L_i(0))} = \frac{1.3223 \%}{(1+0.5 \cdot 0.05)^4} = 1.1979 \% \tag{13.15}$$

Example of Algorithm 13.3

The value of the swaption at T_3 is $\hat{V}_3(X_3^k)$ for each scenario and is calculated identically as in the case of Algorithm 13.1; formula (13.5) is applied to forward LIBORs from Scenario Set 1. The results of calculations are listed in Table 13.1.

At time T_2, identically as in case of Algorithm 13.1 and Algorithm 13.2, we need to compare

1) Intrinsic value of swaption – formula (13.6).
2) Value of swaption under assumption that option is continued. This value is approximated by (13.7) with coefficients given by (13.8).

If 1) > 2) then the swaption should be exercised. It means that

$$\hat{V}_2\left(X_2^k\right) = C_2\left(X_2^k\right)$$

Otherwise the swaption should be continued and its value is equal to continuation value estimated by $\hat{U}_2^2\left(X_2^k\right)$. But in case of Algorithm 3 $\hat{U}_2^2\left(X_2^k\right) = \hat{U}_2^1\left(X_2^k\right)$ and from (13.7) we have

$$\hat{V}_2\left(X_2^k\right) = \hat{U}_2^2\left(X_2^k\right) = a_0 + a_1 W_{T_2} + a_2 W_{T_2}^2$$

Where coefficients a_0, a_1, a_2 are given by (13.8).

The results of this calculation are given in Table 13.13 below. Since all calculations in Table 13.13 are performed for Scenario Set 1 then values $C_2\left(X_2^k\right)$ and $\hat{U}_2^2\left(X_2^k\right)$ are identical as these values listed in Table 13.3. However, values $\hat{V}_2\left(X_2^k\right)$ can be different that these listed in Table 13.3 because:

1) For Algorithm 13.1: $\hat{V}_2\left(X_2^k\right) = \hat{V}_3\left(X_3^k\right)$
2) For Algorithm 13.3: $\hat{V}_2\left(X_2^k\right) = a_0 + a_1 W_{T_2} + a_2 W_{T_2}^2$

Table 13.13

Scenario Number	$C_2\left(X_2^k\right)$	$\hat{U}_2^2\left(X_2^k\right) = \hat{U}_2^1\left(X_2^k\right)$	Optimal Decision	$\hat{V}_2\left(X_2^k\right)$
1	0.0000 %	−0.2339 %	Exercise	0.0000 %
2	0.9349 %	0.9301 %	Exercise	0.9349 %
3	0.0000 %	−0.1942 %	Exercise	0.0000 %
4	1.8076 %	1.4370 %	Exercise	1.8076 %
5	3.4595 %	3.2280 %	Exercise	3.4595 %
6	0.0000 %	0.3545 %	Continue	0.3545 %
7	0.0840 %	0.1995 %	Continue	0.1995 %
8	0.0000 %	−0.0450 %	Exercise	0.0000 %
9	0.0000 %	−0.1938 %	Exercise	0.0000 %
10	0.7564 %	0.5628 %	Exercise	0.7564 %

Now we can calculate swaption values at time T_1, $\hat{V}_1\left(X_1^k\right)$. Analogically as for the calculation at T_2 we have:

$$\hat{V}_1\left(X_1^k\right) = \max\left(C_1\left(X_1^k\right), \hat{U}_1^2\left(X_1^k\right)\right)$$

$C_1\left(X_1^k\right)$ is calculated using formula (13.9). $\hat{U}_1^2\left(X_1^k\right) = \hat{U}_1^1\left(X_1^k\right)$ is calculated with formula (13.10). Coefficients a_0, a_1, a_2 are calculated using LSM by fitting (LSM) values $\hat{V}_2\left(X_2^k\right)$ to $1, W_{T_1}, \left(W_{T_1}\right)^2$ (see Table 13.14 below).

Table 13.14

Scenario Number	W_{T_1}	$\hat{V}_2\left(X_2^k\right)$
1	0.142542	0.0000 %
2	−0.142542	0.9349 %
3	−0.06374	0.0000 %
4	0.06374	1.8076 %
5	1.193405	3.4595 %
6	−1.193405	0.3545 %
7	−0.33478	0.1995 %
8	0.33478	0.0000 %
9	−0.30515	0.0000 %
10	0.30515	0.7564 %

As mentioned $\hat{V}_2\left(X_2^k\right)$ can be different than these values calculated with Algorithm 13.1, so the regression coefficients can be different than the coefficients given by (13.11). Indeed, they are equal

$$a_0 = 0.004138$$
$$a_1 = 0.01164$$
$$a_2 = 0.01020$$

The results of calculations are given in Table 13.15 below.

Table 13.15

Scenario Number	$C_1\left(X_1^k\right)$	$\hat{U}_1^2\left(X_1^k\right)=\hat{U}_1^1\left(X_1^k\right)$	Optimal Decision	$\hat{V}_1\left(X_1^k\right)$
1	0.0000 %	0.6005 %	Continue	0.6005 %
2	0.0000 %	0.2685 %	Continue	0.2685 %
3	0.0000 %	0.3437 %	Continue	0.3437 %
4	0.1388 %	0.4922 %	Continue	0.4922 %
5	2.7702 %	3.2562 %	Continue	3.2562 %
6	0.0000 %	0.4769 %	Continue	0.4769 %
7	0.0000 %	0.1383 %	Continue	0.1383 %
8	0.7058 %	0.9180 %	Continue	0.9180 %
9	0.0000 %	0.1535 %	Continue	0.1535 %
10	0.6404 %	0.8641 %	Continue	0.8641 %

Now the value of the swaption at pricing time T_0 is calculated as the average of $\hat{V}_1\left(X_1^k\right)$ across all ten scenarios (see Table 13.15 above). The calculated value is expressed in the numeraire used for simulations (again a zero coupon bond with maturity at T_4) and is equal to

$$\widetilde{S}_{T_0} = 0.75124 \% . \tag{13.16}$$

In order to get value of the swaption we need to multiply (13.16) by the value of the numeraire:

$$S_{T_0} = \frac{\widetilde{S}_{T_0}}{\prod_{i=1}^{4}(1+\delta L_i(T_0))} = \frac{0.75124\,\%}{(1+0.5\cdot0.05)^4} = 0.680586\,\% \qquad (13.17)$$

Example of Algorithm 13.4

The value of the swaption at $T_3\left(\hat{V}_3\left(X_3^k\right)\right)$ under each scenario is calculated identically as in case of Algorithm 13.1; formula (13.5) is applied to the forward LIBORs from Scenario Set 1. The results of calculations are listed in Table 13.1.

At time T_2 the regression coefficients for the function $\hat{U}_2^1\left(W_{T_2}\right)$ are calculated using LSM. These regression coefficients are identical as in case of Algorithm 1 and they are given by (13.8).

Then for each scenario from Scenario Set 1 a new realization of random variable X_3 is generated. Denote $\widetilde{X}_3^k$ as this new realization for scenario k.

$$\widetilde{X}_3^k = \begin{bmatrix} \widetilde{L}_1^k(T_3) \\ \widetilde{L}_2^k(T_3) \\ \widetilde{L}_3^k(T_3) \\ \widetilde{L}_4^k(T_3) \\ \widetilde{W}_{T_3}^k \end{bmatrix}$$

Where following (13.4) $\widetilde{L}_4^k(T_3)$ is generated as:

$$\widetilde{L}_4^k\left(T_2^1\right) = L_4^k(T_2) + L_4^k(T_2)\,\sigma_4\Delta\widetilde{W}_{T_2}^k$$

$$\widetilde{L}_4^k(T_3) = \widetilde{L}_4^k\left(T_2^1\right) + \widetilde{L}_4^k\left(T_2^1\right)\sigma_4\Delta\widetilde{W}_{T_2^1}^k$$

The remaining forward LIBORs (L_1, L_2, L_3) are expired at time T_3. The results of the calculations are presented in Table 13.16 below.

Table 13.16

Scenario Number	$L_4(T_2)$	$\Delta\widetilde{W}_{T_2}$	$\widetilde{L}_4\left(T_2^1\right)$	$\Delta\widetilde{W}_{T_2^1}$	$\widetilde{L}_4(T_3)$
1	3.6873%	0.203855	3.9128%	0.858451	4.9205%
2	5.9281%	−0.20385	5.5656%	−0.85845	4.1322%
3	3.4600%	0.036165	3.4975%	−0.06545	3.4289%
4	6.7847%	−0.03616	6.7111%	0.06545	6.8429%
5	8.3986%	0.07588	8.5898%	−0.13337	8.2461%
6	2.5146%	−0.07588	2.4574%	0.13337	2.5557%
7	5.0881%	−0.01658	5.0628%	−0.29238	4.6187%
8	4.5924%	0.016583	4.6152%	0.292382	5.0201%
9	4.2178%	−0.17968	3.9904%	−0.07605	3.8994%
10	5.7521%	0.179684	6.0622%	0.076048	6.2005%

By analogy to (13.5) the value of the swaption at T_3 is equal:

$$\tilde{V}_3\left(\tilde{X}_3^k\right) = \delta\left(\tilde{L}_4^k - K\right)^+.$$

The value of the swaption at T_2 for each scenario k is calculated as

$$\hat{V}_2\left(X_2^k\right) = \max\left(C_2\left(X_2^k\right), \tilde{V}_3\left(\tilde{X}_3^k\right)\right).$$

The results are given in Table 13.17 below.

Table 13.17

Scenario Number	$\tilde{L}_4(T_3)$	$\tilde{V}_3\left(\tilde{X}_3^k\right)$	$C_2\left(X_2^k\right)$	$\hat{V}_2\left(X_2^k\right)$
1	4.9205 %	0.0000 %	**0.0000 %**	0.0000 %
2	4.1322 %	0.0000 %	**0.9349 %**	0.9349 %
3	3.4289 %	0.0000 %	**0.0000 %**	0.0000 %
4	6.8429 %	0.9210 %	**1.8076 %**	1.8076 %
5	8.2461 %	1.6230 %	**3.4595 %**	3.4595 %
6	2.5557 %	0.0000 %	**0.0000 %**	0.0000 %
7	4.6187 %	0.0000 %	**0.0840 %**	0.0840 %
8	5.0201 %	**0.0100 %**	0.0000 %	0.0100 %
9	3.8994 %	0.0000 %	**0.0000 %**	0.0000 %
10	6.2005 %	0.6000 %	**0.7564 %**	0.7564 %

Note that the intrinsic value at time T_2, $C_2\left(X_2^k\right)$, is rewritten from Table 13.3.

Now, in order to calculate $\hat{V}_1\left(X_1^k\right)$ we need to generate the alternative realization of random variable $X_2 - \tilde{X}_2^k$. Analogically as in previous time steps we calculate $\tilde{L}_3^k(T_2)$, $\tilde{L}_4^k(T_2)$ using Euler approximation (13.4):

$$\tilde{L}_3^k\left(T_1^1\right) = L_3^k\left(T_1\right) + L_3^k\left(T_1\right)\left(-\frac{\delta\sigma_3\sigma_4 L_4^k\left(T_1\right)}{1 + \delta L_4^k\left(T_1\right)}\Delta t + \sigma_3\Delta\tilde{W}_{T_1}\right)$$

$$\tilde{L}_3^k\left(T_2\right) = \tilde{L}_3^k\left(T_1^1\right) + \tilde{L}_3^k\left(T_1^1\right)\left(-\frac{\delta\sigma_3\sigma_4\tilde{L}_4^k\left(T_1^1\right)}{1 + \delta\tilde{L}_4^k\left(T_1^1\right)}\Delta t + \sigma_3\Delta\tilde{W}_{T_1^1}\right)$$

$$\tilde{L}_4^k\left(T_1^1\right) = L_4^k\left(T_1\right) + L_4^k\left(T_1\right)\sigma_4\Delta\tilde{W}_{T_1}$$

$$\tilde{L}_4^k\left(T_2\right) = \tilde{L}_4^k\left(T_1^1\right) + \tilde{L}_4^k\left(T_1^1\right)\sigma_4\Delta\tilde{W}_{T_1^1}$$

The results are given in Table 13.18 below.

Table 13.18

Scenario Number	$L_3^k(T_1)$ $L_4^k(T_1)$	$\Delta\widetilde{W}_{T_1}$	$\widetilde{L}_3^k(T_1^1)$ $\widetilde{L}_4^k(T_1^1)$	$\Delta\widetilde{W}_{T_1^1}$	$\widetilde{L}_3^k(T_2)$ $\widetilde{L}_4^k(T_2)$
1	4.9924%		5.5844%		6.5096%
	4.9976%	0.3970971	5.5930%	0.554286	6.5230%
2	4.5640%		4.0180%		3.3481%
	4.5700%	−0.397097	4.0256%	−0.55429	3.3562%
3	4.8993%		5.7618%		6.4314%
	4.9047%	0.5886339	5.7708%	0.389461	6.4451%
4	5.0903%		4.1881%		3.6965%
	5.9590%	−0.588634	4.9067%	−0.38946	4.3334%
5	6.7856%		8.1842%		8.3470%
	6.7921%	0.6895267	8.1971%	0.069242	8.3674%
6	3.2074%		2.5428%		2.4892%
	3.2119%	−0.689527	2.5475%	−0.06924	2.4946%
7	4.4551%		4.3666%		3.3388%
	4.4599%	−0.064557	4.3735%	−0.78301	3.3462%
8	5.4580%		5.5604%		6.8632%
	5.4643%	0.0645575	5.5701%	0.783007	6.8786%
9	4.5005%		3.9546%		4.3658%
	4.5058%	−0.402708	3.9614%	0.348092	4.3751%
10	5.4157%		6.0668%		5.4292%
	5.4213%	0.4027079	6.0763%	−0.34809	5.4417%

Now we can calculate values $\widetilde{V}_2\left(\widetilde{X}_2^k\right)$:

$$\widetilde{V}_2\left(\widetilde{X}_2^k\right) = \max\left(C_2\left(\widetilde{X}_2^k\right), H\left(\alpha_{\min}^2, \widetilde{X}_2^k\right)\right)$$

Where the intrinsic value of the swaption $C_2\left(\widetilde{X}_2^k\right)$ is by analogy to (13.6):

$$C_2\left(\widetilde{X}_2^k\right) = \left[\left(1 + \delta\widetilde{L}_3^k\right)\left(1 + \delta\widetilde{L}_4^k\right) - 1 - \delta K\left[\left(1 + \delta\widetilde{L}_4^k\right) + 1\right]\right]^+$$

And

$$H\left(\alpha_{\min}^2, \widetilde{X}_2^k\right) = a_0 + a_1 \widetilde{W}_{T_2}^k + a_2\left(\widetilde{W}_{T_2}^k\right)^2$$

$$\widetilde{W}_{T_2}^k = W_{T_1} + \Delta\widetilde{W}_{T_1} + \Delta\widetilde{W}_{T_1^1}$$

Coefficients a_0, a_1, a_2 are calculated during the previous time step of simulation and they are expressed by (13.8).

The results of calculation are listed in Table 13.19 below.

Table 13.19

Scenario Number	$H\left(\alpha_{min}^2, \widetilde{X}_2^k\right)$	$C_2\left(\widetilde{X}_2^k\right)$	$\widetilde{V}_2\left(\widetilde{X}_2^k\right)$
1	1.4147 %	**1.5409 %**	1.5409 %
2	−0.1980 %	**0.0000 %**	0.0000 %
3	1.1185 %	**1.4613 %**	1.4613 %
4	−0.2290 %	**0.0000 %**	0.0000 %
5	3.2352 %	**3.4272 %**	3.4272 %
6	**0.3577 %**	0.0000 %	0.3577 %
7	−0.1710 %	**0.0000 %**	0.0000 %
8	1.5713 %	**1.9029 %**	1.9029 %
9	−0.2070 %	**0.0000 %**	0.0000 %
10	**0.6862 %**	0.4413 %	0.6862 %

Then $\hat{V}_1\left(X_1^k\right)$ are calculated as

$$\hat{V}_1\left(X_1^k\right) = \max\left(C_1\left(X_1^k\right), \widetilde{V}_2\left(\widetilde{X}_2^k\right)\right)$$

Where the intrinsic value, $C_1\left(X_1^k\right)$, is given by formula (13.9). Calculation results are listed in Table 13.20 below.

Table 13.20

Scenario Number	$C_1\left(X_1^k\right)$	$\widetilde{V}_2\left(\widetilde{X}_2^k\right)$	$\hat{V}_1\left(X_1^k\right)$
1	0.0000 %	**1.5409 %**	1.5409 %
2	0.0000 %	**0.0000 %**	0.0000 %
3	0.0000 %	**1.4613 %**	1.4613 %
4	**0.1388 %**	0.0000 %	0.1388 %
5	2.7702 %	**3.4272 %**	3.4272 %
6	0.0000 %	**0.3577 %**	0.3577 %
7	0.0000 %	0.0000 %	0.0000 %
8	0.7058 %	**1.9029 %**	1.9029 %
9	0.0000 %	0.0000 %	0.0000 %
10	0.6404 %	**0.6862 %**	0.6862 %

The value of the swaption expressed in the assumed numeraire is then calculated as the average of $\hat{V}_1\left(X_1^k\right)$ across all ten scenarios.

$$\widetilde{S}_{T_0} = 0.9515\,\%$$

Then value of the swaption expressed in currency is:

$$S_{T_0} = \frac{\widetilde{S}_{T_0}}{\prod\limits_{i=1}^{4}\left(1+\delta L_i(0)\right)} = \frac{0.9515\,\%}{\left(1+0.5\cdot 0.05\right)^4} = 0.86201\,\%$$

13.3   CALCULATION RESULTS

In order to verify the accuracy of algorithms described above we have made simulation using 5,000 scenarios (2,500 base scenarios and 2,500 antithetic ones). For each of Algorithms 13.1–13.5 the simulation has been repeated 100 times. We have also changed, in comparison to the example described above, the parameters of simulation and parameters of the priced swaption. Now, we have four time steps within each LIBOR period, so time step of simulation $\Delta t = 0.125$, swaption holder has a right to enter into swap that pays float and receives fixed rate $K = 5\%$. The maturity of the swap is $T_{15} = 7.5$. We allow the swaption to be exercisable at times $T_9, T_{10}, T_{11}, T_{12}, T_{13}, T_{14}$. Initial values of all forward LIBORs are equal 5%, their volatilities are 30% and all LIBORs are assumed to be perfectly correlated (calculations are performed under one factor model). Simulation is done under the forward measure associated with zero coupon bond maturing at $T_{20} = 10$. Regressions have been done to polynomials:

$$H(\alpha, W_T) = \prod_{j=0}^{N} a_j (W_T)^j$$

For $N = 10, 20, 50$

Our results are presented in Tables 13.21–13.23 below.

Table 13.21   Calculation results for polynomial of 10th degree

	Average	Stdev of single simulation result	Stdev of average
Algorithm 13.1	2.930 %	0.110 %	0.011 %
Algorithm 13.2	2.900 %	0.120 %	0.012 %
Algorithm 13.3	3.100 %	0.150 %	0.015 %
Algorithm 13.4	2.870 %	0.120 %	0.012 %
Algorithm 13.5	2.950 %	0.100 %	0.010 %

Table 13.22   Calculation results for polynomial of 20th degree

	Average	Stdev of single simulation result	Stdev of average
Algorithm 13.1	2.935 %	0.120 %	0.012 %
Algorithm 13.2	2.910 %	0.110 %	0.011 %
Algorithm 13.3	3.090 %	0.150 %	0.015 %
Algorithm 13.4	3.100 %	0.900 %	0.900 %
Algorithm 13.5	2.950 %	0.110 %	0.011 %

Table 13.23   Calculation results for polynomial of 50th degree

	Average	Stdev of single simulation result	Stdev of average
Algorithm 13.1	2.935 %	0.130 %	0.013 %
Algorithm 13.2	2.850 %	0.110 %	0.011 %
Algorithm 13.3	3.390 %	1.100 %	1.100 %
Algorithm 13.4	8882.000 %	63440.000 %	6344.000 %
Algorithm 13.5	2.935 %	0.110 %	0.011 %

In order to verify the accuracy of the algorithms we also price the swaption using binomial trees (see Chapter 10, Approximations of the BGM model). We receive the value 0.0295.

13.4 SOME THEORETICAL REMARKS ON OPTIMAL STOPPING UNDER LSM

The goal of this subsection is to investigate from a theoretical point of view reasons for under- or over-estimation generated by a described algorithm. In order to do it we estimate the systematic error of one step of simulation. Systematic error is defined:

$$\Delta(x) = \left| E\left(\hat{V}_n \left(X_n^k \right) \middle| X_n^k = x \right) - V(x) \right| \tag{13.18}$$

All algorithms of optimal stopping described in this chapter have one common generic form:

Begin
  If $C_n \left(X_n^k \right) > \hat{U}_n^1 \left(X_n^k \right)$ **then**
    $\hat{V}_n \left(X_n^k \right) = C_n \left(X_n^k \right)$
  Else
    $\hat{V}_n \left(X_n^k \right) = \hat{U}_n^2 \left(X_n^k \right)$
  End If
End

Now we calculate $E\left(\hat{V}_n \left(X_n^k \right) \middle| X_n^k = x \right)$ under the assumption that estimator $\hat{U}_n^1 \left(X_n^k \right) \equiv \hat{U}_n^2 \left(X_n^k \right)$ is unbiased. $\rho(\cdot)$ is a conditional distribution of the random variable $\hat{U}_n^1 \left(X_n^k \right) - U_n \left(X_n^k \right)$ under condition $X_n^k = x$

$$E\left(\hat{V}_n \left(X_n^k \right) \middle| X_n^k = x \right) = \int_{-\infty}^{+\infty} \max\left(C_n(x), U_n(x) + y \right) \rho(y)\, dy$$

$$= \int_{-\infty}^{C_n(x) - U_n(x)} C_n(x) \rho(y)\, dy + \int_{C_n(x) - U_n(x)}^{+\infty} \left(U_n(x) + y \right) \rho(y)\, dy \tag{13.19}$$

Now, let us consider two cases:

1) $C_n(x) \geq U_n(x)$

From (13.19)

$$E\left(\hat{V}_n \left(X_n^k \right) \middle| X_n^k = x \right) = \int_{-\infty}^{C_n(x) - U_n(x)} C_n(x) \rho(y)\, dy + \int_{C_n(x) - U_n(x)}^{+\infty} \left(C_n(x) + y + (U_n(x) \right.$$

$$\left. - C_n(x)) \right) \rho(y)\, dy$$

$$= \int_{-\infty}^{+\infty} C_n(x) \rho(y)\, dy + \int_{C_n(x) - U_n(x)}^{+\infty} \left(y + (U_n(x) - C_n(x)) \right) \rho(y)\, dy$$

And since

$$V_n(x) = \max(C_n(x), U_n(x)) = C_n(x)$$

We obtain

$$E\left(\hat{V}_n\left(X_n^k\right)\middle| X_n^k = x\right) = V_n(x) + \int_{C_n(x)-U_n(x)}^{+\infty} (y + (U_n(x) - C_n(x)))\rho(y)\,dy > V_n(x)$$

$$(13.20)$$

2) $C_n(x) < U_n(x)$

From (13.19)

$$E\left(\hat{V}_n\left(X_n^k\right)\middle| X_n^k = x\right) = \int_{-\infty}^{C_n(x)-U_n(x)} (U_n(x) + (C_n(x) - U_n(x)))\rho(y)\,dy$$

$$+ \int_{C_n(x)-U_n(X)}^{+\infty} (U_n(x) + y)\rho(y)\,dy = \int_{-\infty}^{+\infty} U_n(x)\rho(y)\,dy$$

$$+ \int_{-\infty}^{C_n(x)-U_n(x)} (C_n(x) - U_n(x))\rho(y)\,dy + \int_{C_n(x)-U_n(x)}^{+\infty} y\rho(y)\,dy.$$

Since

$$V_n(x) = \max(C_n(x), U_n(x)) = U_n(x)$$

And

$$\int_{-\infty}^{C_n(x)-U_n(x)} (C_n(x) - U_n(x))\rho(y)\,dy + \int_{C_n(x)-U_n(x)}^{+\infty} y\rho(y)\,dy > \int_{-\infty}^{+\infty} y\rho(y)\,dy = 0.$$

We obtain

$$E\left(V_n\left(X_n^k\right)\middle| X_n^k = X\right) = V_n(x) + \int_{-\infty}^{C_n(x)-U_n(x)} (C_n(x) - U_n(x))\delta(y)\,dy$$

$$(13.21)$$

$$+ \int_{C_n(x)-U_n(x)}^{+\infty} y\rho(y)\,dy > V_n(x).$$

The results mean that if we use the same estimator of $U_n\left(X_n^k\right)$ for determining exercise barrier and the same estimator for calculate value of priced instrument we can obtain overestimated result. In our numerical test algorithms that use the same estimator of $U_n\left(X_n^k\right)$ for both purposes are Algorithm 13.3 and Algorithm 13.4. It is also the case of the most naive algorithm of optimal stopping $\left(\text{where } \hat{U}_n^1 \left(X_n^k \right) = \hat{U}_n^2 \left(X_n^k \right) = V_{n+1} \left(X_{n+1}^k \right) \right)$:

Algorithm 13.6
Begin

  For each scenario k calculate:

    If $C_n \left(X_n^k \right) > V_{n+1} \left(X_{n+1}^k \right)$ **then**

    $V_n \left(X_n^k \right) = C_n \left(X_n^k \right)$

    Else

    $V_n \left(X_n^k \right) = V_{n+1} \left(X_{n+1}^k \right)$

    End If

  Next k

End of algorithm 13.6

Now calculate $E \left(\hat{V}_n \left(X_n^k \right) \middle| X_n^k = x \right)$ under the assumption that estimators $\hat{U}_n^1 (x)$ and $\hat{U}_n^2 (x)$ are independent. $\rho_1 (\cdot)$ and $\rho_2 (\cdot)$ in the formula below are distributions of the random variables $\hat{U}_n^1 (x) - U_n (x)$ and $\hat{U}_n^2 (x) - U_n (x)$ respectively, conditionally that $X_n^k = x$

$$E \left(\hat{V}_n \left(X_n^k \right) \middle| X_n^k = x \right) = 1_{\hat{U}_n^1(x) > C_n(x)} \int_{-\infty}^{+\infty} (U_n (x) + y_2) \rho_2 (y_2) \, dy_2$$

$$+ 1_{U_n^1(x) \le C_n(X)} \int_{-\infty}^{+\infty} (C_n (x) + y_2) \rho_2 (y_2) \, dy_2$$

$$= U_n (x) \int_{C_n(x) - U_n(x)}^{+\infty} \rho (y_1) \, dy_1 + C_n (X) \int_{-\infty}^{C_n(x) - U_n(x)} \rho (y_1) \, dy_1 \tag{13.22}$$

$$\le \max (U_n (x), C_n (x)) = V_n (x)$$

and the inequality in (13.22) becomes equality only if $C_n (x) = U_n (x)$. So, in this case calculations can lead to an underpricing of a valued claim.

Now, we compare the systematic error (13.18) for the two described cases:

1) $\hat{U}_n^1 (x) \equiv \hat{U}_n^2 (x)$
2) $\hat{U}_n^1 (x)$ and $\hat{U}_n^2 (x)$ are independent

Let us assume that both random variables: $\hat{U}_n^1 (x) - U_n (x)$ and $\hat{U}_n^2 (x) - U_n (x)$ are standard normal variables.

The results of the calculations are listed in the Table 13.24 below.

We look at the systematic error:

1) For $\hat{U}_n^1(x) \equiv \hat{U}_n^2(x)$

(a) $C_n(x) > U_n(x)$

From (13.20) and features of the standard normal distribution:

$$\left| V_n(x) - E\left(\hat{V}_n\left(X_n^k \right) \middle| X_n^k = X \right) \right| = \int_{C_n(X)-U_n(X)}^{+\infty} (y + (U_n(x) - C_n(x)))\rho(y)\,dy$$

$$= \frac{1}{\sqrt{2\pi}} \int_{\frac{(C_n(x)-U_n(x))^2}{2}}^{+\infty} e^{-z}\,dz$$

$$+ (U_n(x) - C_n(x)) N(U_n(x) - C_n(x))$$

$$= \frac{1}{\sqrt{2\pi}} e^{\frac{-(C_n(x)-U_n(x))^2}{2}}$$

$$+ (U_n(x) - C_n(x)) N(U_n(x) - C_n(x))$$

$$C_n(x) \le U_n(x)$$

From (13.21) and features of the standard normal distribution:

$$\left| V_n(x) - E\left(\hat{V}_n\left(X_n^k \right) \middle| X_n^k = x \right) \right| = \int_{-\infty}^{C_n(x)-U_n(x)} (C_n(x) - U_n(x))\rho(y)\,dy$$

$$+ \int_{C_n(x)-U_n(x)}^{+\infty} y\rho(y)\,dy$$

$$= (C_n(x) - U_n(x)) N(C_n(x) - U_n(x))$$

$$+ \frac{1}{\sqrt{2\pi}} \int_{\frac{(C_n(x)-U_n(x))^2}{2}}^{+\infty} e^{-z}\,dz = \frac{1}{\sqrt{2\pi}} e^{\frac{-(C_n(x)-U_n(x))^2}{2}}$$

$$+ (C_n(x) - U_n(x)) N(C_n(x) - U_n(x))$$

2) $\hat{U}_n^1(x)$ and $\hat{U}_n^2(x)$ are independent

From (13.21) and features of the standard normal distribution:

$$\left| V_n(X) - E\left(\hat{V}_n\left(X_n^k \right) \middle| X_n^k = x \right) \right|$$

$$= \max(U_n(x), C_n(x)) - U_n(x) \int_{C_n(x)-U_n(x)}^{+\infty} \rho(y_1)\,dy_1 - C_n(x) \int_{-\infty}^{C_n(x)-U_n(x)} \rho(y_1)\,dy_1$$

$$= \max(U_n(x), C_n(x)) - U_n(x) N(U_n(x) - C_n(x)) - C_n(x) N(C_n(x) - U_n(x))$$

Systematic error results are listed in Table 13.24 below.

Table 13.24

$C_n(X)$	$U_n(X)$	Systematic error for case 1)	Systematic error for case 2)
10	13	0.000382	0.00405
10	12.7	0.00106	0.009361
10	12.4	0.00272	0.019674
10	12.1	0.006468	0.037515
10	11.8	0.014276	0.064675
10	11.5	0.029307	0.100211
10	11.2	0.056102	0.138084
10	10.9	0.100431	0.165654
10	10.6	0.168673	0.164552
10	10.3	0.266761	0.114627
10	10	0.398942	0
10	9.7	0.266761	0.114627
10	9.4	0.168673	0.164552
10	9.1	0.100431	0.165654
10	8.8	0.056102	0.138084
10	8.5	0.029307	0.100211
10	8.2	0.014276	0.064675
10	7.9	0.006468	0.037515
10	7.6	0.00272	0.019674
10	7.3	0.00106	0.009361
10	7	0.000382	0.00405

13.5 SUMMARY

Among tested Algorithms, only Algorithm 13.1 and Algorithm 13.5 give appropriate accuracy. Algorithm 13.3 and Algorithm 13.4 are examples of algorithm where the same estimator of continuation value is used for both purposes of:

1) Determining if swaption should be continued.
2) Calculation of swaption value.

In another words $\hat{U}_n^1(x) \equiv \hat{U}_n^2(x)$.

According to our theoretical divagation in section 13.4 'Some theoretical remarks on optimal stopping under LSM' Algorithms 13.3 and 13.4 should lead to overestimation and our numerical tests confirm this.

Algorithm 13.2 is an example of an algorithm where both estimators of $U(x)$ are independent and, consistently with our theoretical reasoning, it leads to underestimation.

And finally one important remark on Algorithm 13.1. If the regression polynomial has an appropriatly high degree we have:

$$\sum_{k=1}^{M} \left(\hat{V}_{n+1}\left(X_{n+1}^k\right) - H\left(\alpha, X_n^k\right) \right)^2 = 0$$

Meaning that for each scenario:

$$\hat{V}_{n+1}\left(X_{n+1}^k\right) = H\left(\alpha, X_n^k\right)$$

And Algorithm 13.1 becomes the naive Algorithm 13.6.

References

Andersen, L. (1999/2000) A simple approach to the pricing of Bermudan swaptions in the multifactor LIBOR market model, *The Journal of Computational Finance*, **3**, 5–32.

Andersen, L. and Andreasen, J. (2000) Volatility skews and extensions of the LIBOR market model, *Applied Mathematical Finance*, **7**(1), 1–32.

Balland, P. and Hughston, L.P. (2000) Markov market model consistent with cap smile, *International Journal of Theoretical and Applied Finance*, **3**, 161–82.

Bennett, M.N. and Kennedy, J.E. (2005) Common Interests, *Risk*, **18**(3), 73–7.

Bjork, T. (2004) *Arbitrage Theory in Continuous Time*, 2nd Edn, Oxford University Press.

Black, F. and Karasinski, P. (1991) Bond and options pricing when short rates are lognormal, *Financial Analysts Journal*, **47**, 52–9.

Black, F., Derman, E. and Toy, W. (1990) A one-factor model of interest rates and its application to treasury bond options, *Financial Analysts Journal*, **46**, 33–9.

Borovkov, A.A. (1998) *Ergodicity and Stability of Stochastic Processes*, John Wiley & Sons, Ltd.

Brace, A., Gatarek, D. and Musiela, M. (1997) The market model of interest rate dynamics, *Mathematical Finance*, **7**, 127–56.

Brigo, D. and Mercurio, F. (2001) *Interest Rate Models: Theory and Practice*, Springer-Verlag.

Brigo, D. and Mercurio, F. (2003) Analytical pricing of the smile in a forward LIBOR market model, *Quantitative Finance*, **3**, 15–27.

Brigo, D., Mercurio, F. and Rapisarda, F. (2004) Smile at the uncertainty, *Risk*, **17**, 97–101.

Carriere, J. (1996) Valuation of early-exercise price of options using simulations and nonparametric regression, *Insurance: Mathematics and Economics*, **19**, 19–30.

Cox, J.C., Ingersoll, J.E. and Ross, S.A. (1985) A theory of the term structure of interest rates, *Econometrical*, **53**, 385–407.

Daniluk, A. and Gatarek, D. (2005) A fully lognormal LIBOR market model, *Risk 9*, **18**, 115–18.

Doberlein, F. and Schweizer, M. (2001) On savings accounts in semimartingale term structure models, *Stochastic Analysis and Applications*, **19**, 605–26.

Duffie, D. and Singleton, K. (1997) An econometric model of the term structure of interest rate swap yields, *Journal of Finance*, **52**, 1287–1323.

Errais, E. and Mercurio, F. (2004) Yes, LIBOR models can capture interest rate derivatives skew: a simple modelling approach, IMI Banca working paper, http://ssrn.com/abstract=680621.

Gatarek, D. (2006) Nonparametric calibration of forward rate models, in L. Hughston and D. Brody (Eds), *Fixed Income Developments: Credit Derivatives, Credit Risk and Interest Rate Derivatives*, John Wiley & Sons, Ltd, submitted for publication.

Glasserman, P. (2003) *Monte Carlo Methods in Financial Engineering*, Springer.

Heath, D., Jarrow, R.A. and Morton, A. (1992) Bond pricing and the term structure of interest rates: a new methodology for contingent claims valuation, *Econometrica*, **60**, 77–105.

Hull, J. (1999) *Options, Futures, and Other Derivative Securities*, 4th Edn, Prentice-Hall.

Hunt, P. and Kennedy, J. (1999) *Financial Derivatives in Theory and Practice*, John Wiley & Sons, Ltd.

Hunt, P., Kennedy, J. and Pelsser, A. (2000) Markov-functional interest rate models, *Finance & Stochastics*, **4**, 391–408.

Hunter, C.J., Jaeckel, P. and Joshi, M.S. (2001) Drift approximations in a forward-rate-based LIBOR market model, Royal Bank of Scotland working paper.

Jaeckel, P. (2002) *Monte Carlo Methods in Finance*, John Wiley & Sons, Ltd.

Jamshidian, F. (1997) LIBOR and swap market models and measures, *Finance and Stochastics*, **1**, 293–330.

Jarrow R., Li, H. and Zhao, F. (2006) Interest rate caps 'smile' too! But can the LIBOR market models capture it? *Journal of Finance*, submitted for publication.

Joshi, M.S. (2003) *The Concepts and Practice of Mathematical Finance*, Cambridge University Press.

Joshi, M. and Stacey, A. (2006) New and robust drift approximations for the LIBOR market model, University of Melbourne working paper.

Karatzas, I. and Shreve, S.E. (1988) *Brownian Motion and Stochastic Calculus, Graduate Texts in Mathematics*, Springer-Verlag, 113.

Krynicki, W. (2003) Calibration of BGM interest rate model (in Polish), Warsaw University, Masters Thesis.

Longstaff, F.A. and Schwartz, E.S. (2001) Valuing American options by simulation: a simple least-squares approach, *Review of Financial Studies*, **14**, 113–47.

Longstaff, F., Santa-Clara, P. and Schwartz, E. (2001) Throwing away a billion dollars: the cost of suboptimal exercise strategies in the swaptions market, *Journal of Financial Economics*, **62**(1), 39–66.

Maurin, K. (1967) *Methods of Hilbert Spaces*, PWN.

Miltersen, K., Sandmann, K. and Sondermann, D. (1997) Closed form solutions for term structure derivatives with log-normal interest rates, *J. Finance*, **52**, 409–30.

Musiela, M. and Rutkowski, M. (1997a) Continuous-time term structure models: Forward measure approach, *Finance Stoch*, **1**(4), 261–91.

Musiela, M. and Rutkowski, M. (1997b) Martingale methods in financial modelling, *Applications of Mathematics 36*, Springer Verlag.

Pelsser, A. (2000) *Efficient Methods for Valuing and Managing Interest Rate Derivative Securities*, Springer Verlag.

Pietersz, R., Pelsser, A. and Van Regenmortel, M. (2004) Fast drift-approximated pricing in the BGM model, *Journal of Computational Finance*, **8**(1), Fall.

Piterbarg, V. (2003) Mixture of models: a simple recipe for a . . . hangover? (July 18). http://ssrn.com/abstract=393060.

Rebonato, R. (2002) *Modern Pricing of Interest-Rate Derivatives: The LIBOR Market Model and Beyond*, Princeton University Press.

Rebonato, R. (2004) *Volatility and Correlation: The Perfect Hedger and the Fox*, John Wiley & Sons, Ltd.

Schoenmakers, J. (2005) *Robust LIBOR Modelling and Pricing of Derivative Products*, Chapman & Hall.

Shreve, S. (2004) *Stochastic Calculus for Finance II, Continuous-Time Models*, Springer.

Shreve, S. (2005) *Stochastic Calculus for Finance I, The Binomial Asset Pricing Model*, Springer.

Simon, B. (1974) *The Euclidian (Quantum) Field Theory, Princeton Series in Physics*, Princeton University Press.

Triantafyllopoulos, K. (2003) On the central moments of the multidimensional Gaussian distribution, working paper.

Vasiček, O. (1977) An equilibrium characterization of the term structure, *Journal of Financial Economics*, **5**, 177–88.

Wieczorkowski, R. and Zieliński, R. (1997) *Computer Generators of Random Numbers*, WNT.

Zühlsdorff, C. (2002) *Extended LIBOR Market Models*, Verlag Dr. Kovac.

Further Reading

Alexander, C. (Ed.) (1999) *The Handbook of Risk Management and Analysis*, John Wiley & Sons, Ltd.

Alexander, C. (2003) Common correlation and calibrating the lognormal forward rate model, *Wilmott Magazine*, 68–78.

Andersen, L. and Andreasen, J. (2001) Factor dependence of Bermudan swaption prices: fact or fiction? *Journal of Financial Economics*, **62**(1), 3–37.

Andersen, L. and Broadie, M. (2004) Primal-dual simulation algorithm for pricing multidimensional American options, *Management Science*, **50**(9), 1222–34.

Andersen, L. and Brotherton-Ratcliffe, R. (2005) Extended LIBOR market models with stochastic volatility, *The Journal of Computational Finance*, **9**(1), Fall.

D'Aspremont, A. (2003) Interest rate model calibration using semidefinite programming, *Applied Mathematical Finance*, **10**(3), 183–213.

D'Aspremont, A. (2005) Risk-management methods for the LIBOR market model using semidefinite programming, *The Journal of Computational Finance*, **8**(4), Summer.

Avellaneda, M. and Laurence, P. (1999) *Quantitative modelling of derivative securities: from theory to practice*, CRC Press.

Baviera, R. (2003) Vol-Bond: an analytical solution, *Quantitative Finance*, **3**, 285–7.

Baviera, R. (2005) Bond market model, (February 16) http://ssrn.com/abstract=710902.

Baxter, M. and Rennie, A. (1997) *Financial Calculus*, Cambridge University Press.

Bingham, N.H. and Kiesel, R. (2004) *Risk-Neutral Valuation: Pricing and Hedging of Financial Derivitives*, 2nd Edn., Springer.

Black, F. (1976) The pricing of commodity contracts, *Journal of Financial Economics*, **3**, 167–79.

Black, F. and Scholes, M. (1973) The pricing of options and corporate liabilities, *Journal of Political Economy*, **81**, 637–54.

Boyle, P. (1977) Options: a Monte Carlo approach, *Journal of Financial Economics*, **4**, 323–38.

Brace, A. (1996) Non-bushy trees for Gaussian HJM and lognormal forward models, UNSW working paper.

Brace, A. (1998a) Dual swap and swaption formulae in forward models, FMMA working paper.

Brace, A. (1998b) Rank-2 swaption formulae, FMMA working paper.

Brace, A. (1998c) Simulation in the GHJM and LFM models, FMMA working paper.

Brace, A. and Musiela, M. (1994) A multifactor Gauss Markov implementation of Heath, Jarrow, Morton, *Mathematical Finance*, **4**, 259–83.

Brace, A. and Musiela, M. (1997) Swap derivatives in a Gaussian HJM framework, in M.A.H. Dempster and S.R. Pliska (Eds) *Mathematics of Derivative Securities*, Cambridge University Press. Publ. Newton Inst., 336–68.

Brace, A. and Womersley, R.S. (2000) Exact fit to the swaption volatility matrix and semidefinite programming, UNSW working paper.

Brace, A., Musiela, M. and Schloegl, E. (1998) A simulation algorithm based on measure relationships in the lognormal market models, UNSW working paper.

Brace, A., Dun, T. and Barton, G. (2001) Towards a central interest rate model, in E. Jouini, J. Cvitanić and M. Musiela (Eds) *Handbooks in Mathematical Finance, Topics in Option Pricing, Interest Rates and Risk Management*, Cambridge University Press.

Brigo, D., Mercurio, F. and Morini, M. (2005) The LIBOR model dynamics: approximations, calibration and diagnostics, *European Journal of Operational Research*, **163**(1), 30–51.

Broadie, M. and Glasserman, P. (1997) Pricing American style securities using simulation, *Journal of Economic Dynamics and Control*, **21**, 1323–52.

Broadie, M. and Detemple, J.B. (2004) Option pricing: valuation models and applications, *Management Science*, **50**(9), 1145–77.

Carr, P. and Yang, G. (2001) Simulating Bermudan interest rate derivatives, in M. Avellaneda, (Ed.) *Quantitative Analysis of Financial Markets*, Vol. II, 295–316, Singapore.

Choy, B., Dun, T. and Schlögl, E. (2004) Correlating market models, *Risk*, 17 September, 124–9.

Corr, A. (2000) Finite dimensional representability of forward rate and LIBOR models, Thesis, University of New South Wales.

Dai, Q. and Singleton, K. (2003) Term structure dynamics in theory and reality, *Rev. Financ. Stud.*, **16**, 631–78.

Da Prato, G. and Zabczyk, J. (1992) Stochastic equations in infinite dimensions, *Encyclopaedia of Mathematics and Its Applications*, **44**, Cambridge University Press.

Derman, E. (1997) The future of modelling, *Risk*, **10** (December), 164–7.

De Jong, F., Driessen, J. and Pelsser, A. (2001a) Estimation of the LIBOR market model: combining term structure data and option prices, University of Amsterdam working paper.

De Jong, F., Driessen, J. and Pelsser, A. (2001b) LIBOR market models versus swap market models for pricing interest rate derivatives: an empirical analysis, *European Finance Review*, **5**(3), 201–37.

Duffie, D. (1996) *Dynamic Asset Pricing Theory*, Princeton University Press.

Dupire, B. (1999) (Ed.), *Monte Carlo*, RISK Books.

Filipovic, D. (2000) Consistency problems for HJM interest rate models, PhD Thesis, ETH, Zurich.

Filipovic, D. (2001) *Consistency Problems for Heath-Jarrow-Morton Interest Rate Models*, Springer.

Gatarek, D. (1996) Some remarks on the market model of interest rates, *Control and Cybernetics*, **25**, 1233–44.

Gatarek, D. (2000) Modelling without tears, *Risk*, **13**, (September) S20–S24.

Gatarek, D. and Maksymiuk, R. (1999) Applying HJM to credit risk, *Risk*, **12** (May), 67–8.

Geman, H., El Karoui, N. and Rochet, J.C. (1995) Changes of numeraire, changes of probability measures, and pricing of options, *Journal of Applied Probability*, **32**, 443–58.

Glasserman, P. and Kou, S.G. (1999) The term structure of simple forward rates with jump risk, Columbia working paper.

Glasserman, P. and Zhao, X. (1999) Fast Greeks by simulation in forward LIBOR models, *The Journal of Computational Finance*, **3**, 5–39.

Glasserman, P. and Zhao, X. (2000) Arbitrage-free discretization of lognormal forward LIBOR and swap rate models, *Finance Stochastics*, **4**(1), 35–68.

Glasserman, P. and Merener, N. (2003a) Cap and swaption approximations in LIBOR market models with jumps, *The Journal of Computational Finance*, **7**(1) (Fall).

Glasserman, P. and Merener, N. (2003b) Numerical solution of jump-diffusion LIBOR market models, *Finance Stochastics*, **7**, 1–27.

Goldys, B. (1997) A note on pricing interest rate derivatives when LIBOR rates are lognormal, *Finance Stochastics*, **1**, 345–52.

Goldys, B. and Musiela, M. (2001) On partial differential equations related to term structure models, in E. Jouini, J. Cvitanić and M. Musiela (Eds) *Handbooks in Mathematical Finance, Topics in Option Pricing, Interest Rates and Risk Management*, Cambridge University Press.

Goldys, B., Musiela, M. and Sondermann, D. (2000) Lognormality of rates and term structure models, *Stochastic Anal. Appl*, **18**(3), 375–96.

Harrison, J.M. and Kreps, D. (1979) Martingales and arbitrage in multiperiod securities markets, *Journal of Economic Theory*, **2**, 381–408.

Harrison, J.M. and Pliska, S. (1983a) Martingales and stochastic integrals in the theory of continuous trading, *Stochastic Processes and Their Applications*, **11**, 215–60.

Harrison, J.M. and Pliska, S. (1983b) A stochastic calculus model of continuous trading: complete markets, *Stochastic Processes and Their Applications*, **15**, 313–16.

Henrard, M. (2003) Explicit bond option and swaption formula in one factor Heath-Jarrow-Merton model, *International Journal of Theoretical and Applied Finance*, **6**(1), 57–72.

Ho, T. and Lee, S. (1986) Term structure movements and pricing interest rate contingent claims, *Journal of Finance*, **41**, 1011–29.

Hughston, L. (Ed.) (1996) *Vasicek and Beyond*, Risk.

Hull, J.C. and White, A. (1990) Pricing interest rate derivative securities, *Review of Financial Studies*, **3**, 573–92.

Hull, J.C. and White, A. (2000) Forward rate volatilities, swap rate volatilities and the implementation of the LIBOR market model, *Journal of Fixed Income*, **10**, 46–62.

Hunt, P.J. and Kennedy, J.E. (1998a) Implied interest rate pricing models, *Finance & Stochastics*, **2**, 275–93.

Hunt, P.J. and Kennedy, J.E. (1998b) On multi-currency interest rate models, University of Warwick working paper.

Hunt, P.J., Kennedy, J.E. and Pelsser, A. (1998) Fit and run, *Risk*, **11**, 65–7.

Hunter, C., Jäckel, P. and Joshi, M. (2001) Getting the drift, *Risk*, **14** (July).

James, J. and Webber, N. (2000) *Interest Rate Modelling*, John Wiley & Sons, Ltd.

Jamshidian, F. (1989) An exact bond options pricing formula, *Journal of Finance*, **44**, 205–9.

Jamshidian, F. (1991) Bond and option evaluation in the Gaussian interest rate models, *Research in Finance*, **9**, 131–70.

Jamshidian, F. (1996) Sorting out swaptions, *Risk*, **9**, 59–60.

Jamshidian, F. (2001) LIBOR market model with semimaringales, in E. Jouini, J. Cvitanić and M. Musiela (Eds) *Handbooks in Mathematical Finance, Topics in Option Pricing, Interest Rates and Risk Management*, Cambridge University Press.

Joshi, M.S. (2003) Rapid computation of drifts in a reduced factor LIBOR market model, *Wilmott Magazine*, (May), 84–5.

Joshi, M.S. and Rebonato, R. (2003) A displaced-diffusion stochastic volatility LIBOR market model: motivation, definition and implementation, *Quantitative Finance*, **3**, 458–69.

Jouini, E., Cvitanić, J. and Musiela, M. (Eds), *Handbooks in Mathematical Finance*, Cambridge University Press.

Kawai, A. (2002) Analytical and Monte Carlo swaption pricing under the forward swap measure, *The Journal of Computational Finance*, **6**(1), Fall.

Kawai, A. (2003) A new approximate swaption formula in the LIBOR market model: an asymptotic expansion approach, *Applied Mathematical Finance*, **10**(1), 49–74.

Kerkhof, J. and Pelsser, A. (2002) Observational equivalence of discrete string models and market models, *The Journal of Derivatives*, **10**(1), 55–61.

Kurbanmuradov, O., Sabelfeld, K.K. and Schoenmakers, J. (2002) Lognormal random field approximations to LIBOR market models, *The Journal of Computational Finance*, **6**(1), Fall.

London, J. (2004) *Modeling Derivatives in* C++, John Wiley & Sons, Ltd.

Longstaff, F., Santa-Clara, P. and Schwartz, E. (2001) The relative valuation of caps and swaptions: theory and empirical evidence, *Journal of Finance*, **56**(6), 2067–2109.

de Malherbe, E. (1999) L'évaluation des instruments indexés sur taux d'échéance constante dans le modéle de marché, *Banque & Marchés*, **40**, 16–29.

de Malherbe, E. (2002) Correlation analysis in the LIBOR and swap market model, *International Journal of Theoretical and Applied Finance*, **5**(4), 401–26.

Musiela, M. (1995) General framework for pricing derivative securities, *Stochastic Processes*, **55**(2), 227–51.

Neftci, S.N. (2000) *An Introduction to the Mathematics of Financial Derivatives*, 2nd Edn, Academic Press.

Neftci, S.N. (2003) *Principles of Financial Engineering*, Academic Press.

Pedersen, M.B. (1999) Bermudan swaptions in the LIBOR market model, SimCorp working paper.

Pelsser, A. and Pietersz, R. (2004) Risk Managing Bermudan Swaptions in a LIBOR Model, *Journal of Derivatives*, **11**(3), 51–62.

Pelsser, A. and Pietersz, R. (2004) Swap vega in BGM: pitfalls and alternatives, *Risk*, **17**(3), 91–3.

Piterbarg, V.V. (2003/04) Computing deltas of callable LIBOR exotics in forward LIBOR models, *The Journal of Computational Finance*, **7**(2), Winter.

Piterbarg, V.V. (2004) Risk sensitivities of Bermuda swaptions, *International Journal of Theoretical and Applied Finance*, **7**(4), 465–510.

Piterbarg, V.V. (2004/05) Pricing and hedging callable LIBOR exotics in forward LIBOR models, *The Journal of Computational Finance*, **8**(2), Winter.

Rebonato, R. (1998) *Interest-Rate Models*, John Wiley & Sons, Ltd.

Rebonato, R. (1999a) Calibrating the BGM Model, *Risk*, **12**, 74–9.

Rebonato, R. (1999b) On the pricing implications of the joint lognormal assumption for the swaption and cap market, *The Journal of Computational Finance*, **2**, 57–76.

Rebonato, R. (1999c) On the simultaneous calibration of multifactor lognormal interest rate models to Black volatilities and to the correlation matrix, *The Journal of Computational Finance*, **2**, 5–27.

Rebonato, R. (1999d) *Volatility and Correlation in the Pricing of Equity, FX, and Interest-rate Options*, John Wiley & Sons, Ltd.

Rebonato, R. (2001a) Accurate and optimal calibration to co-terminal European swaptions in a FRA-based BGM framework, Royal Bank of Scotland working paper.

Rebonato, R. (2001b) The stochastic volatility LIBOR market model, *Risk*, **14**(10), 105–9.

Rebonato, R. (2003/04) Interest-rate term-structure pricing models: a review, Proc Royal Soc London A Mat 460; 667–728.

Rebonato, R. and Joshi, M. (2002) A joint empirical and theoretical investigation of the modes of deformation of swaption matrices: implications for model choice, *International Journal of Theoretical and Applied Finance*, **5**(7), 667–94.

Rutkowski, M. (1996) On continuous-time models of term structure of interest rates. In H.J. Englebert, H. Föllmer and J. Zabczyk, (Eds) *Stochastic Processes and Related Topics*, Gordon and Breach Publishers.

Rutkowski, M. (1998) Dynamics of spot, forward, and futures LIBOR rates, *Int. J. Theor. Appl. Finance*, **1**(3), 425–45.

Rutkowski, M. (1999a) Models of forward LIBOR and swap rates, *Applied Mathematical Finance*, **6**, 29–42.

Rutkowski, M. (1999b) Self-financing trading strategies for sliding, rolling-horizon, and consol bonds, *Math Finance*, **9**(4), 361–85.

Rutkowski, M. (2001) Modeling of forward LIBOR and swap rates, in E. Jouini, J. Cvitanić and M. Musiela (Eds) *Handbooks in Mathematical Finance, Topics in Option Pricing, Interest Rates and Risk Management*, Cambridge University Press, 336–95.

Samuelides, Y. and Nahum, E. (2001) A tractable market model with jumps for pricing short-term interest rate derivatives, *Quantitative Finance*, **1**, 270–83.

Sandmann, K. and Sondermann, D. (1997) A note on the stability of lognormal interest rate models and the pricing of Eurodollar futures, *Math Finance*, **7**(2), 119–25.

Santa-Clara, P. and Sornette, D. (2001), The dynamics of the forward interest rate curve with stochastic string shocks, *The Review of Financial Studies*, **14**(1), 149–85.

Schoenbucher, P. (1999) A LIBOR market model with default risk, Bonn University working paper.

Schoenbucher, P. (2003) *Credit Derivatives Pricing Models: Models, Pricing and Implementation*, John Wiley & Sons, Ltd.

Schoenmakers, J.G. and Coffey, B. (1999) LIBOR rate models, related derivatives and model calibration, WIAS-working paper No. 480.

Schoenmakers, J.G. and Coffey, B. (2000) Stable implied calibration of a multi-factor LIBOR model via a semi-parametric correlation structure, WIAS-working paper No. 611.

Schoenmakers, J.G. and Coffey, B. (2003) Systematic generation of parametric correlation structures for the LIBOR market model, *International Journal of Theoretical and Applied Finance*, **6**(5), 507–19.

Shiryayev, A.N. (1978) *Optimal Stopping Rules*, Springer Verlag.

Sidenius, J. (2000) LIBOR market models in practice, *The Journal of Computational Finance*, **3**, 5–26.

Sundaresan, S.M. (2000) Continuous-time methods in finance: a review and an assessment, *Journal of Finance*, **55**, 1569–1622.

Svoboda, S. (2003) *Interest Rate Modelling*, Palmgrave Macmillian.

Sztuba, P. and Weron, A. (2001) Pricing forward-start options in the HJM framework; evidence from the Polish market, *Applicationes Mathematicae*, **28**(2), 211–24.

Tang, Y. and Lange, J. (2001) Non-exploding bushy tree technique and its applications to the multifactor interest rate market model, *The Journal of Computational Finance*, **4** (Autumn).

Teugels, J. and Sundt, B. (Eds) (2004) *Encyclopaedia of Actuarial Science*, John Wiley & Sons, Ltd.

Thomas, S., Ho, Y. and Lee, S.B. (2004) *The Oxford Guide to Financial Modeling*, Oxford University Press.

Weigel, P. (2004) Optimal calibration of LIBOR market models to correlations, *The Journal of Derivatives*, Winter.

Wilmott, P. (1999) *Derivatives: The Theory and Practice of Financial Engineering*, John Wiley & Sons, Ltd.

Wilmott, P. (2000) *Paul Wilmott on Quantitative Finance*, John Wiley & Sons, Ltd.

Wu, L. (2001) Optimal calibration of LIBOR market models. Working paper, HKUST.

Wu, L. (2002/03) Fast at-the-money calibration of the LIBOR market model using Lagrange multipliers, *The Journal of Computational Finance*, **6**(2), Winter.

Wu, L. and Zhang, Z.Y. (2003) Optimal low-rank approximation to a correlation matrix, *Linear Algebra Appl*, **364**, 161–87.

Zabczyk, J. (1999) Infinite dimensional diffusions in modelling and analysis, *Jahresber. Dtsch. Math.-Ver.*, **101**(2), 47–59.

Index

Printed and bound by CPI Group (UK) Ltd, Croydon, CR0 4YY

23/04/2025

14660970-0001